Consuming
Visions

IINFRSITY

Consuming Visions

Accumulation and Display of Goods in America 1880–1920

EDITED BY

Simon J. Bronner

PUBLISHED FOR
The Henry Francis du Pont Winterthur Museum
WINTERTHUR, DELAWARE

W·W·Norton & Company
NEW YORK   LONDON

Copyright © 1989 by The Henry Francis du Pont Winterthur Museum, Inc.
All rights reserved.

Published simultaneously in Canada by Penguin Books Canada Ltd., 2801
John Street, Markham, Ontario L3R 1B4.

Printed in the United States of America.

The text of this book is composed in Electra, with display type set in Gara-
mond. Composition and manufacturing by The Maple-Vail Book Manufacturing Group.

First Edition.

Editing and production by Deborah Gould Huey, Winterthur Museum.

Library of Congress Cataloging-in-Publication Data
Main entry under title:

Consuming visions : accumulation and display of goods in America,
    1880–1920 / edited by Simon J. Bronner. — 1st ed.
    p.   cm.
    "Published for the Henry Francis du Pont Winterthur Museum,
Winterthur, Delaware."
    Includes index.
    1. Display of merchandise—United States—History.
2. Advertising, Point-of-sale—Social aspects—United States—
History.   3. Consumer behavior—United States—History.
I. Bronner, Simon J.   II. Henry Francis du Pont Winterthur Museum.
HF5845.C68   1989
659.1'57—dc19   89-2916

ISBN 0-393-02709-0 ✓
ISBN 0-393-96002-1 PAPERBACK

W. W. Norton & Company, Inc., 500 Fifth Avenue, New York, N.Y. 10110

W. W. Norton & Company Ltd., 37 Great Russell Street, London WC1B 3NU

1 2 3 4 5 6 7 8 9 0

Contents

Acknowledgments

I planted the seed for this book during my tenure as National Endowment for the Humanities Research Fellow at Winterthur Museum in 1984. Having opened several lines of inquiry into the intellectual and cultural history of American consumership, a relatively new field, I sought to make connections among the field's scattered workers. Kenneth L. Ames, chairman of the Office of Advanced Studies at Winterthur, encouraged me to bring these scholars to the museum for an interdisciplinary forum. With funding from the Delaware Humanities Council and the University of Delaware and the cooperation of the Pennsylvania State University at Harrisburg, the forum occurred November 7 and 8, 1986, and this book grew out of that enlightening experience.

Others at Winterthur and Delaware were extremely helpful; I want to acknowledge the assistance of Deborah Gould Hucy, Scott T. Swank, Richard Bushman, Deborah A. Federhen, Dini Silber, and Barbara McLean Ward. My gratitude also goes out to the many helpful hands at Penn State Harrisburg. Darrell Peterson lent his technical expertise to the preparation of photographs, Donna Horley kept on top of the correspondence, Thea Hocker and John Patterson provided valuable suggestions, Carol Kalbaugh typed the manuscript, Jacqueline Guida proofread the manuscript and hounded authors, and many wonderful students and colleagues pondered the ideas found here. Special thanks are due William Mahar, division head of humanities at Penn State Harrisburg, for nurturing the project and to Ian M. G. Quimby, director of the Publications Office at Winterthur, for coaxing me along. Finally, to the late Warren Susman goes a tribute for his advising and provoking; this was a book he wanted to see.

Introduction

Simon J. Bronner

This volume examines a consumer way of life in America as it unfolded in the late nineteenth and early twentieth centuries. The book explores the visions that guided this spreading way of life and the figures, events, and institutions that projected these visions. The scenes and sights of consumption that Americans took in with aplomb and style are shown through studying the arts, advertisements, amusements, advisers, manuals, sermons, novels, furnishings, fairs, stations, hotels, museums, schools, and stores that set the stage for an engaging cultural fin de siècle drama and, indeed, laid the backdrop for performances of consumption that still command our attention today.

The consumer system dominates the landscape as well as the economy, the society as well as the culture, as evidenced by giant malls with everything under one roof, mail-order catalogues offering everything under one cover, and billboards inviting us to shop for our own good and the good of the nation. During the nineteenth century, as the nation moved from life revolving around the local market to the consumer center, the idea of how life was properly lived changed and led us to where we are today. The essays in this book explore the ways that distinctive visions of a consumer culture were formed and accepted and how they have affected our society, our worldview, and our lives.

More than simply a matter of economics, the cultural web of consumption is related to the rise of American mass culture. Many advances in communication, transportation, and education were geared toward the needs of an expanding consumer world as the scale and audience of business changed. From the secure but limited range of the local market, business imagined the growth and profits offered by coast-to-coast distribution; from a sure but limited audience of elite customers, business contemplated the potential of ready-made, nonessential goods available through mass transportation to the common man in the hinterlands. Both these changes involved risks, for both demanded speculation on future orders, which meant possible overproduction and loss. But several bold business leaders were willing to push the venture and educate the nation in their way of doing things. As Boston department-store magnate Edward Filene argued, "Mass production demands the education of the masses . . . masses must learn to behave like human beings in a mass production world." Again setting a standard, Richard Sears used advertising to educate as well as to sell. In 1905 Louis Asher told Sears's correspondents, "Our advertising is another class, an entirely different proposition, a simple proposition, the simplest and plainest in the world, and that is to get our announcements regarding merchandise read by the people, to put into their hands our catalogues and price lists, to study our ways and means by which we can make it easiest for the farmer, the laborer, or mechanic to buy his goods from us, save money and feel that the transaction has been satisfactory, so that the second order comes to us too." Many Americans received education—"object lessons" as they were called in the rhetoric of the day—in schools and museums which responded quickly to the demand for orientation to commercial design, display, and management.[1] But many more Americans received their education through the aisles of department stores, the long recitations of advertising copy, the lessons provided by holiday celebrations reoriented toward consumer behavior, and the parables of exposition displays.

Our inheritance of this education had received scant attention by students of history and culture until recently. In 1954 David Potter opened American abundance for scrutiny with *People of Plenty*. Connecting the American character to its condition of copiousness, Potter identified the "consumer orientation" of American society. He explained

---

[1] Stuart Ewen, *Captains of Consciousness: Advertising and the Social Roots of the Consumer Culture* (New York: McGraw-Hill Book Co., 1976), p. 54; Boris Emmet and John E. Jeuck, *Catalogues and Counters: A History of Sears, Roebuck and Company* (Chicago: University of Chicago Press, 1950), p. 65. See also Burton J. Bledstein, *The Culture of Professionalism: The Middle Class and the Development of Higher Education in America* (New York: W. W. Norton, 1976), pp. 248–334; and Simon J. Bronner, "Object Lessons: The Work of Ethnological Museums and Collections," elsewhere in this volume.

that as the nation shifted from an orientation of production to one of consumption in the late nineteenth century, institutions such as advertising agencies arose. With those institutions, the mythology of pioneer scarcity gave way to the imagery of easy abundance and expandable supply. In an often-cited passage, Potter explained:

In a society of scarcity, or even of moderate abundance, the productive capacity has barely sufficed to supply the goods which people already desire and which they regard as essential to an adequate standard of living. Hence the societal imperative has fallen upon increases in production. But in a society of abundance, the productive capacity can supply new kinds of goods faster than society in the mass learns to crave these goods or to regard them as necessities. If this new capacity is to be used, the imperative must fall upon consumption, and the society must be adjusted to a new set of drives and values in which consumption is paramount.[2]

Although Potter was credited for raising the issue of American cultural transformation for scholarly discussion, he was also criticized for failing to explain how and why this adjustment occurred. His work suffered for its apparently vain attempt to locate an overarching American character and its biased vantage in the prosperous 1950s.

During the 1970s and 1980s interdisciplinary combinations of popular culture studies, material culture studies, folklore studies, women's studies, and American studies fostered provocative forays into the life of consumers. The emphasis was on things and the meanings they held—from Chippendale chairs to Levittown houses, from mail-order catalogues to fast-food chains. With this body of evidence, questions of process and theory once again arose. In 1983 Richard Wightman Fox and T. J. Jackson Lears published *Culture of Consumption*, a flagship work that rallied many scholars to the serious consideration of the cultural web of consumption. The editors raised the vital point that, although it appeared that the American culture of consumption emerged full-blown in the 1950s, historical evidence showed a path of development leading from the late nineteenth century. They declared, "Consumer culture is more than the 'leisure ethic,' or the 'American standard of living.' It is an ethic, a standard of living, and a power structure."[3]

[2] David M. Potter, *People of Plenty: Economic Abundance and the American Character* (Chicago: University of Chicago Press, 1954), p. 173.

[3] Richard Wightman Fox and T. J. Jackson Lears, eds., *The Culture of Consumption: Critical Essays in American History, 1880–1980* (New York: Pantheon Books, 1983), p. xii.

In *No Place of Grace* (1981) Lears introduced at least one provocative answer to Potter's inquiry about the source of the cultural transformation during the late nineteenth century. Lears suggested that the process owed to a "cultural hegemony" where dominant social groups win the spontaneous consent of the great masses of the population to the general direction imposed on their cultural life.[4] He argued that one could read the subtle but powerful wielding of persuasion in symbolic texts such as advertising, world's fairs, and utopian literature. Further, in a closer humanistic reading of the lives and ideas of elites and members of the masses, one could find the tensions and negotiations that occur in a process of culture.

This idea of cultural hegemony received criticism from other interpreters of the consumer culture. In *Culture as History* (1984) Warren Susman complained of two methodological problems. First he claimed that the new historians had imposed their values onto their data. He wrote that "the culture of abundance was not largely the result of evil machinations that control and distort human life . . . and it would be a serious methodological error not to attempt first to understand the culture on its own terms." Second, Susman thought that the new historians assumed "that the world today (whatever its nature and however correct their critical evaluation) is simply the direct and the only consequence that could follow from the world developing at the turn of the century."[5] Susman presented his own view of the cultural transformation which occurred at the turn of the century. He saw a shift in technology from the hand to the machine which, in addition to changing social patterns, produced new ways of thinking about providing for one's needs. He saw an intellectual basis as well in the shift from the moral communal concern for "character" in the nineteenth century to the secular, individualistic emphasis on "personality" in the twentieth century.

Daniel Horowitz meanwhile contributed an intellectual history of nineteenth- and twentieth-century writing on the consumer culture.

[4]T. J. Jackson Lears, *No Place of Grace: Antimodernism and the Transformation of American Culture, 1880–1920* (New York: Pantheon Books, 1981), p. xvii. See also T . J. Jackson Lears, "The Concept of Cultural Hegemony: Problems and Possibilities," *American Historical Review* 90, no. 3 (June 1985): 567–93; and Robert W. Rydell, *All the World's a Fair: Visions of Empire at American International Expositions, 1876–1916* (Chicago: University of Chicago Press, 1984).

[5]Warren I. Susman, *Culture as History: The Transformation of American Society in the Twentieth Century* (New York: Pantheon Books, 1984), p. xxix.

Expanding on Susman's notion of changing moral attitudes, Horowitz also had a methodological suggestion. Looking at both the critics and the supporters of a "morality of spending," Horowitz called for a more reciprocal model than Lears's, "one that emphasizes the power of the economic system and elites to set the framework of consumer culture but does not forget the ability of people, within limits, to shape the meaning of their consumption patterns." The reciprocal model that Horowitz had in mind came from the anthropological work of Mary Douglas, whose *World of Goods* (1979) presented an outline of messages, functions, and symbols provided by the exchange and consumption of goods. Instead of the power struggle that Lears saw or the technological tension that Susman found in the rise of American consumer culture, Douglas observed consumption as a fundamental form of human communication prone to cultural variation.[6]

Thus, although this volume is not the first word on the cultural and historical issues of consumption, it is among the first to sponsor an interdisciplinary exchange among scholars of the subject before a wide audience. Before preparing this volume, I worked on a book called *Grasping Things* (1986), which explored the material life of Americans. While checking museum collections, evaluating my field research, and perusing library sources, I uncovered a limitation of the historical study of objects. The bias in these materials leaned heavily toward production apart from the consumption of objects. To fill out my picture of material culture, however, I wanted to know who bought, promoted, and collected the objects we glorify as art and artifact. Emphasizing creative production is a natural bias drawn from the genteel regard for aesthetics and creation in the humanities. But as scholarship has moved more toward uncovering cultural context to analyze the meaning and significance of goods in everyday life, questions of the social and economic systems of consumption in which our material lives are played out demand answers.[7]

[6] Daniel Horowitz, *The Morality of Spending: Attitudes toward the Consumer Society in America, 1875–1940* (Baltimore: Johns Hopkins University Press, 1985), p. 168; Mary Douglas and Baron Isherwood, *The World of Goods: Towards an Anthropology of Consumption* (New York: W. W. Norton, 1979).

[7] See Simon J. Bronner, *Grasping Things: Folk Material Culture and Mass Society in America* (Lexington: University Press of Kentucky, 1986); Simon J. Bronner, ed., *American Material Culture and Folklife* (Ann Arbor: UMI Research Press, 1985); Ian M. G. Quimby, ed., *Material Culture and the Study of American Life* (New York:

The chapters in this book address two fundamental questions: one historical and one cultural. Taking up the challenge of David Potter, we ask the historical question of what happened during the late nineteenth and early twentieth centuries that made this time distinctive. This "age of excess," "age of optimism," "age of energy," and "age of enterprise," as it has been called, usually has been framed by the years 1880 and 1920.[8] At one end lies the end of Reconstruction and the vigorous growth of incorporation, immigration, urbanization, transportation, and communication; at the other end lies the shadow of World War I and the new "modern era." At the beginning of the period, the work of Charles Darwin and Herbert Spencer gave the era a fervor for evolutionary metaphors of progress and civilization; at its end, Einstein's idea of relativity expanded into an intellectual and social doctrine for the modern era. In this volume especially, we explore what people thought and envisioned during this period.

Taking up the challenge of Jackson Lears, we ask how this period reflected the transformation of American culture. What arts, customs, and institutions expressed the culture of consumption? What were the

---

W. W. Norton, 1978); Thomas J. Schlereth, ed., *Material Culture: A Research Guide* (Lawrence: University Press of Kansas, 1985); Thomas J. Schlereth, *Artifacts and the American Past* (Nashville: American Association for State and Local History, 1980); Mihalyi Csikszentmihalyi and Eugene Rochberg-Halton, *The Meaning of Things: Domestic Symbols and the Self* (Chicago: University of Chicago Press, 1981); Harvey Green, *The Light of the Home: An Intimate View of the Lives of Women in Victorian America* (New York: Pantheon Books, 1983); John R. Stilgoe, *Common Landscape of America, 1580 to 1845* (New Haven: Yale University Press, 1982); Clifford Edward Clark, *The American Family Home, 1800–1960* (Chapel Hill: University of North Carolina Press, 1986); Deborah Anne Federhen et al., *Accumulation and Display: Mass Marketing Household Goods in America, 1880–1920* (Winterthur, Del.: Winterthur Museum, 1986); Richard A. Gould and Michael B. Schiffer, eds., *Modern Material Culture: The Archaeology of Us* (New York: Academic Press, 1981); and Wolfgang Fritz Haug, *Critique of Commodity Aesthetics: Appearance, Sexuality and Advertising in Capitalist Society*, trans. Robert Bock (Minneapolis: University of Minnesota Press, 1986).

[8] See Ray Ginger, *Age of Excess: The United States from 1877 to 1914* (New York: Macmillan Publishing Co., 1965); James Laver, *Manners and Morals in the Age of Optimism* (New York: Harper and Row, 1966); Howard Mumford Jones, *The Age of Energy: Varieties of American Experience, 1865–1915* (New York: Viking Press, 1971); and Robert H. Walker, *Life in the Age of Enterprise* (New York: Paragon/G. P. Putnam's Sons, 1979). See also Carl Degler, *The Age of the Economic Revolution, 1876–1900* (Glenview, Ill.: Scott, Foresman, 1967); Stephen Kern, *The Culture of Time and Space, 1880–1918* (Cambridge, Mass.: Harvard University Press, 1986); and Robert Wiebe, *The Search for Order, 1870–1920* (New York: Hill and Wang, 1967).

sources and consequences of the cultural processes affecting American society such as the shift from production to consumption, from an emphasis on the touch and feel of things to the look and style of commodities, and from a small-town ethos to the rising cosmopolitan ideal? And what were the sources and consequences of the rise of professionalism and a reliance on therapeutic services, the increasing nationalization of services and goods, and the accelerating pace of communication and transportation? With regard to the cultural processes, the authors examine the active pursuit of status objects for possession and display in a conspicuous manner, the reliance on accumulating goods as measures of economic, cultural, and political identity, and the concomitant emergence of a scholarship and literature concerned with the effect of consumer goods. By exploring such processes, the authors interpret the versions, and visions, of abundance in America.

Each author provides an ideological perspective and a bit of material culture to consider. I admit to a material culture bias in the organization of the topics. An important contribution of this volume is to bring material culture studies more significantly into the historical and cultural inquiry of consumption. Devoted to the artifacts of American life, the scholarship of material culture has been an essential, although often overlooked, source for the cultural history to be found in American production and consumption.[9] To be sure, the authors offer something as well from their training in history, folklore, museology, sociology, psychology, art, anthropology, semiotics, and literature. But in a spirit of unity, the authors address the issues of consumption under the tent of American studies, for their approaches to the study of consumption bring an integrative, humanistic inquiry to bear on the symbols and meanings of American civilization.

The rhetoric of describing the cultural values influenced by consumer behavior has varied among writers in this field. Looking back at the early twentieth-century foundations of the consumer culture, Stuart Ewen defined *consumerism* as "the mass participation in the values of the mass-industrial market." Roots of the consumer system in the United

[9] See Thomas J. Schlereth, ed., *Material Culture Studies in America* (Nashville: American Association for State and Local History, 1982); Schlereth, ed., *Material Culture*; Quimby, ed., *Material Culture*; Bronner, ed., *American Material Culture*; and Robert B. St. George, ed., *Material Life in America, 1600–1860* (Boston: Northeastern University Press, 1987).

States predate the twentieth century and can be followed well back to the seeds of the New Republic, although the mass proportions to which Ewen refers arise distinctly in the late nineteenth century.[10] Mass retailing at fixed prices, national distribution of advertising, and elaborate displays were signs of new relations toward goods, shifting attitudes toward society, and fresh arguments over society's future direction. Given these conditions, Ewen's term *consumerism* struggles to describe the complexities of the changes occurring in the turn-of-the-century economy and culture. It is evident that the meaning of consumerism can be misleading—first, because today we often associate it with the protection of consumers rather than their behavior; and second, because it speaks to a state of being a consumer rather than to the processes involved. Pointing to the overarching cultural effects of mass consumption, many scholars prefer to use terms such as *consumer culture, consumptive culture,* or *culture of consumption.*

The contributors to this volume share this concern with our national cultural history, but I sense a new perspective emerging from the new work on the subject. Concerned with the specific behavior and thought that generates a material culture, students in the last decade have shaped a perspective oriented toward the lives, aesthetics, and actions of craftsmanship. With craftsmanship steeped in the touch-oriented, local world of production, I believe that *consumership* arose for the sight-oriented, broader world of consumption from the older web of production, and the term can be effectively used for analysis. A historical irony is that as Americans became more aware of the threat of mechanization to traditional village crafts, the principles of craftsmanship and the dictates

[10] Ewen, *Captains of Consciousness*, p. 54. For discussions of consumption before the late nineteenth century, see Edgar W. Martin, *The Standard of Living in 1860* (Chicago: University of Chicago Press, 1942); John J. McCusker and Russell R. Menard, *The Economy of British America, 1607–1789* (Chapel Hill: University of North Carolina Press, 1985), pp. 277–94; Gloria L. Main, *Tobacco Colony: Life in Early Maryland, 1650–1720* (Princeton: Princeton University Press, 1982), pp. 140–236; Alice Hanson Jones, *Wealth of a Nation to Be: The American Colonies on the Eve of the Revolution* (New York: Columbia University Press, 1980); Carole Shammas, "Consumer Behavior in Colonial America," *Social Science History* 6, no. 1 (Fall 1982): 67–86; Carole Shammas, "How Self-Sufficient Was Early America?" *Journal of Interdisciplinary History* 13, no. 2 (Autumn 1982): 247–72; Lorena S. Walsh, "Urban Amenities and Rural Sufficiency: Living Standards and Consumer Behavior in the Colonial Chesapeake, 1643–1777," *Journal of Economic History* 43, no. 1 (March 1983): 109–17; and Regina Lee Blaszczyk, "Ceramics and the Sot-Weed Factor: The China Market in a Tobacco Economy," *Winterthur Portfolio* 19, no. 1 (Spring 1984): 7–19.

of technique became more important in turn-of-the-century America. Immensely popular "how-to" books, etiquette books, and social advisers used a rhetoric of technique to turn the consuming passions of turn-of-the-century Americans into productive activities. Noting the emphasis on craftsmanship during this period, historian Howard Mumford Jones pointed out that it differed from that of the earlier "romantics in its demand for a fusion of technical competence and artistic invention." One adviser, *Art in Every Day Life*, boldly told its middle-class readers:

Taste is molded, to a very large extent, by the things which surround one, and the family taste is trained by the objects selected by the homemaker. There is, therefore, a distinct obligation in the home to set the highest possible standards of beauty. This is becoming widely recognized and there is an ever growing demand for information which will help people to become more intelligent customers. Since art is involved in most of the objects which are seen and used every day, one of the great needs of the consumer is a knowledge of the principles which are fundamental to good taste. . . . Solving these problems of purchasing and arranging requires the same knowledge of the principles of art as goes into the creation of objects.[11]

Like this adviser, the contributors in this volume aim to uncover hidden principles. They present consumership for analysis, and they refer to the style and skill associated with being a consumer and its intellectual and cultural sources.

I arranged the contents to proceed from the intellectual background of consumership to its objects and settings. The book opens with essays on the philosophies behind accumulation and display. Michael Barton, Jackson Lears, and I discuss the technique, appeal, and style of influential consumer "texts" as well as their authors and critics. Sermons, polemics, novels, poems, photographs, illustrations, cities, and advertisements are texts of the age in which can be read emerging concepts of fashion, performance, and well-being. Barton interprets the changing ways that the Bible, certainly a critical text, was read during the nineteenth century for attitudes toward accumulation and display

[11] Simon J. Bronner, *Chain Carvers: Old Men Crafting Meaning* (Lexington: University Press of Kentucky, 1985); Bronner, *Grasping Things*, pp. 1–22, 87–210. For the term *consumership*, see Dallas Smythe, "Buy Something: Five Myths of Consumership," in *In the Marketplace: Consumerism in America*, ed. Editors of Ramparts Magazine with Frank Browning (San Francisco: Canfield Press, 1972), pp. 167–74. Jones, *Age of Energy*, p. 224; Harriet Goldstein and Vetta Goldstein, *Art in Every Day Life* (rev. ed.; New York: Macmillan Publishing Co., 1932), pp. 2–5.

in American society. Lears and I delve into the secular reading that took on a growing importance in dictating values and outlooks for Victorian Americans. Chapters by William Leach and Jean-Christophe Agnew mark a move from intellectual criticism to aesthetic criticism. They tour shop windows, house interiors, paintings, and novels and find a grammar of consumership that continues to influence our rhetoric of goods.

Essays that follow cover influential patterns and institutions in the culture of consumption. Karen Halttunen offers a close reading of the changes in the interior design of the family home as signs of the shift from an emphasis on *character* to a modern sense of *personality*. Robert Rydell provides a tour through the spectacles of American world's fairs and their influence on the mass scale, or the imperial ethos as some would have it, of modern consumption. As the world's fairs intended ethnological exhibits to carry meaning for consumers, so too did museums. Toward an understanding of this meaning, I contribute a look at the accumulation and display of ethnological museums and their relation to consumership. Jay Mechling considers the history of yet another institution using ethnological precepts in shaping its principles of accumulation and display, in his analysis of the founding and growth of the Boy Scouts and other youth movements in his psychological interpretation of the "collecting self."

Authors of the next group of essays explore some of the settings that were centerpieces of America's realignment in the culture of consumption. William R. Taylor opens with a study of the meaning of public space in the symbolically important display of New York City as a commercial capital. He surveys several significant artifacts in the showcase city, from the Woolworth Building and Grand Central Terminal to the less monumental but nonetheless important "comfort stations." Eugene Rochberg-Halton takes us inland to Chicago, the nation's heart, a city that was remarkable for its rapid growth and great wealth, as well as its active literary and sociological circles. Rochberg-Halton makes connections between this important city, its social concern and study, and its image of consumption. Thomas J. Schlereth then takes us to the countryside, where consumption took distinctive forms and led to a truly national phenomenon.

Taken together, the authors in this volume might be said to work from the inspiration of that great observer of American character, Alexis de Tocqueville, who identified a distinctive American acquisitiveness in his classic tome *Democracy in America*. The authors indeed speak to Tocqueville's prophetic speculation that in America, "the love of well-being" expressed through consumption is "displayed as a tenacious, exclusive, universal passion." In America's democracy it was not the enormous European palace or castle that held attention, Tocqueville pointed out, but "to be always making life more comfortable and convenient, to avoid trouble, and to satisfy the smallest wants without effort and almost without cost." Tocqueville thought these were "small objects, but the soul clings to them." Their importance, as well as our need for understanding them, is compounded because the soul "dwells upon them closely and day by day, till they at last shut out the rest of the world and sometimes intervene between itself and heaven."[12]

[12] Alexis de Tocqueville, *Democracy in America* (1835, 1840; abridged ed., New York: Modern Library, 1981), p. 426.

Reading Consumer Culture

Simon J. Bronner

An especially telling period in American cultural history occurred when the nation, poised in the late nineteenth century, paused to consider its future in the twentieth century. Americans hoped for a unified vision, but confusion appeared to blur the road ahead. The rise of a consumer culture and the wealth that accompanied it created cultural, societal, and individual dilemmas. Wealth was power, and to show this intangible relationship, wealth was made tangible. The accumulation and display of goods expressed the power to manage people by directing production through consumption. It also provided something that the absence of family name and breeding could not—taste. Following an evolutionary model, preachers for wealth argued that affluence lifted culture above ungodly states of barbarism and savagery. They contended that much as conditions and nature propelled the refined human over the primitive ape, so too would the refinement of consumption lead Americans to a new age of ease and abundance. In short, wealth in America promised the flowering of a sprawling, glorious American civilization.

Still, there was worry that the humane spirit of the country was submerged beneath the surface allure of having and displaying possessions in the rising consumer culture. Beneath the uniformity of mass consumption, could individuality spring forth? Behind the trappings of "gimcrackeries," as William Dean Howells referred to the new ostentatious goods, could people still touch and inspirit each other?

Americans looked to expressive texts such as novels, artifacts, and communities to provide interpretations of unresolved ideas and experiences toward the goal of resolution. The rise of a consumer culture provided compelling new texts for society to behold and read. These texts gained their significance by working through ambivalent feelings by putting them into symbols and parables that could be vividly comprehended. By interpreting symbols within concrete texts, people had the chance to pause to evaluate the rapid changes occurring around them and to dramatize emotions, extend ideas, and gain an instrument of persuasion. Yet because of the immediacy of these texts, the significance of their metaphors was not always realized. In the rhetoric of accumulation and display, goods increased their roles as mediators and conveyors of cultural values, human emotions, and social priorities.

This essay examines what was read and how the texts might be studied in order to understand their symbols. This interpretation differs from approaches that previously treated *text* narrowly as a narrative read for its content.[1] In a broader view, text, suggestive of its linguistic origin in "a woven thing," has structure, style, pattern, and function that convey meaning. This meaning for an age is illuminated by reference to a text's cultural and historical context, the background of its creation, in this case especially the rise of a consumer culture. In this essay I move from a literal to metaphorical use of *text*, from literature to artifact to community. With communication dramatically diversifying in the form of films, telephones, and periodicals during the late nineteenth century, different kinds of texts were subjects for intense scrutiny as the nation became more literate and more aware of reading and using symbols in media other than print. Concerns for the appearance and composition of things ranged from the rhetoric of a novel to the dimensions of goods in a store display to the layout of a community. In structure, style, pattern, and function, texts espoused ways of thinking and acting and posed dilemmas of the age.

The Rhetoric of Accumulation in Literature

A character in William Dean Howells's *Hazard of New Fortunes* asks, "Does anything from without change us? We're brought up to think so

---

[1] For further discussion of this type of interpretation, see D. W. Meinig, ed., *The Interpretation of Ordinary Landscapes* (New York: Oxford University Press, 1979); Clifford Geertz, *The Interpretation of Cultures* (New York: Basic Books, 1973); Mary Douglas, *Implicit Meanings* (London: Routledge and Kegan Paul, 1975); and Alan Dundes, *Interpreting Folklore* (Bloomington: Indiana University Press, 1980).

by the novelists, who really have the charge of people's thinking nowadays." In the wake of rapid changes—many of them material—felt at the end of the nineteenth century, characters in Howells's popular novel went beyond reading literature for reminders of values to illustrations and things. Indeed, Howells used the establishment of new reading material in the form of a magazine as the organizing principle of the novel. This magazine is different because it has illustrations suited to "the twilight of the nineteenth century." The magazine, expanded to a biweekly, is a hit with consumers. The innocent editor from intellectual Boston transplanted to commercial New York feels the pull of the consumer world and realizes how things—"gimcrackeries," he calls them— were read for values as much as his words. His wife reminds him, "I remember that when we were looking for a flat you rejected every building that had a bell ratchet or a speaking tube, and would have nothing to do with any that had more than an electric button; you wanted a hallboy, with electric buttons all over him. I don't blame you. I find such things quite as necessary as you do." He admits that "having and shining" are held up at this time "as the chief good of life." They signify "material civilization . . . a culture that furnishes showily, that decorates, and that tells."[2]

In 1899 Thorstein Veblen's *Theory of the Leisure Class* described a "leisure class" comprising financiers, manufacturers, and merchants cashing in on the opportunities of industrial America. According to Veblen, the class used consumption to herald a newly attained status by displaying their excesses and by demonstrating the ease, idleness, and self-gratification with which wealth and success were enjoyed. Veblen noted that the man's cane conveyed the infirmity associated with idle wealth; the clean-shaven face demonstrated the ample time that a man had to worry about an unnecessary chore and the ability to afford the many accessories needed for the task. As interpreted by Veblen, the upsurge in consumption was driven by the need to clarify uncertain social status by accumulating material things, and it also created a model of fashion for others to follow. The model designated a hierarchy from the leisure class downward: those below would strive toward the position and display of wealth demonstrated by the leisure class; that class, because

[2] William Dean Howells, *A Hazard of New Fortunes* (1890; reprint, New York: New American Library, 1980), pp. 422, 13, 262, 380–81.

of its vested interests, would profit further from the consumption created.[3]

Although Veblen's view appeared harsh, others calling themselves visionaries saw in the new order opportunities for a more benevolent prosperity and egalitarianism only dreamed of earlier. Personal wealth and stories of consuming wealth abounded by the turn of the century. The rags-to-riches mythology pervaded much of the popular literature, although in reality mobility was rather restricted. Still, the image that wealth in America was infinitely expandable, that accumulation of goods provided well-being, and that opportunity was everywhere encouraged "buying into" the system. The "million dollar corner" in New York City was one engaging popular symbol of success supporting this image and its upscaled consuming vision. In 1911 a widely circulated newspaper story told of Robert S. Smith, who had come to New York before the end of the century with six dollars in his pocket and bought what seemed then to be a remote property at Thirty-fourth Street and Broadway. Smith eventually sold his tiny parcel for one million dollars, a record price per square foot, to make way for a towering department store. Meanwhile, Fifth and Sixth avenues in New York became nationally known showcases full of a visible mythology of unlimited goods available to upwardly aspiring cosmopolitans who lined the avenues wide-eyed and put themselves on display as a stream of consuming shoppers engulfing the avenues (fig. 1).[4]

[3] See Thorstein Veblen, *The Theory of the Leisure Class* (1899; reprint, New York: Penguin Books, 1979); Joseph Dorfman, *Thorstein Veblen and His America* (1934; reprint, New York: Viking-Penguin, 1961); John P. Diggins, *The Bard of Savagery: Thorstein Veblen and Modern Social Theory* (New York: Seabury Press, 1978); David Riesman, *Thorstein Veblen: A Critical Interpretation* (New York: Charles Scribner's Sons, 1960); Bernard Rosenberg, *The Values of Veblen: A Critical Appraisal* (Washington, D.C.: Public Affairs Press, 1956); and Jackson Lears, "Beyond Veblen: Rethinking Consumer Culture in America," elsewhere in this volume.

[4] For contemporary contrasts to Veblen's leisure class, see Marlys J. Harris, "The Theory of the Busy Class," *Money* 16, no. 4 (April 1987): 203–20; and John Brooks, *Showing Off in America: From Conspicuous Consumption to Parody Display* (Boston: Little, Brown, 1981). For the rags-to-riches mythology in popular literature and the American idea of success, see Moses Rischin, ed., *The American Gospel of Success: Individualism and Beyond* (Chicago: Quadrangle Books, 1965); John G. Cawelti, *Apostles of the Self-Made Man* (Chicago: University of Chicago Press, 1965); Richard M. Huber, *The American Idea of Success* (New York: McGraw-Hill Book Co., 1971); Herbert Gutman, "The Reality of the Rags-to-Riches 'Myth,'" in *Work, Culture and Society in Industrializing America*, ed. Herbert Gutman (New York: Alfred A. Knopf, 1976), pp. 211–33; Ralph D. Gardner, *Horatio Alger; or, The American Hero Era* (New York: Arco Publishing, 1971); and Celeste MacLeod, *Horatio Alger: Farewell, the End of the Amer-*

Fig. 1. Sixth Ave. near Seventeenth St., New York, Christmas, ca. 1900. (Library of Congress: Photo, George Grantham Bain.)

The sentiment of acquisitiveness was a favorite theme of late-Victorian chronicles and novels. The central character in Theodore Dreiser's *Sister Carrie* (1900) finds the "lure of the material" as she wanders around a Chicago department store:

ican Dream (New York: Seaview Books, 1980). The social origins and the mobility of business elites are discussed by Frances W. Gregory, "The American Industrial Elite in the 1870s," and William Miller, "American Historians and the Business Elite," in *Men in Business: Essays on the Historical Role of the Entrepreneur* (New York: Harper Torchbooks/Harper and Row, 1952), pp. 193–211, 309–28. The "image of unlimited good" is discussed in Alan Dundes, "Folk Ideas as Units of Worldview," *Journal of American Folklore* 84, no. 331 (January–March 1971): 93–103; and Patrick Mullen, "The Folk Idea of Unlimited Good in American Buried Treasure Legends," *Journal of the Folklore Institute* 15, no. 3 (September–December 1978): 209–20. The story of the "million dollar corner" was circulated by the Bain News Service, December 13, 1911 (Prints and Photographs, George Grantham Bain Collection, Library of Congress). For further discussion of the imagery of the public and its streams, see William R. Taylor, "The Evolution of Public Space in New York City: The Commercial Showcase of America," elsewhere in this volume.

Carrie passed along the busy aisles, much affected by the remarkable displays of trinkets, dress goods, stationery, and jewelry. Each separate counter was a showplace of dazzling interest and attraction. She could not help feeling the claim of each trinket and valuable upon her personally, and yet she did not stop. There was nothing there which she could not have used—nothing which she did not long to own. The dainty slippers and stockings, the delicately frilled skirts and petticoats, the laces, ribbons, hair-combs, purses, all touched her with individual desire.

Entering a restaurant, Carrie noticed "the tables were not so remarkable in themselves, and yet the imprint of Sherry upon the napery, the name of Tiffany upon the silverware, the name of Haviland upon the china, and over all the glow of the small, red-shaded candelabra and the reflected tints of the walls on garments and faces, made them seem remarkable. Each waiter added an air of exclusiveness and elegance by the manner in which he bowed, scraped, touched, and trifled with things."[5]

Examined alone, Dreiser's work appears to suggest an unusual preoccupation with habits of accumulation and display, but the attention to the minutest details of consumption carries over to a variety of literary works of the period. The central theme of Harold Frederic's *Damnation of Theron Ware*, a bestseller of 1896, is the Hawthorne-like downfall of a Methodist minister who succumbs to various worldly temptations. The name *Theron Ware* is a clue to the theme of consumption in the novel (*Theron* is usually linked to an ancient tyrant; *Ware* suggests salable, often manufactured goods). This is not to suggest that Theron Ware is a tyrant; rather, that he falls prey to many forces, including the material lure of an emerging consumer society. He confronts temptation in a new department store called Thurston's (a name that plays on the sense of thirst or consumption it provides for some and drought for others) located in the village of Octavius (the Roman name usually associated with wealth and the name of the emperor in whose reign Christ was born).

"Thurston's" was a place concerning which opinions differed in Octavius. That it typified progress, and helped more than any other feature of the village to bring it up to date, no one indeed disputed. One might move about a great deal, in truth, and hear no other view expressed. But then again one might

---

[5] Theodore Dreiser, *Sister Carrie* (1900; reprint, New York: W. W. Norton, 1970), pp. 47, 51, 17, 235. For further discussion of Dreiser's views of consumption, see Rachel Bowlby, *Just Looking: Consumer Culture in Dreiser, Gissing, and Zola* (New York: Methuen, 1985).

stumble into conversation with one small store-keeper after another, and learn that they united in resenting the existence of "Thurston's," as rival farmers might join to curse a protracted drought. Each had his special flaming grievance.

After visiting Thurston's, Ware resolves "to preach a sermon on the subject of the modern idea of admiring the great for crushing the small," but the sermon is never written. Ware is lured, almost blindly, by the things and the ease of acquiring them in Thurston's, although he feels ignorant about making consumer choices, particularly in selecting a piano for the church. He later returns to buy a piano accompanied by Celia (an anagram for his loyal wife, Alice, as well as the name of the patron saint of music and the blind), the organist of the Catholic church for whom he feels sinful longing: "There were a good many pianos in the big showroom overhead, and Theron found himself almost awed by their size and brilliancy of polish, and the thought of the tremendous sum of money they represented altogether." But Celia cooly declares, "There's nothing here really good. It is always much better to buy of the makers direct." Replying with one of the great romantic lines of Victorian writing, Ware asks, "Do they sell on the installment plan?"[6]

Harry Leon Wilson produced another—perhaps the ultimate—parable of consumption in *The Spenders*. It is the story of a family fortune made in mining in the rugged but arcadian West, only to be squandered by the younger cosmopolitan generations back East. It joins a host of earlier novels, including Howells's *Hazard of New Fortunes* and *Rise of Silas Lapham*, about character and the consequence of new wealth. The novels were popular reading for the way in which they worked through new experiences and values in contrast to the past. Like other novels of the period, *The Spenders* often offers a display-window or catalogue style of narrative to gain its effect. Early in the novel, the contrast of a humble "what-not" in the sitting room and a newly purchased "Empire cabinet" in the parlor commands several pages of commentary. The contrast between these things reflects the differences between the older and newer generations, a reflection of the family strife that wealth has produced.

The what-not, once the cherished shrine of the American home, sheltered the smaller household gods for which no other resting place could be found. [The] "what-not" [contains] a tender motto worked with the hair of the dead; a "Rock

---

[6]Harold Frederic, *The Damnation of Theron Ware*, ed. Everett Carter (1896; reprint, Cambridge, Mass.: Harvard University Press, 1960), pp. 56–57, 216–17.

of Ages" in a glass case, with a garland of pink chenille around the base; two dried pine cones brightly varnished; an old daguerreotype in an ornamental case of hard rubber; small old album; two small China vases of the kind that came always in pairs, standing on mats of crocheted worsted; three sea-shells; and the cup and saucer that belonged to grandma. . . . [But] the new cabinet, haughty in its varnished elegance, with its Watteau dames and courtiers, and perhaps the knowledge that it enjoys widespread approval among the elect—this is a different matter. In every American home that is a home, to-day, it demands attention. The visitor, after eyeing it with cautious side-glances, goes jauntily up to it, affecting to have been stirred by the mere impulse of elegant idleness. Under the affectedly careless scrutiny of the hostess he falls dramatically into an attitude of awed entrancement. Reverently he gazes upon the priceless bibel-ots within: the mother-of-pearl fan, half open; the tiny cup and saucer of Sevres on their brass easel; the miniature Cupid and Psyche in marble; the Japanese wrestlers carved in ivory; the ballet-dancer in bisque; the coral necklace; the souvenir spoon from the Paris Exposition. . . . The what-not is obsolete. The Empire cabinet is regnant. Yet though one is the lineal descendant of the other— its sophisticated grandchild—they are hostile and irreconcilable.

Similarly, department store windows and hotel lobbies become studies in the power and symbolism of things and wealth by showing the unrelenting force of accumulation, the blinding qualities of display, and the commonly fleeting surface rewards. The revealing name "Hightower Hotel" is used in the novel as "an instructive microcosm of New York. . . . It overwhelms with its lavish display of wealth, it stuns with its tireless, battering energy. But it stays always aloof, indifferent if it be loved or hated; if it crush or sustain."[7]

Writers stepped forward to point out a disturbing gap between publicly obvious consumers and the often hidden, shunned bottom of the scale. This gap was more disturbing because of the republican and Christian ideals of egalitarianism that Americans traditionally claimed. Howells brought home the troubling situation to Americans in his biting commentary on the fading vision of a republican past, *A Traveler from Altruria*, about an altruistic visitor to the United States from a land where American egalitarian ideals are actually lived out. By setting the reality of life in America against life as Americans imagined it, the book forced a reflection on the "progress" of the new order.

This dilemma of the age was plain to Sir Philip Burne-Jones, an

---

[7] Harry Leon Wilson, *The Spenders* (Boston: Lothrop, 1902), pp. 34–38, 152, 218.

Englishman who recorded his observations of turn-of-the-century America in *Dollars and Democracy:* "The doctrine of equality, though of course it lends itself . . . to ridicule or ludicrous satire, is in reality a fine idea, and it lies at the root of all that America once held most sacred when she began the new life a hundred years ago—the theory that every man born in the country should have a fair and equal chance. . . . it is this spirit that has inspired the whole people since it has existed as a separate nation." Yet matters of money forced elitism and class protectionism upon Americans: "In snatches of conversation caught in the streets, the restaurants, and the cars, the continual cry is always 'dollars—dollars—dollars!' You hear it on all sides perpetually, and money does truly here, as politics in England, seem to be an end in itself, instead of a means to an end." Burne-Jones noted that, unlike in England, where family title and land-based wealth allowed lasting security, in America status was often fleeting; thus, it had to be displayed rather than inherited. Therefore, the power of American wealth was obsessively turned over to the consumption of things that conveyed one's station in life or the station to which one aspired. Even those without money often neglected basic needs to seek things that offered a taste of luxury.[8]

Contrasted with frequent reports of the preoccupation with excess were reformist titles such as Jacob Riis's *How the Other Half Lives* and Lincoln Steffens's *Shame of the Cities,* which gave a vivid reminder of how much wealth had been gained and who had been left behind in its acquisition. Waves of immigrants and rural migrants swelled the ranks of the urban poor and appeared starkly captured before the great industrial advance. The growing city sought to reconcile its excessive fortunes and excessive privations. The paradox of conditions that allowed for great wealth while promoting great poverty again forced Americans to contemplate the institutions they had molded for the new age. Questions lingered among reformers over whether the lot of the poor could be improved by teaching them to save or consume better, by having the city and industry serve them better, or by having them become more urbane and industrious.[9]

[8] Sir Philip Burne-Jones, *Dollars and Democracy* (New York: D. Appleton, 1904), pp. 70–71, 74, 107–16.
[9] See Jacob A. Riis, *How the Other Half Lives: Studies among the Tenements of New York* (Williamstown, Mass.: Corner House, 1890); Lincoln Steffens, *The Shame of the Cities* (New York: McClure, Phillips, 1904); Charles Richmond Henderson, *The Social*

From his editor's post at *Atlantic Monthly* and later *Harper's Monthly*, Howells became an observer, a critic, and the conscience of the changing nation. His move from Boston to New York in 1888 drew notice as representing a symbolic shift of the nation's character from its intellectual center in old New England to the commercial colossus. In *Traveler from Altruria*, Howells cited accumulation as the culprit of a scheme gone awry: "Men's minds and men's hands were suddenly released to an activity unheard of before. Invention followed invention; our rivers and seas became the warp of commerce where the steam-sped shuttles carried the woof of enterprise to and fro with tireless celerity. Machines to save labor multiplied themselves as if they had been procreative forces; and wares of every sort were produced with incredible swiftness and cheapness." Accumulation became a force in its own right: "The Accumulation, as we called this power, because we feared to call it by its true name, rewarded its own with gains of twenty, of a hundred, of a thousand per cent, and to satisfy its need, to produce the labor that operated its machines, there came into existence a hapless race of men who bred their kind for its service, and whose little ones were its prey, almost from their cradles."[10]

Despite Howells's literary influence in warning of the dire consequences of this consumer system, the advance of consumer behavior accelerated. At least in part, Americans seemed to be moved more by cultural conventions that averred a faith in consumption. The late-Victorian interior was overstuffed, filled with manufactured accessories such as layers of drapes and many pillows. Furniture often tended to be excessively ornate and heavy, and popular pieces suited for eclectic display such as étagères, sideboards, and cabinets were used to stuff and

---

Spirit in America (Chicago: Scott, Foresman, 1901); C. Hanford Henderson, *Pay-Day* (Boston: Houghton Mifflin Co., 1911); Herbert David Croly, *The Promise of American Life* (New York: Macmillan, 1914); Scott Nearing, *Poverty and Riches: A Study of the Industrial Regime* (Philadelphia: John C. Winston, 1916); Lewis Filler, ed., *Late Nineteenth-Century American Liberalism* (Indianapolis: Bobbs-Merrill, 1962); Arthur Myron Weinberg, ed., *The Muckrakers: The Era in Journalism that Moved America to Reform* (New York: Van Nostrand, 1974); and Steven Kesselman, *The Modernization of American Reform* (New York: Garland Publishing, 1979).

[10] William Dean Howells, *A Traveler from Altruria* (1894; reprint, New York: Sagamore Press, 1957), p. 274. For more of "Altruria" as a literary setting, see William Dean Howells, *The Altrurian Romances* (1895; reprint, New York: Arno Press, 1971).

layer crowded exhibits of ceramics, souvenirs, novelties, plants, and exotic shells into the Victorian parlor.

Equally overstuffed were world's fairs, which attracted millions of people to Philadelphia, Chicago, St. Louis, San Francisco, and other boastful cities to see elaborate, crowded mixtures of commercial spectacles of industrial progress and imperial expansion. At the 1901 Pan-American Exposition in Buffalo, visitors saw the vision of consumption celebrated at the central "Fountain of Plenty" in the "Court of Abundance." Illustrator Thomas Fleming made a splash by satirizing the consuming vision of "the Pan" with drawings of classical sculptures selling advertising space, preindustrial "primitives" on the midway doing the bidding of crass Yankees, and commercial exhibits producing comical hypnotizing effects. Fleming drew out a compelling message of the fairs—consumption basked in the glow of "educational" entertainment—while manufacturing radiated the vital energy of a progressive civilization.[11]

Economist George Gunton chided the critics for standing against the side of "social progress." He argued that a nation of workers, many of them immigrants, could be indoctrinated into an uplifting democratic experience through the cultural education of consumption. To Gunton, grandiose displays such as George Vanderbilt's 250-room Biltmore mansion led "the way to a new direction of devoting American wealth to the uplifting of the American standard of taste and social cultivation." Using an evolutionary model, Gunton beheld in con-

---

[11] Thomas Fleming, *Around the "Pan" with Uncle Hank: His Trip through the Pan-American Exposition* (New York: Nut Shell Publishing, 1901), p. 187. For connections between the scale of the Victorian interior and the fairs, see Alan Gowans, *Images of American Living: Four Centuries of Architecture and Furniture as Cultural Expression* (New York: Harper and Row, 1976), pp. 363–86. Other discussions of the stuffing and layering of the Victorian interior include Gail Caskey Winkler and Roger Moss, *Victorian Interior Decoration: American Interiors, 1830–1900* (New York: Henry Holt, 1986); Edgar de N. Mayhew and Minor Myers, Jr., *A Documentary History of American Interiors from the Colonial Era to 1915* (New York: Charles Scribner's Sons, 1980), pp. 193–310; and Meyric R. Rogers, *American Interior Design: The Traditions and Development of Domestic Design from Colonial Times to the Present* (New York: W. W. Norton, 1947), pp. 130–68. For analyses of particular Victorian furniture pieces and their strong display functions, see Kenneth L. Ames, "Meaning in Artifacts: Hall Furnishings in Victorian America," in *Material Culture Studies in America*, ed. Thomas J. Schlereth (Nashville: American Association for State and Local History, 1982), pp. 206–21; Kenneth L. Ames, ed., *Victorian Furniture: Essays from a Victorian Society Autumn Symposium* (Philadelphia: Victorian Society in America, 1983).

sumption the promise for America of "entering upon the threshold of the leisured phase of its societary development."[12] Gunton argued that expanding the system of consumption would bring increased comfort, leisure, and refinement to working Americans.

The promise of consumption drew considerable comment in the wave of utopian writing during the late nineteenth century. In *Looking Backward*, Edward Bellamy foresaw a contented army that supplied goods to central warehouses for mass distribution to the public of the year 2000. Itself a milestone of consumption, Bellamy's book sold more than 125,000 copies within one year of its publication. Bellamy had a vision of progress and abundance, with stores not more than ten minutes away from the new consumers. Befitting his nineteenth-century concern over the upheaval of striking tradesmen, Bellamy downplayed the individual productive worker and told of an overarching, formal organization that replaced the old republican localism with a corporate nationalism. He viewed the architectural adornment of nationalism as a "female ideal of Plenty, with her cornucopia," the same emblem that graced the cover of Sears, Roebuck, and Company's catalogues in the late nineteenth century.[13]

Bradford Peck's *World a Department Store* provided another striking illustration of the vision of consumption. Like Bellamy's hero, in Peck's novel Percy Brantford (a play on the author's name) falls asleep and wakes up years later to encounter a world where all productive activities, even cooking, are ordered out. Services are paid for and regulated by a credit system: the world "is indebted to the system formerly used in the department stores for our present wise condition of life," and the system is taught to the young through competitions and "object lessons." Dedicated to "suffering toilers in all walks of life," Peck imagined city planning around neat aisles and rows with clear divisions for residences, services, and supply stores. Brantford eventually exclaims, "It is like awakening in heaven. All the wonderful changes I have thus

---

[12] George Gunton, *Principles of Social Economics, Inductively Considered and Practically Applied, with Criticisms on Current Theories* (New York: G. P. Putnam's Sons, 1891); Daniel Horowitz, *The Morality of Spending: Attitudes toward the Consumer Society in America, 1875–1940* (Baltimore: Johns Hopkins University Press, 1985), p. 45.

[13] Edward Bellamy, *Looking Backward, 2000–1887* (1888; reprint, New York: Modern Library, 1982), p. 72; see also John F. Kasson, *Civilizing the Machine: Technology and Republican Values in America, 1776–1900* (1976; reprint, New York: Penguin Books, 1977), pp. 191–202.

far seen, the methods and customs which are now in vogue, shows how systematic all things are. No hurry, no worry, no bustle, yet all laboring for a grand and noble existence."[14]

Dimensions of Display in Artifact

Historians have long held that Americans broke with the agrarian past after the Civil War with their embrace of industrialization, urbanization, and incorporation. Often overlooked is another lasting sign of the times—the flowering of consumer behavior in mass proportions. As more Americans earned wages rather than made or grew products for trade, they increasingly relied on ready-made goods. Having basic goods more widely available because of mass production techniques did not satisfy the craving for ready-made goods; rather, it created a demand for more to become available. It did not popularize the traditional ethic of self-sacrifice and saving; instead, the cry went out to bring down the cost of basic goods, and as costs went down more goods became "nec essary" to buy. The "good life" became more materially defined as the accumulation of goods appeared to offer status, mobility, and self-confidence. Luxury items came within the reach and desire of more buyers, and variants of basic goods and "necessary" innovations proliferated. Advertisers and promoters saw to it that demand for more goods, especially novel or "improved" ones, continued. Economist Simon Patten observed, "The new morality does not consist in saving, but in expanding consumption." Howard Mumford Jones later summarized, "Wealth in this period expressed itself in the acquisition of things."[15]

In unprecedented numbers Americans shopped for standardized,

[14] Bradford Peck, *The World a Department Store* (1900; reprint, New York: Arno Press, 1971), pp. 142–45, 242–43.
[15] See Daniel Horowitz, *Morality of Spending*; Thomas C. Cochran, *Frontiers of Change: Early Industrialism in America* (New York: Oxford University Press, 1981); Neil Harris, "The Drama of Consumer Desire," in *Yankee Enterprise: The Rise of the American System of Manufactures*, ed. Otto Mayr and Robert C. Post (Washington, D.C.: Smithsonian Institution Press, 1981), pp. 189–216; and Ethel Hoover, "Retail Prices after 1850," in *Trends in the American Economy in the Nineteenth Century* (1960; reprint, New York: Arno Press, 1975), pp. 142–63. Simon N. Patten, *The New Basis of Civilization* (New York: Macmillan, 1907), p. 213; Howard Mumford Jones, *The Age of Energy: Varieties of American Experience, 1865–1915* (New York: Viking Press, 1971), pp. 17–18; Henry James, "The Old Things," *Atlantic Monthly* 77, no. 463 (May 1896): 681.

ready-made goods that were distributed nationally. The department store was the great palace of the new consumer culture where an abundance of goods was proudly displayed and sold, and where shopping became an emotional experience. Americans beheld the promise and prestige of new goods in advertisements, catalogues, magazine illustrations and stories, novels, theaters, train stations, restaurants, hotels, expositions, and fairs. More than a new way of providing for one's sustenance, consumer behavior spawned new professions, institutions, desires, and outlooks.

The prevailing wisdom of business practice late into the nineteenth century was to provide specialized goods on demand for selected clients, thus ensuring a reputable and secure income. For the protection of their stock, most stores displayed few goods. Select customers asked for merchandise they often had not seen beforehand. The goods were brought out and handled by store managers. Department stores were original at their dawning because of their high-volume, fixed-price sale of many varieties of goods available for viewing and handling, which introduced a level of speculation and pandering into business that many economic advisers found shocking.

In Philadelphia on Monday, March 12, 1877, a men's dry-goods merchant named John Wanamaker opened what he called a "New Kind of Store." The store was devoted to open aisles of men's and women's clothing and other items all "under one roof" and "conveniently arranged" by departments (fig. 2). Coming one year after the mass spectacle of the Centennial Exhibition in Philadelphia, the expansion and rearrangement of Wanamaker's business were influenced heavily by the grand exhibits of the fair (fig. 3). The influence was not lost on the Philadelphia *Press*, which reported:

As is very commonly remarked, a view of the main floor from the antique gallery west of the Chestnut entrance strikingly recalls the Centennial Exhibition. There is the same width of display extending about as far as the eye can reach, the riches of the world brought together from all lands, and representing all departments of art and industry, tastefully arranged to be shown with advantage. There is the same sense of spaciousness and, what is specially noticeable, the same ample illumination, the whole place being light, bright and cheerful.[16]

[16] John Wanamaker, *Golden Book of the Wanamaker Stores* (Philadelphia: John Wanamaker, 1911), pp. 43–56, 71. For further discussion of the relation of world's fairs and department stores, see Russell Lewis, "Everything under One Roof: World's Fairs and Department Stores in Paris and Chicago," *Chicago History* 13, no. 3 (Fall 1983): 28–47.

Fig. 2. John Wanamaker's "Grand Depot," Philadelphia, before 1902. From John Wanamaker, *Golden Book of the Wanamaker Stores* (Philadelphia: John Wanamaker, 1911), p. 56.

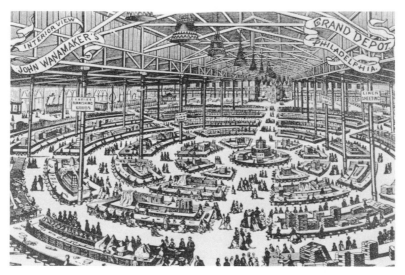

Fig. 3. Interior of John Wanamaker's "Grand Depot," after 1877. From John Wanamaker, *Golden Book of the Wanamaker Stores* (Philadelphia: John Wanamaker, 1911), p. 52.

The opening of this "Grand Depot" store provoked additional commentary in an editorial by the Philadelphia *Public Ledger:*

There are thirty-three blocks of counters, numbering 129 in all, and aggregating two-thirds of a mile in length, and in front of which are 1,400 stools for the convenience of shoppers. There are elegantly fitted rooms for such goods as ladies' finished suits, and other departments, besides parlors, retiring rooms, etc., for the comfort of customers. The store, No. 1313 Chestnut street, has been purchased by Mr. Wanamaker and entirely demolished in order to make room for a beautiful arcade, leading from Chestnut street into his great store. The entrance is handsomely ornamented, and the arcade is tiled with marble and lighted by day by means of stained glass skylights, and by night by elaborate chandeliers.[17]

Wanamaker met with opposition from shopkeepers for treading over the traditional lines of merchandising and opening up commerce to greater numbers of consumers. Wanamaker promoted his new institution by the use of mass advertising in newspapers and circulars. The technique was suggested by the Centennial Exhibition, which engendered a boom in newspaper circulation and influence thanks to the throngs descending on Philadelphia looking for a souvenir of the fair. Newspapers left the local realm of the city and, with runs of hundreds of thousands, were scattered throughout the country. Taking a cue from this boosterism, Wanamaker created large-scale ads with glitzy enticements unprecedented in advertising. One month after the store opened, *Sunday Gazette* hurled the following barb at the store: "Billions of Millions! more or less, of Ladies and Gentlemen, Boys and Girls, Spitzdogs and Poodles, have visited our Immense Emporium during the first week of its existence and the mammoth headquarters of Monopoly is now an established fact, and must remain a monument to the Gullibility of the Public as long as there is a Public to be gulled."[18]

Sunday Mercury predicted that Wanamaker's store and its maverick ideas would fold within three months. Instead the store prospered and expanded into more merchandising lines and provided more customer services. Estimates were that as many as 40,000 shoppers came to the store daily. Wanamaker became an internationally known figure, and his store was proclaimed a progressive, "modern" institution. In

[17] Wanamaker, *Golden Book*, pp. 51–53.
[18] Wanamaker, *Golden Book*, pp. 57–60.

1884 an editorial by Wanamaker declared, "Seven years ago the winds of old trade customs were dead in our faces. Never did Kansas cyclones blow more fiercely. We could only do our best and trust the good common sense of the people to set things to rights. We have not been disappointed." In 1900 Wanamaker announced, "Where there was one large dry goods store twenty-five years ago there are ten today—so well have the people supported the new codes and practices of business dealing. We have never secured patents on our system; but on the contrary, have given our best strength and experience to educate generals and soldiers of every rank for the mercantile army." Wanamaker stirred the public imagination by offering the lure of cheaper prices and conveniences (including rest rooms, elevators, and fountains, which were novelties at the time), the promise of equal treatment and fair trading for anyone with cash, and the aura of artistic spectacle and machinelike order. He also made use of mass advertising, grand displays, and educational devices to train and attract enlightened consumers to the abundant world of goods available for viewing and handling. A contemporary of Wanamaker noted: "The underlying idea of Mr. Wanamaker's great undertaking is to bring the producer and consumer into the closest possible relations; to offer the article wanted with the least possible amount of intermediate handling. This idea of yours has greatly excited the town. I stand by you on the old proverb: 'The greatest good to the greatest number.' "[19]

That Wanamaker's store set standards for techniques of merchandising, advertising, and store design is not the essential point; rather, it is that such standards became part of our culture and created symbols for the age. These standards found symbolic extension in custom, literature, art, and even city planning. Wanamaker assumed that commerce was "the great civilizer." As consumers participating in new economic and social patterns, Americans embraced new ways of living, seeing, and thinking. The vice-provost of the University of Pennsylvania conveyed the idea in 1909 that Wanamaker's store had become a metaphor for progress, a reference for the present and future, when he declared, "A thorough knowledge of what the Wanamaker Store really represents in its relation to the work of the world is in itself a broad education, for within this building are found in operation almost every

[19] Wanamaker, *Golden Book*, pp. 61–63.

Fig. 4. "The Loan Exhibition at the National Academy of Design,"
Harper's Weekly 22, no. 1140 (November 2, 1878): 872–73. From John
Grafton, *New York in the Nineteenth Century* (New York: Dover Pub-
lications, 1977), p. 144.

law of political economy, almost every application of scientific knowledge to the service of man, or the results of such application."[20]

Central to the behavior of the new consumers were the connected
patterns of accumulation and display. Although reformers during the
late nineteenth century sometimes used the pejorative term *materialism*
to describe emerging patterns of consumer behavior, others recognized
the more specific descriptions of accumulation and display as the foundations upon which the changing way of American life was built. A
well-known Victorian illustration splashed across two full pages of *Harper's Weekly* for November 2, 1878, demonstrated the excitement generated by accumulation and display for a society that traded in its
mythology of pioneer scarcity for the prospect of material abundance
(fig. 4). Bragging of the "effective arrangement" of the objects and the
way they filled the rooms to abundance, a writer declared, "A few years

[20]Wanamaker, *Golden Book*, p. 133.

Fig. 5. Advertisement for the "Hoffman House" Bouquet Cigar, Foster Hilson Co., ca. 1900. (The New-York Historical Society, Bella C. Landauer Collection.)

ago it would have been impossible to form such a collection in New York; and considering that nearly all these beautiful and interesting objects have been loaned by our citizens at very short notice, and that many persons who would gladly have contributed are absent in Europe, the exhibition certainly speaks well for the art culture and liberality of New Yorkers."[21]

By then New York had replaced Philadelphia as the mercantile center of the nation. It became a port of entry for new commercial ideas and the accumulation of things in expositions, museums, hotels, and department stores. Interior details of hotels, like the Hoffman House, thus proliferated to flatter guests and convey a new modern sensibility (fig. 5). Enterprising Americans were developing tasteful skills in accu-

[21]"The Loan Exhibition," *Harper's Weekly* 22, no. 1140 (November 2, 1878): 872–74.

mulating and displaying objects on the floors of department stores and in the lobbies of hotels, serving rooms of restaurants, and exhibits of expositions and museums. Historian Alan Trachtenberg has pointed out that "these places created a unique fusion of economic and cultural values; they were staging grounds for the making and confirming of new relations between goods and people." In a 1911 study of the spending habits of working-class women, Sue A. Clark and Edith Wyatt concluded that workers had adopted "the New York show window-display ideal of life manifested everywhere around them." Far from New York in their classic study *Middletown* (1929), Helen and Robert Lynd observed that the culture of consumption had swept middle America. During the 1890s midwestern residents "lived on a series of plateaus as regards standard of living." By the 1920s it was noted that "the edges of the plateaus have been shaved off, and every one lives on a slope from any point of which desirable things belonging to people all the way to the top are in view." Residents were "running for dear life in this business of making the money they earn to keep pace with the even more rapid growth of their subjective wants."[22]

In the Lynds's Middletown of the 1920s, the automobile—a high-ticket, mass-produced artifact stressing status and mobility in a consumer culture—was a prime symbol of the town's subjective wants. The way for the marketing of the automobile had been paved by the marketing of the bicycle during the 1880s. In 1884 a "safety" bicycle had been introduced, and the demand for it, especially among younger members of the middle class, quickly spread. It offered mobility, the thrill of self-propelled speed, the chance to experience fashionable strenuosity in the street and countryside, and, for many courting couples, the chance for an extended excursion away from the watchful eyes of chaperons (fig. 6). The design of the safety bicycle, with two wheels of equal size, abandoned the danger and achievement of the craftsman-like high-wheelers for the ease and convenience of a standardized industrial product. But there was not as yet a standard bearer for the

---

[22] Alan Trachtenberg, *The Incorporation of America: Culture and Society in the Gilded Age* (New York: Hill and Wang, 1982), p. 133; Sue A. Clark and Edith Wyatt, *Making Both Ends Meet: The Income and Outlay of New York City Working Girls* (New York: Macmillan, 1911), p. 23; Robert S. Lynd and Helen M. Lynd, *Middletown: A Study in American Culture* (1929; reprint, New York: Harcourt Brace Jovanovich, 1956), pp. 82–83, 87.

Fig. 6. H. A. Thomas and Wylie Lith. Co., sheet-music cover, 1896. Lithograph; H. 10″, W. 8½″. (The New-York Historical Society, Bella C. Landauer Collection.)

mass distribution of the bicycle; many independent manufacturers distributed the luxury item for local markets. Introducing more mass production techniques, many sewing machine and arms manufacturers entered the trade and further fragmented the market. The intense competition for the growing craze spawned an advertising war in national magazines. By 1898, 10 percent of all advertising featured bicycles. Frank Presbrey commented, "Especially is the development of magazine advertising indebted to the bicycle, for the bicycle gave the magazine a measure of recognition as a medium which encouraged the use of large space and more frequent insertions by advertisers in general.

Fig. 7. Advertisement for the Columbia Bicycle, Pope Manufacturing Co., Boston, ca. 1890. Poster; H. 14″, W. 10″. (The New-York Historical Society, Bella C. Landauer Collection.)

. . . It was bicycle manufacturers who first proved that an article of luxury costing $100 could be sold to the mass."[23]

[23] See David A. Hounshell, *From the American System to Mass Production, 1800–1932: The Development of Manufacturing Technology in the United States* (Baltimore: Johns Hopkins University Press, 1984), pp. 189–216; E. Benjamin Andrews, *The History of the Last Quarter-Century in the United States, 1870–1895*, 2 vols. (New York: Charles

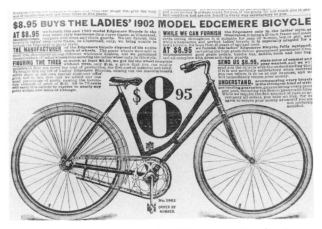

Fig. 8. Advertisement for the Edgemere Bicycle, Sears, Roebuck, and Co., 1902. From Sears, Roebuck, and Company, *Consumers Guide*, no. 111 (1902): 276.

With his keen understanding of the potential of mass consumption, Richard Warren Sears stepped into the market in the late 1890s with now-familiar techniques. Foreseeing a large market for an already developed product, Sears contracted for huge volume, offered easy installment plans, slashed prices, and advertised profusely in mass circulation outlets. He shifted the prevailing advertising pitch from speed and distance, a kind of manly utilitarian concern (fig. 7), to the mass cultural appeals of style, status, fashion, and easy availability—in short, pushing an object "everybody else has" or should want (fig. 8). Sears published his own circulars promoting bicycles and offered a free bicycle to anyone who brought in ten orders from the circulars. Corporate historians Boris Emmet and John E. Jeuck have claimed that Sears's own hand is evident in editorials such as one found in *American Woman:*

Last year retailers succeeded in reducing the price of all $100 bicycles to $75, and then they held the trade at home; but what are they going to do now when a new 1898 bicycle is offered at only $5.00, on easy conditions?—other latest

Scribner's Sons, 1896), 2:288–90; "An Outline of Bicycle History," *Bicycle News* 11, no. 10 (October 1926): 16. Frank Presbrey, *The History and Development of Advertising* (New York: Doubleday, Doran, 1929), pp. 363, 410–12.

models outright at $13.95 and $19.75, on free trial. It appears the monopoly on the finest grade seamless bicycle tubing has been broken, and where the best tubing alone for a bicycle formerly cost about $18 it is now reduced to less than $4, and Sears, Roebuck and Co., of Chicago, at these special prices, are waging war on all bicycle dealers. They send a Bicycle Catalogue free to anyone who asks for it, and, we are told, shipping several hundred bicycles every day to every state, direct to the riders at $5 to $19.75, on free trial before paying. If Sears, Roebuck and Co. continue to wage their bicycle war throughout the season it will be a boon to all those who want bicycles, but a sad blow to bicycle dealers and manufacturers.[24]

Despite promoting his products as a victory against the bicycle monopoly, the end result was that Sears virtually formed one of his own. In one year Sears set records by selling 100,000 bicycles, and he put new models on the market to encourage replacing the buyer's old one with the latest and best Sears had to offer.

The bicycle was "a trail-blazing pioneer" for encouraging advertising and mass consumption. In 1900 an official of the Census Bureau made the claim that because the bicycle helped to break down isolation and differentiation of the sexes, not to mention limited mobility, "few articles ever used by man have created so great a revolution in social conditions." Ethnologist W. J. McGee opined that with its arousal of invention and mass production, stimulation of commerce, encouragement of strong character (especially a unified national character), and development of "individuality, judgment, and prompt decision on the part of its users more rapidly and completely than any other device," the bicycle "weighed by its effect on body and mind as well as on material progress must be classed as one of the world's great inventions." Although invented in Europe, the bicycle was "redevised" in the United States, "and native genius made it a practical machine for the multitude; now its users number millions, and it is sold in every country."[25]

Although Europe experienced an earlier blossoming of consumer behavior among the middle classes, by the late nineteenth century America boasted of mail-order catalogues, department stores, and expo-

[24] Boris Emmet and John E. Jeuck, *Catalogues and Counters: A History of Sears, Roebuck and Company* (Chicago: University of Chicago Press, 1950), pp. 70–72.
[25] Presbrey, *History and Development*, p. 363; Arthur M. Schlesinger, *Political and Social Growth of the American People* (New York: Macmillan Co., 1941), p. 218; W. J. McGee, "Fifty Years of American Science," *Atlantic Monthly* 82, no. 491 (September 1898): 311–12.

sitions that reached more people with more ready-made goods—from bicycles to stoves and boots to suits—than any European counterpart. Even before the full flowering of an American consumer system, Alexis de Tocqueville's classic tome *Democracy in America* (1840) described a distinctive proprietary sense among Americans: "A native of the United States clings to this world's goods as if he were certain never to die." Tocqueville believed the "passion for physical comforts is essentially a passion of the middle classes; with those classes it grows and spreads, with them it is preponderant. From them it mounts into the higher orders of society and descends into the mass of the people." Rarely content with their possessions, Americans were quick to replace their goods with "fresh gratifications":

At first sight there is something surprising in this strange unrest of so many happy men restless in the midst of abundance. The spectacle itself, however, is as old as the world; the novelty is to see a whole people furnish an exemplification of it. Their taste for physical gratifications must be regarded as the original source of that secret disquietude which the actions of Americans betray and of that inconstancy of which they daily afford fresh examples. . . . Besides the good things that he possesses, he every instant fancies a thousand others that death will prevent him from trying if he does not try them soon.[26]

The Organization of Abundance in Community

Tocqueville's characterization of the restless nation is now considered prophetic, but even he might have been surprised at the nation's growth

[26] For discussions of European consumption, see Neil McKendrick, John Brewer, and J. H. Plumb, *The Birth of a Consumer Society: The Commercialization of Eighteenth-Century England* (Bloomington: Indiana University Press, 1982); Rosalind H. Williams, *Dream Worlds: Mass Consumption in Late Nineteenth-Century France* (Berkeley: University of California Press, 1982); and Whitney Walton, " 'To Triumph before Feminine Taste': Bourgeois Women's Consumption and Hand Methods of Production in Mid-Nineteenth-Century Paris," *Business History Review* 60, no. 4 (Winter 1986): 541–63. For the triumph of American consumption, see Daniel J. Boorstin, *The Americans: The Democratic Experience* (New York: Vintage/Random House, 1973), pp. 89–164, 411–50; Richard Wightman Fox and T. J. Jackson Lears, eds., *The Culture of Consumption: Critical Essays in American History, 1880–1980* (New York: Pantheon Books, 1983); Peter E. Samson, "The Emergence of a Consumer Interest in America, 1870–1930" (Ph.D. diss., University of Chicago, 1980); and Paul Mazur, *The Standards We Raise: The Dynamics of Consumption* (New York: Harper and Brothers, 1953). For "fresh gratifications," see Alexis de Tocqueville, *Democracy in America* (1840; abridged, New York: Modern Library, 1981), pp. 422–34.

and its move to the cities. Between 1850 and 1900 the population tripled; from 1859 to 1919 manufactured goods increased in value fivefold; from 1860 to 1900 the rail system increased ninefold; between 1880 and 1910 the industrial labor force grew from 2.75 million to over 8 million; and the number of cities with populations over 100,000 mounted from nine to fifty. Despite rapid urbanization and industrialization that promised dominance over the American landscape, the nation's numbers still gave the edge to the nonurban domain. But the clear trend toward urban life-styles spurred much reflection, speculation, and debate about a made-over future. Moralists pointed to a vast difference in the character of life and mores between the city and country, and wondered whether the agrarian ideals of family, home, and God could be preserved in the wake of rapid change. With a rhetoric that set the tone for debate, their tracts harped on the contrast between the traditional small town with its easy familiarity and the faceless, mass scale of the urban industrial empire.[27]

With this contrast, community took on a symbolic quality apparent to the eye. The common progression of change—from lone settlement to farm village to market town to city—became a parable of modernization. The organization of the community took on new significance as a visible reminder to outsiders of what to expect. Among the early forms of community, the New England village commons with its towering church steeple suggested communal ownership and a legacy of Christian inspiration. As geographer D. W. Meinig points out, "An idealized image of the New England village became so powerfully impressed upon such a broad readership as to become a national symbol, a model setting for the American community." It suggested the nation's colonial roots, and an older way of viewing land as something spiritual rather than commercial. When the image gave way to other forms of settlement in America, the change—and the recognition of one form differentiated from another—produced texts to read. This

[27] See David E. Shi, *The Simple Life: Plain Living and High Thinking in American Culture* (New York: Oxford University Press, 1985); Morton White and Lucia White, *The Intellectual versus the City: From Thomas Jefferson to Frank Lloyd Wright* (Cambridge, Mass.: Harvard University Press, 1962); Peter Schmitt, *Back to Nature: The Arcadian Myth in Urban America* (New York: Oxford University Press, 1969); James H. Tufts, *The Real Business of Living* (New York: Henry Holt, 1918), pp. 299–333; and Michael Barton, "The Victorian Jeremiad: Critics of Accumulation and Display," elsewhere in this volume.

change drew comment at nineteenth-century world's fairs in America, which typically featured rustic "olde tyme" New England kitchens representing an old domestic harmony in the midst of towering commercial exhibition buildings arranged by modern principles of city planning. The change in the late nineteenth century that formed communities into texts of consumer culture was the growth of cosmopolitan cities out of the market towns.[28]

A historical account of Harrisburg, Pennsylvania (designated an "All-American City" in 1985 by the National Municipal League), chronicles a common story of the rise of a cosmopolitan spirit that infused the consumer culture. Often the attention to changes on a mass scale obscures the smaller settings that are replete with cultural dramas and meanings of a very immediate and human kind. As a moderate-sized city set against the backdrop of the frugal Pennsylvania "Dutch" country, a German settlement that established an agricultural and folk-cultural stronghold, Harrisburg wore its conflicts on its sleeve. By the 1920s a threshold literature (in contrast to the futurist utopian literature of the 1880s) came pouring out, chronicling the passing of an old age and the brink of a new one, such as Marian Inglewood's *Then and Now in Harrisburg* and George P. Donehoo's *Harrisburg: The City Beautiful, Romantic and Historic.* Donehoo reflected: "The old town commenced to sink into the memories of the past and the city of Harrisburg began to materialize." Its physical and social conversion to the cosmopolitan spirit represented the kind of resolution that swayed the nation. It was this spirit that led syndicated columnist Mary McGrory to announce, "Harrisburg might indeed be America."[29]

[28] D. W. Meinig, "Symbolic Landscapes: Some Idealizations of American Communities," in *Interpretation of Ordinary Landscapes*, ed. D. W. Meinig (New York: Oxford University Press, 1979), pp. 164–92; John Brinckerhoff Jackson, *The Necessity for Ruins and Other Topics* (Amherst: University of Massachusetts Press, 1979), pp. 113–26; John Brinckerhoff Jackson, *American Space: The Centennial Years, 1865–1876* (New York: W. W. Norton, 1972); Rodris Roth, "The New England, or 'Olde Tyme,' Kitchen Exhibit at Nineteenth-Century Fairs," in *The Colonial Revival in America*, ed. Alan Axelrod (New York: W. W. Norton, 1985), pp. 159–83; Alan Trachtenberg, *The Incorporation of America: Culture and Society in the Gilded Age* (New York: Hill and Wang, 1982), pp. 208–34; Harold M. Mayer and Richard C. Wade, *Chicago: Growth of a Metropolis* (Chicago: University of Chicago Press, 1969).

[29] I chose Harrisburg partly because I live and work there, but also because it provides a counterpoint to the usual examples of large eastern metropolitan cities. George P. Donehoo, *Harrisburg: The City Beautiful, Romantic and Historic* (Harrisburg, Pa.:

Harrisburg rests along the shores of the Susquehanna River, which in its early years provided an economic lifeline of trading and logging. The city was founded in 1785 as a frontier outpost, a cluster of three hundred houses, behind which was a host of new farms and mills founded by hearty German and Scots-Irish immigrants. As the population of Pennsylvania moved west toward Harrisburg, agitation increased to move the capital of the state inland from Philadelphia. After much debate, Harrisburg was chosen as the capital in 1812 and proceeded to grow as a center of government, trade, and agriculture. As the town grew, the pattern of consumption changed: "When it was still but a frontier village, everybody had his own garden and raised his own fruits and vegetables, but as the place became more thickly settled, the citizens of Harrisburg were forced to depend more and more upon the farmers who lived round about."[30]

The response was to build market houses, which were considered to be "the first evidences of its trend toward city ways." In 1807 the first market houses, little more than sheds, were built on the central square—called Market Square—for the cost of $915.86 each. Although the "capacious buildings" of Market Square became the heart of the town (fig. 9), market buildings were built in each of the neighborhoods of the town. "Most every family, rich and poor alike went to market. . . . This was a way of life," reminisced Ralph "Cub" Huston, an old Harrisburg resident. In addition to carrying regular foodstuffs, the markets provided sources for many regional and ethnic folk foods, particularly Pennsylvania German varieties such as "smier kase" (a kind of soft cheese) and "lep kuche" (a kind of gingerbread). The markets contributed to the incorporation of Harrisburg as a city in 1860 while preserving the neighborhood and ethnic patterns of the town. The markets offered some unprecedented shopping—and serving—performances. Huston recalled:

Practically all the sellers were real farmers or real butchers. In season, each stall would have lettuce, endive, carrots, turnips, beets, eggs, tomatoes, potatoes,

---

Stackpole Books, 1927), p. 175. McGrory as quoted in Paul B. Beers, *Profiles from the Susquehanna Valley* (Harrisburg, Pa.: Stackpole Books, 1973). McGrory announced this shocking discovery in 1972 while covering the setting of the famous trial of the so-called Harrisburg 8.

[30] Marian Inglewood, *Then and Now in Harrisburg* (Harrisburg, Pa.: Minnie I. Etzewiler, 1925), p. 51.

Fig. 9. Market house, Market Square, Harrisburg, Pa., ca. 1880. (Dauphin County Historical Society.)

cabbage, celery, and corn. These were regular items. Then there were special seasons, including one with the most delectable, sweetest strawberries from York County. . . . Markets also provided opportunities for boys to earn money. Those of us having wagons would park outside the entrances and bid for the chance to haul the baskets to the homes of the shoppers. You had no set rate, as you were at the mercy of the customer. You learned the tricks of the trade. You learned to tip your cap, smile at the right time, how to be careful at curbs, and how to show appreciation. You also learned which customers were generous, and which ones to avoid if you could.[31]

Permanent grocery stores opened to meet the immediate needs of wage earners, especially after some industries came to Harrisburg after the Civil War. The stores were small establishments entrenched in the class- and ethnic-based neighborhoods (fig. 10). Innovations made by

[31] Inglewood, *Then and Now*, p. 51; Michael Barton, *Life by the Moving Road: An Illustrated History of Greater Harrisburg* (Woodland Hills, Calif.: Windsor Publications, 1983), pp. 101–2; Inglewood, *Then and Now*, p. 52; Barton, *Life*, pp. 102–3.

Fig. 10. H. G. Hagenberger's Grocery, Harrisburg, Pa., late nineteenth century. (Dauphin County Historical Society.)

grocery stores included adding consumer goods, such as tableware and
clothing, to their regular inventory of food and stocking prepackaged
edibles. Grocers "had long, hard days. They opened their stores at six
or seven in the morning. Men coming from their nightshifts would stop
to buy the things that had been written on a list the night before. The
grocer's day continued until late at night. Neighborhood stores were
seldom longer than a home living room; in fact, many were located in
what would have been the parlor. Yet, in that small space you could
find everything a family would need for survival."[32]

But as the family bought goods in that small space, the distance
between producer and consumer grew. New worlds of assorted choices
filled in the gap. Huston recalled the introduction of a new commercial
novelty as an example—the candy store: "The Gods with barrels of
ambrosia were not any richer than a kid with a penny in a candy store.
With a penny one had a choice of a most wonderful assortment. Perhaps the most difficult decisions we made in our lifetime were those

[32] Barton, *Life,* p. 100.

made in front of candy counters. You would feast your eyes from left to right, from right to left, from front to back, and even diagonally. You had to decide not only on taste, but also on which items gave the most for your money. . . . Boys had fun buying licorice, because they could emulate their elders by pretending they were chewing tobacco."[33]

The candy store was one of many new stores to sprout around the markets and eventually replace them. Besides carrying a wider assortment of goods in a smaller space, the stores were open almost every day of the week. Less crowded and less communally oriented than the markets, the stores enabled customers to feel unique and upwardly mobile. In the quiet, enclosed spaces of the stores, merchants used displays of goods that created an attractive environment for private consumption. The stores offered more of the ready-made goods (besides food) that residents sought for convenience. By changing displays to remind shoppers of new conveniences, the stores conveyed the look of keeping up-to-date and expert. The stores offered the pull of novelty, the appeal of modernity, and the promise of flattering attention. Customers were increasingly "served" in the stores.

By the 1880s a streetscape of small shops lined the avenues and pushed out the markets. The markets and the avenues came into conflict, because the markets created crowded neighborhood "centers" within traffic areas. To spur the commercial growth of the cosmopolitan city, civic leaders envisioned "streams" of traffic moving up the citywide avenues. Citing the hazards to traffic that the markets caused, the courts decreed on behalf of the merchants that the central market houses obstructed a highway—the new economic lifeline—and should be removed. Farmers came to the city now to buy rather than to sell. The last market day was held January 19, 1889. As Inglewood described the scene, "It seemed like the passing of old friends when those market houses were torn down, even if every one knew the march of progress made it necessary. . . . As for the buildings around the Square, they, too, have changed as radically as the Square itself, and have grown up from little log cabins into quite respectable looking semi-skyscrapers." Among the sights was the hardware store of Kelker and Brother, who had "just about everything in their large store that was in any way con-

[33] Barton, *Life*, pp. 103–4. The role of the consuming child in the city is discussed in David Nasaw, *Children of the City: At Work and at Play* (New York: Oxford University Press, 1986), pp. 115–37.

Fig. 11. Fahnestock's department store, Harrisburg, Pa., 1895. (Dauphin County Historical Society.)

nected with hardware, iron, or steel, from files, nails, and horseshoes up to anvils, circular saws, and Fairbanks scales. They even were agents for Meneely's church bells, something you'd scarcely expect to find in a hardware store of today."[34]

There were other stores that had things that residents hardly expected, most notably William Fahnestock's (fig. 11). Originally a ladies' clothing store, Fahnestock's built on its appeal to the influx of women earning wages at new factories in the city.[35] Although no longer a "ladies" store, Fahnestock added furniture, bicycles, toys, and rugs to lure the growing numbers of women who accounted for most of the city's consumer purchases. Fahnestock's feminine appeal was a contrast to the somber manly look of the Kelkers' hardware store, and the department

[34] Inglewood, *Then and Now*, p. 55.
[35] "Harrisburg Great Factories Employ Thousands of Girls," *Board of Trade Journal* 2, no. 10 (October 1907): 13; "Women Are Forming Clubs to Patronize Clean Shops," *Board of Trade Journal* 2, no. 11 (November 1907): 20. See also William Leach, "Transformations in a Culture of Consumption: Women and Department Stores, 1890–1925," *Journal of American History* 71, no. 2 (September 1984): 319–42; and Susan Porter Benson, *Counter Cultures: Saleswomen, Managers, and Customers in American Department Stores* (Urbana: University of Illinois Press, 1986).

store quickly outdistanced its competitor in business. Taking a cue from Philadelphia department stores, Fahnestock packed his show windows with bright mannequin-filled displays and hired well-dressed, enthusiastic sales clerks. The store was later taken over by Woolworth's and helped to make the downtown area a lively "shopping district."

Harry Robinson went further than Fahnestock in establishing the attraction of consumer dry goods in his department store. Robinson pushed the showcase of goods to three floors, each floor brandishing an airy window display (fig. 12). He invited workers to spend their days off ("dollar days," he called them) leisurely shopping for their labor's rewards.

Fig. 12. Robinson's department store, Harrisburg, Pa., 1902. (Dauphin County Historical Society.)

Fig. 13. *From left:* Dauphin Deposit Bank, Commonwealth Hotel, and John Wanamaker Arch, Market St. off Market Square, Harrisburg, Pa., 1896. (Dauphin County Historical Society.)

Overlooking the old Broad Street Market, Robinson's overshadowed the market in a neighborhood stronghold and expanded department store shopping outside the center of the city. He openly advertised prices and offered luxurious items as well as bargain items to lure shoppers to midtown from every neighborhood. Robinson was the harbinger of a cosmopolitan consumer identity for the city.[36]

Other sights and organizations confirmed the movement into the consumer age. The Harrisburg National Bank, founded in 1814, took on a new interior that resembled the designs of grand railroad stations. Established in 1845, Dauphin Deposit Bank off Market Square bragged of its commercial strength by brandishing huge classical pillars at its entrance (fig. 13). A new capitol was erected in 1897 boasting the design of the resplendent domes at the 1893 World's Columbian Exposition in

[36] For the importance of the department store to turn-of-the-century cities, see Gunther Barth, *City People: The Rise of Modern City Culture in Nineteenth-Century America* (New York: Oxford University Press, 1980), pp. 110–47; and Trachtenberg, *Incorporation of America*, pp. 130–36.

Fig. 14. Capitol, Harrisburg, Pa., erected 1897. (Photo, Simon J. Bronner, 1985.)

Chicago (fig. 14). The governor at the time declared, "The Capitol which in its mass of granite reigns over the city seems to throw a shadow of power and richness over everything."[37] Just as the capitol reigned over the city, the new Commonwealth Hotel towered over Market Square and became a center of social activity. When John Wanamaker ran for the United States Senate in 1896, a grand arch announced his entry into town past the hotel (see fig. 13). A stately Board of Trade was completed in 1898 on Market Street near the square (fig. 15), and the board shortly thereafter put out a magazine to attract more consumer development. The boom also produced some eccentric organizations like the Sons of Rest, young members of the new leisure class who gathered together to watch others work whenever a large new building was constructed downtown. Members of the uniformed Harrisburg Wheel Club, composed of merchants and professionals such as Fahnestock, compensated for their sedentary life-styles by riding the rough old high wheelers on strenuous outings to unspoiled natural outskirts (fig. 16).

[37] Donehoo, *Harrisburg*, p. 170.

Fig. 15. Board of Trade Building, Market St., Harrisburg, Pa., 1898. (Dauphin County Historical Society.)

John O'Hara captured the flavor of turn-of-the-century Harrisburg in *Rage to Live* (1949). O'Hara recalled the city from his childhood, and he returned to Market Square to talk to old-timers about the city's emergence "simply to record reality." In O'Hara's view, Harrisburg was a city turned from the farmers with their sense of tradition to the merchants with their vision of the future; it was a city where the "snappiest," rather than the richest inhabitants, now set the tone in manners. With his eye for family dynamics and hometown details, O'Hara described social changes apparent behind the city's new look: the dining-out that workers felt obliged to do rather than going home for lunch; the increased attention to appearances, and expensive ones at that; the growing concern for having what others had; and the passing of the leisurely cere-

Fig. 16. Harrisburg Wheel Club at Natural Bridge, Va., 1888. William Fahnestock is standing at far right, first row. (Dauphin County Historical Society.)

monial pipe for the anxiously consumed cigarettes that both men and women now smoked. O'Hara wrote that Harrisburg "went in for a metropolitan social life, with consequent prosperity for dressmakers, tailors, shoemakers, and jewelers at home and away."[38]

Still, residents nostalgically recalled older ways. Old Home Week was a celebration that was instituted in 1905 to tour and "read" the community texts of an earlier time. As a result of the tourist development of the Amish settlement, which included the promotion of markets, city residents were able to escape back to a preindustrial way of life. From the few market houses still left standing, "people gathered up the bits of wood as mementoes of the good old times they typified, and today in many a Harrisburg home, you'll find a cane, paper weight, or fancy ornament made from the wood of the old market houses on the Square."[39]

In spite of the romantic stirrings of the old neighborhood and mar-

[38] Frank MacShane, *The Life of John O'Hara* (New York: E. P. Dutton, 1980), pp. 141–42; John O'Hara, *A Rage to Live* (New York: Random House, 1949), p. 49.
[39] Inglewood, *Then and Now*, p. 54.

ket system, civic leaders viewed the changes as progress that had transformed the city into "a busy industrial center, in which is made almost
every article used by man, from steel and iron to silk and knitted goods,
with a valuation of $218,810,400 of the products made. And instead of
a hundred Indian traders, representing the total of the industrial
employees, they would find an army of 28,258 men and women engaged
in the 302 industries in the country."[40]

Conclusion

Sources of texts varied from the intellectuals who produced novels to
the corporate executives who designed new products to the merchants
who built a vivid streetscape, but a common agenda can nonetheless be
discerned. Judging by what people read in the signs of the times, the
preoccupation of the age was with wealth: new wealth, consuming wealth,
widespread wealth. Americans wondered what to make of this recent
good fortune, what to do with it, how to show it, and what it meant for
the future. They embraced it, but worried about it.

Progress was a key word in the perception of texts, for it was defined
by a condition marked by an abundance of goods and ease of life.
Regardless of the many plaints that emerged during the late nineteenth
century, the texts bowed before the inevitable force of progress defined
materially. Progress so defined provided a vivid measure of advancement for the society, the culture, and its children. The real struggle was
ensuring that matters of spirit and human compassion remained part of
the essence of life. Within that struggle was the harnessing of wealth to
social advantage and welfare while gratifying the self. Texts reminded
readers of the alluring, hypnotizing effects of available goods. Although
people swore that their character did not change with the accumulation
and display of goods, texts often conveyed the idea that changes were
occurring typically outside of one's awareness. Swept up by the tide of
goods, turn-of-the-century Americans attentively read new texts geared
to the consumer culture to understand what had happened to them and
could happen to them in the future. In this they found pause, if not
parting. It ironically confirmed the culture even as it questioned its

[40] Donehoo, *Harrisburg*, p. 188.

patterns. In text and symbol, characters basked in the glory of attainment and lost something in the process. The question was whether progress had created this dilemma—for society, for culture, and for the individual.

The impression of a society of consumers raised images of breaking down the isolation of people. Shared goods meant having more in common; therefore, a scattered society still could be close, even if it meant that strangers could hide behind the facade of their things. People could create status differences not through their character, but through their accumulation of luxuries. A society with ready-made goods available to them could also be more expansive. Not tied to the local market and environment, Americans were free to explore new sights. The consumer system reached across the land, advancing in apparent defiance of the land. Advertisements proclaimed and artifacts offered that whatever was desired was possible if a rational and efficient way of doing things was adopted, inspired by the very machines that brought this possibility to reality. Freedom of movement and the promise of ease replaced the power of self-reliance. The power of consumption and its heightened capacity to order goods replaced the power of production and its capacity to produce goods.

As the question for society concerned effects on people, the question for culture emphasized what happened to socially shared ideas expressed in customs, arts, and institutions. Texts were more important in a consumer system, since people who were increasingly strangers to one another relied on signs to communicate. Within the older familiarity of the rooted village, more knowledge was inherited and assumed. People on the move needed more signs to guide them through the changing landscape and their changing lives. And once settled in new situations, people looked to vivid texts to offer advice and tradition. Further, with the broader scope of the consumer system, the importance of appearance represented a shift from the reliance on handwork and complemented this shift and produced a textual world of color, light, and spectacle emanating from goods.[41]

Yet as Howells and others observed, "it looked a little dull" because it was a veneer over deep-spirited feelings found in the individuality of

---

[41] For further discussion of this textual world, see William Leach, "Strategists of Display and the Production of Desire," elsewhere in this volume.

handwork and the unrestrained expression of primitive tastes. On Sunday on Madison Avenue, according to Howells, "The men's faces were shrewd and alert, and yet they looked dull; the women's were pretty and knowing, and yet dull. It was probably the holiday expression of the vast, prosperous, commercial class, with unlimited money and no ideals that money could not realize; fashion and comfort were all that they desired to compass." In contrast the Bowery had a "gay ugliness—the shapeless, graceless, reckless picturesqueness." Madison Avenue presented a culture of plays and operas; the Bowery culture existed in the style of conversation and books with a "prevailing hideousness that always amused . . . in that uproar to the eye which the strident forms and colors made."[42] The consumer culture promised a perfection of design and taste to inspire all Americans, but it was the rough-hewn spirit that suggested depth and meaning. The depth came from the feeling of rooted community and compassion associated with an older system of exchange. The surface quality of consumer goods expanded the sense of community, of belonging to the nation, while at the same time flattering the self of the person who owned the goods.

What of the self, the individual, in the texts of the consumer culture? In many texts, the self triumphs over the society to propel the advance of an enlightened civilization. Many of the novels of the period are about great, noble figures who declare themselves through the accumulation and display of goods, but who only realize themselves through the spirit when they have lost everything. The boom in decorating with mirrors during the Victorian period focused attention on the appearance and flattery of the self. Meanwhile advertising texts told Americans that goods mediated and conveyed human relations while they protected the self—that goods could replace deeds. The Victorian stuffed interior comforted guests so that human hands did not have to. The late nineteenth-century traditions of the giving of flowers as gifts, the leaving of cards, and the stuffing of Christmas stockings with presents were examples of emerging expressions of obligatory kindness mediated by goods. The easy offering of emotions through consumer goods allowed for a growing sense of restraint in human relations, which raised questions again in texts about the real meaning and feeling of facades in a consumer landscape of signs.

[42] Howells, *Hazard of New Fortunes*, pp. 262, 159.

Howells answered his central, poignant question for his generation, "Does anything from without change us?" by stating, "Conditions *make* character." But beneath the surface of things, he cautioned, "we must put some of the blame on character." The emphasis on the external and the artificial in changing the way we live pervades the texts of the period. The nagging thought that something in the human character suffers or lays dormant instills a tension into many of the symbols presented in the texts. While many of the texts took what seemed like an antimodernist tone to their plaints, they nonetheless accepted the direction of "modernity" toward the emphasis on the consumption of goods. Steeped in the evolutionary principles of the day, most readers were convinced that material progress was inevitable. They felt that one could not turn back to the rootedness of the small face-to-face community and achieve the sense of a rising civilization. In symbol and text, Victorians struggled to grasp the meaning of the consumer culture that heralded the future.

The Victorian Jeremiad
Critics of Accumulation and Display

Michael Barton

Ambivalence about luxury is a national tradition. Americans have honored the rich and admired their possessions, at the same time imagining their corruption and comforting their enemies. This essay explores the rise of the critical side of this tradition in the late nineteenth century, the effort I call the Victorian jeremiad, although it has earlier republican roots. While it features the stylistic qualities of hyperbolic advertising, the Victorian jeremiad draws its energy and motive from the moral sentiments of the Bible. This essay examines how the jeremiad, thus powered by the Bible, criticized the emerging culture of consumed luxury in the Gilded Age and how the jeremiad was shaped by luxurious culture itself. It also presents the triumphant counter-reaction to the jeremiad, also religiously inspired, which consisted of the greatest praise ever showered upon wealth.

The historic, textual source of American mixed feelings about riches was the Bible, that everyday constitution of the United States, wherein the faithful could learn in one verse that wealth and splendor were divine, or in a later parable that such extravagance was devilish, or in still another proverb that spirituality and materialism might coexist. The Old Testament is a holy book about power, glory, and dominion, among other things, and this leads to occasions in the text for descriptions of extravagant display. The author of 2 Chronicles notes:

King Solomon passed all the kings of the earth in riches and wisdom.
And all the kings of the earth sought the presence of Solomon, to hear his wisdom, that God had put in his heart.

And they brought every man his present, vessels of silver, and vessels of gold, and raiment, harness, and spices, horses, and mules, a rate year by year. [2 Chron. 9:22–24]

Solomon's prayers to God for wisdom and knowledge were rewarded as God answered:

Because this was in thine heart, and thou hast not asked riches, wealth, or honour. . . .
I will give thee riches, and wealth, and honour, such as none of the kings have had that have been before thee, neither shall there any after thee have the like. [2 Chron. 1:11–12]

The passage implied that riches should not come first, but that they may come at last as a reward for being good and wise.

The same promises and precautions about riches are present elsewhere in the Old Testament. Wealth in itself was not considered to be regrettable, but the manner and purpose of getting it could be: "Wealth gotten by vanity shall be diminished: but he that gathereth by labour shall increase" (Prov. 13:11). Jeremiah warned that wealth was acceptable so long as it was not vain and paramount in life: "Let not the wise man glory in his wisdom, neither let the mighty man glory in his might, let not the rich man glory in his riches" (Jer. 9:23).

The New Testament's approach is different. Its unmistakable blessing of poverty would appear more obviously distinctive and possibly confounding to Americans. Mark's gospel tells of a man who asked Jesus what he should do in order to inherit eternal life. Jesus told him, "One thing thou lackest: go thy way, sell whatsoever thou hast, and give to the poor, and thou shalt have treasure in heaven: and come, take up the cross, and follow me." The man went away grieved, "for he had great possessions." Then Jesus denied the value of wealth twice to his disciples:

And Jesus looked round about, and saith unto his disciples, How hardly shall they that have riches enter into the kingdom of God!
And the disciples were astonished at his words. But Jesus answereth again, and saith unto them, Children, how hard is it for them that trust in riches to enter into the kingdom of God!
It is easier for a camel to go through the eye of a needle, than for a rich man to enter into the kingdom of God.
And they were astonished out of measure. [Mark 10:21–26]

The Gospels are harmonious in their opinions about the poor; Christians could scarcely ask for a clearer warning against accumulation, and it came from their humble Messiah himself.

Paul's teachings on riches were equally radical.

We brought nothing into this world and it is certain we can carry nothing out.

And having food and raiment let us be therewith content.

But they that will be rich fall into temptation and a snare, and into many foolish and hurtful lusts, which drown men in destruction and perdition.

For the love of money is the root of all evil. [1 Tim. 6:7–10]

In James's epistle Americans read:

Go to now, ye rich men, weep and howl for your miseries that shall come upon you.

Your riches are corrupted, and your garments are motheaten.

Your gold and silver is cankered; and the rust of them shall be a witness against you, and shall eat your flesh as it were fire. [James 5:1–3]

No muckraker was ever more vivid than that.

The import of this radical New Testament message, and sometimes even its exact words, can be found in the most critical indictments of American life pronounced between 1880 and 1920, when conspicuous consumption was the hallmark of the Gilded Age. The diatribes of labor organizer Mother Jones echo those of the Bible almost exactly, even though she called herself a "hell-raiser" and "Bolshevist from the top of my head to the bottom of my feet." On the first page of *Miner's Magazine*, published in 1915, she was at the acme of her ire. She wrote:

I called the other day to see Mrs. J. Borden Harriman at the Colony Club. While I sat in the reception room waiting to be received I watched the fashionable women come and go. Nearly all of them, if you asked them, would tell you proudly that they belonged to society. . . . The word society, as applied to women of today, stands for idleness, fads, extravagance, and display of wealth. They posed and strutted before me like the poor, ignorant geese that they are, and probably imagined that I was impressed. I was, but not in the way they intended. . . . I pitied them. My pity was not without censure, however, because in these times of suffering the idle rich woman who parades her finery before the hungry and poverty-stricken is a modern inquisitor turning the thumb-screws of envy and despair into the very vitals of those who are in reality her sisters.

Mother Jones was even more repulsed by the "average city woman":

She is always overdressed, and although she wears gloves she is careful to leave her right hand bared so that she can display her fingers crowded to their utmost with jewels. Whenever I see that sort of display, I think of the gems as representing the blood of some crucified child. The woman of today—the woman of the "upper classes" I mean—is a sad commentary on civilization, as we are pleased to call it. Everywhere I go in a city I see this same display of jewelry. The women even go to church on Sunday with their fingers and breasts ablaze with diamonds. This includes the wives of ministers themselves. We never heard of Christ wearing diamonds.[1]

The sentiments of Mother Jones were shared by Adolph Fischer, who wrote the following complaint in 1886. An elegant "idler" was smoking a Havana cigar, his hands protected by kid gloves, his starched shirt glittering with a diamond stickpin, his vest festooned with a gold watch chain. Fischer followed him and saw him

enter a wonderfully beautiful house—a palace. Costly pictures decorated the massive walls of its parlors, precious carpets covered the floors and golden chandeliers were suspended from the ceilings. The safes and pantries were bursting with its tempting contents, and the tables covered with choice wines and delicacies. In short, everything good and agreeable could be enjoyed here in abundance. This contrast between the busy toiler and the idle bystander did not fail to impress itself upon my mind. . . . I perceived that the diligent, never resting human working bees, who create all wealth and fill the magazines with provisions, fuel and clothing, enjoy only a minor part of their products and lead a comparatively miserable life, whilst the drones, the idlers, keep the ware-houses locked up and revel in luxury and voluptuousness. Was I wrong, or was the world wrong?[2]

In Chicago it was decided that Fischer was wrong, not the world, and they hanged him and three other men for allegedly throwing the bomb that killed police at the Haymarket Riot.

Still another indictment is provided by sociologist Edward Alsworth Ross in his lecture on "the outlook for plain folk" in 1909. Ross looked to the effects of conspicuous consumption on the community:

[1] Philip S. Foner, ed., *Mother Jones Speaks: Collected Writings and Speeches* (New York: Monad Press, 1983), pp. 468–71. For recent studies of topics closely related to the criticism of accumulation and display, see Daniel Horowitz, *The Morality of Spending: Attitudes toward the Consumer Society in America, 1875–1940* (Baltimore: Johns Hopkins University Press, 1985); and David E. Shi, *The Simple Life: Plain Living and High Thinking in American Culture* (New York: Oxford University Press, 1985).

[2] Philip S. Foner, ed., *The Autobiographies of the Haymarket Martyrs* (New York: Monad Press, 1977), p. 75.

The startling inequalities of wealth that have sprung up in a generation threaten to establish class distinctions hostile to democracy. For the tendency of such abysmal contrasts is thus: The ultra-rich vie in extravagance. The spectacle of their baronial estates, princely houses, liveried lackeys, Sybaritic luxury, and elaborate ostentation infects even the worthy with the workshop of wealth. Success comes to be measured by the sheer cash standard. . . . People fall apart into as many social groups as there are styles of living. . . . The rule is, snobbishness toward those below you, and toadyism toward those above you. The rich are gangrened with pride, the poor with envy. There is no longer a public opinion, there are only class opinions. . . . Unless democracy mends the distribution of wealth, the mal-distribution of wealth will end democracy.[3]

Frederick Townsend Martin's writing provides another example of the highly decorated prose opposing wretched excess. He described himself as a banker and a conservative, and that made his *Passing of the Idle Rich* a tattler on its class in 1911. The book was so popular that it was rewritten as a play and performed widely. Martin may have been richer than the other scolds, but his nostalgia for a more egalitarian and righteous American past was the same. As a boy he lived in "a true American home [where] we knew there was a God. We were positive as to just what was right and what was wrong. The Bible, the Declaration of Independence, the Constitution of the United States, . . . our faith in these was our Rock of Ages." At the turn of the century, however, Martin felt that all those verities had lost their hold: "Instead of Hawthorne we read Zola and Gorky; instead of Longfellow and Bryant, Ibsen and Shaw. . . . I do not know whither we are going, but I do know that we are going." Then Martin proceeded to document the consequences of the "feverish search for some new sensation that can be had only at a tremendous cost." Such compulsive consumption, he said, was far from "the healthy, wholesome spending of money for amusements, pleasures, and recreations," an escape clause in his complaint which showed how far even he had strayed from his true American ancestors. Martin reported extensively on the excesses of the rich, citing anecdotes about elaborate banquets and balls and extravagant behavior. Martin's lurid anecdotes included one about an owner of a little mutt dog who gave a banquet in the animal's honor. Men in evening clothes and women in gowns attended to watch the dog be rewarded with a diamond collar worth $15,000. Another man gave a "poverty social," where his

[3] Edward Alsworth Ross, *Changing America: Studies in Contemporary Society* (1909; reprint, Chautauqua, N.Y.: Chautauqua Press, 1915), p. 18.

guests arrived in rags, ate food scraps on wooden plates, and drank beer
from tin cans while they sat on broken soapboxes and used newspapers
for napkins. Another anecdote describes a millionaire who turned an
imported motor car into what may have been the first recreational vehicle—he refitted it with two small rooms, hot and cold traveling water,
a small bathtub, and a kitchen. Further, Martin wrote, "At the conclusion of an elaborate affair in New York City, the guests leaned back in
their chairs to listen to the singers. The cigarettes were passed around.
. . . Each was rolled, not in white paper, but in a one hundred dollar
bill and the initials of the host were engraved in gold letters." With
images of excess constantly circulating—Martin said, "Our papers are
full of them"—it was to be expected that Americans would learn "to
hate great wealth."[4]

Mother Jones, Adolph Fischer, Edward Ross, and Frederick Martin had passionate contempt for extravagance and idleness. A publicly
accessible extravagance—a palatial post office, for example—they could
justify and even admire; the idleness of the exhausted poor, they would
expect and forgive. The culpability of the extravagant and idle rich,
however, they could never excuse. To socialists like Jones, the idle rich
man was the symbol of all that had gone wrong with the economy—
the growth of industrial monopolies, the decline of the skilled craftsman, and the injustice of the inverse relation between hard work and
great wealth. To conservatives like Martin, the same man was a demonstration of something gone wrong with traditional morality—the growth
of self-indulgence, the decline of civic virtue, and the frustration of
God's will for his people. The combined complaints of the socialists
and conservatives amounted to a Victorian-industrial phase of the
American jeremiad, the larger phenomenon literary historian Sacvan

---

[4] Martin's book has become the encyclopedia of extravagance for American historians. In 1975 Arno Press reprinted it, along with forty-one other "classics" of consumption
in their "Leisure Class in America" series. See Frederick Townsend Martin, *The Passing
of the Idle Rich* (London: Hodder and Staughton, 1911), pp. 14–16, 29, 23–58, 111.
Joseph Conlin demonstrates how current college textbooks are paying more attention to
the material lives of the Victorian rich by including Martin's vignette "The Last Dance
of the Idle Rich: The Bradley Martin Ball of 1897" in his text; see Joseph R. Conlin, *The
American Past: A Survey of American History* (2d ed.; San Diego: Harcourt Brace Jovanovich, 1987), pp. 493–99, 501. Martin's description of the Bradley Martin Ball is also
"boxed" in James A. Henretta, W. Elliot Brownlee, David Brody, and Susan Ware,
America's History, 2 vols. (Chicago: Dorsey Press, 1987), 2:561.

Bercovitch has recently identified as "a ritual designed to join social criticism to spiritual renewal."[5]

From Bercovitch's scholarly perspective, we see that American anxieties about material indulgence did not spring fresh from fin de siècle United States, but were descendants of both Puritan and early republican theories of virtue. For example, John Adams wrote to Thomas Jefferson in 1819, "Will you tell me how to prevent riches from becoming the effects of temperance and industry? Will you tell me how to prevent riches from producing luxury? Will you tell me how to prevent luxury from producing effeminacy, intoxication, extravagance, Vice, and folly?" In 1829 the Reverend Lyman Beecher expressed fear that "the power of voluntary self-denial is not equal to the temptation of an all-surrounding abundance." William Leggett, a Jacksonian journalist and leader of New York's Loco Foco party, wrote in 1834 that American "aristocratic airs" were "supremely ridiculous." He asked, "Does a man become wiser, stronger, or more virtuous and patriotic because he has a fine house over his head? Does he love his country the better because he has a French cook and a box at the opera?" In *The American Frugal Housewife* (1832), Lydia Maria Child warned:

The prevailing evil of the present day is extravagance. . . . [L]augh as we may at the sage advice of our fathers, it is too plain that our present expensive habits are productive of much domestic unhappiness, and injurious to public prosperity. . . . A luxurious and idle REPUBLIC! Look at the phrase!—The words were never made to be married together; everybody sees it would be death to one of them.

In the first issue of *Atlantic Monthly*, published in November 1857, Parke Godwin further lamented:

[5] I will not hold Bercovitch responsible for my use of the jeremiad idea, which is perhaps too liberal here; my attitude about its meaning is closer to Perry Miller's, which is wisely discussed in Sacvan Bercovitch, "Introduction: The Puritan Errand Reassessed," in Sacvan Bercovitch, *The American Jeremiad* (Madison: University of Wisconsin Press, 1978), pp. xi, 3–30; see also Perry Miller, "Errand into the Wilderness," in *Errand into the Wilderness*, ed. Perry Miller (Cambridge, Mass.: Harvard University Press, 1958), pp. 8–9. As Miller said of the Puritan jeremiads, I also find guise and ambiguity in the Victorian versions. Treatment of another jeremiad is found in David Howard-Pitney, "Enduring Black Jeremiad: The American Jeremiad and Black Protest Rhetoric, from Frederick Douglass to W. E. B. Du Bois, 1841–1919," *American Quarterly* 38, no. 3 (Bibliography 1986): 481–92.

Here is a whole commercial society suddenly wrecked . . . values sink to the bottom . . . great money-corporations fall to pieces . . . as soon as we get one dollar, we run in debt for ten. We must have fine houses, fine horses, fine millinery, fine upholstery, troops of servants, and give costly dinners, and attend magnificent balls. . . . When the time comes—as come it will—for paying for all this glorious frippery, we collapse, we wither . . . we sink into the sand.[6]

The Victorian jeremiad should not be mistaken for quotidian left-ist rhetoric. The jeremiad's jargon was not simply the staple of radical speeches of the time. Prominent leftists either declined or neglected to condemn accumulation and display explicitly—the speeches of Eugene Debs and Norman Thomas, for example, lack the antimaterialist imagery and precision of Fischer's statements. The jeremiad's complaint was not the maldistribution of wealth; it was the inequality of consumption that galled. Victorian Jeremiahs could be distinguished from conventional leftists because their anger came from the rising expectation that every-one, not just plutocrats, should be a consumer; they were resentful not because they were oppressed, but because their consuming vision was unfulfilled. The Victorian jeremiad, in short, had more panache than other forms of contemporary social criticism, and that plumed, confi-dent style was derived from the culture of luxury itself. But before we become too entertained by this luscious censure of extravagance, we should realize that the prophets of affluence, not the Jeremiahs, swayed the larger crowds in the late nineteenth century.

The prophets of affluence never approved of indulgence or idle-ness—advertisers would take that mission later—but neither did they gainsay the bounty of industrialism and the prosperity of its captains. In

---

[6] Lester J. Cappon, ed., *The Adams-Jefferson Letters*, 2 vols. (Chapel Hill: University of North Carolina Press, 1959), 2:187. See also the discussion of this text in Daniel T. Rodgers, *The Work Ethic in Industrial America, 1859–1920* (Chicago: University of Chicago Press, 1978), p. 103. Lyman Beecher, "The Gospel the Only Security for Eminent and Abiding National Prosperity," *National Preacher* (1829), as quoted in Rodgers, *Work Ethic*, pp. 99–100; William Leggett, *A Collection of the Political Writings* (New York, 1840), 1:106, as quoted in Henry Steele Commager, ed., *The Era of Reform, 1830–1860* (New York: Van Nostrand Reinhold Co., 1960), p. 95. Although Child warned against extravagance, elsewhere in her book she gave advice on how to cleanse gold, perhaps in case any extravagant women were reading her book: "Wash it in warm suds made of delicate soap, with ten or fifteen drops of salvolatile in it. This makes jewels very brilliant"; Mrs. [Lydia Maria] Child, *The American Frugal Housewife, Dedicated to Those Who Are Not Ashamed of Economy* (12th ed., 1832; reprint, Columbus: Friends of the Libraries of the Ohio State University, 1985), pp. 21, 89, 99. Parke Godwin, as quoted in *Atlantic Monthly* 250, no. 5 (November 1982): 4.

the end, their positive approach to accumulation and display was socially functional and politically acceptable. By drawing the line just this side of conspicuous indulgence and idleness, they implicitly legitimized all lesser forms of mass consumption and recreation that were practiced on their side. Their moral optimism prevailed over the Jeremiahs' demanding negativism. They revived the Old Testament's truce with wealth and understated the New Testament's assault on it.

More Americans believed Russell Conwell's panegyric than Mother Jones's jeremiad. Certainly more Americans heard his oration, for he delivered the ultimate lecture, *Acres of Diamonds*, more than 6,000 times after 1870. The lecture is a series of stories within stories about men searching in remote places for riches—diamonds, gold, and oil—only to discover that "the opportunity to get rich . . . is here . . . now, within the reach of almost every man and woman." *Acres of Diamonds* survives as a classic form of motivational speech. When it was delivered by Conwell it was "studied, analyzed, marked off into sections, and its every element weighed and measured" for its fiery ideas:

I say that you ought to get rich, and it is your duty to get rich. . . . to make money honestly is to preach the gospel. . . . Money is power, and you ought to be reasonably ambitious to have it. You ought because you can do more good with it than you could without it. Money printed your Bible, money builds your churches, money sends your missionaries, and money pays your preachers. . . . While we should sympathize with God's poor . . . let us remember there is not a poor person in the United States who was not made poor by his own shortcomings, or by the shortcomings of some one else. It is all wrong to be poor, anyhow.

Regarding love, money, and the love of money, Conwell stated:

Love is the grandest thing on God's earth, but fortunate the lover who has plenty of money. . . . the man who idolizes simply money, the miser that hoards his money in the cellar, or hides it in his stocking, or refuses to invest it where it will do the world good, that man who hugs the dollar until the eagle squeals has in him the root of all evil.[7]

Conwell's emphatic defense of the profit system, market economics, and the work ethic was the most ingenious heterodoxy in American religion, all the more amazing because it came from a Baptist minister. Underscoring the Parable of the Talents, condemning only the worship

[7] Russell H. Conwell, *Acres of Diamonds* (New York: Harper and Brothers, 1915).

of money itself, and saying nothing against luxury unless it was dramatically selfish, he was able to disestablish the church's suspicion of consumption. Conwell had redefined the problem into nonexistence; he had turned a temptation into an opportunity. This was not simply another reading of the New Testament's position on wealth: it was a landmark rewriting of Christian social policy. He could say he had reduced the Gospel to its essence—love—and then insist that making and spending money were modern forms of caring, inasmuch as one man's economic activity was the cause of another man's livelihood. He had exchanged the theory of the deserving poor for the ideal of the deserving rich. His admonitions would become the spiritual common sense of the middle class.

The other Victorian counterjeremiads may be read as footnotes to Conwell. In 1869 the controversial Reverend Lewis Tappan tried to stimulate, even provoke, his readers with an essay titled *Is It Right to Be Rich?* He repeated first the New Testament's warnings against wealth, advising that it was wrong to "hoard" and "pursue" wealth. "As a general rule," he thought, children who inherited great wealth would be "injured." Nevertheless, at the end of his analysis he granted that it could be acceptable to be rich. Quoting the Bible again, he drew attention to the promise that a man who was a good steward "over a few things" was a man whom God would make a "ruler over many things," the presumption being that Heaven, if not earth, might be crowded with accumulation and display. Tappan's warning was against excess on earth.[8]

In *The Message of Jesus to Men of Wealth* (1891), the Reverend George Davis Herron, a Social Gospeler, preached that "sin is pure individualism," and he denounced the exploitative acts of predatory financiers. He concluded, however, "you can make the market as sacred as the church. You can make the whirl of industrial wheels like the joyous music of worship. . . . You can give work to the wageless; teach the thriftless and ignorant; seat the poor in the best pews of your churches."[9] Herron urged "repentance unto this mammon-worshiping

    [8] Lewis Tappan, *Is It Right to Be Rich?* (2d ed.; New York: Anson D. F. Randolph, 1869), pp. 22, 24.
    [9] George D. Herron, *The Message of Jesus to Men of Wealth* (New York: Fleming H. Revel Co., 1891), reprinted in Ernest J. Wrage and Barnet Baskerville, eds., *American Forum: Speeches on Historic Issues, 1788–1900* (New York: Harper and Brothers, 1960), pp. 276–82.

generation," and he condemned William Graham Sumner's and Herbert Spencer's social Darwinism as a philosophy that would have "astounded Moses" and sounded "barbarous to Abraham." The important point was that Herron did not criticize middle-class accumulation and display. He implied that one could be a committed consumer and still qualify as his brother's keeper. Daniel Seely Gregory's *Christian Ethics*, a widely used textbook in the 1870s and 1880s, concurred with Herron, noting, "By the proper use of wealth man may greatly elevate and extend his moral work. It is therefore his duty to seek to secure wealth for this high end. . . . The Moral Governor has placed the power of acquisitiveness in man for a good and noble purpose." Mark Hopkins, president of Williams College, informed his scholars, "The acquisition of property is required by love, because it is a powerful means of benefiting others." He would give a failing mark only to "a selfish getting of property," which was "better than a selfish indolence or wastefulness" but "not to be encouraged."[10]

The Right Reverend William Lawrence, Episcopal bishop of Massachusetts, offered in 1901 an even more elaborate and religious defense of prosperity than those mentioned so far. He began his essay with virtually the same question John Adams had asked Jefferson—"whether in the long run material prosperity does not tend toward the disintegration of character." He cited the Bible's warnings and history's lessons and determined that at least there was moral danger in great wealth. But it was not necessary, he concluded, that wealth should have to lead to "demoralization"; indeed, it was man's nature to become strong and therefore rich, and it must be the divine plan that "Godliness is in league with riches." Lawrence considered "the yachts, the palaces, and the luxuries that flaunt themselves before the public" to be only a fraction of the national wealth and argued that a much greater sum was stored in the savings of thousands of ordinary men. Witnessing an occasional vulgar extravagance was a small price to pay, he thought, for the

[10] Daniel Seely Gregory, *Christian Ethics: The True Moral Manhood and Life of Duty* (Philadelphia: Eldredge and Brother, 1875), p. 224, as quoted in Ralph Henry Gabriel, *The Course of American Democratic Thought* (2d ed.; New York: Ronald Press Co., 1956), p. 157. Gabriel's complete chapter is worth reading as an early piece of American studies scholarship on this topic; see Ralph Henry Gabriel, "The Gospel of Wealth of the Gilded Age," in Gabriel, *Democratic Thought.* The same is true of Merle Curti, *Growth of American Thought* (2d ed.; New York: Harper, 1951), esp. chap. 25; Mark Hopkins, *The Law of Love and Love as Law* (New York, 1868), p. 183, as quoted in Gabriel, *Democratic Thought*, p. 157.

general system of material prosperity, which actually made the millionaire reinvest most of his earnings. As for the man who simply tries to
increase his comforts, Lawrence approved him as a natural advance in
civilization, a fellow simply exercising his faculties and developing "self-
respect and self-mastery." Some would fall into the clutches of drink,
lust, and laziness, but "the great body of the American people are
marching upwards in prosperity through the mastery of their lower tastes
and passions to the development of the higher." Moreover, an increasingly prosperous man, Lawrence said, will be increasingly sociable and
civic-minded, as opposed to the poor man with his "intense self-cen-
tralization and hardness."[11]

After explaining away most of the dangers, Lawrence admitted that
perils still remained in prosperity. The spirit of commercialism could
become too pervasive, the political system might not be mature enough
to deal wisely with the great corporations, and finally, "the ability to
have what you want" might lead men to want the wrong things. The
concrete examples he offered suggested that Lawrence objected to the
democracy of wealth rather than its concentration: "To me the vulgarest
of all is not the diamond-studded operator, but the horde of mothers
crushing each other around the bargain counter." In any case, he forecast that prosperity was inevitable and that Americans would need the
character to accept and use it, not shrink from it: "Material prosperity
is helping to make the national character . . . more Christlike."[12]

Of all the panegyrics to wealth, Andrew Carnegie's is the most
surprising and ironic, for this most wealthy man was the least tolerant
of accumulation and display. In his article for the *North American Review*
in 1889, he confronted the social problem head-on and right off: "The
problem of our age is the proper administration of wealth, so that the
ties of brotherhood may still bind together the rich and poor in harmonious relationship." As a successful capitalist he knew the social alien-
ation that could attend the modern form of industrial organization: "We
assemble thousands of operatives in the factory . . . of whom the employer
can know little or nothing, and to whom the employer is little better
than a myth. All intercourse between them is at an end . . . and often

[11] Reverend William Lawrence, "The Relation of Wealth to Morals," *World's Work*
(January 1901), reprinted in Gail Kennedy, ed., *Democracy and the Gospel of Wealth*
(Lexington, Mass.: D. C. Heath, 1949), pp. 68–76.
[12] Lawrence, "Relation of Wealth," pp. 68–76.

there is friction between employer and the employed, between capital and labor, between rich and poor. Human society loses homogeneity." Carnegie offered his solution just as surely and efficiently as he had posed the basic question: "This, then, is held to be the duty of the man of Wealth: First, to set an example of modest, unostentatious living, shunning display or extravagance; to provide moderately for the legitimate wants of those dependent upon him; and after doing so to consider all surplus revenues . . . simply as trust funds . . . the man of wealth thus becoming the mere agent and trustee for his poorer brethern." Carnegie would not leave the definition of modesty a hostage to any rich man's self-serving indecision: "Whatever makes one conspicuous offends the canon," he declaimed, using the word *conspicuous* ten years before Thorstein Veblen published *Theory of the Leisure Class.* Carnegie concluded, "The community will surely judge [what is conspicuous] and its judgments will not often be wrong."[13]

We can judge how Victorian men and women responded to the jeremiads and panegyrics of the time from observing the visual records of their habits of accumulation and display. Most Americans appeared to live as if they had never seriously considered the possibility that consumption could be corrupting. For instance, hundreds of photographs of late Victorian homes demonstrate that urban middle-class families decorated their residences obviously and self-consciously, putting themselves figuratively into their decor as effectively as any shopkeeper portrayed his purpose in his display window. Their models were the celebrated interiors of the rich and famous (figs. 1, 2).[14] This generalization holds true even as we acknowledge that decorating tastes changed significantly from 1880 to 1920, to the effect that there was less Victorian stuffing and clutter at the end.

On the American frontier, Solomon Butcher's renowned photographs of western Nebraska homesteaders demonstrate that isolated farm families decorated wherever they could, showing off whatever was at hand: their livestock, tools, instruments, and toys; their dead; and most

---

[13] Andrew Carnegie, "Wealth," *North American Review* 148, no. 391 (June 1889): 653–64.

[14] See William Seale's remarkable, almost lurid collection of photographs of "object-filled rooms" in William Seale, *The Tasteful Interlude: American Interiors through the Camera's Eye, 1860–1917* (2d ed., rev. and enl., Nashville: American Association for State and Local History, 1981).

Fig. 1. Sitting room, Adm. George Dewey house, Washington, D.C., 1912. (Courtesy, The Mariners Museum, Newport News, Va.)

of all, themselves (fig. 3).[15] Sodbusters thus documented (no doubt with the photographer's encouragement) that they were still civilized, as evidenced by their portage and possession of decent, eastern things. Indeed, it could be that photography at this time was causative as well as indicative in relation to accumulation and display. It stimulated Americans to pose and exhibit themselves as decorously and proudly as a newspaper advertisement featured a smoked ham or as a mail-order catalogue pictured a steel plow.

Victorian parents taught the same habits of accumulation and display to their children, especially at Christmastime, when the "fetishism of commodities" was most pronounced and glorified and valued things were most numerous and mysterious. The irony here is the transformation of an antimaterialist's birthdate into a commercial celebration. It is difficult to imagine a more pointed and effectual socialization for

[15] These matchless frontier photographs have finally been collected by John E. Carter, *Solomon D. Butcher: Photographing the American Dream* (Lincoln: University of Nebraska Press, 1985).

Fig. 2. Drawing room, Edward Lauterbach house, New York, 1899.
(The Byron Collection, Museum of the City of New York: Photo, Byron.)

Fig. 3. David Hilton family, with possessions, Custer Co., Neb., 1887.
(Solomon D. Butcher Collection, Nebraska State Historical Society.)

Fig. 4. Thomas Nast, "Merry Old
Santa Claus." From *Harper's Weekly*
25, no. 1253 (January 1, 1881): 8–9.

consumption than Christmas, wherein concrete enjoyments are hoped
for and appear out of nowhere, apparently under the benevolent sponsorship of a supernatural, prosperous elder (fig. 4). In the festival of the
Victorian Christmas, God was at peace with the worldly.[16]

The Victorian jeremiad that appeared by the late nineteenth century was a particularly concrete and imaginative method of moral criticism. The ascetism of the New Testament—a basic American cultural
text—was its justification and energy. It was a period complaint provoked by the economic conditions of the time—both millionaires and
the middle class had more opportunities to display their growing prosperity, which also widened the visible gap between them and the poor.
Seeing this, the Jeremiahs condemned luxury, but they used the same

---

[16] See Clarence P. Hornung, ed., *An Old-Fashioned Christmas in Illustration and
Decoration* (2d ed., enl., New York: Dover Publications, 1975), which contains more
than 250 examples from English and American publications such as *Harper's, Ballou's
Pictorial Drawingroom Companion*, and *Frank Leslie's Illustrated Newspaper*. The sheer
crowding of playthings into these illustrations demonstrates the urge to accumulate and
display.

hyperbolic language advertisers invented to sell commodities.[17] They became connoisseurs of glorious consumption, even its press agents, in the process of identifying and excoriating it. The jeremiad produced, at first, a successful defense of wealth by such counter-Jeremiahs as Russell Conwell and, eventually, a strategic change in the public lives of the very rich, who developed a form of self-control called "good taste"— a subtle form of display that would not excite mass envy. Thus, the jeremiad was effective, but not in the way its authors intended.

The rich showed their countrymen how to consume life as well as things. By their mastery of grace and style, they made unnatural advantage seem ordinary and easy to bear. They exuded self-confidence and offered a gospel that said the consumed world was finally good and just. Expecting social equality and biblical virtue in America, the critics reviled the rich and their habits of accumulation and display, prophesying and advertising their influence on the unfolding patterns of consumption.

[17]The "extravagant puff" and "tall talk" of advertising rhetoric during the Gilded Age is described in Daniel Boorstin, *The Americans: The Democratic Experience* (New York: Vintage Books, 1974), pp. 137–45. For further discussion of advertising and the critical tradition, see Jackson Lears, "Beyond Veblen: Rethinking Consumer Culture in America," and Simon J. Bronner, "Reading Consumer Culture," elsewhere in this volume.

Beyond Veblen
Rethinking Consumer Culture in America

Jackson Lears

A portrait of Thorstein Veblen in the faculty lounge at Yale University shows him leaning back in his chair, one leg tossed easily over the other, smoking a cigarette. He is surveying the passing scene of academic pomp with just the hint of a twinkle in his eye. Despite his mythic marginality, Veblen looks more bemused than embittered. And were he alive today, Veblen might be pardoned some bemusement. The ideas of the celebrated iconoclast have become part of the conventional wisdom about American society and conspicuous consumption. Many serious analysts of American culture have clasped Veblen to their bosoms, and more than a few would agree with Max Lerner's assertion that Veblen possessed "the most creative mind American social thought has produced."[1]

In many ways the reputation is deserved. Veblen broke new ground, much of which is still neglected. He was one of the first theorists to move away from the producer orientation of nineteenth-century economics and focus on consumption as an important category of social and economic behavior. He rejected the utilitarian psychology of orthodox economic thought, demolished through caricature the "Economic Man," and effectively focused on the irrationality and absurdity inherent in many acts of consumption. Having immersed himself in anthropological literature, Veblen could add a cultural dimension to Karl Marx's famous distinction between use-value and exchange-value. Much of

---

[1] Max Lerner, ed., *The Portable Veblen* (New York: Viking Press, 1948), back cover.

73

what passed for exchange-value, he noted, was also a form of symbolic value. The orgies of display at Newport and the parading of ornamental wives on Fifth Avenue corresponded to similar ceremonies among "primitive" tribes: the captain of industry, like the Kwakiutl chieftain, was eager to demonstrate his prowess by showing off his trophies. But unlike many anthropologists of his own time or ours, Veblen preserved a keen sense of hierarchical social structure and of how that structure was reinforced by patterns of consumption. By remaining sensitive to the interaction between culture and power relations, Veblen plunged forward where orthodox Marxism pulled up short. He was able to see how subordinate groups could develop allegiances to a dominant culture that may not have reflected their own best interests. He anticipated some of Antonio Gramsci's insights into the ways dominant groups exercise cultural hegemony under organized capitalism.[2]

Despite Veblen's achievements, his persistent influence has been a mixed blessing. His republican moral commitments prevented him from realizing the near universality of conspicuous consumption and conspicuous display. He himself habitually resorted to conspicuous display in the guise of antidisplay. Veblen's unkempt appearance and bizarre attire, his thick woolen stockings supported by pins clipped to his trouser legs, were aspects of costume that contributed crucially to his legendary status as a bohemian intellectual. Despite his anthropological perspective, he could not see accumulation and display as patterns interwoven by different social groups throughout the whole fabric of a culture. He insisted on attributing the dominant patterns of consumption to the pernicious influence of a parasitic "leisure class." His assumption that cultural influences flow only from the top downward is not borne out by the historical record. Lois Banner's recent and comprehensive study of American fashion, for example, demonstrates that the pacesetters in the beauty sweepstakes were courtesans and chorus girls who were often aped by their social betters.[3]

[2] Thorstein Veblen, *The Theory of the Leisure Class: An Economic Study in the Evolution of Institutions* (New York: Macmillan Co., 1899); John Patrick Diggins, *The Bard of Savagery* (New York: Seabury Press, 1978); T. J. Jackson Lears, "The Concept of Cultural Hegemony: Problems and Possibilities," *American Historical Review* 90, no. 3 (June 1985): 567–93.

[3] Lois Banner, *American Beauty* (New York: Alfred A. Knopf, 1983). For an influential discussion of consumption as a way that various groups throughout a society can create cultural meaning, see Mary Douglas and Baron Isherwood, *The World of Goods:*

Veblen's top-down model of cultural domination melded with his desire to stress the irrationality of consumption. As a result, his psychology remained narrow. His thinking was, to be sure, a step beyond the simple-minded utilitarianism of orthodox economics, but he still reduced complex social rituals to one-dimensional examples of "pecuniary emulation." Nothing—from a funeral to a wedding to any form of "devout observance"—was allowed its true, multivalent significance. Veblen realized that all consumption enacted cultural meaning, but he was willing to assign it only one meaning: status-striving. Moreover, since nearly all cultural artifacts and practices contain elements of display, Veblen's furious assault on display amounted to an "attack on culture" itself, as Theodor Adorno recognized more than forty years ago.[4] Veblen's polemical intent led him to a sweeping dismissal of art, religion, and nearly all sensuous or material cultural forms in the name of a utopian alternative: a rational state where sturdy producer-citizens would be ruled by the discipline of the machine rather than the irrationalities of consumption.

What is amazing is how often this bleak vision has continued to inspire critics of consumer culture, particularly on the Left, and how often they have perpetrated Veblen's misconceptions.[5] Why has Veblen's influence been so durable? In part, I would suggest, because his critique resonates with a long tradition in Anglo-American Protestant culture: the Puritan's plain-speak assault on theatrical artifice and effete display. The ensuing essay furthers this argument by situating Veblen historically by tracing the tensions between authenticity and artifice in nineteenth-century American market culture and by suggesting how those tensions were reorchestrated during the period from 1880 to 1920, the period when Veblen consolidated his data base.

Towards an Anthropology of Consumption (New York: W. W. Norton, 1979). For a somewhat more sophisticated version of this argument, see Mihaly Csikszentmihalyi and Eugene Rochberg-Halton, *The Meaning of Things: Domestic Symbols and the Self* (New York: Cambridge University Press, 1981).

[4]Theodor Adorno, "Veblen's Attack on Culture" (1941), reprinted in Theodor Adorno, *Prisms*, trans. Samuel and Sherry Weber (Cambridge, Mass.: MIT Press, 1981), pp. 73–94.

[5]See, for example, Stuart Chase, *The Tragedy of Waste* (New York: Macmillan, 1925); John Kenneth Galbraith, *The Affluent Society* (New York: New American Library, 1958); and John Kenneth Galbraith, *The New Industrial State* (Boston: Houghton Mifflin Co., 1967).

The origins of the plain-speech tradition lay in a fundamental project of the Protestant Reformation: the effort to create an alternative to the method of constructing meaning through the assemblage and display of objects, the method that anthropologists claim is virtually universal and timeless. The pietist tradition in Protestantism insisted that salvation lay in faith rather than works, in inner being rather than outward form. They believed that the objective surface of things concealed rather than revealed meaning. Appearances, for the early Protestant, were always deceptive.[6]

The problem of appearances was exacerbated by the emergence of a modern, placeless market, as Jean-Christophe Agnew has persuasively argued. Theatrical modes of artifice were detached from their customary ritual moorings; they became modes of self-aggrandizement in the fluid, boundless world of market relations.[7] Puritan and later evangelical Protestants aimed to create a new and tighter set of boundaries around the simple, striving self and to control the flood of meanings unleashed in market society by insisting on unadorned communication in language as well as material goods. Plain speech complemented plain living: both served the vision of social transparency; that is, a society where people said what they meant and meant what they said. That vision, of course, remained provokingly just out of reach, as market society multiplied goods and the meanings attached to them.

The tension between authenticity and artifice transferred slowly to American shores. American public culture was born in opposition to European-style luxury and display, nurtured in dreams of Spartan simplicity. But by the early and mid nineteenth century, representatives of the national and international market began to fan out from the cities into a countryside that was still dominated in many areas by household production. We are just beginning to glimpse the ways that this expanding world of goods was represented in popular culture, but preliminary evidence suggests that it may be a mistake to argue a shift from the

---

[6] This issue is discussed in Edmund Morgan, *Visible Saints: The History of a Puritan Idea* (New York: New York University Press, 1963); and the issue is deftly brought into the nineteenth century in Karen Halttunen, *Confidence Men and Painted Women: A Study of Middle-Class Culture in America, 1830–1870* (New Haven: Yale University Press, 1982), esp. p. 45.

[7] Jean-Christophe Agnew, *Worlds Apart: The Market and the Theater in Anglo-American Thought, 1550–1750* (New York: Cambridge University Press, 1986).

plodding nineteenth century to the carnivalesque twentieth: the carnival may have been in town all the time.[8]

Certainly the nineteenth-century market signified entertainment and exoticism, offering new sensations as well as new goods. Exotica were the stock-in-trade of museum promoters from P. T. Barnum to his backwoods emulators; Barnum's first and most famous estate—itself a gigantic advertisement for his work—was Iranistan, a fabulous oriental villa built in 1846. From the 1830s on, many consumer goods (such as clothing, cosmetics, jewelry, patent medicines) were surrounded by an aura of sensuous mystery, even magical self-transformation. The mysterious East had long been associated with marketable goods, and mid Victorian writers kept that link before the reading public. "India is the Ophir of commerce," a *Godey's Lady's Book* contributor announced in 1853. Fashion magazines printed engravings of bare-breasted brown ladies, such as "The Circassian Beauty" in *Peterson's* for 1851, providing a kind of sanctioned Victorian pornography. By the 1850s, fashionable clothes were often surrounded with exotic attributes: the Turkish shawl, the Castilian cloak, the Echarpe Orientale. New York department store magnate A. T. Stewart chose oriental motifs for the interior of the store he built at Broadway and Tenth Street in 1863, complete with "luxurious hassocks . . . soft Persian mats . . . [and] fairy-like frostings of lace draperies." The tie between the market and exotic oriental goods was firmly implanted in the bourgeois imagination.[9]

[8] Here I do not mean to abandon my own and other historians' stress on the late nineteenth century as a period of crucial transformation. But I now believe that an understanding of that transformation requires a subtler conceptual framework than simply the notion of a shift from a Protestant "producer culture" to a secular "consumer culture." For statements of that earlier view, see T. J. Jackson Lears, "From Salvation to Self-Realization: Advertising and the Therapeutic Roots of the Consumer Culture, 1880–1930," in *The Culture of Consumption: Critical Essays in American History, 1880–1980*, ed. Richard Wightman Fox and T. J. Jackson Lears (New York: Pantheon Books, 1983), pp. 3–38; and Warren I. Susman, *Culture as History: The Transformation of American Society in the Twentieth Century* (New York: Pantheon Books, 1984), esp. Introduction.

[9] P. T. Barnum, *Struggles and Triumphs; or, Forty Years' Recollections of P. T. Barnum* (Buffalo: Warren, Johnson, 1872), p. 263; Henry P. Haynes, "The East," *Godey's Lady's Book* 47 (July 1853): 33; engraving, "The Circassian Beauty," in *Peterson's* 29, no. 3 (September 1851), frontispiece; "Work Department: The Ottoman," *Godey's Lady's Book* 56 (June 1858): 555; advertisement for "The Castiglione" in *Godey's Lady's Book* 58 (January 1858): 9; Emily May, "The Echarpe Orientale," *Peterson's* 27, no. 1 (January 1855): 89–90; "Chitchat upon Prevailing Fashions," *Godey's Lady's Book* 48 (May 1854): 479–80; Alice B. Haven, "A Morning at Stewart's," *Godey's Lady's Book* 66 (May 1863): 429–33.

Representatives of the market reinforced those connections. Many, to be sure, were complaisant shopkeepers; but many others were more aggressive and intrusive peddlers whose wares were sometimes just as enticing as those found in the fashionable shops.

For many Americans, particularly those outside the urban upper classes, the market was personified in the itinerant peddler. The primal scene of the emerging market culture in the mid nineteenth century was the peddler entering the isolated village or rural community, laden with glittering goods that were ornamental as well as useful: scissors, knives, tools, tinware, clocks, patent medicines, jewelry, perfumes, and fabrics. The peddler embodied a multitude of cultural associations. Certainly he was a trickster figure, a confidence man who achieved his goal through guile rather than strength, particularly through a skillful theatricality. What was perhaps most striking about the peddler was his liminality. He was constantly on the move, scurrying along the fringes of established society. He occupied the threshold not only between the village and the cosmopolitan world beyond but also between the natural and the supernatural. He was an emissary of the marvelous, promising his audience magical transformations not through religious conversion, but through the purchase of a bit of silk, a pair of earrings, or a mysterious elixir. Like the traditional conjurer multiplying rabbits, doves, or scarves, the peddler opened his pack and presented a startling vision of abundance. (In Clement Moore's famous poem "A Visit from St. Nicholas" [1822], Santa Claus himself "looked like a peddler opening his pack.") Despite his secular concerns, the peddler, particularly if he was the impresario of a patent medicine show, had much in common with the evangelical ministry: itineracy, a special appeal to women, and a rhetorical style that combined exhortation with the invocation of testimonials from the saved. From Johnson Jones Hooper's Simon Suggs to Mark Twain's Beriah Sellers, humorists presented the confidence man as preacher, and vice versa.[10]

[10]The standard works on peddlers are Richardson Wright, *Hawkers and Walkers in Early America: Strolling Peddlers, Preachers, Lawyers, Doctors, Players, and Others, from the Beginning to the Civil War* (Philadelphia: J. B. Lippincott Co., 1927); and J. R. Dolan, *The Yankee Peddlers of Early America* (New York: Clarkson N. Potter, 1964). Also helpful are Frazar Kirkland, *Cyclopedia of Commercial and Business Anecdotes*, 2 vols. (New York: D. Appleton, 1864); and B. A. Botkin, *A Treasury of New England Folklore* (rev. ed.; New York: Crown Publishers, 1965). The concept of liminality is associated with the work of Victor Turner, who is threatening to displace Clifford Geertz

The peddler's persona resonated with magic and religion. Those resonances varied depending on regional or ethnic circumstances. Folklore tended to label all peddlers (at least up to the Civil War) as either Yankees or Jews. Both groups were proverbially alleged to be rootless and conniving avatars of the market, aggressively penetrating the countryside, and both provoked a mingling of fear, hostility, and fascination. After the 1830s, as German Jews became a more palpable presence in peddling and its lore, popular assumptions tended increasingly to conflate the peddler's mobility and marginality with his Jewishness. "The Jews are proverbially a restless, roving class," announced Luke Shortfield, the hero of John Beauchamp Jones's *Western Merchant* (1849). "The Shylocks prefer to be on navigable streams, where it is convenient for them to take passage for 'parts unknown,' should their necessities or indications render it expedient for them to do so." Mid Victorian imagery presented the Jew as a liminal figure who was even more exotic than the Yankee. "These wonderful people bear the imprint of their Oriental origin even to this day," wrote novelist Joseph Holt Ingraham in 1860. In physical appearance and social behavior, the Jewish peddler epitomized the commercial arts of the mysterious East. Beginning with *The Monk*, written by Monk Lewis in 1796, the literary Wandering Jew was gradually transformed from an exemplar of Christian doctrine to "a black magician whose sorcery was interesting on secular grounds." The peddler was a Wandering Jew with a pack on his back, promising a brief deliverance through the magical powers of purchase.[11] Whatever his

---

as the anthropologist most cited by historians. The most relevant writings on liminality include Victor Turner, *The Ritual Process: Structure and Anti-Structure* (Chicago: University of Chicago Press, 1969), esp. chap. 3; and Victor Turner, *Dramas, Fields, and Metaphors* (Ithaca: Cornell University Press, 1974), esp. chaps. 1, 6, 7. On the link between ancient conjuring lore and dreams of fantastic abundance, see Paul Bouissiac, *Circus and Culture: A Semiotic Approach* (Bloomington: Indiana University Press, 1975), p. 78. See also Clement Moore, "A Visit from St. Nicholas" (1822), reprinted as *The Night before Christmas* (Philadelphia: J. B. Lippincott Co., 1954); Johnson Jones Hooper, *Adventures of Capt. Simon Suggs* (Philadelphia: T. B. Peterson Co., 1846); Samuel L. Clemens and Charles Dudley Warner, *The Gilded Age: A Tale of To-Day* (1872; reprint, Indianapolis: Bobbs-Merrill, 1972).

[11] John Beauchamp Jones, *The Western Merchant* (Philadelphia: Grigg, Elliot, 1849), p. 289; Joseph Holt Ingraham, *The Sunny South; or, The Southerner at Home, Embracing Five Years' Experience of a Northern Governess in the Land of Sugar and the Cotton* (1860; reprint, New York: Negro Universities Press, 1968); Edgar Rosenberg, *From Shylock to Svengali: Jewish Stereotypes in English Fiction* (Stanford: Stanford University Press,

ethnic persuasion, the peddler became a lightning rod for the anxieties and aspirations of a developing market society. The encounter between the peddler and his prospective customer was exciting but also disturbing. It prefigured later, more structured rituals of purchase in department stores and other urban settings.

The common link between earlier and later cultural forms was the tendency to see selling as seduction. The peddler was not only a potential poacher on what the husband conceived to be his private sexual realm but also a participant in the mysterious power of "influence"—the Victorian belief in the capacity of one individual to form or deform another's malleable character forever. The peddler—like that other liminal confidence man, the mesmerist—seemed particularly adept at influencing women. If he sold patent medicine, he also resembled the mesmerist in his access to hidden lore: the word *nostrum* derives from *our secret*. If he sold clothes, perfume, and jewelry, he dealt in "fascination" and "glamour"; both words originally referred to magic spells.[12]

The peddler's brand of influence had powerful connotations; at its worst, it could even promote a kind of addiction. This was suggested by Ann Porter's "Banishment of the Peddlers," a *Godey's* poem published in 1848, deep enough into the era of German Jewish peddling to contain a harsh note of anti-Semitism. The poem tells the story of a small town where the ladies decide to boycott the shopkeepers until they refuse to sell any more liquor. All but one yield.

> "Ladies," said he, "you know full well,
>   That peddlers haunt this place,
> And for their knick-knacks take your cash,
>   A low and vulgar race.

1960), p. 206. See also Louis Harap, *The Image of the Jew in American Literature, from the Early Republic to Mass Immigration* (Philadelphia: Jewish Publication Society, 1974); Rudolf Glanz, *The Jew in the Old American Folklore* (New York: Privately printed, 1961), esp. pp. 2–8, 187 n. 21; and Mac E. Barrick, "The Image of the Jew in South-Central Pennsylvania," *Pennsylvania Folklife* 34, no. 3 (Spring 1985): 133–38.

[12]On influence, see Halttunen, *Confidence Men*, pp. 4–5. The explicitly sexual connotations of mesmerism are discussed in John Haller, *American Medicine in Transition, 1840–1910* (Urbana: University of Illinois Press, 1974), p. 105. For the etymologies mentioned in this paragraph, see the relevant entries in *Oxford English Dictionary*, s.v. "fascination," "glamour." On fascination in particular, see Herbert Leventhal, *The Shadow of the Enlightenment* (New York: New York University Press, 1974), pp. 138–39.

But if you will refuse to trade,
With this same Jewish clan,
I'll quit the sale of spirits now,
Nor sell a dram again."

Although "the ladies had some feeling for these men of heavy packs,"
they bow to the will of the "brave man": peddlers and liquor alike are
banished from the village. This poem dramatizes a developing social
conflict between established Protestant retailers and itinerant Jewish
peddlers: it is not consumption per se that is equated with addiction to
alcohol, but consumption from a particularly "influential" source. In
suggesting that equation, "The Banishment of the Peddlers" identified
the act of purchase as an arena of gender conflict; it also evoked the fear
that, without proper boundaries, the market could undermine self-
control.[13]

That fear lay at the heart of Victorian moralism. Participation in
the market, given its associations with avarice and exotic sensuality,
posed fundamental temptations. The moralists' nightmarish vision was
that the self's moral and intellectual gyroscope would spin out of control
as it entered the magnetic field of market relations, resulting in the
pursuit of worldly goods that would lead to madness and death. Novelist
Catherine Sedgwick, recalling the speculative fever of the 1830s, charged,
"the atmosphere was poisoned, and the silly and the wise alike went
mad." Popular fiction confirmed the threat, as the mad speculator became
a stock figure. An 1858 *Godey's* story introduced a Mr. Brandon, who,
"in the reckless spirit of the age, had entered speculation after speculation until success had made him mad; and when failure had met him
he still madly persisted until inevitable ruin stared him in the face."
Nor were women immune. A *Peterson's* editorial of 1866 presented an
imaginary conversation between a doctor and another male observer at
a fashionable ball; their decorous exchange is frequently interrupted by
the screeching "mad laugh" of a lovely and elegant young matron, the
most fashionably dressed and wittiest woman in the room. The doctor
believes that he detects insanity in her laugh, and, sure enough, after
her husband's death in a warehouse accident six months later, the woman
has to be admitted to an asylum. The quest for social brilliance could

---

[13] Ann E. Porter, "The Banishment of the Peddlers," *Godey's Lady's Book* 37 (October 1848): 227.

be as perilous as the speculative plunge, sapping one's resources and leaving one vulnerable to psychic as well as financial collapse.[14]

The fears of self-ruination, rooted in a persistent Puritan-republican ethos, pervaded bourgeois culture throughout much of the nineteenth century. So it should come as no surprise that the proliferation of marketable goods and sensations generated protest as well as fascination. Among artisans and farmers, heirs of the plain-speech tradition mounted a powerful critique of individual accumulation at the expense of the social whole, a critique energized by the principles of labor republicanism. Among intellectuals, dreams of social transparency led to discomfort amid a new world of manufactured appearances, expressed as longings to strike through the pasteboard mask of artifice (as Melville's Ahab said), and experience unmediated life directly.[15] Longings could be expressed in the idiom of romantic transcendentalism or, later, as austere positivist scientism. Veblen participated in this latter trend; nearly all his work is pervaded by the desire to unmask the duplicities of polite society or conventional wisdom.

During the mid nineteenth century (1840–80), the arbiters of taste in fashion magazines and other popular periodicals groped for a middle ground between authenticity and artifice. Sensing that market relations could be integrated into bourgeois society only if their centrifugal impact were controlled, these makers of mainstream culture sought an idiom that would meld aristocratic fashion and republican simplicity. They wanted to penetrate behind the veil of appearances, but not too far. They implicitly anticipated an idea articulated by Joseph Conrad, Henrik Ibsen, and Sigmund Freud at the end of the century: the notion that civilization was in some sense dependent on a delicate tissue of necessary lies.

Longings for sincerity persisted, however, and led to a bit of a muddle. Fashion was justifiable only insofar as it expressed the true self within; appearances meant everything and nothing.[16] Aesthetic moral-

---

[14] Mrs. C. M. Sedgwick, "Wilton Harvey," *Godey's Lady's Book* 24 (March 1842): 122; "Blanche Brandon," *Godey's Lady's Book* 56 (April 1858): 306; "Editor's Table," *Peterson's* 50, no. 3 (September 1866): 210.

[15] Herman Melville, *Moby Dick; or, The White Whale* (1851; reprint, New York: New American Library, 1961), p. 167.

[16] "All is not gold that glitters" was an obsessive theme in women's magazines throughout the 1840–80 period; for example, see Harriet Beecher Stowe, "Art and Nature," *Godey's Lady's Book* 19 (September 1839); Ellen Ashton, "Keeping Up Appearances," *Peterson's*

ists wanted to maintain a tightly controlled equipoise between respectability and extravagance, authenticity and artifice. As expressed by Charles J. Peterson, editor of *Peterson's* magazine, in 1873, "Wise men or women make their dress so thoroughly in accordance with their person or character, that no one notices it any more than the frame of a picture; but to be clothed shabbily in the hopes that our inner perfections will overshadow our dress, is but the extreme of vanity." Yet in the same magazine, one finds extraordinarily elaborate directions for assembling the appropriate ensemble at the appropriate time, as in these comments on the chemisette from an 1851 issue: "The undersleeves should correspond as nearly as possible, in style and pattern, with the collar and chemisette with which they are intended to be worn. This rule should be observed whether the undersleeves are open or closed at the end. We may mention that undersleeves should be reserved exclusively for evening dress, or at least confined to indoor wear." One can find similar descriptions in almost any issue of *Peterson's*, *Godey's*, or other fashion magazines during the middle decades of the nineteenth century, coexisting with obsessive references to simplicity and suitability. The editors recognized the need to express one's true self, but also to fit in, not to appear eccentric.[17] A sense of unified character began to erode gradually beneath the layers of appearances. What emerged was an antifashionable ideology of fashion, in which the authentic self became a constructed objet d'art, carefully framed by its material surroundings.

Fashion ideologues constantly emphasized the control and care with which clothes and other goods should be presented to the world. The meanings associated with goods, especially fashionable or luxury goods, were always shifting, unstable, and perhaps even dangerous; they embodied the decadence of the aristoi, the sybaritic delights of the demimonde, and the exotic sensuality of the "uncivilized" periphery. Madness, the literature implied, bubbled just beneath the surface of

24, no. 6 (December 1853): 283–84; and L. MacDonnell, "Grace Eversleigh's Golden Hair," *Peterson's* 62, no. 1 (July 1872): 23–24.

[17] "Editor's Table," *Peterson's* 63, no. 6 (June 1873): 442; "Fashions for September," *Peterson's* 20, no. 3 (September 1851): 134. See also "Editor's Table," *Peterson's* 28, no. 6 (December 1855): 410; "Descriptions of Fashions," *Godey's Lady's Book* 18 (January 1839); "The Art of Dress," *Godey's Lady's Book* 57 (October 1848); and "New Furniture," *Godey's Lady's Book* 40 (February 1850): 152–53.

select society. So there was a constant need to organize the meanings attached to consumption—to domesticate and moralize them. This was the role played by fashion magazine editors and authors of advice literature.

The tendency to link the glittering theatricality of consumer culture with a frightening loss of control was more than puritanism; it was rooted in the insecurities of everyday life in an expanding market society. Popular fiction and the files of Dun and Bradstreet were pervaded by tales of rapid rise and overnight ruin. In searching for explanations for wild fluctuations of fortune, moralists predictably conflated the impersonal operations of the market with personal moral choice, in particular the choice of extravagance or overconsumption. They flayed men for indulging in wine, cigars, and stag outings and criticized women for improvident expenditures on clothes and household furnishings.[18]

The idiom of control was sentimental moralism, and its material embodiment was the domestic household. Home became the necessary counterweight to the centrifugal forces unleashed by the market. Few scenes were more distressing to moralists than the forced auction of household goods—the invasion of the home by the corrosive powers of cash. Used repeatedly as a symbol of doom in popular fiction, the unwise purchase of a Brussels carpet meant that the household gods would soon be toppled from their pedestals and the auctioneer's red flag would soon be hoisted over the family home. In "The New Carpets" (1881), Fannie Swift decides that she must have new carpets even though things are difficult financially for her husband, Charlie. Charlie's banker sees the carpets being delivered, considers the purchase to be a wild extravagance, given Charlie's current financial condition, and decides that Charlie is a poor credit risk. Three weeks after the banker turns down Charlie for a crucial loan, the auctioneer's flag signals the dissolution of the Swift home. It is a bitter lesson, but Fannie learns it. Through industry and economy, she and Charlie fight their way back from ruin. In this story, as in many others, not only extravagance but also the

[18] Mrs. Lambert, "Margaret Compton," *Lady's National* 4, no. 4 (October 1843): 109–18; Alice B. Neal, "Furnishing; or, Two Ways of Commencing Life," *Godey's Lady's Book* 41 (November 1850): 299–305; Mrs. Child, "Our Treasury: Hints about Furniture," *Godey's Lady's Book* 46 (June 1853): 467–68; Charles J. Peterson, "Waifs by the Wayside," *Peterson's* 32, no. 3 (September 1857): 247; Mrs. J. E. M'Conaughey, "Saving Matches," *Peterson's* 69, no. 2 (February 1876): 109–10.

appearance of extravagance is the key to a disastrous fall. Appearances, so often dismissed as nothing, again turn out to be everything.[19]

Overall, during the period from 1840 to 1880, fashion ideologues were engaged in a continuing search for some means of organizing and controlling the chaotic potential of the proliferating meanings attached to commodities. The search was pervaded by tension between simplicity and extravagance, as well as authenticity and artifice, and by the implicit realization that obsessive preoccupation with either authenticity or artifice could lead to catastrophe. The result was the well-known Victorian compromise, respectability, rooted in tense ambivalence.

From 1880 to 1920, the period when Veblen began to survey the dominant culture, the tensions between authenticity and artifice increased for a wide variety of reasons. The most obvious reasons involved the increase of wealth, the elaboration of ornament, and the strutting social performance among elites—the tendencies that Veblen anatomized and anathematized in *The Theory of the Leisure Class* (1899). Another reason was the rise of European aestheticism, which exalted fluid theatricality and the manipulation of surfaces. The career of Oscar Wilde personified these tendencies. His delight in language as artifice, as well as his flamboyant self-fashionings, rejection of conventional gender roles, and dramaturgical conception of life, all dramatized the blurring of boundaries that Victorians attempted to control. Americans' ambivalent fascination with Wilde deserves closer scrutiny. It is worth noting that a character in an 1882 story names her rooster after him and that trade cards for goods from fertilizer to perfume satirized Wildean poseurs through the 1890s. An additional reason for increasing anxiety over issues of authenticity and artifice was the arrival of immigrants from non-Protestant traditions of ritual and carnivalesque display. Finally, within what might be called the vernacular entrepreneurial tradition, there was a continuing elaboration of exotic, sensuous display in trade card iconography and, as William Leach and John Kasson have shown, the rise of two new institutions for popularizing exoticism and commercial theatricality: department stores and amusement parks. It is not surprising that Veblen and other, more conventional plain speakers felt ill

[19]Mrs. J. E. M'Conaughey, "The New Carpets," *Peterson's* 80, no. 2 (August 1881): 148–49. See also Edgar Wayne, "Eleanor Hartley," *Lady's National* 11, no. 6 (June 1847): 201; and Helen B. Thornton, "The Red Flag," *Peterson's* 58, no. 2 (August 1870): 101–2.

at ease in this developing cultural environment.[20]

At the same time, the fin de siècle also saw a new and more rigorous search for dark truth behind the veil of appearances. For J. G. Frazer, Freud, and others, the surface of civilization was nothing, a mere veneer covering primal irrationality. In both high and popular cultures, one can see an emergent fascination with instinctual experience unmediated by surface conventionality, a quest for what D. H. Lawrence called "blood knowledge." As Lionel Trilling suggested, the Victorian ideal of simplicity was becoming the modernist ideal of authenticity: more rigorous, demanding, and dangerous.[21]

Both the spread of exotic theatricality and the recovery of primal irrationality involved the resurfacing of instinctual energy that was submerged, although never absent, in the Victorian imagination. Both pointed toward the upsetting of equipoise, the loss of control, and the renewed need to balance tension between authenticity and artifice. Fortunately for the survival of civilization as we know it, cultural elites did develop new means of orchestrating familiar tensions—new ways of mediating the meanings attached to goods, domesticating fashion, and sanitizing exoticism. The idiom of mediation shifted from moralism to professionalism as new structures of control arose, including professional associations, national corporations, and bureaucratic organizations of all kinds. Licensing laws stopped the mobile peddler in his tracks and put him behind the counter of a department store, transforming him from a liminal figure into a complaisant shopkeeper. Advertising sought to shed its Barnumesque inheritance and achieve professional respectability. Corporations acquired unprecedented control over the visual and verbal images attached to goods. These changes helped to reorganize cultural meanings in many different arenas of consumption, of which two are particularly representative: the domestic interior and the body. There was a similar pattern in both cases: a moralized nature

[20]Veblen, *Theory*, pp. 33–131; Mary Hayes, "An Esthete's Heart," *Peterson's* 81, no. 5 (November 1882): 371–77; John F. Kasson, *Amusing the Millions: Coney Island at the Turn of the Century* (New York: Hill and Wang, 1978); William Leach, "Transformations in a Culture of Consumption: Women and Department Stores, 1890–1925," *Journal of American History* 71, no. 2 (September 1984): 319–42.

[21]James G. Frazer, *The Golden Bough: A Study in Comparative Religion*, 2 vols. (London and New York: Macmillan Co., 1890); Sigmund Freud, *The Interpretation of Dreams*, trans. A. A. Brill (New York: Macmillan Co., 1913); D. H. Lawrence, *Studies in Classic American Literature* (1924; reprint, London: William Heinemann, 1937), p. 86; Lionel Trilling, *Sincerity and Authenticity* (Cambridge, Mass.: Harvard University Press, 1972).

Fig. 1. Queen Anne dining room, William Owen Goodman residence, Chicago, ca. 1885. From David Lowe, *Chicago Interiors* (Chicago: Contemporary Books, 1979).

had become increasingly surfeited with lush and decadent imagery. Professional designers on the one hand and professional advertisers on the other sought to sanitize that imagery and to purge it of unhealthy exoticism.

The nineteenth-century interior was the woman's sphere. Women not only provided moral uplift but also gave constant attention to the messy details of biological existence often ignored or denied by the male world outside. It is therefore no surprise that the Victorian interior embodied the iconography of female experience; it domesticated and moralized natural fecundity and sexual energy with floral wallpaper, globular lamps, cavorting cupids in the bedroom, and Ceres in the dining room. The vogue of potted plants epitomized the pattern of a domesticated nature straining at the seams of its civilized constraints (fig. 1).[22] For men—and for some more privileged women—the inte-

---

[22] Bonnie G. Smith, *Ladies of the Leisure Class: The Bourgeoises of Northern France in the Nineteenth Century* (Princeton: Princeton University Press, 1981), pp. 82–85, 87; Mario Praz, *An Illustrated History of Furnishing from the Renaissance to the Twentieth*

rior was associated with retreat to a world of private revery and leisured aesthetic contemplation. Late Victorian architects aimed to individualize and compartmentalize interior space as much as possible. Alongside natural imagery, exoticism and theatrical display intensified during the last two decades of the nineteenth century. Curio cabinets filled with bric-a-brac from many lands, the Turkish corner, the Egyptian booth, the vogue of chinoiserie, and the riot of eclectic architectural motifs, all betokened the rise of the interior as a stage set for private fantasy. As fiction and advice literature makes clear, some parts of that domestic stage could also be set for fashionable social performance.[23]

But by the turn of the century, there was a growing sense of oppressiveness, nearly suffocation, amid the clutter of theatrical props. Male fantasies of entombment, which pervaded the work of Edgar Allan Poe, Joris-Karl Huysmans, and Gustav Klimt, became more widespread and less gender-specific. In Charlotte Perkins Gilman's "Yellow Wallpaper" (1891), for example, the narrator not only recoils from the "sprawling, flamboyant patterns" in the wallpaper but also associates its "florid arabesque" with a nightmarish vision of fecundity—a fungus: "if you could imagine a toadstool in joints, an interminable string of toadstools, budding and sprouting in endless convolutions—why, that is something like it." Here and elsewhere, domestic artifice can hardly contain the monstrous energies of nature.[24]

The more drastic aesthetic response to this oppressive anxiety was enacted by the European modernists, who preached a gospel of secular

---

Century, trans. William Weaver (New York: George Braziller, 1964), p. 327; Carroll Smith-Rosenberg, "The Female World of Love and Ritual," *Signs* 1, no. 1 (Autumn 1975): 1–29; Catharine E. Beecher and Harriet Beecher Stowe, *The American Woman's Home; or, Principles of Domestic Science; Being a Guide to the Formation and Maintenance of Economical, Healthful, Beautiful, and Christian Homes* (1869; reprint, Hartford, Conn.: Stowe-Day Foundation, 1975).

    [23] Walter Benjamin, "Paris, Capital of the Nineteenth Century," in Walter Benjamin, *Reflections*, trans. Edmund Jephcott (New York: Harper and Row, 1978), esp. pp. 154–56; Gwendolyn Wright, *Moralism and the Model Home: Domestic Architecture and Cultural Conflict in Chicago, 1873–1913* (Chicago: University of Chicago Press, 1980), pp. 28–40.

    [24] Charlotte Perkins Gilman, "The Yellow Wallpaper" (1891), in *A Charlotte Perkins Gilman Reader*, ed. Anne Lane (New York: Pantheon Books, 1980), pp. 3–20. For other examples of these developing claustrophobic sentiments, see Joris-Karl Huysmans, *Against the Grain*, trans. John Howard (New York: Modern Library, 1930); and Carl Schorske, *Fin de Siècle Vienna: Politics and Culture* (New York: Alfred A. Knopf, 1980), esp. chap. 5.

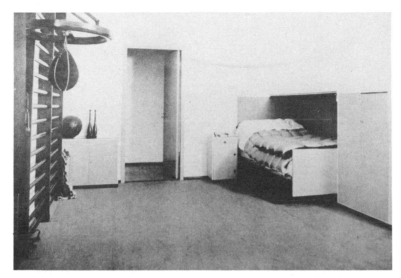

Fig. 2. Bedroom, Piscator apartment, Berlin, 1927, by Marcel Breuer. From Christopher Wilk and Marcel Breuer, *Furniture and Interiors* (New York: Museum of Modern Art, 1986).

puritanism, rationality, and efficiency in the guise of liberation from the airless, closed box of the nineteenth-century interior. In a sense, European modernism was a return to plain speech in architectural style. Severe functionalists like Ludwig Mies van der Rohe and Gerrit Rietveld were animated by a blend of Dutch Calvinsim and German pietism; the bedrooms designed by Marcel Breuer began to look like gymnasiums (fig. 2).[25] Anglo-Americans never warmed to this sterilized vision, although there was a brief flurry of scientific management in the home. Ellen Richards introduced "euthenics"—the "science of the controlled environment"—to middle-class audiences who were initially enthusiastic, but the appeal of euthenics never went beyond a few ideologues. It is also true that *House Beautiful* magazine and the arts and crafts movement attacked "the tyranny of things" and "the poor taste of

[25] Herbert Bayer, Walter Gropius, and Ise Gropius, *Bauhaus, 1919–1928* (2d ed.; Boston: Houghton Mifflin Co., 1952), esp. p. 126; Charles Edouard Jeanneret-Gris [Le Corbusier, pseud.], *The New World of Space* (New York: Reynal and Hitchcock, 1948), p. 48; Hans Ludwig C. Jaffee, *De Stijl 1917–1931: The Dutch Contribution to Modern Art* (Amsterdam: J. M. Meulenhoff, 1956), pp. 5, 42, 59.

the rich," warring against clutter in the name of taste, health, and sanity. They argued in the new professional/scientific language of expertise to do away with heavy drapes that sheltered microbes and "nervous, discordant" colors that bred neurasthenia. The overall result of American design reform, however, was a compromise between puritanical plain speech and riotous ornament.[26]

Frank Lloyd Wright's prairie houses expressed that compromise perfectly. He opened up and deindividualized the floor plan, providing fewer opportunities for morbid introspection and private fantasy. He brought the outdoors indoors, using the large, flat sheets of plate glass that were industrially available for the first time in the 1880s. These were moves in the direction of Bauhaus-style functionality. Wright used wood and stone rather than steel in keeping with the "organic" preoccupations of the arts and crafts movement. And he never fully rationalized the domestic ideal; he aimed to impart a sacramental aura to traditional family gathering places like the hearth and the dining room. In the pages of *House Beautiful* and other decorating magazines, the compromise was even more apparent (fig. 3). A good deal of ornament survived the assault on clutter, and by the 1910s a Morrisite commitment to "sincerity" in design—always an ambiguous goal at best—had given way to a tasteful eclecticism.[27]

The sanitizing of late Victorian imagery was even more apparent in the commercial iconography of the body. There was a dramatic movement away from exoticism and display, toward rationality and control. The vernacular entrepreneurial tradition of trade cards and patent medicine almanacs yielded to national corporate advertising planned by bureaucratic organizations—called advertising agencies—in New York City. These organizations were staffed overwhelmingly by educated, upper-class, WASP men with the same social and cultural background

[26] See, for example, Helen Campbell, "Household Art and the Microbe," *House Beautiful* 6, no. 5 (October 1899): 218–20: Esther Morton, "The Tyranny of Things," *House Beautiful* 36, no. 4 (September 1914): 113; Katherine W. Hand, "Nerves and Decoration," *House Beautiful* 37, no. 6 (May 1915): 184–85; and Wright, *Moralism*, pp. 234, 291. On feminist efforts to create alternative household arrangements, see Dolores Hayden, *The Grand Domestic Revolution* (Cambridge, Mass.: MIT Press, 1981).

[27] Here I follow the stimulating suggestions of Robert Twombly, "Saving the Family: Middle Class Attraction to Wright's Prairie House, 1901–1909," *American Quarterly* 27, no. 1 (March 1975): 57–72. See, for example, Claude Bragdon, "The Architecture of the Home: Some Fundamental Principles," *House Beautiful* 16, no. 1 (June 1904): 10; and Richard Bowland Kimball, "Keeping the House Alive," *House Beautiful* 47, no. 5 (May 1920): 404.

Fig. 3. Dining room, Elsie de Wolfe residence, New York, after 1898, by Elsie de Wolfe. From Allen Tate and C. Ray Smith, *Interior Design in the Twentieth Century* (New York: Harper and Row, 1986).

as the Protestant arbiters of nineteenth-century taste.[28]

Through the late nineteenth century, patent medicine advertising had preserved an exotic aura. Advertisements were steeped in herbalist lore and claims of primitive tribal origin (fig. 4). They fell into a common imperialist pattern: the white man penetrates the dark interior of a tropical land, extracts mysterious remedies, and puts them to the service of "civilization." A Warner's Safe Remedy pamphlet from 1882 captures the imperialist pattern; it shows a white man's head on a muscular brown body, paddling a canoe toward the heart of primitive darkness.[29]

---

[28] On the social background of advertising agency people, see Roland Marchand, *Advertising the American Dream: Making Way for Modernity, 1920–1940* (Berkeley: University of California Press, 1985), pp. 130–38; and Wallace Boren, "Bad Taste in Advertising," *JWT Forum*, January 7, 1936 (J. Walter Thompson Company Archives, New York).

[29] *Wright's Indian Vegetable Pills* (Philadelphia, 1844), box 33, Lyon Manufacturing Co., *Morning, Noon, and Night* (1872), box 20, *Peruvian Catarrh Cure* (New York, 1890), box 25, *Warner's "Safe" Remedies* (Rochester, N.Y., 1883), box 34, in Patent Medicines, Warshaw Collection of Business Americana, National Museum of American History, Smithsonian Institution.

Fig. 4. Cover, *Warner's "Safe" Remedies* (Rochester, N.Y.:
Privately printed, 1883). (Warshaw Collection, National
Museum of American History, Smithsonian Institution.)

Advertising for cosmetics also wallowed in exotic settings redolent
of luxuriant sensuality during the late nineteenth century. Often advertisements toyed with overt eroticism in displaying the languorous ease
of voluptuous women from the subculture of sensuality (fig. 5). Corsets

Fig. 5. Trade card, London Toilet Bazaar Co., 1886. (Warshaw Collection, National Museum of American History, Smithsonian Institution.)

were associated with images of explosive fecundity and even peep show-style prurience (fig. 6). These advertisements suggest a more complex picture of late Victorian culture than the prim and bloodless one presented by its early twentieth-century critics.[30]

After 1900 exoticism survived within the entrepreneurial tradition, inscribed on the walls of restaurants and movie theaters; however, in corporate iconography, it declined or was channeled into more productive outlets. Advertisers who promoted the tanning vogue of the early twentieth century, for example, detached dark skin from overtones of tropical sensuality and linked it with bracing outdoor vigor. The imperialist pattern was transformed from extraction of dark secrets to imposition of white values. In an Ivory soap series from 1900, for instance, an assembly of Plains Indians recalled that their blankets had been smeared with "grease and stains / from buffalo meat and settlers' veins" until "Ivory soap came like a ray / of light across our darkened way." Cleanliness had been a key emblem of refinement for at least half a century;

---

[30] In addition to those illustrated, see trade cards for F. J. Taney and Co. Angostura Bitters, 1876, box 31a, Patent Medicines, and Love's Incense, 1880, and Taylor's Premium Cologne, ca. 1890, box 108, Cosmetics, Warshaw Collection. For other examples of nineteenth-century exoticism, see Banner, *American Beauty*, esp. pp. 111–17.

Fig. 6. Trade card, Warner's Coraline Corsets, ca. 1890.
(Warshaw Collection, National Museum of American
History, Smithsonian Institution.)

what emerged after the turn of the century was a certain kind of cleanliness, purged of decadent hedonistic associations, oriented toward productive activism and a broader agenda of control. In corporate advertising, there was a growing emphasis on standardized, sanitized images of

Fig. 7. Advertisement, Gillette Sales Co., 1909. (Warshaw Collection, National Museum of American History, Smithsonian Institution.)

youthful physical perfection: the voluptuous woman and the bearded man yielded to smoother, cleaner, more activist and athletic models of beauty (fig. 7). The sanitation of body imagery was paralleled by an increased sensitivity to odors, culminating in the drive for "an absolute cleanliness of person, a real surgical cleanliness" announced by Zonite antiseptic in 1932. Euthenics triumphed in advertising, if not in actuality; a Lysol campaign from the early 1930s showed a cellophane-wrapped guest at a suburban front door, claiming, "If callers also arrived in sanitary packages, we wouldn't need Lysol."[31]

[31] Advertisement for Mennen's Borated Talcum Powder, in *Town and Country*, June 19, 1909, in box 109, Cosmetics, Warshaw Collection; Ivory Soap Co., *What a Cake of Soap Will Do* (ca. 1900), in box "Proctor and Gamble," Soap, Warshaw Collection; advertisement for Zonite Antiseptic, *Good Housekeeping* 92, no. 4 (April 1931): 126; advertisement for Lysol Antiseptic, *Good Housekeeping* 90, no. 4 (April 1930): 143. The upper-class counterattack on the belle ideal of voluptuous womanhood is discussed in Banner, *American Beauty*, pp. 130–31.

There are a number of explanations for this intensified emphasis on control of the biological universe. One involves the consolidation of scientific authority because of therapeutic breakthroughs and the growing preoccupation with the germ theory of disease. Another encompasses the broad process that Max Weber identified as the "disenchantment of the world": the reduction of nature, including one's own body, to a commodity, a manipulable thing. But there are more specific historical reasons as well, involving the ethnic, class, and intellectual background of the ad men themselves. They were members of a WASP elite group surrounded by swarming immigrants and troubling Darwinian theories. If one had apes for ancestors and Hottentots for cousins, the old cultural boundaries between civilization and barbarism, body and soul, no longer seemed so clear. Anglo-Saxon elites felt a strong need to distinguish themselves from primitives, exotics, and the "lower races"—the whole lot of brute creation. As Mary Douglas has suggested, a concern with bodily purification can reflect broader anxieties; pollution taboos reassert the reality of established social boundaries. The American preoccupation with sanitized, hairless bodies and sterile households was a means of redrawing familiar boundaries in a period of critical social stress. The standardized model of physical perfection offered a distinct alternative to the simian stereotypes of immigrant ethnic groups, the sort of people that Attorney Gen. A. Mitchell Palmer characterized in 1919 as "alien filth with sly and crafty eyes, lopsided faces, sloping brows, and misshapen features." Correct appearance became a mark of political normality and of civilization itself. More dramatically than in the domestic interior, in the iconography of the body one sees a farewell to exoticism, a triumph of control, and a steering away from both primitivism and decadence in favor of a moderate norm.[32]

[32] On the consolidation of authority by the mainstream medical profession, see Paul Starr, *The Social Transformation of American Medicine* (New York: Basic Books, 1982), esp. chap. 3. The best concise explication of disenchantment is Peter Berger, *The Sacred Canopy: Elements of a Sociological Theory of Religion* (Garden City, N.Y.: Doubleday, 1967). For an insightful discussion of late Victorian anxieties about the blurred boundaries between humanity and animality, see James Turner, *Reckoning with the Beast: Animals, Pain, and Humanity in the Victorian Mind* (Baltimore: Johns Hopkins University Press, 1980), esp. pp. 63–69. The classic analysis of the relationship between pollution taboos and social boundaries is Mary Douglas, *Purity and Danger: An Analysis of Concepts of Pollution and Taboo* (London: Routledge and Kegan Paul, 1966). Palmer is quoted in Michael Paul Rogin, *Ronald Reagan, the Movie, and Other Episodes in Political Demonology* (Berkeley: University of California Press, 1987), pp. 238–39.

One can only imagine what Veblen would think of this analysis. Maybe he would see the rationalizing tendencies I have described as a partial vindication of his own critique, a process by which the American ruling class refused to become a leisure class, instead creating new sanctions for self-control and disciplined achievement. And perhaps he would recognize that the reorganization of cultural meaning between 1880 and 1920 was too complex to be captured in any linear scheme of progress or decline. What is particularly suspect is the idea, derived partly from Veblen, that the emergence of new ways of assigning meaning to goods meant the rise of self-indulgent materialism and hedonism. We have always had materialism with us, in the sense that people have always used material goods to make cultural meaning; the history of hedonism has yet to be written.

Meanwhile, the tension between authenticity and artifice is still very much alive. Indeed it has acquired a global significance, as multinational corporations cry their commodities in every corner of the "developing" world. The cacophony helps to conceal older, quieter relationships of imperial coercion, at least from postmodern theorists in the West who have taken to celebrating the agreeably meaningless signifiers of mass cultural fashion. But the discourse of authenticity survives outside Anglo-Saxon traditions of plain speech, among anti-imperialist leaders in the third world who invoke national or tribal loyalties in their attempts to exorcise the demons of Western artifice. Whether their project will be any more successful than Veblen's remains to be seen.

Strategists of Display and the Production of Desire

William Leach

"What a stinging, quivering zest they display," novelist Theodore Dreiser wrote in 1902 of the show windows on Fifth Avenue in New York, "stirring up in onlookers the desire to secure but a minor part of what they see, the taste of a vibrating presence, and the picture that it makes." And again, fifteen years later, in his diary: "We go across 34th to 5th Avenue, and up to 42nd, looking in windows. Wonderful display. . . . We visit Arnold, Constable, Franklin Simon and Co., Lord and Taylor, and Macy. . . . It is getting colder. These great stores are so fascinating in the winter." Wherever Dreiser lived or traveled in urban America, he visited the big stores, excited by the way they looked, both inside and out. In their size and power, their human bustle, and their capacity to make people hungry for pleasure and wealth, the stores epitomized the great city for Dreiser, which he called "the gorgeous storehouse . . . heaped in glittering masses."[1] Above all, the stores embodied new forms of display and decoration that attracted Dreiser and countless

[1] Theodore Dreiser, *Color of a Great City* (New York: Charles Scribner's Sons, 1923), p. 4; Theodore Dreiser diary, November 10, 26, 1917, in *Theodore Dreiser, American Diaries, 1902–1926*, ed. Thomas Riggio (Philadelphia: University of Pennsylvania Press, 1982), pp. 204, 222; Theodore Dreiser, "Reflections," *Ev'ry Month* 3, no. 10 (October 1896): 6–7, republished as Theodore Dreiser, "The City," in *A Selection of Uncollected Prose*, ed. Donald Pizer (Detroit: Wayne State University Press, 1977), p. 98. For other cities Dreiser visited, see Dreiser diary, November 6, 1919, May 12, 1920, April 24, May 5, 1921, December 9, 1925, in Riggio, ed., *Theodore Dreiser*, pp. 288, 314, 354, 365, 418.

other urban and suburban Americans. Although traces of these new forms can be found earlier in the United States, it was not until the late nineteenth century that they became the reigning forms of representation, recreating both the look and the meaning of commodities and commodity environments. Never before had Americans mobilized aesthetic energies so completely in this fashion—and never so completely in the commercial sphere. Unlike Europeans, who often articulated aesthetic desires in high art, Americans channeled their desires almost entirely, and seemingly without equivocation, into the creation of mass commercial forms.

After 1890 display and decoration were year-round, nocturnal, and diurnal endeavors. They were syncretic and surrealist—syncretic because they incorporated all traditions and myths (religious and secular, folk and foreign) for commercial purposes; surrealist because they tried to invest artificial and material things, whole urban spaces, with plasticity and life, breaking down the barriers between the animate and the inanimate. Commercial designers shifted the improvising power of the imagination away from natural and religious things toward artificial and secular things. They strove for theatrical effects and for a new enchantment, systematically interpreting and dramatizing commodities and commodity environments in ways that disguised and transformed them into what they were not.

Conditions for the Emergence of Display and Decoration

Several overlapping conditions created the foundation for the emergence of modern approaches to display and decoration. The most obvious condition was the rapid shift of American capitalism from its agrarian base in the early nineteenth century to industrial manufacturing, which generated a great abundance of commodities for the domestic market and created unprecedented distributive requirements. In the short space of just thirty years (1890–1920), American society had established the institutional basis for a consumer society. Where once large retail businesses clustered only in a few urban centers, now, in cities across the country, a whole spectrum of stores—grocery, hardware, cigar, drug, dry-goods, chain, and department—had come into being. What was remarkable about this growth was that, almost uniformly, it far outpaced the needs of the population.

Commercial entrepreneurs therefore became obsessed with the distribution, flow, and traffic of goods. They labored to make urban space and time completely amenable to the circulation of commodities, and they focused increasingly on removing constraints on the expression of consumer desire and on expanding that desire. They had to cultivate in far greater measure than ever before the already well-entrenched desire of Americans for new and better things. They had to build on the American longing for individual material well-being, happiness, and pleasure.

Contributing to the rise of the new styles in display and decoration was a popular readiness to receive and welcome them, fostered by the improvements in the standard of living, by the growth of disposable income, and above all by changes in work and by new attitudes toward play, leisure, and consumption. In the early nineteenth century, most white American men were self-employed, owners of their own property, and producers of foodstuffs and raw materials for a burgeoning Atlantic economy. Relatively free from the dangers of manufacturing, which relied on disciplined work rhythms and a dependent work force to churn out goods, Americans rejoiced in their widely diffused prosperity and their relaxed work habits, calling America the "Land of Comfort" for all.[2] Gradually these circumstances were altered, until by the 1890s large numbers of men (and many women) worked in factories and in big corporate bureaucracies that demanded differing degrees of professional expertise. In both instances, these people had lost individual control over their own work and were subject to new disciplines and stresses that often rendered the work they performed wearying and unsatisfying.

Such a situation also transformed the meaning of leisure and consumption, as both became more and more the focus of individual fulfillment. This change in emphasis, perceivable as early as the 1850s in major American cities, was reinforced by the weakening of religious, domestic-familial, and republican scripts that had once vigorously mediated between people and an expanding market economy, protecting them from what Dreiser called in 1898 "the boundless, limitless desire within our hearts."[3]

By the 1890s America had evolved from the "Land of Comfort" into the "Land of Desire." It was this upsurge in desire, occurring at

---

[2] Joyce Appleby, *Capitalism and the New Social Order* (New York: New York University Press, 1984), p. 44.
[3] Dreiser, "Reflections," p. 85.

the deepest levels of consciousness and affecting all classes, that so strikingly marked the psychological turmoil of the period and fostered greater
freedom and inventiveness in display and decoration by merchants, who
themselves were affected by these changes. Florence Peck, a young Boston librarian, reflected in her diary for 1903, "Have you ever had the
desire, the awful longing for something, some one that you could not
have—away down in your heart—that dreadful longing for something,
some one." This upsurge in longing would trouble Americans for many
decades, especially middle-class Americans, who would struggle to sub-
due and rationalize it and to understand its meaning and significance.
From at least the 1880s the term *desire* entered American discourse at
all levels. In the very year that Peck anguished over her "dreadful desire,"
Lester Ward, the founder of American sociology, defined consumption
as the "satisfaction of desire." At the same time, dry-goods merchant
John Wanamaker announced to his customers in bold type that his
advertising "EDUCATES DESIRE. . . . It tells all the beauty or benefits of
the articles. It also tells how easy it is to possess these things. . . . At
length desire ripens. And where desire is earnest, the means can always
be found." In another advertising editorial in 1906, John Wanamaker
described America as the "Land of Desire."[4]

Another related factor underlying the formation of new merchandising strategies was the emergence of schools and institutes to teach
commercial skills ranging from decorative architecture to commercial
design and display. Already by 1900 such countries as Germany and
France had erected their own institutions to teach commercial skills;
after 1900 a comparable and even more powerful apparatus appeared in
the United States. New York City alone offered Pratt Institute, Cooper
Union (both converted into commercial art schools after 1905), and
Parson School of Design (originally called New York School of Fine
and Applied Arts), as well as great museums and universities, which
increasingly offered specialized instruction in commercial subjects. The
skills taught in these institutions—the skills of commodity exchange,
representation, and interpretation—were developed in response to the

    [4]Florence Peck diary, April 12, 1903, Manuscripts Division, New York Public Library;
North American (April 5, 1906), clipping in scrapbook, Wanamaker Archives, Philadelphia; *Dry Goods Economist*, March 14, 1903, p. 12; Lester F. Ward, *Pure Sociology: A
Treatise on the Origin and Spontaneous Development of Society* (New York: Macmillan,
1903), pp. 282–83.

needs of modern manufacturing and merchandising and on the heels of the decline of skills in the productive sector, signified by the devaluation of craft labor.

The new display and decorative strategies also emerged because merchants had at their disposal an astonishing arsenal of color, glass, and light, the visual vocabulary of desire, which guaranteed the means to translate readiness into action. Long before this time, of course, these materials (particularly color and light) had been marshaled in both overlapping and contesting ways by the court and the church, as well as by the theater and the marketplace, to please and delight, to transform lifeless objects into icons worthy of worship, and to excite loyalty and devotion. Their exploitation, however, was not only technically but also culturally limited by restrictions on indulgence in leisure, play, and luxury. Especially in Protestant cultures, both color and light were viewed with deep suspicion, their use perceived as ethically dangerous and demonic and as an engenderment to longing and desire.[5]

By the modern period, restrictions on the use of these materials were being lifted partly for the reasons discussed above but also because of the influx of Catholic and Jewish immigrants who were accustomed to the visual density of aesthetic representation. For the first time, commercial entrepreneurs had at their fingertips totally new kinds of color, glass, and light and an unrivaled abundance of each: artificial colors made from aniline coal-tar dyes, which exceeded in brilliance anything in nature and required the invention of color standards so that people could recognize the differences among colors; large quantities of domestically made plate glass by the 1890s; glass that was frosted, etched, rolled, and figured, as well as wire glass, carrara glass, prism glass; and, of course, artificial electrical light in many forms. Of these three materials, light was the most determinant, shaping in many ways the evolution of color and glass. Artificial light revolutionized modern architecture. "The sheer abundance of light," wrote architectural historian Reyner

[5] Lee Simonson, *The Stage Is Set* (1932; reprint, New York: Dover Publications, 1946), pp. 249–50; Michael R. Booth, *The Victorian Spectacular Theater, 1850–1910* (London: Routledge and Kegan Paul, 1981), pp. 24–25; Peter Burke, *Popular Culture in Early Modern Europe* (London: Temple Smith, 1978); Mikhail Bakhtin, *Rabelais and His World*, trans. Helene Iswolsky (Cambridge, Mass.: MIT Press, 1968); Le Roy Ladurie, *Carnival in Romans* (New York: George Braziller, 1979); Richard D. Altick, *The Shows of London* (New York: Oxford University Press, 1978); Neil Harris, *Humbug: The Art of P. T. Barnum* (Chicago: University of Chicago Press, 1973).

Banham, "effectively reversed all established visual habits by which buildings were seen. For the first time it was possible to conceive of buildings whose true nature could only be perceived after dark, when artificial light blazed out through their structure."[6]

From the 1880s onward, the application of color, glass, and light spread rapidly throughout the domain of popular entertainment and consumption. Opera houses, ballet companies, restaurants, hotels, department stores, and amusement parks, as well as fairs and (later) museums, incorporated color, glass, and light into exterior and interior spaces. Similar "architectural hocus-pocus" amplified the "atmospherics" of movie and vaudeville houses, inviting customers into "another system of aesthetics."[7] The luxury of the movie screen or the theatrical stage was reflected in luxurious mirrors and colored lights in lobbies and by lavish murals that often decked the interior walls. The existence of such a matrix of similar urban commercial institutions, whose display and decorative strategies resembled one another and were often designed by the same architects, hastened the innovative use of color, glass, and light. No single institution could have achieved this, but several, interlinked and cross-fertilizing one another, endowed the display aesthetic with a secure life of its own.

When integrated, these materials produced stunning visual effects in city streets and in specific commercial icons of the times. In many American cities after 1900, urban jeweled forms appeared as vertical monuments flooded with light, symbols of the fairy-tale orientalism that overtook public dream culture. The prototype was the Tower of Jewels at the 1915 San Francisco World's Fair, a festival totem pole of 50,000 jewels in five colors. A year later Chicago's municipal Christmas tree was made from the gems taken from the Tower of Jewels. To commem-

[6] Matthew Luckiesh, *Torch of Civilization: The Story of Man's Conquest of Darkness* (New York: G. P. Putnam's, 1940); Warren C. Scoville, *Revolution in Glassmaking: Entrepreneurship and Technological Change in the American Industry, 1880–1920* (Cambridge, Mass.: Harvard University Press, 1948); Pittsburgh Plate Glass Company, *Glass History* (Pittsburgh: Pittsburgh Plate Glass Co., 1923); Faber Birren, *Color and Human Response* (New York: Van Nostrand Rheinhold Co., 1978); Krishnasami Venkataraman, *The Chemistry of Synthetic Dyes* (New York: Academic Press, 1952); Reyner Banham, *The Architecture of the Well-Tempered Environment* (Chicago: University of Chicago Press, 1969), p. 70.

[7] Lewis Mumford, as quoted in Lary May, *Screening Out the Past: The Birth of Mass Culture and the Motion Picture Industry* (Chicago: University of Chicago Press, 1983), p. 156.

orate the homecoming of the troops in 1919, both Chicago and New York erected huge jeweled arches "symbolic of the Living Light of Democracy triumphant over the darkness and evil of militarism." In New York, American troops flowed under the arch with its two jewel-encrusted obelisks, topped by radial sunbursts and joined together by a necklace of multicolored, prismatic glass, a structure that would reappear again as the El Arco de Brilliantes to celebrate San Francisco's Diamond Jubilee in 1925. In 1923 New York constructed the Fountain of Jewels, which was installed at the center of an industrial exposition in the Grand Central Palace, to honor the Silver Jubilee of the unification of the five boroughs. These jeweled forms signified a new way of life, welcoming Americans into the pleasures of a new consumer age.[8]

By 1920 merchants had great access to color, glass, and light, and they had more money to spend on them and more desire to exploit them than any comparable group in history. This is a fact of considerable importance, for any class or any group that could acquire control over these paradisiacal materials could dominate the character of cultural life. Commercial entrepreneurs commanded these materials, which explained why so many gifted people trained in art and architecture gravitated to the commercial sector, excited not only by the prospects of big salaries but also by the chance to experiment with color, glass, and light.

The last factor underpinning the articulation of modern display and decoration was the development of a complex institutional infrastructure that supported it in every way. This infrastructure encompassed merchandising institutions and schools, museums, hotels, restaurants, theaters, and similar consumer institutions—the entire urban educational hierarchy—as well as the government at all levels, above all the federal government, which by 1920 had placed its imprimatur on the expansion of display and decoration. All these institutions worked closely and harmoniously together to generate new strategies of display

[8]"Celebrations: Silver Jubilee," pt. 2, Subject Files, 1919–26, box 174, and Mayor's Committee, 2, 1918, pt. 2, Departmental Letters Received, 1918-M, box 22, Mayor John Hylan Papers, Municipal Archives, New York; San Francisco's Diamond Jubilee Illumination, Photographic Archives, General Electric Co., Schenectady, N.Y.; Matthew Luckiesh, *Artificial Light: Its Influence on Civilization* (London: Century Co., 1920), pp. 304–5; Juliet James, *Palaces and Courts of the Exposition* (San Francisco: California Book Co., 1915), pp. 64–65.

and decoration and, by extension, the consumer culture that issued from them.

Show Windows and the Land of Oz

Every commercial and entertainment industry of the time applied some variant of display and decoration. The American middle-class department store was representative of these industries in its focus on three major facets of merchandising display and decoration: show windows, merchandising interiors, and the color and light displays of the 1920s. Department stores, taking their recognizable shape by the mid 1890s, pushed the entire merchandising sector into a revolutionary direction. By 1920 department stores had become, in the words of well-known ethnologist and museum curator Stewart Culin, "the aesthetic centers of urban communities . . . schools for taste transcending every other I know."[9]

Before 1890 *display* as a term denoting systematic treatment of goods did not exist, nor would it be part of everyday merchandising language until World War I. What display did exist was primitive, as trimmers crowded goods together inside the windows or, weather permitting, piled them up outside on the street. Sometimes merchants massed and obscured commodities into baroque architectural structures concocted from outrageous quantities of silks and linens, a practice that persisted into the twentieth century. Many stores, like Arnold Constable's in New York, exhibited nothing at all in the windows, relying on them merely to light interiors. Other store owners viewed display as tasteless, and most simply did not know what to do with the manufactured goods that inundated their shelves. By and large, from store to store, the lighting was poor, the glass was of inferior quality, and the display fixtures were makeshift (for example, boxes, cheesecloth, piece goods, or random materials dredged up from back rooms).[10]

The first steps toward a modern display aesthetic can be dated specifically in 1889 when an influential journal of the period, *Dry Goods*

[9] Stewart Culin, "Color in Window Displays," *Men's Wear* 6, no. 6 (June 9, 1926): 72.

[10] John Crawford Brown, "Early Days of Department Stores," in *Valentine's Manual of Old New York*, ed. Henry Collins Brown (New York: Charles Scribner's Sons, 1921), pp. 134–45.

Economist, shifted its format from the mechanics to the theatrics of commodity exchange. First published in 1858, this New York–based organ offered little to merchants on retailing methods for the next thirty years; it reported on money markets, banking, real estate, and stocks and featured a weekly religious column on evangelical activities full of appeals to merchants to pursue selfless and Spartan Christian paths. In 1889 *Dry Goods Economist* dropped all of this to focus entirely on the retailing sector. Year by year more material on display appeared in its pages, until by the late 1890s, in a climate of unprecedented prosperity and intense store rivalry, new directions had clearly opened in the practice of display.

It is perhaps appropriate that the first significant advocate of display was the greatest of all American fairy-tale writers, L. Frank Baum, creator of the Land of Oz. Baum was among the earliest architects of the dream life of the consumer age; he wrote in a new language tailored to consumer aspirations, and he created the first literature on display in the world. He articulated the new ideas on display, urging merchants to rid their windows of clutter and crowding, to treat their goods aesthetically, to immerse them in color and light, to place them in the foreground and single them out, and to make them come "alive."

Baum was born in 1856 at Roseland, his family's comfortable estate in upstate New York. Although his father made a fortune in the oil business, Baum cared nothing for industrial production or work. He believed instead in the virtues of consumption and leisure and, like many of his contemporaries (such as Lester Ward, Simon Patten, and Edward Bellamy), in lifting taboos on the expression of desire. Baum wrote, "To gain all that meat from the nut of life is the essence of wisdom, therefore, 'eat, drink, and be merry'—for *tomorrow* you die." Baum disparaged saving over spending, had a genial contempt for established religion, and opposed prohibition and Sunday enforcement laws. As the son-in-law of Matilda Joslyn Gage, a leading feminist of the nineteenth century, Baum defended women's rights, and his fictional characters—above all, Dorothy—were derived in part from his feminist convictions.[11]

[11] *Aberdeen Saturday Pioneer,* May 10, 1890; Frank Joslyn Baum and Russell P. MacFall, *To Please a Child: A Biography of L. Frank Baum, Royal Historian of Oz* (Chicago: Reilly and Lee, 1951), pp. 17, 44–45; *Aberdeen Saturday Pioneer,* March 15, 19, November 6, 1890; M. J. Gage, "The Dakota Days of L. Frank Baum," *Baum Bugle* 2, no. 8 (Autumn 1966): 7.

Baum's stories reflect the polymorphous nature of the commodity market and of the new urban world in which the market took its grandest expression. His stories are the literary apotheosis of commodity flow. In the Land of Oz, things are always animated, always metamorphosing; landscapes shift again and again in color and hue, boundaries are magically crossed, and pathways go in many directions at once. Gender lacks fixity, as boys change into girls, girls into boys, with a lyrical fluidity unparalleled in American fantasy writing.[12] Far from being disturbed by this volatility, Baum celebrated it in fiction marked by an abundance of color and light. He aesthetically celebrated technological interventions into space (above and below the ground) that made possible market expansion and the artificial world of commodities that flowed from it.

Baum transplanted the artificial and the technological into seemingly natural settings to create a kind of upbeat surreal chemistry that may have tended in its effect to accustom Americans to living in artificial environments. His tales echoed Ward's view that "the artificial is superior to the natural." They were the literary outgrowth of something begun in the mid nineteenth century when Americans aestheticized machinery and probably completed by 1915 with the building of countless pleasure palaces that institutionalized a new aesthetic of artificiality—more attractive, it was hoped, than any naturalist one.[13]

The sources for Baum's fantasies lay partly in his love of technology, his fascination with artificial color and glass, and his passion for electrical light. Although Baum practiced no conventional faith, he believed in spiritualism and was "eager to penetrate the secrets of Nature." He was amazed by the magic of modern science, particularly by discoveries of electrical waves, radium, and X rays, which seemed to reveal a living presence at the heart of inanimate things. Baum would have understood the conviction of his near-contemporary Albert Einstein "that

---

[12] For these gender transformations, see L. Frank Baum's *Emerald City of Oz* (Chicago: Reilly and Britton, 1919), *Ozma of Oz* (Chicago: Reilly and Britton, 1907), *John Dough and the Cherub* (Chicago: Reilly and Britton, 1906), and *Land of Oz* (Chicago: Reilly and Britton, 1904).

[13] Lester Ward, "Some Economic and Social Paradoxes (1888)," reprinted in *Lester Ward and the Welfare State*, ed. Henry Steele Commager (Indianapolis: Bobbs-Merrill, 1967), pp. 118–89. On the early aestheticizing of machinery, see John F. Kasson, *Civilizing the Machine: Technology and Republican Values in America, 1776–1900* (New York: Grossman Publishers, 1976).

there had to be something behind objects that lay deeply hidden." In 1910 Baum wrote the first major science-fiction tale in America, *The Master Key: An Electrical Fairytale*, dressing what he called "the demon of electricity" in a "gorgeous vest of all colors of the rainbow into a flashing, resplendent mass." Urban commercial institutions had an equally deep claim on Baum's imagination. As a young man he operated a chain of small theaters originally purchased by his father and produced spectacular traveling shows. As he grew older, Baum experimented with mechanical wizardry, staging his own tales as musical extravaganzas in settings radiated with color and light and glutted with jewels. In mandatory "transformation scenes," fairy choruses danced on rainbows or dissolved in snowstorms of "frosty blues and greens."[14]

Baum dabbled in photography and motion pictures. In the first decade of the twentieth century, he toured the country with his "fairylogues" and "radio shows," made up of lectures, stereopticon slides, and hand-tinted movies. And no one enjoyed hotel life more than Baum. He wrote many of his best fantasies while staying in the luxurious Hotel del Coronado, a hotel in southern California that so delighted him that he designed the crown-shape lighting fixtures for its Crown Dining Room, which still hang there. He called the hotel a tourist "paradise," "a year-round carnival," and a "fairyland."[15]

Most important, Baum was a merchant who was occupied for almost twenty-five years with the concrete work of commodity interpretation. At the same time that he managed a string of theaters in his youth, he owned a retail business. Later, in the early 1890s, he was lured to Chicago by retailing prospects and by an impending world's fair; he made his living as a china and glassware salesman and peddled fireworks as a sideline. Then in 1897 Baum founded *Show Window*, the first magazine ever devoted to such a subject and acclaimed by H. Gordon Selfridge of Field's department store as indispensable to merchants. The next year Baum assembled the first National Association of Window

[14] *Aberdeen Saturday Pioneer*, January 25, 1890; Albert Einstein, as quoted in Richard Rhodes, *The Making of the Atomic Bomb* (New York: Simon and Schuster, 1987), p. 70; L. Frank Baum, *The Master Key: An Electrical Fairytale* (1901; reprint, Westport, Conn.: Greenwood Press, 1974), pp. 9–10; Alla T. Ford and Dick Martin, *The Musical Fantasies of L. Frank Baum* (Chicago: Reilly and Britton, 1958), p. 14.

[15] Russell MacFall, "L. Frank Baum and the Radio Plays," *Baum Bugle* 3, no. 8 (August 1962): 2; Scott Olsen, "The Coronado Fairyland," *Baum Bugle* 18, no. 12 (Winter 1976): 1.

Trimmers; in 1900, the year he wrote *The Wizard of Oz* and left merchandising permanently, Baum published *The Art of Decorating Show Windows and Dry Goods Interiors*, the first book of its kind.[16]

Baum's display strategy reflected the combined weight of all the other things that mattered to him—fairy tales, the theater, hotels, new visual technologies, and the attractions of the modern urban commercial world. Display was fantasy, childhood, theater, technological play, and selling all rolled into one for Baum, as it would be for later display artists infatuated with the same urban commercial forms.

Baum raised the status of the show window to first place among advertising strategies. He advised retailers to have larger windows and to deepen them, to install wooden or scenic backgrounds, and to stretch out the glass surface as far as it would go. He urged trimmers to learn everything about color and light, adding, "An up-to-date trimmer must be his own electrician" and should know the properties of color and its impact on the senses. Like so many displaymen (few women practiced window display in those early days), Baum advocated spectacular windows, architectural displays, and devices intended not so much to display goods as to attract attention: flasher lights, electrical waving flags, and electrically illuminated fountains. At the same time, his fanciful imagination, so saturated in spiritualism and in the concentrating playfulness of a child, readily grasped the magical potential of a single, isolated commodity. In 1898 Baum wrote that the finest commercial art should be employed to "arouse in the observer a cupidity and longing to possess the goods." He advised merchants to look for the "possibilities laying dormant in the beautiful goods" and to transform and reconstitute the everyday goods by sharpening their outlines in order to highlight their individuality: "Tastefully display a single apron."[17]

The Arsenal and Strategy of Display

In the years immediately following Baum's departure from retailing, a whole new system of expertise developed to shape and reshape the com-

---

[16] Baum and MacFall, *To Please a Child*, pp. 75–78, 95; Robert Baum, "The Autobiography of Robert Baum," *Baum Bugle* 13, no. 12 (Christmas 1970): 2; L. Frank Baum, *The Art of Decorating Show Windows and Dry Goods Interiors* (Chicago: National Window Trimmer's Assn., 1900), pp. 22–23, 113–26.

[17] Baum, *Art of Decorating*, pp. 7–9, 14, 82–140, 213–44; *Show Window* 3, no. 7 (April 1899): 66.

modities in the windows. The first professional schools to teach display appeared; manuals and books on display multiplied; professional displaymen's organizations sprang up at the city, state, and regional levels; and the National Association of Window Trimmers matured into a major vehicle of trade standardization. For the first time, the term *display* was used to describe what merchants did with their commodities. In 1912 *trimmer* was dropped for *display manager* as the operative term, a shift in nomenclature "indicative of the change in the whole aspect of the retail profession," according to Percy Straus of R. H. Macy and Company. In 1914 the National Association of Window Trimmers was renamed the International Association of Displaymen.[18] Nothing of this kind of voluntary professional ferment existed elsewhere. In Europe, the state directed and shaped the development of professional merchandising standards, but it could not match, at least in these early years, the energy and inventiveness of American commercial business.

Store display staff and budgets quadrupled in size over ten or fifteen years. In 1890 Field's had no display staff, but by 1915 it employed over fifty painters, sculptors, and craftsmen to do the displays. John Wanamaker's had a comparable staff, as did Strawbridge and Clothier, Siegel-Cooper, and Jordan Marsh, among others. The new visual technologies of color and light contributed greatly to the arsenal of display and were embraced as the "key" materials of representation. After 1915 spotlighting and floodlighting slowly came into vogue. The displaymen's repertoire expanded to include colored glass caps and sheets of colored glass, projectors to flood the windows with color, light dimmers, electric eyes, and movable colored screens rheostatically controlled to achieve the best color impressions.[19]

Independent display companies played a major role in the evolution of professional display, supplying stores with pedestals, millinery stands, velours and other fabrics, decorative backgrounds, expensive wooden backs (essential to display until the late 1920s), and a remarkable new fixture: mannequins. Throughout most of the nineteenth century, people could see full-bodied mannequins only in dime museums.

[18] *Merchants' Record and Show Window* 30, no. 2 (February 1912): 40–41; 37, no. 2 (August 1915): 40–44; 35, no. 4 (October 1914): 52.

[19] *Merchants' Record and Show Window* 50, no. 2 (February 1922): 36–7; 72, no. 1 (January 1933): 3; 54, no. 1 (July 1924): 7–26; 52, no. 2 (February 1923): 14–18; 53, no. 5 (November 1923): 48–50; 51, no. 3 (September 1922): 11–14. *Dry Goods Economist*, July 7, 1917, July 2, 1921, pp. 59, 79; Matthew Luckiesh, *Light and Color in Advertising and Merchandising* (New York: G. P. Putnam's, 1923), pp. 146–70, 207–17.

During the late 1880s, however, the first American wax industry appeared, although only a few stores drew on this domestic supply. The commonest dress fixtures were still "headless dummies—no arms, or heads—no feet," draped in expensive yard goods. By the turn of the century, in the wake of the growth of the ready-to-wear clothing industry, female mannequins (and most mannequins were female until the 1970s) were assured a central place in merchandising. The use of mannequins provided the first visual persuasion to women that ready-to-wear clothing was as good, if not better, than any they might construct from dress materials at home. By 1912 mannequins had gained a "wonderful popularity"; even Field's, long a holdout for the headless form, began to pose them in the windows.[20]

The first mannequins were primitively made, doll-like wax figures that were expressionless and static, very much like the stylized figures that appeared earlier in such magazines as *Godey's Lady's Book* and *Peterson's*. And they tended to melt quickly in hot weather. After 1915 mannequins were placed increasingly in temperature-controlled window spaces and were molded from a more reliable blend of papier-mâché and wax. They were endowed with authentic-looking hair, natural facial features, "animated attitudes," and adjustable limbs. "As many types of wax figures" existed "as there were human beings," although mannequins continued to be principally female. By the late 1920s realistic mannequins were replaced temporarily by fantastic, modernist figures in various abstract shapes, but they returned again in even greater force and were better designed in the mid 1930s. "The figures seem to live to be occupied with one another," wrote Lester Gaba, the premier mannequin designer, about his "personality" mannequins, "so that, as you look at them in the window, you seem almost to be intruding on their privacy."[21]

[20] Arthur Frazer, "Lloyd Lewis Interviews," *Merchants' Record and Show Window* 33, no. 5 (November 1913): 20–21, 40–44; 34, no. 6 (June 1914): 20–21, 36–39; 22, no. 4 (April 1908): 16–19; "The Evolution of Expression," *Visual Merchandising* 5, no. 2 (February 1978): 49–51; "Mannequins from the Beginning," *Visual Merchandising* 4, no. 5 (May 1980): 42; *Department Store* 3, no. 4 (April 1914): 61–3; *Show Window* 3, no. 1 (January 1, 1899): 12; *Dry Goods Economist*, October 12, 1889, December 10, 1898, pp. 15, 12.
[21] Lester Gaba to John Nichols, October 12, 1938, records of Wanamaker displayman Howard Kratz, Howard Kratz Papers, Wanamaker Archives; *Women's Wear Daily*, November 19, December 24, 1927, pp. 12, 10; Marcus, *American Store Window*, pp. 34–35; *Dry Goods Economist*, August 18, 1908, July 26, 1913, February 21, April 14, 1914, October 27, 1917, July 12, 1919, November 19, 1921, pp. 3, 8, 3, 3, 17, 14, 23.

Female mannequins were perhaps the most radical display fixtures ever to appear in the store window. They helped transform the character of the public female image. Unlike the female statuary of the past, which personified such classical virtues as justice and truth, as well as the domestic virtues of purity and maternal nurture, these figures owed little allegiance to earlier traditions. They invoked individual indulgence in luxury as often as they did traditional domestic behavior. Indeed, as devices to excite desire for goods, mannequins were used explicitly to suggest not one kind of behavior, but a range of behaviors and roles. The same process was at work in other forms of representation. Partly as a result of technological advances in color illustration, photography, and motion pictures, the female image was gradually thrust out of its older protective cultural shelter. The image was stylized in a new way to show, among other things, concrete movement, exuberance, frivolity, and sensuality. Jules Cheret's and Eugene Grasset's poster girls, kicking their feet and throwing their arms in the air, pioneered this type of representation.[22]

A new generation of displaymen orchestrated this arsenal of materials to forge selling windows of considerable effect. Goods were no longer crowded together or shaped into architectural structures, but were foregrounded, isolated, and singled out. One New York displayman reported: "We used to put twenty-one hats in a single window . . . now we have no more—possibly less—in a whole window stretch." Mass-manufactured, ready-made goods—above all, clothing—were the first merchandise to be treated in this theatrical manner. Over time, all commodities, including everyday manufactured commodities as well as canned goods and yard goods, were similarly displayed.[23]

By 1915 many department stores were strategically bathing goods with color and light to create the illusion of dramatic depth and of an almost living and organic energy—a "halo of bliss," a "glamorous lustre," a "vibrating presence," as Dreiser described it as early as 1902. Mannequins amplified the drama. They riveted the eyes to a few goods, contributed to making centered ensembles, and "created an atmosphere

---

[22]On early poster art, see *Poster* 1, no. 1 (January 1896): 1–24; and *Outdoor Advertising Association News*, December 1941, p. 3.

[23]*Dry Goods Economist*, November 1, 1913, p. 35; Lorin F. Deland, "Imagination in Business," *Atlantic Monthly* 103, no. 4 (April 1909): 433–47; *Merchants' Record and Show Window* 46, no. 3 (March 1920): 30; Arthur Frazer, interview by Lloyd Lewis, 1946, "Lloyd Lewis Interviews," Marshall Field Archives, Chicago.

of reality that aroused enthusiasm and acted in an autosuggestive manner."[24]

The Lord and Taylor windows of 1914 in New York were notable for their simplicity: a gown or two shown at one time, accompanied by spare clusters of slippers, fans, and laces. In July 1919 one hat and one glove were cast against a gold-color background. Raymond Loewy, French-born displayman at Macy's who later became a famous industrial designer, introduced a startling window in 1919 which today would be viewed as commonplace: he used only a single mannequin in a black evening gown with a fur and a few accessories "scattered" on the floor: "I left the window in semi-darkness. The only illumination came from three powerful spotlights focused on the figure. The result was a contrast of violent shadows. It was dramatic, simple, and potent."[25]

Color alone often seemed sufficient to serve the displayman's goal. After Edmund Rostand's *Chanticleer* was performed on Broadway in 1910 with brightly colored birds in leading roles, a stream of red flowed through the New York City windows. Hats, parasols, hosiery, and slippers appeared in ensembles of chanticleer red; brilliant red drapes hung on window backs; and in one B. Altman window, a trimmer covered a dress form (not a mannequin) with scarlet silk and black chanticleer lace in a rooster pattern. A decade later Field's displaymen dressed each of the store's State Street windows in a single color of the spectrum, starting with the darkest tints at the bottom of the windows to the lightest and most delicate tints at the top. Store decorators relished the charms of colored light. Every window at Gimbel's in New York in February 1916 was dramatized by a different color: purple light on silverware, green on silk, blue on furniture, and red on a Japanese bedroom set. In April 1920 James McCreery and Sons on Fifth Avenue presented a full series of color windows called "Sunbeams," "Nature's Palette," "A Midsummer's Night Dream," and "Scheherazade's Basket." "Sunbeams" displayed a balanced composition of two jade green suits on either side of a silver-green tree against a background of sand-color marble. By means of a revolving gelatin screen placed on an overhead spotlight, a rotation of color was thrown on a space behind the artifacts, suggesting the dancing of sunlight. These windows added vastly to an

---

[24] *Women's Wear Daily*, October 22, December 22, 1927, pp. 1, 1; *Merchants' Record and Show Window* 77, no. 1 (July 1935): 17–18.
[25] Quoted in Marcus, *American Show Window*, pp. 20–21.

expanding commercial environment of color. There was so much mar-shaling of color by the 1920s that, according to the *New York Times*, the term *colorful* entered the English language as common usage for the first time.[26]

Under the influence of European modernism in the 1920s, dra-matic and simplified window treatment came completely into its own, forming the foundation for all future window strategies in the big stores. Norman Bel Geddes, who served as displayman for Franklin Simon for two years in New York, pioneered this modernist inflection of simpli-fied aesthetic selling. Bel Geddes rejected anything that blocked the foregrounding of the commodity in the window; he rid his windows of their old stationary backs, stationary lighting, and clutter. His key word was *flexibility*: variable and interchangeable backgrounds of glass, wood, metal, and textiles that could be developed in radically different direc-tions; flexible, high-intensity, invisible spotlights thrown from any source or angle; and a standardized amount of color (he used thirty-seven shades at Franklin Simon) that could be linked directly to the goods and sug-gest any psychological mood. With the same kind of improvisational playfulness that distinguished the imagination of Baum, Bel Geddes wanted to transform goods into "luminous images" in order to "kindle emotional excitement." Like Baum, he sought to stir up a "cupidity and longing to possess the goods."[27]

European display managers who visited this country were fasci-nated with this uniquely American way of selling—by the mingling of art with goods in the window. European department stores were proud of their elaborate, artistic "prestige windows" that had little or nothing to do with selling; they boasted of the height and depth of their windows that exceeded anything in America, and they drew attention to their display fixtures made by craftsmen and not (as in America) by industrial mass-production methods. Yet for all of this, the Europeans still jum-bled goods in the "selling" window. As one German displayman reported

[26] *Merchants' Record and Show Window* 46, no. 2 (February 1920): 42–45; *Dry Goods Economist*, March 5, 1920, p. 3. The use of *colorful* is quoted in *Merchants' Record and Show Window* 67, no. 3 (September 1930): 40.

[27] *Women's Wear Daily*, November 19, 1927, pp. 1–2, 18. *Merchants' Record and Show Window* 61, no. 1 (July 1927): 33; 61, no. 4 (October 1927): 30–31; 63, no. 1 (July 1928): 44. Norman Bel Geddes, *Miracle in the Evening: An Autobiography* (New York: Doubleday, 1960), pp. 160, 259–67, 278–93; Norman Bel Geddes, *Horizons* (New York: Simon and Schuster, 1932), pp. 259–71.

years after American display style had achieved dominance, Americans understood how to "allure the imagination" and "to stir up insatiable appetites." The German selling windows were "beneath contempt," while the American windows were splendid: "The leaven of artistic selection, arrangement, and decoration permeates the entire system of American department stores. . . . The motto of the American window dresser is rapidly coming to be 'I'll make it beautiful if it kills me.' " Americans had learned "how to transform goods into roses."[28]

What any culture or commercial system chooses to dramatize identifies its priorities and expectations. By 1920 urban Americans had radically altered the meaning of commodities through dramatic treatment, investing them with an emotional power that set them off and above other things. But Americans did more than visually dramatize goods; they attempted to give them associative power as well. "Associate goods with people and events," one decorator implored, and not with "the idea of buying and selling: in this manner you command attention." Glamour, stardom, luxury, sensuality, and leisure activities were all enlisted to attract consumers to the goods. In 1911 in Philadelphia a simple Wanamaker's millinery display composed against a portrait of a voluptuous woman in the manner of John Singer Sargent summoned the idea of sensual pleasure. Trimmings placed in velveteen settings at Greenhut's in New York brought "constantly to mind" the impending excitement of "evening activities." Displaymen inscribed different scenes in window spaces, giving symbolic meaning to the goods. Pastoral, vacation, and holiday scenes, even colorful swimming pools with realistic mannequins in the act of diving off boards and swimming, were put into windows.[29] At a time that America excluded Japanese and Chinese immigrants from this country, there were no quotas placed on Oriental culture, design, and beauty, which displaymen everywhere were systematically and freely incorporating into strategies of display.

Women's underwear was displayed on mannequins in exotic settings. In the early stages of the shift to the production of ready-to-wear women's clothing, women's white underwear was never shown explic-

---

[28] *Women's Wear Daily*, November 26, 1927, p. 1.

[29] *Signs of the Times* 3, no. 2 (December 1912): 3; *Display World* 2, no. 6 (June 1923): 69; *Dry Goods Economist*, December 6 , 1917, p. 10; *Merchants' Record and Show Window* 47, no. 4 (October 1920): 29–30, 36–40; Wanamaker's show window photographs, 1911, Wanamaker Archives.

itly. Merchants ordinarily displayed underwear by massing it into architectural structures such as arches or cones that left dormant the potential sensual character of the garments. By the outbreak of World War I, merchants were not only selling colored lingerie and corsets on the mass market for the first time but also displaying them on expressively posed mannequins against fancy backgrounds. This policy was popular in May, the month of "underwear events" when, according to one expert, it was appropriate to appeal to "everywoman's natural appetite for beautiful, dainty lingerie." In April 1917 New York's Franklin Simon store on Fifth Avenue presented three mannequins in "boudoir costumes" from three lands: Turkey, Hawaii, and America. Ten years later, Wanamaker's in New York installed a "humanly adorable mannequin . . . at one end of her quite modern boudoir with her quite modern underthings," elegantly thrown in relief by a costly tapestry depicting the French countryside. Sometimes live models trying on corsets, corselettes, lingerie, and bathrobes were featured in department store windows.[30]

These displays were often so unusual when they first appeared that they caused street crowding and occasionally some rioting, and they did not take hold without resistance. Benjamin Altman, who died in 1913, detested mannequin displays on moral grounds; out of homage to his memory, Altman's did not have mannequins until 1927. A Field's executive objected not only to the displays but also to the underwear itself (especially the silk underwear), which he thought was too "Frenchy," fit only for "prostitutes and madams." Women's clubs launched crusades against the "immoral use" of such displays in 1899, followed by ever-weakening periodic yearly assaults. Yet for reasons that probably reflected both general public acceptance and merchandising imperatives, department stores remained undaunted in their commitment to these displays. "If the trade demands underwear," one major spokesman for the display industry wrote in 1919, the "house that does not show it will lose out."[31]

Commodities of all kinds were immersed in dreamlike surroundings, a strategy that issued in the self-conscious surrealist windows of

---

[30] *Display World* 5, no. 11 (November 1924): 43.
[31] *Merchants' Record and Show Window* 44, no. 6 (June 1919): 12–13; 61, no. 6 (December 1927): 3. *Fame* 3, no. 6 (May 1899): 3; *Department Store* 2, no. 8 (August 1914): 3; *Dry Goods Reporter*, August 15, 1908, p. 13; Emily Kimbrough, *Through Charlie's Door* (New York: Harper's, 1952), pp. 101–3.

the 1930s. As one display expert noted, "Display managers have realized more and more that nothing is impossible, that people expect display windows to reflect in some measure their own experiences, their own daydreams, and childhood fantasies. Windows today tell stories, fantastic fairy tales, which bring people back to a dimly remembered childhood in a peaceful world without stress or strain. They may tell a story that is the exact opposite to the one that people live in other ways." "Sell them their dreams," advised another authority, "visions of what might happen if only. . . . After all, people don't buy things, they buy hope."[32]

Arthur Frazer of Field's, by all accounts "America's leading display director," excelled in these sensual and fantastic inscriptions. Frazer was hired by Field's during the mid 1890s at a time when the store was just making its conversion to retailing after many years as a wholesale house. By 1907, the year he first commanded display, his windows opened the fall and spring shopping seasons. Frazer put the goods into richly colored and harmoniously unified contexts. He forged an immediate relationship between these settings and the commodities. For months he and his staff studied the style of architecture and furniture most suited to the goods in vogue. In 1923 fashions were influenced by Japanese and Persian art, so Frazer filled his windows with golden temples and pillars, rose-red velvet and lavender metallic hangings, carved animals, green and blue drapes, plush cushions, mythic female artifacts, and huge goddess figures, all methodically reproduced from Persian and Japanese models. The colors mimicked exactly the colors of the merchandise to form integrated color pictures that made a "most wonderful effect that one can never tire in looking at." A year later, modernized East Indian designs were displayed "in a riot of red and purple." In one window, an Indian slave boy served candy to "gorgeously gowned women." Dana O'Clare, head of display at Lord and Taylor during the 1930s, still remembers Frazer today as "his great star": "I used to go to Chicago on business, and I looked at Frazer's windows. I thought how wonderful this man is."[33]

[32] *Retail Ledger*, June 6, 1923, p. 6; *Display World* 49, no. 8 (August 1946): 90.

[33] Frazer, as quoted by Lewis, "Lewis Interviews," Field Archives; S. H. Ditchett, *Marshall Field and Co.: The Life of a Great Concern* (New York: Charles Scribner's Sons, 1922), pp. 87–88; *Dry Goods Economist*, October 5, 1907, p. 3; *Merchants' Record and Show Window* 27, no. 3 (September 1910): 20; 53, no. 4 (October 1923): 9; 55, no. 4 (October 1924): 7–9; 78, no. 6 (June 1936): 4. Interview with Dana O'Clare, June 11, 1985.

Although Frazer mounted extravagant windows—and was often attacked by modernists for this excess—he believed that he never lost the relationship between the commodity in the foreground and the background. The point always was to awaken desire for the goods. But Frazer's displays were also intended to stir up longing for the sensuous and luxurious life inhabiting the window space. He hoped to "create in the mind of the viewer a psychological harmony, a sort of 'glimpse into the interior of the temple' that is an inherent desire in all of us."[34]

Merchandising Interiors

Merchandising interiors underwent the same kind of aesthetic transformation that marked the evolution of the show window. Before 1895 department store and dry goods interiors were largely dull and uninviting, in spite of the splendor of much of the architectural design. Interiors were poorly heated, ventilated, and lighted, with ugly fixtures exposed to view. Goods were inadequately displayed; they were piled up on wooden counters, crowded together, used to decorate walls, or hidden away on shelves. Between 1895 and 1925 there was a revolution in interior "atmospherics," overturning all these earlier conditions.

Merchants connected related departments and displayed individual commodities against accessories to encourage ensemble buying. The "quick sellers," as well as the elevators, were grouped far away from the store entrances, compelling customers to pass by the most expensive goods on the main floor; individual floors and departments were arranged according to the same principle. For example, in 1916 the Abraham and Straus store in Brooklyn completely altered its floor-covering department by displaying the expensive oriental rugs near the elevators and hustling the cheaper grades and carpet yardage to the rear.[35]

As a general policy, merchants openly displayed their goods for the first time, clearly individualizing them on display fixtures (counter stands, cornice and suspended fixtures, and dress forms) and in glass showcases illuminated by concealed light that was brighter than store light and

---

[34] *Merchants' Record and Show Window* 56, no. 2 (February 1925): 31.

[35] *Dry Goods Economist*, March 25, 1916, p. 25; *Merchants' Record and Show Window* 32, no. 6 (June 1913): 12–13; 50, no. 1 (January 1922): 13–17, 23–25; Bureau of Foreign and Domestic Commerce, *Retail Store Planning* (Washington, D.C.: Government Printing Office, 1924), pp. 2–4.

often backed by mirrors. Displaymen assembled commodities into "merchandise pictures" or ensembles, placing the goods into aesthetically pleasing display pavilions, salon rooms, little arcade shops, "unstorelike" special rooms, and especially model showrooms, which were first built during the late 1880s and 1890s and then reached epic proportions by the outbreak of World War I.[36] At the same time that commodities were aesthetically displayed, the store as a whole was decoratively and theatrically changed. Bronze embellishments, mahogany woodwork, and marble displaced the old iron and wooden interiors; carpets were laid; mirrors glittered on store columns. After 1915 interior color schemes were in vogue everywhere in the big stores. Merchants decorated walls, ceilings, entrances, and exits with visual art.

Department stores also hastened the evolution of artificial light. By World War I, new indirect lighting systems, marketed under such utopian names as Planetlight and Celestialite, illuminated interiors with a soft radiance approaching the "light of a spring morning." Decorators increased this natural effect by organically fusing new light fixtures with the interior architecture: luminous pilasters or shallow lighted columns affixed to walls; niches and alcoves built into walls and lined with illuminated panes of glass; entire glass floors radiating light; and recessed lighting shielded by frosted and opal glass.[37]

Merchants enlisted the aesthetic resources of many artists to transform the interiors. In 1910 Dreiser spotted one of the first modernist murals ever displayed in this country, painted in a fauvist style by Anne Estelle Rice for Wanamaker's in Philadelphia, hung above the elevators on the first floor. In 1929 Boardman Robinson, a socialist artist who earlier illustrated for the *Masses* and the *Liberator*, painted a huge pan-

[36] *Dry Goods Economist*, April 24, September 18, 1897, April 30, September 24, 1898, April 14, 1900, January 21, 1905, January 29, 1916, pp. 39, 22, 62, 9, 4, 55, 62. *Merchants' Record and Show Window* 32, no. 3 (March 1913): 17; 30, no. 2 (February 1912): 40–41. *Housefurnishing Review*, February 1904, clipping in scrapbook, Woodward and Lothrop Archives, Washington, D.C.; John Wanamaker, *Betty Comes to Town: A Letter Home* (New York: John Wanamaker, 1909), pp. 11–15; *Wanamaker Originator* 2, no. 11 (November 1908): 2. John Wanamaker to "my dear friend," February 20, 1886, "JW—personal—letters, 12/22/85–12/2/86," p. 145, and Howard Kratz to Rodman Wanamaker, November 14, 1924, Christmas photograph album of 1924, Wanamaker Archives.

[37] *Dry Goods Economist*, May 20, 1905, p. 2; *Merchants' Record and Show Window* 67, no. 5 (November 1930): 7–8; 67; no. 6 (December 1930): 27, 52; 77, no. 1 (July 1935): 16–18.

oramic mural for Kaufmann's department store in Pittsburgh, which depicted the evolution of commercial capitalism and did more than any single artwork to revitalize American mural painting.[38]

Reflecting the constantly shifting priorities of the commodity market, particularly fashion and taste, much of this art was discarded almost as soon as it appeared, although a few major installations remained, including Field's green, blue, and gold opalescent glass dome, the largest single piece of iridescent glass mosaic in the world. The dome was designed in 1902 by Louis Tiffany, the passionate colorist, who considered it "the acme of his most artistic work." It drew its inspiration from Blakean mysticism and consisted of three concentric circles intended to convey the illusion of open-ended space, of a heavenly domain without limits—a perfect symbol for this consumer setting.[39]

Joseph Cummings Chase, an artist who garnered a minor reputation by painting portraits of subjects ranging from Clara Bow to Rin Tin Tin, carved out a career in merchandising interior decoration. After graduating from Pratt Institute in 1898, Chase studied in Paris where he "discovered all he could about color—at any price, at any sacrifice." He understood the therapeutics of color, how it affected the senses, states of mind, and the power of concentration. "If the ceiling of your best room is painted a tint of lemon yellow," Chase explained, focusing on his favorite color, "it will be easier for you to read your Sunday morning newspaper. . . . The ceiling will look softer and quieter, but it will give more light in the room." In 1914 McCreery's department store in Manhattan, whose president viewed the "color question" as one of "great importance," invited Chase, at a salary of $30,000 a year, to redecorate the store. For the next fifteen years, Chase changed the show windows, the main-floor decorations, and the interior color scheme, completing his finest work in 1926 when nearly every floor at McCreery's was painted a different hue: orange cream for the main floor's ceiling, sidewalls, and columns; yellow orange (the "sunshine color") for the

[38] Albert Christ-Janer, *Boardman Robinson* (Chicago: University of Chicago Press, 1946), pp. 28–31, 50–52; Lloyd Goodrich, "Mural Paintings by Boardman Robinson," *Arts* 16, no. 2 (February 1930): 390–93, 438; Wanamaker index to store paintings, "Among the work of art . . . at the Store," Wanamaker Archives.

[39] "Educational Values of a Great Shop," *House and Garden* 13, no. 5 (May 1904): 21–25; Samuel Howe, "One Source of Color Values," *House and Garden* 10, no. 9 (September 1906): 105–13; Robert Koch, *Louis C. Tiffany's Art Glass* (New York: Crown Publishers, 1977).

children's floor; and lemon yellow for the ceiling of the women's intimate apparel department, complemented by orchid-color walls. Chase
selected each color with an eye toward comfort and "suggestive
atmosphere."[40]

Among the most gifted artists to work for the stores was Joseph
Urban, a pioneering decorative architect who, according to one of his
biographers, "added a tremendous stimulation in the use of color in this
country." Urban was born in Vienna in 1872, rose to fame as a member
of a radical group of secessionist artists in that city, and later resigned
from the secession to form a splinter group, the Hagenband, over which
he presided. Urban created some of the first modern museum interiors.
He designed the stage sets for Debussy's *Peleas and Melisande* and drew
further acclaim for his color illustrations of fairy tales, including a new
edition of *Grimm's Fairy Tales*. Urban had the mind of a fairy-tale
writer; he was a fantasist and a dreamer whose imagination delighted in
primitive and pagan transfigurations.[41]

In 1911 Urban immigrated to America, perhaps seeing there greater
opportunities for his kind of aesthetic expression than anywhere else in
the world. Until his death in 1932, he left his imprimatur on practically
every major consumer and theatrical institution, setting standards of
decoration and display that other artists admired and emulated. Urban
was an architectural utopian with a fundamentally pagan ethical perspective. He believed in nothing save the "Joy of Life" and in making
beauty the pathway to joy. He was certain that beautiful architectural
spaces in and of themselves had the power to transform consciousness
and ameliorate the human condition. This profoundly bourgeois belief
explained his infatuation with color and light. "He looked at everything, including life," wrote architectural critic Otto Teagan, in "terms
of color." Urban longed to "build colorful structures" that would "charm
on gloomy days as well as when the sunlight tints them, and at night
all degrees of the lights and shadows, of artificial illumination will have

---

[40] Joseph Cummings Chase, *Face Value: Autobiography of the Portrait Painter* (New
York: Rolton House, 1962), p. 57; Joseph Cummings Chase, *Artist Talks* (London:
Chapman and Hall, 1933), pp. 12–13; *Merchants' Record and Show Window* 59, no. 2
(August 1926): 19; 53, no. 6 (December 1923): 17–18; 50, no. 3 (March 1922): 28–29.
Women's Wear Daily, December 22, 1927, p. 1; Chase, *Face Value*, pp. 101–2.

[41] Otto Teagan, "Joseph Urban's Philosophy of Color," Deems Taylor, "The Scenic
Art of Joseph Urban," and Otto Teagan, "Joseph Urban," *Architecture* 69, no. 5 (May
1934): 258, 275, 256.

their part in modifying and enhancing them."[42]

By today's standards, it may appear surprising that artists invested so much utopian energy in commercial design. As early as the late 1880s, such architects as John Root and Louis Sullivan were thrilled by the prospects of using color in commercial spaces. Root looked to the development of color as the art of the future; Sullivan, whose Auditorium Building and Carson, Pirie, Scott department store in Chicago are landmarks, was perhaps the first American decorative architect to integrate color and artificial light effectively into interior design. One of Sullivan's students, Frank Lloyd Wright, celebrated the utopian promise of color, glass, and light, writing in 1928: "Imagine a city iridescent by day, luminous by night, imperishable! Buildings, shimmering fabrics, woven in rich glass." Wright (and Urban as well) was influenced by an eccentric architectural utopian, Paul Scheerbart, a German who dreamed of a "glass architecture" so vast, so splendid, and so multicolored that "we should have paradise on earth and no need to watch in longing expectation for the paradise in heaven."[43]

Urban decorated the interiors and exteriors of hotels and restaurants. His barrooms and supper rooms for such places as Paradise Restaurant and Central Park Casino in New York, William Penn Hotel in Pittsburgh, and Congress Hotel in Chicago were masterfully composed, integrated spaces usually forged around a centrally located mural. The mural determined the color schemes of everything in these rooms from the carpets to the table services; in the evening the colors were augmented by colored lights. At the Urban Room in Congress Hotel, the colored lights were arranged so that the entire room could be alternately bathed in red, blue, yellow, white, and even the bluish green color named for Urban himself.[44]

Urban joined American stage designers Lee Simonson and Norman Bel Geddes (both of whom also designed for department stores) in

[42]Otto Teegan, lead typescript in collection catalogue, Joseph Urban Papers, Butler Library, Columbia University; Teegan, "Urban's Philosophy," pp. 257–71.

[43]Paul Scheerbart, *Glass Architecture*, ed. Dennis Sharp and trans. James Palmes (1914; reprint, New York: Praeger Publishers, 1927), p. 46; Frank Lloyd Wright, as quoted in introduction by Sharp, *Glass Architecture*, p. 27; Harriet Monroe, *John Wellborn Root: A Study of His Life and Work* (1896; reprint, Park Forest, Ill.: Prairie School Press, 1966), pp. 207–46; Robert Twombly, *Louis Sullivan: His Life and Work* (New York: Viking Press, 1986), pp. 163–96, 247–79, 337–47.

[44]Teegan, "Urban's Philosophy," pp. 258–61.

reconceiving the theatrical stage into a totally integrated, three-dimensional space that "we could vicariously inhabit." He transformed the stage decor for the Ziegfeld Follies, Boston Opera Company, and Metropolitan Opera House in New York, as well as for innumerable Broadway musical comedies. People came to see his sets (the voluptuous "Harem Scene" or the "Temple of Color" at the Ziegfeld Theater during the early 1920s, for instance) rather than the performances. Composer and music critic Deems Taylor wrote, "[Urban] proved that scenery for an ordinary run-of-the-mill commercial Broadway show should be beautiful, and that the public should respond to that beauty." During the 1920s he designed the most spectacular motion picture sets ever imagined up to that time. On both stage and screen, Urban introduced modernist principles: he repudiated artificial scenic painting and excessive ornamentation for authentically contrived interiors and relied on color and light to create moods and atmospheres.[45]

Urban's desire was to establish a more festive and fluent relationship between patrons and commercial environments. In 1926 he designed the largest oil painting in the world, a carnivalesque mural for the Ziegfeld Theater in Manhattan, with floriated patterns, replete with harlequins, that flowed over the interior walls of the auditorium. Here again, the mural, which epitomized Urban's aesthetic thinking, determined and unified the colors in the rest of the theater. More important, by reflecting the "gaiety and laughter" on the stage, the mural was supposed to liquefy the boundaries between the audience and the players, to make "the audience feel itself part of the whole occasion." Urban called it the "Joy of Life": "The Painting has no tale to tell, no continuous action as its basis. Under a roof of flowers and foliage, among castles and hamlets, in meadows and in woods, hunting and laughing, running, leaping, music-making, singing, kissing, loving—human beings in mad, happy medley—no deep meaning, no serious thoughts or feelings—only joy, happiness, and a veritable trance of color."[46]

[45] Both Simonson and Bel Geddes were, like Urban, passionate advocates of theatrical color and light; see Simonson, *Stage Is Set*, p. 359; Lee Simonson, "The Painter and the Stage," *Theatre Arts* 2, no. 12 (December 1917): 1–12; and "Norman Bel Geddes: His Art and Ideas," *Theatre Arts* 3, no. 7 (July 1919): 181–92. Taylor, "Scenic Art," pp. 286–90; *Boston Advertiser*, May 23, 1920; *Architectural Review* (July 1921): 31, and *Moving Picture World*, July 30, 1920, clippings in scrapbook, Urban portfolio no. 38, pts. 1, 50, Urban Papers.

[46] Joseph Urban and Thomas Lamb, "The Ziegfeld Theater, New York," *Good Furniture* 46, no. 5 (May 1927): 415–19; *Arts and Decoration* 21, no. 3 (January 1927): 43, clipping in scrapbook, Urban portfolio no. 37, pt. 2, Urban Papers.

Several large department stores commissioned Urban to transform their interiors into beautiful spaces. His 1915 design for Gimbel's fall fashion show in New York, "Les Promenades des Toilettes," broke decisively with conventional treatment as Urban split the promenade stage into two parts, each part going in opposite directions. A colorfully illuminated fountain and two orchestras entertained the store patrons, and silver bay trees and blue and silver lamps lined the promenade. Everything in the store's theater (the site of the fashion show), including the ceiling, was decorated in a new French blue.[47]

In the mid 1920s, Kaufmann's department store in Pittsburgh and Bedell's store in New York invited Urban to redesign their interiors and exteriors. Urban theatrically integrated the spaces. Dramatic light and shadow effects transformed Bedell's entrance rotunda; lighted columns "created a rhythm of color and light," and silver embossed the deep-blue of the ceiling. Floriated oriental patterns decorated the interiors of different departments as well as the elevators, which were staffed by young Chinese women dressed in native costumes. Unfortunately the Kaufmann designs were never executed, but had they been, they would have exemplified the best in modernist architecture. The first floor would have been a brilliant futurist space unified by black marble and gleaming metal in the columns and showcases; the marble floor's geometrical star-burst design would have been reflected in the geometrically shaped crystal light fixtures of frosted glass that would have hugged the tops of the columns like melting triangular icicles.[48]

Middle-class department stores reaped considerable rewards from these aesthetic changes. But the stores went further than this: on holidays and special occasions, they reconstituted the interiors into festival, spectacular spaces. Of Wanamaker's in Philadelphia, one woman wrote to another, "I spent all day before yesterday in 'the Store'; no, I cannot call it that; for, except for the basement the commercial atmosphere is not uppermost. . . . It is a place of joyful inspiration." As early as the 1890s merchants were inscribing churches into store interiors. For his Christmas show of 1898, John Wanamaker raised a huge model of a church, complete with organ and choir, above the silk department on

[47] *Merchants' Record and Show Window* 37, no. 4 (October 1915): 40–41.
[48] Urban, "Bedell Department Store," Urban portfolio no. 17, Urban Papers; *Chain Store Age*, April 1929, clipping in scrapbook, Shepard Vogelgesang, "Architectures and Trade Marks," *Architectural Design* (1929), Urban, "Kaufmann Department Store," Urban portfolio no. 33, Urban Papers.

the main floor of his Philadelphia store. Although Wanamaker disliked such attributions, contemporaries compared him with P. T. Barnum and with Imre Kiralfy, the late nineteenth-century pageant specialist who produced such extravaganzas as "Nero and the Destruction of Rome" and the "Fall of Babylon." One of Wanamaker's admirers wrote, "He's the Kiralfy of modern merchandising. . . . The store is a great spectacular show."[49]

Most Americans lacked the money to pay for a trip to France to see the great cathedrals there or to buy the expensive automobiles (expensive at least until after 1920) that made it easy for affluent people like Henry Adams and Edith Wharton to travel from one cathedral to another. But if ordinary Americans could not go abroad, they could nevertheless visit artificially constructed medieval cathedrals in their own backyards. They could see them in the opera and early movie sets designed by Urban or on the theatrical stage designed by Bel Geddes, whose own trip to Chartres put him in touch with "a nobler way of life, a civilization." Or they could go to department stores to see medieval cathedrals designed by such decorators as William L. Larkin of Wanamaker's New York store, who in the early 1920s erected the facade of the cathedral at Rheims in the store's rotunda, with "every one of the innumerable details of the facade faithfully reproduced." For his 1921 Christmas decorations, Howard Kratz, Wanamaker's Philadelphia displayman, included a perfect replica of the rose window in the south transept of Westminster Abbey. Later the number of medieval rose windows doubled, then tripled until, by Christmas 1928, they had become a part of an incredible Cecil B. de Mille–like reproduction of the cathedral at Chartres.[50]

Like Larkin in New York, Kratz researched his displays with the rigor of a museum specialist, relying for thoroughness on the handbook of the American Wing of the Metropolitan Museum of Art. The purpose of both men was far more aesthetic than religious: As Kratz remarked in 1924, "After all, the Decorator is a species of super-showman pre-

---

[49] Ellen Aledeedier to Agnes Barr, November 29, 1925, Wanamaker Archives; *Dry Goods Economist*, April 21, 1900, April 6, 1901, pp. 16, 3; W. H. Barley, "The Power of Store Decoration," *Store Life* 1 (October 1904): 7–8; Harris, *Humbug*, p. 245.

[50] Bel Geddes, *Autobiography*, pp. 278–79; Urban, *New York Tribune*, January 8, 1922, Urban portfolio no. 38, pt. 1, Urban Papers; Kratz, Christmas albums of 1921, 1924, and 1928, Kratz Papers; *Women's Wear Daily*, February 4, 1928, p. 3.

senting really beautiful things—just so quickly will the Public become instilled with the love of beauty; consequently, be of benefit to everyone devoting their energies in lifting the Public educationally to the more beautiful things of life."[51]

The cathedral inscription was but one of a whole succession of mythical worlds, each of equal value, that Wanamaker and other department store merchants installed in store interiors. Today "this Store is an Easter Egg," Wanamaker wrote, tomorrow a "Garden," or a "Rainbow," or an "Autumn Festival," or "Five Miles of Golden Chain," or, far more often than not, an oriental dream. These inscriptions, which overlapped with similar inscriptions in the movies and on the theatrical stage, were the most daring kind of interior transformation practiced by merchants. Together with the show windows, the store color and light, and the concrete display devices, they saturated commodities and commodity environments with new meanings and excitements. They created a separate space distinct from other spaces that "transported" customers "out of the hurley-burley world" into the projected promise of a new paradise, like the one Henry Adams described in *Mont-Saint-Michel and Chartres*, free from "pain, punishment, and damnation" and overseen by a forgiving feminine presence.[52]

Color and Light Displays of the 1920s

The most spectacular application of decoration and display aesthetics took the form of the coordinated color and light displays of the 1920s. This decade was the age of the engineered spectacle, and commercial entrepreneurs grouped their forces on behalf of decoration and display. Although coordinated activities existed well before 1920, they became widespread only in this decade. Throughout the 1920s merchants launched cooperative fashion shows, cooperative show window displays, and cooperative style shows. They worked systematically through their trade associations with other consumer-oriented institutions (such as hotels, restaurants, and theaters) and with city governments to con-

[51] Kratz, Christmas album, 1924, Kratz Papers.
[52] John Wanamaker, "Editorials of John Wanamaker," March 10, 1912, October 2, 10, 1913, September 9, 1914, April 14, 1917, vol. 1, Wanamaker Archives; Henry Adams, *Mont-Saint-Michel and Chartres* (New York: Houghton Mifflin, 1904), p. 62.

trol the shape of urban space and time. At the same time that the stores
sought to widen holiday time, they worked to standardize it in accordance with market needs. They labored to rid the streets of peddlers and
crowds of lunchtime workers and to eliminate disruptive and excessive
parade activity in downtown retail districts, the intense centers of urban
market life.[53]

By the 1920s the stores had helped to erect a powerful institutional
circuit through which merchandising ideas passed and were given aesthetic shape. A variant of this circuit consisted of department stores,
manufactories, art schools, and museums, all of which gained added
power as a result of the roles they played within the circuit. One of the
many generative figures to serve this circuit was Stewart Culin, a curator at the Brooklyn Museum who struggled to upgrade the status of his
institution by placing it within the stream of contemporary urban life.
Like so many people who contributed to the formation of the modern
system of merchandising, Culin's entrée into commerce was through
his nearly lifetime obsession with the magic of primitive things and with
the fairy-tale world of children. Culin was a foremost anthropologist
and folklorist. He toured continents tirelessly to collect primitive artifacts and wrote accounts of primitive games for adults and children
which are still drawn on today, including the ground-breaking *Games
of the North American Indians* (1907). Culin conducted three major
expeditions to study North American Indian cultures in the early 1900s
under John Wanamaker's sponsorship. In 1903 he became the first curator
of the ethnological collection at the Brooklyn Museum, whose president during the 1920s was Edward Blum, head of Abraham and Straus,
the leading department store in Brooklyn.[54]

Culin respected primitive and preindustrial cultures, viewing them
in some ways as superior to industrial cultures, which, he argued, so
often disparaged the primitive as "weak," effeminate, childish, and irra-

---

[53] Fifth Avenue Association, *Annual Report for 1912* (New York, 1913), pp. 2–5;
Report of the Fifth Avenue Association, for the Year 1914 (New York, 1918), pp. 6–7;
Fifth Avenue Association, *Annual Report for 1929* (New York, 1930), p. 11; *Retail Ledger*,
January 17, 1923, p. 8, and First September Issue, 1926, p. 9; *Merchants' Record and
Show Window* 58, no. 2 (February 1926): 20–21; 60, no. 2 (February 1927): 10.

[54] Ira Jacknis, "Biographical Sketch," pp. 1–4; and Edward Blum to Culin, March
16, 1922, October 31, 1927, Stewart Culin Papers, Brooklyn Museum. For further discussion of Culin, see Simon J. Bronner, "Object Lessons: The Work of Ethnological
Museums and Collections," elsewhere in this volume.

tional. He shared the same goals with Baum and Urban: to resurrect the "magical" enchantment of primitive and exotic times and to breathe a new life, a new animism into modern things, which machine production and rationalized machine processes seemed to have abstracted away. Culin wanted especially to bring back the "magic of color," that "concrete expression of nature's most vital forces." Culin said, "I had the child's eagerness and color desire," and "I still sympathize with the craving in children." In the mid 1920s he revolutionized museum display by exhibiting his ethnological collection in Rainbow House, inspired by a Zuni myth. The exhibit consumed most of a museum floor and was "as brightly decorated as an Easter Egg," painted in the "gayest tints" of pink, red, yellow, and green. The point was to "make the artifacts live and to stimulate the imagination."[55]

Culin fed the institutional commercial circuit of manufactories, art schools, and department stores with his primitivist ideas. Indeed, his anthropology, as well as the anthropology and archaeology of this period that exhumed so many exotic riches, constituted a crucial part of this commercial circuit. Culin made the Brooklyn Museum "a centre of the artistic industries," fulfilling a dream he and other museum curators had as far back as the 1890s. He designed a special room in the museum filled with primitive artifacts from Africa, eastern Europe, India, and North America and opened it to the scrutiny of the commercial designers who used it as a source for design ideas. Costume and textile designers from different manufacturing firms flocked there from all over the country; their commodities were soon found on department store shelves.[56]

Culin circulated information throughout the commercial world by writing articles for *Women's Wear Daily* and other merchandising journals. Students from Pratt Institute in Brooklyn attended his museum lectures, and he, in turn, lectured at Pratt. Culin helped speed up the process by which Pratt made its conversion from a manual-labor college

[55] Stewart Culin, "The Road to Beauty" (Address delivered to the Teachers of Drawing in the Public Schools of New York City, December 1925, Culin Papers; Stewart Culin, "The Magic of Color," *Merchants' Record and Show Window* 52, no. 3 (March 1923): 8, 9; Culin, "Color in Window Displays," pp. 71–72; *New York Times*, August 7, 1927, p. 23.

[56] Culin to Edward Blum, November 17, 1926, to Lockwood deForest, December 14, 1918, to M. D. C. Crawford, January 1, 1919, and to Franz Boas, January 1, 1928, Culin Papers.

to a first-rate commercial art school in the 1920s. Pratt turned out students who often ended up as industrial designers or as display people in department stores. Culin completed the circuit by lecturing at department stores during the 1920s on folk materials and the history of furniture and clothing. The stores, he believed, "made it possible for us all to participate in the creative thought of a new revolutionary era."[57] Culin lent merchants peasant costumes and primitive materials for their show window displays, and he served as a judge for window display contests. In 1923 Culin organized an exhibit of western African handmade fiber textiles at the Brooklyn Museum simultaneously with show window exhibits at Bonwit Teller on Fifth Avenue, which displayed manufactured goods modeled after the African designs and sportswear made from "Congo Cloth."[58]

Out of this elaborate institutional circuitry, which assumed many different guises by the 1920s, the authority and power of a new commercial urban culture emerged. It took even grander form in the cooperative color and light festivals of the decade conducted by many department stores together. These festivals embraced entire retail districts and were given full support by governments at all levels. Color and light, of course, had always played roles in merchandising events, but after 1920 they were the focus of celebration, a practice that would assume its most extravagant expression at the 1932 World's Fair in Chicago when Urban integrated three miles of heterogeneous buildings into the brightest color and light scheme ever devised for public architectural display. The fair was essentially a spectacular tribute to commercial color and light.[59]

Almost invariably, the city festivals announced the introduction of new lighting technology into retail districts, an effort pioneered by the big stores in their determination to cultivate the night for shopping. The

[57] Culin to Frederic Pratt, October 7, 1926, Culin Papers. For the beginnings of Pratt's shift into commercial art, see "Reports—The Art School, 1901–1906," vol. 3, and "Reports—The Art School, 1916–1921," vol. 6, Pratt Archives, Brooklyn. Note by Culin, appended to Booth Hubbett (store manager for Abraham and Straus) to Culin, January 27, 1928, Culin Papers.

[58] Felix Meyer to M. G. Wallace, c/o Marshall Field's, March 6, 1923, Edgar Kaufmann to Culin, January 21, 1927, Estelle Hamburger (Bonwit Teller) to Culin, October 11, 1926, Charles Nausmy (Namm's department store, Brooklyn) to Culin, October 23, 1926, Ernest Wilkinson (Jordan Marsh) to Culin, February 21, 1928, and Dorothy Shaver (Lord and Taylor) to Culin, May 24, 1923, Culin Papers.

[59] Teegan, "Urban's Philosophy," pp. 266–67.

most famous was the Chicago State Street Illumination Festival of 1926. Nearly fifty businesses—theaters, hotels, specialty houses, and department stores—combined to sponsor the event. The big stores provided most of the capital, led by Field's, whose advertising manager, Roy Schaeffer, assembled the forces. The purpose of the festival was to celebrate the new lighting standards installed by General Electric and paid for by the merchants. This new system furnished State Street with light two-and-one-half times brighter than any street light in the world. As Schaeffer claimed in his promotional literature, it was not a blinding or dazzling light, but a diffused and soft light, a light to "please" and "invite," a light "as close to artificial daylight as possible." For the first time in its history, State Street was closed to traffic for three successive nights of festivity. It was the biggest merchandising "party" ever thrown in Chicago. Immense colored searchlights radiated the streets and buildings; arches and towers, covered with crystal jewels, were erected; jazz bands played; scantily dressed women rode on floats; and the entire history of artificial light was portrayed in a pageant parade that began the minute President Calvin Coolidge flipped the switch that turned on the flood of light. Carnival confetti drifted through the air. On the first night the crush of the crowds was so great that the parade had to be stopped. Police were called in to protect the store windows from breakage. On the following evening, merchants conducted "impromptu parades" to make up for the failure of the night before. In a *Chicago Tribune* interview, errand boy Louis Gianzola reported, "It was a great sight. . . . I hardly knew the street last night."[60]

The evolution of display and decorative strategies helped domesticate Americans to the commodity world. But they did more than this: they helped forge a new commercial aesthetic that would henceforth dominate the visual space of urban Americans and against which all other aesthetics would be either measured or forgotten. This commercial aesthetic carved out a wide terrain of desire and longing and contained the elements of a new secular carnivalesque, one that played at the margins of unacceptable thought and behavior. It celebrated meta-

<hr/>

[60] Roy Schaeffer, promotional statement, "Two thousand lumens per linear foot make State Street the 'Pathway to Beauty' "; "List of those participating in the State Street Celebration"; "State Street Light Festival Publicity, October 1926," *Chicago Tribune*, October 15, 1926; *Chicago American*, October 8, 1926; *Herald Examiner*, October 15, 1926; and *Chicago Post*, October 15, 16, 1926—all clippings in scrapbook, Field Archives.

morphosis, the violation of boundaries, and the blurring of lines between hitherto opposed categories—luxury and necessity, artificial and natural, night and day, male and female, the expression of desire and its repression, the primitive and the civilized. The new strategies of display and decoration produced a radiant sensual center at the heart of American cities, attracting thousands of people who were drawn not only to commodities but also to the sensual, fluid, and radiant density of the center itself, where, as the tormented boy in F. Scott Fitzgerald's short story "Absolution" says, "There was something ineffably gorgeous . . . that had nothing to do with God." Indeed, this commercial aesthetic expressed the direction of a new commodity culture that challenged at its core the moral heritage of the nineteenth century.

A House of Fiction
Domestic Interiors and the Commodity Aesthetic

Jean-Christophe Agnew

Commodity aesthetic is admittedly not a term that runs trippingly off the tongue. It is awkward; more than that, it is incongruous. To join the two words together is to risk the same odd and confused impression that would be produced in clamping a dime-store frame on an original Vermeer. So ill-fitted does the term *commodity* seem in relation to the values of beauty and feeling comprehended by the term *aesthetic* that one might regard the marriage of the terms not just as a lapse of taste but as a lapse of logic as well. What could the concept of a commodity aesthetic mean, then, and how could it operate as a useful category of American cultural history? In particular, how could the concept help us understand the history of the "consuming vision" in America?

The brief history of the "interior" that follows is a provisional answer to that question. Yet I want to make it clear from the outset that insofar as I consider the incongruities of my category to be of a piece with the contradictory experiences and meanings it attempts to encapsulate, I use the notion of a commodity aesthetic to isolate a body of cultural representations rather than to explain them. If indeed there is a logic that has joined the priceless and the priced, the familiar and the unfamiliar, the world of goodness and the world of goods—in nineteenth-century terms, the dwelling place and the marketplace—that logic has been historically, not universally, given. And we are that logic's heirs.

To give a sense of that inheritance and at the same time to make a start upon my definition of a commodity aesthetic, I will begin with an illustration drawn from one of the most popular and profitable works of fiction published in the last decade: Judith Krantz's *Princess Daisy*. The passage can serve as my dime-store frame for this essay because it initially served as a kind of "establishing shot" in Krantz's narrative, an extended description that works to situate an important character named Ram.

Ram was thirty. He lived in a perfect house on Hill Street, only a step away from Berkeley Square, a house decorated by David Hicks in severe bachelor sumptuousness. . . . His suits, which cost nine hundred dollars each, were made at Huntsman and Sons, the best tailor in England, as were all his riding clothes. He was counted one of the best shots in the British Isles and owned a pair of shotguns made to his measurements, from James Purdey and Sons, a firm that had existed in the time of George III. It had taken three years before they were completed, at fifteen thousand dollars the pair, and they were, Ram thought, well worth waiting for. His shoes and boots came, of course, from Lobb's and cost from two-hundred and fifty-five dollars a pair upwards, depending on the style and the leather. He collected rare books in a major way and avant-garde sculpture in a minor way. He wore white silk pajamas piped in sober burgundy, heavy silk dressing gowns and shirts made of the finest Sea Island cotton, all made to order at Turnbull and Asser. He considered sulka vulgar. He never left the house without his umbrella from Swaine, Adeney, Brigg and Sons. It was made of a single piece of exceptional hickory. He drew the line at a hat—perhaps in ten years, but not now, except for fishing, riding and yachting, and his dark hair was cut in the privacy of one of the ancient wooden rooms at Trumper on Curzon Street. He dined out every night, except on Sunday.[1]

This is not parody; every phrase is designed to ring true. The oxymoronic image of "severe bachelor sumptuousness" is meant to impress the reader in much the same way as the vague hint of Sabbatarian restraint hanging over Ram's orgy of consumption. Here is a character who has managed to assemble himself in the marketplace without at the same time losing the handmade touch. Here indeed is a man who

[1] Judith Krantz, *Princess Daisy* (New York: Ballantine Books, 1980), pp. 217–18; for a different approach to the topic, see Wolfgang Fritz Haug, *Critique of Commodity Aesthetics: Appearance, Sexuality and Advertising in Capitalist Society*, trans. Robert Bock (Minneapolis: University of Minnesota Press, 1986).

appears to live in the marketplace—except, that is, on Sundays. From the "perfect house" he already owns to the hat he only looks forward to owning, Ram is virtually indistinguishable from the brand-name shelters that are home to his suitably elusive spirit. His style and fashion may vary (although not in any capricious way), but his aesthetic is emphatically that of the commodity—its power, the reflected power of purchase.

A commodity aesthetic may be defined as a way of seeing the world in general, and the self and society in particular, as so much raw space to be furnished with mobile, detachable, and transactionable goods. A commodity aesthetic is a point of view that celebrates those moments when the very boundaries between the self and the commodity world collapse in the act of purchase. Such an aesthetic regards acculturation as if it were a form of consumption and consumption, in turn, not as a waste or use, but as deliberate and informed accumulation. As a literary character, Ram operates according to a particular version of this aesthetic, but it is of course more accurate to take that aesthetic as the cultural premise upon which Krantz sets out to render Ram a plausible, indeed an intimidating presence. It is just such premises and their origins that this essay attempts to explore in three ways: in the literature of design and decoration of houses, in the genre painting of domestic interiors, and in the novels that used such interiors as their primary theater of action in the late nineteenth and early twentieth centuries.

As these three categories of evidence indicate, this is not strictly an essay in material culture; that is, it does not seek to read particular material artifacts as documents of popular taste or culture between the wars. I confine myself to those aesthetic presuppositions that were more or less deliberately laid down in the relevant prescriptive and descriptive "texts" of the time. I leave open the question of how most American householders actually *presented* themselves through their commodity choices in order to compare the ways in which a small group of American artists and writers imaginatively *represented* those choices to themselves and to others. It is to the problem of representation, then, as distinct from the problem of representativeness, that this essay is addressed. In any event, one should not test the historical pervasiveness of such a formidable abstraction as a commodity aesthetic without first making some effort to determine whether any historical actors were disposed to abstract it for themselves.

Thorstein Veblen's now familiar notion of conspicuous consumption could very well count as just such an instance of contemporaneous rumination about the social role of the commodity in America. At the very least one may see Veblen's effort to reinterpret—to re-present—Gilded Age consumption as having launched a long and rich tradition of ethnographic thought about the communicative functions of accumulation and display. Commodities do convey important information about the class and gender, freedom and constraint, and knowledge and competence of their owners. From this information the careful ethnographic historian can systematically reconstruct the "social life of things" in much the same way as one might strip and restore an old house, with each brick or plank serving as a clue to the exact sequence of meaning and use to which the artifacts were put over the years.[2]

But the house I have in mind to reconstruct here, or rather the house I believe my subjects to have had in mind, was not a thing of bricks and planks. It was a fictional house, for it was only with the freedom granted to them by their fantasies of the interior that these artists and writers could confront, however obliquely, the lived relation of commodity forms. In this light, goods appeared to them not just as reflective objects but also as objects of reflection. Thus, as the consumption of mass-produced household furnishings expanded after the Civil War, American novelists, painters, and aestheticians seized upon the goods themselves as the most appropriate and compelling idiom in which to represent their changing sense of the human self and its relations.[3] The purchased interior thereby became for many observers a convenient metaphor with which to convey the new powers and predicaments that they were beginning to discern in their own bourgeois existence. In their hands the commodified home became something more than a likeness or even an expression of the selves placed within it: it became something interchangeable with those selves, something out of which those selves were at once improvised and imprisoned, constructed and confined. To the extent, then, that a commodity aesthetic

[2] For examples of this ethnographic approach, see the essays in Arjun Appadurai, ed., *The Social Life of Things: Commodities in Cultural Perspective* (Cambridge, Mass.: Cambridge University Press, 1986); Mihaly Csikszentmihalyi and Eugene Rochberg-Halton, *The Meaning of Things: Domestic Symbols and the Self* (Cambridge, Mass.: Cambridge University Press, 1981).

[3] For a different treatment of the "language of commodities," see Mary Douglas and Baron Isherwood, *The World of Goods: Towards an Anthropology of Consumption* (New York: W. W. Norton, 1979).

may be said to emerge under the brush of, say, Eastman Johnson or William Paxton, or under the pen of Edith Wharton or Henry James, it suggests not just a way of seeing but a way of being as well.

The Tasteful Interior

To focus on the American interior in the late nineteenth century would seem at first to run against the grain of one's most cherished and familiar images of the period. After all, the Gilded Age suggests, if anything, a preoccupation with *exteriors*, with the unrestrained appetite for luxury long associated with flamboyant robber barons and political bosses. Yet against this broad-brush portrait of an expansive, grasping society, it is possible to trace a countervailing or centripetal movement toward social and cultural isolation: a movement of "interiorization."[4] Even so intrusive a work as Jacob Riis's famous exposé of New York slum life in *How the Other Half Lives* (1890) depended for its appeal on a new, yet increasingly common assumption among its readers that, for the first time in American history, classes had somehow become inaccessible to one another. Why else resort to the midnight visit to East Side tenements or to the "candid" snapshot of groggy basement lodgers if such images and information were otherwise readily available to Riis's middle-class audience? The realism of *How the Other Half Lives* was a blunt and graphic inversion of the *House Beautiful* ideal. Not only did it promise, in the language favored by realists, an "unvarnished" view of things, but it did so in a way that effectively mimicked the voyeurism of the society columns.

The isolated and enclosed world that Riis strove to depict was a reverse image of that protected terrain occupied by the detached house, the country and metropolitan club, the college fraternity, the preparatory school, and the professional society into which both old and new bourgeois were withdrawing during the late nineteenth century.[5] It is

[4] I have drawn this term from Celia Betsky, *Inner Spaces* (New York: Viking Press, forthcoming). Although the manuscript pursues different aims, I found it especially helpful. For further discussion of Gilded Age representation, see also Jay Mechling, "The Collecting Self and American Youth Movements," elsewhere in this volume.

[5] For a general overview of these developments, see E. Digby Baltzell, *The Protestant Establishment: Aristocracy and Caste in America* (New York: Vintage Books, 1964); Burton J. Bledstein, *The Culture of Professionalism: The Middle Class and the Development of Higher Education in America* (New York: W. W. Norton, 1976); and Frederic Cople Jaher, *The Urban Establishment: Upper Strata in Boston, New York, Charleston, Chicago, and Los Angeles* (Urbana: University of Illinois Press, 1982).

not surprising that this gradual segmentation of American society into class, ethnic, and gender enclaves found one of its expressions in a growing middle-class preoccupation with the household interior, both as a practical problem of habitation and as a figurative representation of newly discovered personal and social boundaries. This preoccupation with the interior was expressed most obviously in the occasional writing on interior design and decoration that appeared during the 1870s and 1880s—the centennial years—and that developed soon thereafter into the highly profitable, specialty periodical literature of the 1890s and 1900s. Beyond the immediate inspiration of the Centennial and World's Columbian expositions, there were a number of forces at work behind the emergence of this literature of the interior, among them the growth in the number of private homes (aided by the rise of savings and loan associations, the availability of cheap immigrant labor, and new methods of construction), the decline of handicraft, and the corresponding rise in machine-made furniture, floor coverings, plate glass, moldings, plumbing, and other fixtures. Specialty magazines provided an ideal showcase through which the new manufacturers of these goods could stimulate and channel the wants of this growing market, through which newly settled readers could glean information about the bewildering array of products, and through which a number of genteel men and women could fashion out of this double set of imperatives the rationale for a new professional calling: interior decoration and design.[6]

The different interests of manufacturers, consumers, and advisers did not always sit easily with one another at first, as the fate of at least one periodical, *Decorator and Furnisher* (1882–98) attests. In keeping with its name, the magazine initially tried to promote itself as both a trade organ for furniture manufacturers and dealers and an adviser for the amateur decorator. After a brief attempt at partitioning the magazine to serve both constituencies, the editors finally settled on the ama-

[6]On these trends, see David P. Handlin, *The American Home: Architecture and Society, 1815–1915* (Boston: Little, Brown, 1979), chap. 4; Jan Cohn, *The Palace or the Poorhouse: The American Home as Cultural Symbol* (East Lansing: Michigan State University Press, 1979); Gwendolyn Wright, *Moralism and the Model Home: Domestic Architecture and Cultural Conflict in Chicago, 1873–1913* (Chicago: University of Chicago Press, 1980), pp. 82–89; and Clifford Edward Clark, Jr., *The American Family Home, 1800–1960* (Chapel Hill: University of North Carolina Press, 1986), chaps. 2–5. See Russell Lynes, *The Tastemakers: The Shaping of American Popular Taste* (1954; reprint, New York: Dover Publications, 1980), chaps. 10–11.

teurs' side in 1895, only to see their readership dwindle into insignificance three years later. By this time, according to authorities like Edith Wharton and Mrs. Burton Harrison, the epoch of amateur decoration (with all its homely tips about savings) had thankfully given way to the trained expertise of the professional aesthetician. Aesthetic laggards might find some comfort in the friendly, unpretentious columns of the *Ladies' Home Journal*, especially as its editor Edward Bok conceived them after 1889. But both the style and the content of the new interior magazines made it clear that there were general principles of acquisition and arrangement that went beyond the vagaries of fashion and finance.[7]

Gone, for example, was the brittle defensiveness about expensive furnishings that had marked Clarence Cook's pioneering book, *The House Beautiful* (1878). Gone as well was the impression of coyness and hesitancy that had characterized Eugene Clarence Gardiner's 1882 parable of interior decoration, *The House that Jill Built, after Jack's Had Proved a Failure*. In 1915 the editor of *House and Garden* declared, "Were every woman her own decorator, a healthy profession would pass out of existence." Indeed, gone entirely was the assumption that the occupant of a room would leave his or her imprint upon it in any other way than by accumulation, selection, and placement. By the 1890s readers were no longer being urged to mask the machine-made origins of household furnishings by means of their own ornamentation.[8] If craft was not to be had through the purchase of antiques—a postcentennial fad—the sense of craft could be had through the mass-produced Eastlake style.

To be sure, these movements within the mainstream of interior decoration encountered a strong countercurrent in the works of the arts and crafts writers inspired by John Ruskin and William Morris. But as several historians have shown, the hostility of the craftsman's ideologues toward the new consumer society was at best problematic when it was

[7] An interesting instance of survival is *Building, Decorator, and Furnisher* (1883–1905), later *House and Home*; see Hardy Green, "Nineteenth Century 'Consumerism' and the Aesthetic Advisers," paper (March 1978), pp. 10–12; and Lynes, *Tastemakers*, pp. 175–78. See also Christopher P. Wilson, "The Rhetoric of Consumption: Mass-Market Magazines and the Demise of the Gentle Reader, 1880–1920," in *The Culture of Consumption: Critical Essays in American History, 1880–1980*, ed. Richard Wightman Fox and T. J. Jackson Lears (New York: Pantheon Books, 1983), pp. 39–64.

[8] Richardson Wright, *Inside the House of Good Taste* (New York: McBride, Nast, 1915), p. iv; Handlin, *American Home*, p. 428. The urge to ornament has of course never been fully suppressed; unfinished or half-finished furniture remains a popular item in the twentieth century.

not, as in the case of Elbert Hubbard, wholly fraudulent.[9] Herbert Stone's *House Beautiful* began publication in Chicago in 1896 as a modest, octavo journal in the *Chap-Book* style, featuring a few advertisements for furniture companies, books, tourism, and interior decoration. By 1904 the magazine had shifted to a large format, added color-tinted cover photographs, and merged its new "Shopping Guide" into an expanded advertising section that included appeals for appliances, cars, telephones, pianos, insurance, real estate, and landscape gardeners, as well as the usual ads for furnishings and interior decorators. New magazines, such as *Suburban Life* (1905–14) and *Indoors and Out* (1905–12), sought to capitalize on the burgeoning sense of life-style (as opposed to housing style) that this ever-expanding horizon of accessories implied. The boundaries of the household interior, it seemed, were gradually dissolving into a suburban landscape reconceived in its image. Henry James perfectly captured this sense of dissolution when, after a visit to New Hampshire, he wrote of its "silver-grey rock" as "cropping through thinly-grassed acres with a placed and 'composed' felicity that suggested the furniture of a drawing room."[10]

From the very outset of this period, the literature of domestic architecture had attacked the excessive compartmentalization and clutter of the late Victorian drawing room and had called for an openness of interior design that James was to find dizzying in its invitation to the performance of private life as public spectacle. Advisers like Cook, for example, railed against the seemingly mindless accumulation of objects found within the contemporary parlor. Cook noted as early as 1878, "What with easels, chairs not meant for use, little teetery stands, pedestals, and the rest of the supernumerary family filling up the room left by the solid and supposed useful pieces, it is sometimes a considerable test of one's dexterity and presence of mind to make one's way from end to end of a long New York drawing-room. . . . Mignon's egg-dance was as nothing to it."[11]

---

[9] Wright, *Moralism*, pp. 128–32, 139–49; T. J. Jackson Lears, *No Place of Grace: Antimodernism and the Transformation of American Culture, 1880–1920* (New York: Pantheon Books, 1981), chap. 2; Eileen Boris, *Art and Labor: Ruskin, Morris, and the Craftsman Ideal in America* (Philadelphia: Temple University Press, 1986).

[10] Henry James, *The American Scene* (Bloomington: Indiana University Press, 1968), p. 16.

[11] James, *American Scene*, pp. 166–67; Clarence Cook, *The House Beautiful: Essays on Beds and Tables, Stools and Candlesticks* (New York: Scribner, Armstrong, 1878), pp. 98–99. For further discussion of the parlor's significance, see Karen Halttunen, "From

What Cook and his colleagues had in mind by simplicity, open-ness, and serviceability, however, would astound a modern minimalist, yet they never ceased to promote those ideals. Readers were expected to prune their possessions, especially their personal keepsakes and heir-looms, in order to bring forth an even more spectacular harvest of new and better-informed purchases. To the increasing numbers of middle-class apartment dwellers of the late 1890s, the domestic interior took on added importance as the ideal of exterior renovation, or for that matter, the ideal of the detached house, fell further out of reach. The monthly magazines' relentless injunctions to buy pressed readers against the decidedly shrinking space of their city dwellings, leaving rigorous selec-tion—"severe bachelor sumptuousness"—as the only alternative to a choking accumulation of decorative objects. Like the window displays of department stores, the domestic interior was increasingly represented as an ever-revolving still life of household furnishings.[12]

In sum, the literature of interior design and decoration collectively projected an imaginary world in which the power of purchase held sway over the older authority of personal mementos and personal craft alike. The constituents of the household interior were no longer to be "built up," as Richardson Wright put it, but "picked up": "For the ideal house is the house that is picked up: A lit-clos from Brittany, a refectory table from Italy, Spanish iron work, roundels from Switzerland, English linen-fold paneling, a German chest. Or it may be that the table comes from Grand Rapids and the chairs from Philadelphia. Already [the con-sumer] has begun the house that is to be his and his alone—his own choice, his own buying." *Taste*—a word whose nineteenth-century rise in popularity had been intimately bound up with the rise of consumer culture—became the operative term for writers like Wright and Elsie de Wolfe, who singled out the act of decorative acquisition as a conso-

---

Parlor to Living Room: Domestic Space, Interior Decoration, and the Culture of Person-ality," elsewhere in this volume.

[12] See, for example, Frank Alvah Parsons, *Interior Decoration: Its Principles and Practice* (Garden City, N.Y.: Doubleday, Page, 1915), p. 7; Parsons also wrote on the principles of advertising design and arrangement. On the rising numbers of renters and shrinking space of middle-class city dwellers, see Wright, *Moralism*, pp. 44–46. On the exterior renovation of apartment dwellings, Donald Warren wrote, "It is pretty generally conceded that it is a mistake for a man, unless he has unlimited wealth at his command, to try to attain much originality, if any, in the exterior of a city house" (*House Beautiful* 5, no. 5 [April 1899]: 203). Gwendolyn Wright, *Building the Dream: A Social History of Housing in America* (New York: Pantheon Books, 1981), p. 85.

lation for the trapped city dweller. Where early nineteenth-century writers had pointed to the whole house as an expression of the owner's individuality, Wright saw the apartment interior as an externalization of the renter's multiple personalities: "In passing from room to room, one should be able to sense not merely a change in periods but a change in personalities as well." An emphasis on structure, so prominent in Wharton's writing on architecture, had yielded to an emphasis on performance. The word *character,* once conceived as an almost lapidary substance upon which life was supposed to have etched its facets and flaws, had given way to the word *personality,* now conceived as a protean effect: a display in which the personal properties of the self mingled with the stage properties of its immediate surroundings.[13]

Rooms without Views

Never was this confusion of properties more vividly represented than in those paintings of genteel domestic scenes that came into vogue during the late nineteenth and early twentieth centuries, under the leadership of the so-called Boston school of painters. William Paxton, Edmund Tarbell, and Philip Hale were among the school's foremost exponents, but intimations of their approach to the interior can be seen as early as the 1870s in the paintings of Eastman Johnson. In Johnson's 1871 portrait of the Hatch family, we can better appreciate, if only by way of contrast, the particular aesthetic that his successors brought to the genre of domestic interiors (fig. 1). Offered is a serviceable portrait of a large family (fifteen people in all) placed within a plush yet homey, Italianate parlor whose details, like those of the figures themselves, have been rather loosely rendered, with little attention to the peculiarities of light, texture, and surface. The painting is basically a conversation piece by

---

[13] Wright, *House of Good Taste,* p. iv; see also Elsie de Wolfe, *The House in Good Taste* (New York: Century Co., 1913), p. 261. On "taste," see Wright, *Building the Dream,* p. 85; Raymond Williams, *Keywords: A Vocabulary of Culture and Society* (1976; rev. ed., New York: Oxford University Press, 1985), pp. 264–66; Wright, *House of Good Taste,* p. iv; and Halttunen, "Parlor to Living Room." On the change from a "character" model to a "personality" model, see Warren I. Susman, *Culture as History: The Transformation of American Society in the Twentieth Century* (New York: Pantheon Books, 1984), pp. 271–85; and Lears, *No Place of Grace,* chap. 1.

Fig. 1. Eastman Johnson, *The Hatch Family*, 1871. Oil on canvas; H. 48″, W. 73⅛″. (Metropolitan Museum of Art, gift of Frederick H. Hatch, 1926.)

which the viewer is given the sense of a family assembled for the purpose of just such a memorialization as the scene provides.

As such, *The Hatch Family* differs sharply from a later Johnson work, *Not at Home* (fig. 2). This painting aims to capture, rather than to arrange, a social drama, one in which an air of mystery is communicated through the treatment of the setting itself. A woman is pictured fleeing from an unwanted caller. The focus of attention is treated in such a way, however, as to reverse the conventional priorities of background and foreground, shading the hall and bathing the parlor (and its lustrous objects) in a golden light. The caller is hidden from the viewer, and the woman herself is half hidden, her escape already figuratively achieved by means of her virtual dissolution into the immediate yet indistinct colors of the staircase. The mystery of her flight suggests another possible meaning to Johnson's title, one in which it is not the caller, but the warm, embracing enclosure of the drawing room that is being

Fig. 2. Eastman Johnson, *Not at Home*, ca. 1872–80. Oil on academy board; H. 26½″, W. 22¼″. (Brooklyn Museum, gift of Miss Gwendolyn O. L. Conkling.)

fled. *Not at Home* is thus a troubling painting in which the inviting and intimidating features of a half-concealed interior are deliberately played off one another.

No such conflicts are to be found, however, in the paintings of William McGregor Paxton. His figures, almost invariably women, are the primary compositional links between household objects from which they are, in visual and tactile terms, indistinguishable. In *The New Necklace* of 1910 (fig. 3), the viewer sees two young women dressed in exquisitely rendered fabrics and posed against the luxurious backdrop of a French escritoire, a Japanese screen, a European painting, and elaborately worked wallpaper. The objects express and complement the figures, and vice versa. The placement and postures of the women repeat

Fig. 3. William McGregor Paxton, *The New Necklace*, 1910. Oil on canvas; H. 35½", W. 28½". (Zoë Oliver Sherman Collection, Museum of Fine Arts, Boston.)

the telescoped, receding planes of the background while at the same time joining them in graceful three-dimensional circles. Both the flesh and the fabric are treated with the same attention to luster and highlight that Paxton lavishes on the porcelain figure, gilt frame, and brass ornaments. The painting is in a sense a visual essay on ornament.

The same interest in symmetry of objects and figures may be seen in Paxton's 1913 *Front Parlor* (fig. 4). Both color and composition are used to merge the figure of the young woman into a room whose intimate dimensions are brilliantly achieved. Her upper torso forms an oval with the vase of flowers, while her lower body forms another oval with the interior modeling of the fireplace, all of which is echoed in the

Fig. 4. William McGregor Paxton, *The Front Parlor*, 1913. Oil on canvas; H. 27″, W. 22″. (Saint Louis Art Museum, bequest of Cora E. Ludwig and Edward Mallinckrodt, Sr.)

repeated ovals of the carpet and wallpaper. The woman is more than absorbed in her letter; she is absorbed into the room itself. She verges on becoming not just a figure *on* the carpet but a figure *in* the carpet.

This impression of figurative dissolution into a more lively background of household objects is perhaps most dramatically (or theatrically) conveyed in Paxton's 1916 *Other Room* (fig. 5). The viewer once again sees a woman performing her compositional services, only to have her own features subordinated to the meticulously rendered details of the objects she is, in effect, connecting. Paxton's framing devices, cou-

Fig. 5. William McGregor Paxton, *The Other Room*, 1916. Oil on canvas; H. 32″, W. 17½″. (El Paso Museum of Art.)

pled with his adroit use of focus, give this painting a peculiarly dream-like quality. As such, it manages to achieve the fusion of self and object that Paxton's literary contemporaries, Wharton and James, were endeavoring to represent through the medium of words. Although neither of these authors confronted the commodity aesthetic with quite the complacency of Paxton, they nonetheless placed it at the heart of their greatest novels—novels that are, in every respect, narratives of the interior.

The House of Fiction

For many writers at the turn of the century, the purchased interior became a convenient metaphor with which to convey the new powers and predicaments that they discerned in their own bourgeois existence. Both Edith Wharton and Henry James thought in architectonic terms about their fiction. Wharton described her choice of narrative perspective as analogous to the selection of a building site, while James saw himself constructing, in his own celebrated phrase, a "house of fiction" through whose million windows the reader was invited to peer. Wharton, who entered the literary marketplace in 1897 as coauthor of *The Decoration of Houses*, used her writings on the domestic interior as a means of emancipating herself from the confinement of the social role to which she, as a bourgeois woman, had been consigned. In this sense, Wharton was able to draw the kind of boundaries between herself and her commodity environment that Lily Bart, the protagonist of Wharton's great novel *The House of Mirth* (1905), is incapable of achieving.[14]

At the outset of the novel, Wharton presents Lily as a beautiful, self-absorbed woman approaching the end of her eligibility in the marriage market of Gilded Age society. The reader first sees Lily through the eyes of one of her admirers, Lawrence Selden, as he walks with her down New York's Madison Avenue:

As she moved beside him with her long, light step, Selden was conscious of taking a luxurious pleasure in her nearness: in the modelling of her little ear, the crisp upward wave of her hair—was it ever so slightly blackened by art?—and the thick planting of her straight black lashes. Everything about her was at once vigorous and exquisite, at once strong and fine. He had a confused sense that she must have cost a great deal to make, that a great many dull and ugly people must, in some mysterious way, have been sacrificed to produce her. He was aware that the qualities distinguishing her from the herd of her sex were chiefly external as though a fine glaze of beauty and fastidiousness had been applied to vulgar clay. Yet the analogy left him unsatisfied, for a coarse texture will not take a high finish; and was it not possible that the material was fine but that the circumstance had fashioned it into a futile shape?

Selden's confusion over the source of Lily's artificiality—did it spring from within or from without?—soon becomes the reader's confusion and, as such, persists throughout the narrative. On the one hand, Lily becomes a figure whose "impenetrable surface suggested a process of

[14] Edith Wharton, *The Writing of Fiction* (New York: Charles Scribner's Sons, 1925), p. 46; Henry James, *The Future of the Novel: Essays on the Art of Fiction*, ed. Leon Edel (New York: Vintage Books, 1956), p. 50. See also Amy Kaplan, "Edith Wharton's Profession of Authorship," *ELH* 53, no. 2 (Summer 1986): 433–57.

crystallization which had fused her whole being into one hard, brilliant substance." On the other hand, Lily remains a figure whose boundaries occasionally dissolve into the ornamental world that surrounds her. She is herself an ornament, as she readily acknowledges, a decorative status that is most strikingly demonstrated in the famous *tableaux vivants* scene that comes midway through the novel. There, in calculated contrast to her rivals, who reproduce the poses and costumes of Titian's and Van Dyck's models, Lily astonishes her jaded audience by posing as herself, by pointing quite deliberately to herself as a work of art and a marriageable commodity. The nominal inspiration for Lily's tableau is a portrait by Joshua Reynolds, but as Wharton describes the scene, "It was as though she had stepped, not out of, but into, Reynolds' canvas, banishing the phantom of his dead beauty by the beams of her living grace."[15]

Lily is forever "stepping into" the gilded frames of various New York interiors, so it is no surprise that her ultimate downfall should come by being quite literally framed. She is, after all, a temperament notoriously open to the suggestion of her surroundings. "Her whole being dilated in an atmosphere of luxury; it was the background she required, the only climate she could breathe." Lily cannot "figure herself as anywhere but in a drawing-room, diffusing elegance as a flower sheds perfume." As her name suggests, Lily *is* a flower, but a "rare flower grown for exhibition" and cultivated indoors. She thrives in the luxuriant, hot-house atmosphere of New York's mansions and begins to die only when she is driven out of them. Their furnishings are her soil; their mirrors are the pools in which she finds the security of her own reflected beauty, so much so that whenever Lily encounters an unexpected reversal of fortune, she invariably rushes to the nearest mirror for reassurance, exchanging electric light for candlelight when the reflection grows too harsh and unflattering. Throughout *The House of Mirth*, Wharton uses the increasingly shabby New York interiors to which Lily is condemned as an index of her inexorable social decline. But Wharton also uses these interiors to bring home, as it were, the arrested character of Lily's emotional development. Because the conditions of Lily's own self-presentation as an ornament—a marriageable commodity—are so overriding, the aesthetic preoccupations of her life

[15] Edith Wharton, *The House of Mirth* (1905; reprint, New York: New American Library, 1964), pp. 7, 198, 141–42.

almost completely displace the moral perplexities they entail. As Wharton puts the case, Lily's "faculty for renewing herself in new scenes and casting off problems of conduct as easily as the surroundings in which they had arisen made the mere change from one place to another seem not merely a postponement, but a solution, of her troubles. Moral complications existed for her only in the environment that had produced them; she did not mean to slight or ignore them, but they lost their reality when they changed their background."[16] Lily thus pursues an almost caricatured form of situational ethics, one in which her moral interior surrenders entirely to the various physical interiors in which she happens to find herself.

Now this would scarcely seem to make Lily Bart an appealing literary character. Yet it is precisely this confusion of boundaries, this narcissistic identification with the immediate commodity environment that, as Joan Lidoff argues, has remained the source of Lily's continuing attraction for readers of Wharton's novel. Lily's life, Lidoff writes, "is nourished, like an infant's, by an amniotic bath of sensual satisfactions," so that even as she plunges toward "darkness and pollution," the reader is made to share Lily's immersion, made to step into a personality that, in turn, diffuses itself into every room she enters. "For all the hard glaze of her exterior," Wharton concludes, Lily is "inwardly as malleable as wax."[17] She dies as she lives, by the pathetic fallacy of a commodity aesthetic.

Much the same may be said of a number of Henry James's characters, especially those of the later novels. But it is not just that so many of his personae lust after dowries, as in *The Portrait of a Lady* (1881). Nor is it simply that they lust after things themselves, as in *The Spoils of Poynton* (1897), a novel that James had once considered entitling *The House Beautiful*. Nor does James's commodity aesthetic confine itself to those cases in which his characters actually consume one another, as they do in *The Sacred Fount* (1901). It is that James himself begins to treat the properties of his characters as if they were in fact properties:

---

[16]Wharton, *House of Mirth*, pp. 29, 106, 329, 203.

[17]Joan Lidoff, "Another Sleeping Beauty: Narcissism in *The House of Mirth*," in *American Realism: New Essays*, ed. Eric J. Sundquist (Baltimore: Johns Hopkins University Press, 1982), pp. 238–58. For the market dimension of the novel, see Wai-chee Dimock, "Debasing Exchange: Edith Wharton's *The House of Mirth*," *Publications of the Modern Language Association* 100, no. 5 (October 1985): 783–92; and Wharton, *House of Mirth*, p. 57.

detachable and exchangeable goods. Nowhere is this impulse more freely indulged than in James's last complete novel, aptly entitled *The Golden Bowl* (1904), a huge literary edifice whose four major inhabitants treat one another as objects in each other's private collection. Adam Verver looks upon his daughter Maggie as a graceful artifact, a "slim draped 'antique' of Vatican or Capitoline halls." Maggie, in turn, refers to her prospective husband, the Prince, as "an object of beauty, an object of price," while the Prince, for his part, regards his former lover, Charlotte, as a commodity, indeed as an assemblage of beautifully framed properties available for his appropriation. In an extraordinary passage in the novel, James describes the Prince as he takes stock of his lover:

But it was, strangely, as a cluster of possessions of his own that these things, in Charlotte Stant, now affected him; items in a full list, items recognized, each of them, as if, for the long interval, they had been "stored"—wrapped up, numbered, put away in a cabinet. While she faced Mrs. Assingham the door of the cabinet had opened of itself; he took the relics out, one by one, and it was more and more, each instant, as if she were giving him time. . . . He knew her narrow hands, he knew her long fingers and the shape and color of her finger-nails, he knew her special beauty of movement and line when she turned her back, and the perfect working of all her main attachments, that of some wonderful finished instrument, something intently made for exhibition, for a prize. He knew above all the extraordinary fineness of her flexible waist, the stem of an expanded flower which gave her a likeness also to some long, loose silk purse, well filled with gold pieces, but having been passed, empty, through a finger-ring that held it together. It was if, before she turned to him, he had weighed the whole thing in his open palm and even heard a little the chink of the metal.[18]

Among other things, *The Golden Bowl* is about Maggie's effort to regain possession of her husband, the Prince, by winning him back from his lover, Charlotte. With the aid of her father, she does win in the end, and in the novel's final scene, the two victors in this possessive struggle—Adam and Maggie—stand looking upon the vanquished—the Prince and Charlotte—as they take their last tea together. In looking

[18] Henry James, *The Golden Bowl* (1904; reprint, New York: Penguin Books, 1966), pp. 153–54, 58–59. For a more extended discussion, see Jean-Christophe Agnew, "The Consuming Vision of Henry James," in *The Culture of Consumption: Critical Essays in American History, 1880–1980*, ed. Richard Wightman Fox and T. J. Jackson Lears (New York: Pantheon Books, 1983), pp. 65–100.

upon the two, father and daughter seem to take a final inventory of their possessions.

The other objects in the room, the other pictures, the sofas, the chairs, the tables, the cabinets, the "important" pieces, supreme in their way, stood out, round them, consciously, for recognition and applause. Their eyes moved together from piece to piece, taking in the whole nobleness. . . . The two noble persons seated, in conversation, at tea, fell thus into the splendid effect and the general harmony: Mrs. Verver and the Prince fairly "placed" themselves, however unwittingly, as high expressions of the kind of human furniture required, aesthetically, by such a scene. The fusion of their presence with the decorative elements, their contribution to the triumph of selection, was complete and admirable.

Despite the evident sense of triumph conveyed in this scene, neither Henry James nor Edith Wharton ever sought to glorify this fusion of human and decorative elements, this representation of persons as "grown" or "made for exhibition." To the very end of their careers, the two writers remained ambivalent toward the attractions of a commodity aesthetic. They were not alone in this conflict. It is difficult to return to Eastman Johnson's painting *Not at Home*, for example, without at the same time recalling Charlotte Perkins Gilman's chilling short story of 1892, "The Yellow Wall-Paper," the semiautobiographical tale of a woman who does indeed lose herself in the amniotic zone of the domestic interior.[19] The "power of purchase," as James referred to it, is an alternately enchanting and engulfing power.

Figures of Consumption

If the ambivalence toward a commodity aesthetic testifies to anything, it is to the imaginative power of that aesthetic in the minds of those writers and artists who, in one way or another, struggled to represent it. For them the very act of imagining could become inextricably enmeshed with the fantasy of acquisition, much to their delight and dismay. This mixture of feelings is understandable if one recalls that one of the results of the mutual entanglement of creative and consuming visions was a

---

[19]James, *Golden Bowl*, p. 541; Charlotte Perkins Gilman, "The Yellow Wall-Paper," *New England* 5, no. 5 (January 1892): 647–56.

visual and rhetorical dismemberment of the self and its reconstitution
as a mobile pastiche of properties, an assemblage of commodities. What
the image of the domestic interior offered these writers and artists was,
in effect, a ready-made laboratory (quite literally, a drawing room) in
which their recombinant versions of personhood could be experimen-
tally refined, safe from the ordinary claims of daily life yet indissolubly
connected to them. Accordingly, the dazzling creatures (Lily, Maggie,
and Paxton's figures) who emerge out of this laboratory of the interior
owe their charismatic powers, such as they are, less to the Promethean
promise of technology than to the protean premise of the market: they
are more Franklins, if anything, than Frankensteins.

To invoke Benjamin Franklin, however, is to remind oneself that
the commodity aesthetic was not the invention of the late nineteenth
century. One may find any number of antecedents from the surrealistic,
composite portraits of sixteenth-century Italian mannerism to the
hyperrealistic interiors of the seventeenth-century Dutch pictorial tradition.[20] Nevertheless, such movements do not become "anticipations"
unless and until posterity grasps them as such; this, as it happened, a
variety of nineteenth-century American artists and writers were quite
prepared to do.

Thus, at the same time that William Paxton and Philip Hale were
reviving Vermeer's reputation in America, Bernard Berenson, described
as a "passionate sight-seer," was putting forward his theory of the importance of tactile values in painting. Berenson declared later, "Tactile
values occur in representations of solid objects when communicated,
not as mere representations (no matter how veracious), but in a way that
stirs the imagination to feel their bulk, heft their weight, realize their
potential resistance, space their distance from us, and encourage us,
always imaginatively, to come into close touch with, to grasp, to embrace,
or to walk around," or, one might add, to hear "the chink of the metal."[21]
The gloss that such aestheticians as Berenson were inclined to put on
the images left to them by their forebears was more than reflective; it

---

[20] In this connection, see Arnold Hauser, *Mannerism: The Crisis of the Renaissance
and the Origins of Modern Art* (New York: Alfred A. Knopf, 1965); and Svetlana Alpers,
The Art of Describing: Dutch Art in the Seventeenth Century (Chicago: University of
Chicago Press, 1983).

[21] Bernard Berenson, *Aesthetics and History in the Visual Arts* (New York: Pantheon
Books, 1948), p. 63.

was positively refulgent. A realism of this order did not so much wish to strip away the varnish of everyday life as to polish it.

Yet the realism of these luxuriously tactile representations was no less "real" for the women who were so often their object and subject. As Rachel Bowlby has argued in her aptly titled study of consumption, *Just Looking*, it was no accident that women so often bore the "sign" of the commodity in late nineteenth-century American and European culture, for they were expected to become "like prostitutes in their active, commodified self-display, and also to take on the role almost never theirs in actual prostitution: that of consumer." Add to this double bind the explicitly gendered setting of the Victorian drawing room, and it becomes additionally clear why the domestic interior functioned so well and so long as the site of an emerging (or perhaps reemerging) commodity aesthetic.[22] At the very least, that aesthetic shows just how much the house of fiction owed to the fiction of houses invented by artists and writers of the late nineteenth and early twentieth centuries.

In our own time, Victorian gentility, like the Victorian parlor, no longer serves as the indispensable credential of a commodity aesthetic, although the elaborate genealogies of the accessories owned by Krantz's Ram suggest that it may still survive as a useful reference point. Still, reference points are notoriously mobile in the contemporary world of designer labels. What began as a modest blurring of bodily and commodity "properties" has long since given way to a blurring of genres, as advertising applies its ever-present airbrush to Berenson's beloved tactile values. Consequently, when one comes upon an image of a woman in a contemporary advertisement (fig. 6), one may immediately recognize the image as that of an advertisement and yet may momentarily wonder

---

[22] Rachel Bowlby, *Just Looking: Consumer Culture in Dreiser, Gissing, and Zola* (New York: Methuen, 1985), p. 11. Several historians have pushed the birthdate of consumer society as far back as the late sixteenth and early seventeenth centuries, in which case this story is but a mere episode in a much longer tale; see Fernand Braudel, *Capitalism and Material Life, 1400–1800*, trans. Mirian Kochan (New York: Harper and Row, 1973), pp. 192–243; Joan Thirsk, *Economic Policy and Projects: The Development of a Consumer Society in Early Modern England* (Oxford: Clarendon Press, 1978); Neil McKendrick, John Brewer, and J. H. Plumb, *The Birth of a Consumer Society: The Commercialization of Eighteenth-Century England* (Bloomington: Indiana University Press, 1982); and Chandra Mukerji, *From Graven Images: Patterns of Modern Materialism* (New York: Columbia University Press, 1983); Colin Campbell, *The Romantic Ethic and the Spirit of Modern Consumerism* (Oxford: Basil Blackwell, 1987).

All you need is
one beautiful drop
to know why Estée Lauder
was keeping
Private Collection Perfume
for herself.

ESTĒE LAUDER

Fig. 6. Advertisement for Private Collection Perfume, Estée Lauder, 1981. (Courtesy, Estée Lauder, Inc.)

what precisely it is selling. In this particular instance, appropriately enough, the commodity happens to be a perfume called Private Collection. But whether one sees in this photograph the image of Henry James's Princess Maggie or Judith Krantz's Princess Daisy, one sees a figure who is at once collector *and* collectible. Of all the exquisite objects in the room, she is the only self-consuming artifact.[23]

---

[23] Berenson, *Aesthetics and History*, p. 63. For a discussion of the hypertactility of advertising images, see Michael Schudson, *Advertising: The Uneasy Persuasion* (New York: Basic Books, 1984), pp. 217–18.

From Parlor to Living Room

Domestic Space, Interior Decoration, and the Culture of Personality

Karen Halttunen

A number of recent popular books with titles such as *What Your House Tells about You*, *What Do You Say to a Naked Room?*, and *Psycho-Decorating* make the central assumption that interior decoration is an important expression of *personality*. These manuals explain, for example, that while glass-top tables reveal aggressiveness, burled wood indicates a strong sense of social justice, and patchwork quilt patterns betray a tendency toward self-criticism. They teach us to read the signs of marital troubles, sexual impotence, or insecurity about shortness of stature in the homes of our acquaintances. They offer "Self-Discovery Testing" so we can learn about our sense of space, color preferences, emotional tendencies, and personal style before we redecorate, and thus avoid costly mistakes. And they warn us that the perils of self-ignorance in interior decoration are not merely financial: "Narcissistic attitudes, defects in identification, oral and anal aggressions, latent homosexuality, a deeply rooted sadomasochistic pattern—any or all of these neurotic phenomena may come bubbling to the surface" when a woman ventures to redecorate without first knowing who she is. Finally, modern interior-decoration manuals indicate that "the living room is the general identity room" of the house, where the expression of personality is most important. *Psycho-Decorating*, for example, offers "Pictures of Living Rooms of Different Personalities," including the Achieving, Deferent, Exhibitionistic, Dominant, Heterosexual, and Friendly living rooms. A man informs a woman seated next to him in a bar, in a *New Yorker* cartoon of 1978, "I've tried to express myself clearly, but for a truly definitive statement of *me* you'd have to see my new living room."[1]

In American cultural history, the living room and the concept of personality both emerged at about the same time. The living room replaced the parlor as the most important room in the middle-class house around the turn of the century, and *personality* displaced *character* as the dominant conceptualization of the self also in the years around 1900. This essay explores the historical relationship between the new social space and the new modal self by tracing the transition from a Victorian domestic culture, which focused on the parlor as the most important arena for the demonstration of character, to an early twentieth-century domestic culture, which focused on the living room as the place to express personality. The new organization of middle-class domestic space around 1900 is shown to be a critical mechanism for the making of what historian Warren Susman called "the culture of personality" in America.[2] This essay also demonstrates that the appearance of "personal decorating"—the effort to decorate houses as the expression of personality—between 1900 and 1930 shaped a new understanding of the meaning of domestic things that has proved crucial to the emergence of mass consumer society in the twentieth century.

At the center of the romantic revival that introduced the Gothic cottage, the Italianate villa, and the bracketed house into American domestic architecture between 1840 and 1870 lay a view of the home as moral force. Rejecting the classical aesthetic, which regarded structural forms as beautiful in themselves insofar as they conformed to timeless standards of harmony and proportion, the romantics argued that

---

[1] M. H. Harmon, *Psycho-Decorating: What Homes Reveal about People* (New York: Wyden Books, 1977), pp. 23–30, 174, chap. 7; Virginia Frankel, *What Your House Tells about You* (New York: Trident Press, 1972), pp. 24–25 and passim; Catherine C. Crane, *What Do You Say to a Naked Room?* (New York: Dial Press, 1979), p. 25. For a general discussion of the "psychology" of interior decoration, see Joan Kron, *Home-Psych: The Social Psychology of Home and Decoration* (New York: Clarkson N. Potter, 1983). Cartoon, as quoted in Gerry Pratt, "The House as an Expression of Social Worlds," in *Housing and Identity: Cross-Cultural Perspectives*, ed. James S. Duncan (New York: Holmes and Meier, 1982), p. 135.

[2] Warren I. Susman, *Culture as History: The Transformation of American Society in the Twentieth Century* (New York: Pantheon Books, 1984), pp. 271–85.

forms were beautiful to the degree that they raised proper thoughts in the mind of the viewer. Andrew Jackson Downing, a landscape designer who emerged as the leader of the romantic revival in the 1840s, stated the romantic aesthetic most simply: *"true taste lies in the union of the beautiful and the significant."* Along with other architects of his generation—men such as Alexander Jackson Davis and Calvert Vaux— Downing was committed to elevating the morals of the American people by enlightening them on the connection between architectural forms and moral ideals. Oliver P. Smith wrote in 1852: "Nothing has more to do with the morals, the civilization, and refinement of a nation, than its prevailing architecture. . . . Our minds and morals are subject to constant influence and modification, gradual yet lasting, by the inanimate walls with which we are surrounded." As participants in the shift of American Protestantism from evangelical revivalism to Christian domesticity in the 1840s and 1850s, romantic architects visibly linked house form with individual moral development, especially in the Gothic house, where the cross-shaped floor plan, vaulted arches, crosses mounted on gables, and stained-glass windows evoked obvious associations of home with church.[3]

If the avowed higher purpose of the Gothic house was to exercise a constant Christian influence upon its inhabitants, the real social function of its ostentatious ecclesiastical design was to proclaim the family's moral stature to the world at large. As Downing wrote, "The home of every family, possessed of character may be made to express that character." For Downing, as for other nineteenth-century proponents of the Protestant ethic, moral character was closely linked to social position. This concern that the house express as well as influence the character of those living within it was most evident not in the exterior style of the Gothic revival house, but in the interior layout of most middle-class houses at midcentury. By 1850 middle-class usage had shaped a widely

[3] Andrew Jackson Downing, "Cockneyism in the Country," in *Rural Essays*, ed. Andrew Jackson Downing (New York: R. Worthington, 1881), p. 227; Smith, as quoted in Colleen McDannell, *The Christian Home in Victorian America, 1840–1890* (Bloomington: Indiana University Press, 1986), pp. 21–22, 24; Clifford E. Clark, Jr., "Domestic Architecture as an Index to Social History: The Romantic Revival and the Cult of Domesticity in America, 1840–1870," *Journal of Interdisciplinary History* 7, no. 1 (Summer 1976): 44; Clifford E. Clark, Jr., *The American Family Home, 1800–1960* (Chapel Hill: University of North Carolina Press, 1986), chap. 1; McDannell, *Christian Home*, chap. 2.

used floor plan that included a front porch, an entrance hall with stairway, a front parlor or drawing room, a sitting or dining room, servants'
workrooms (such as the kitchen, pantry, and scullery), a second staircase at the back of the house, and the upstairs chambers, the nursery,
and the bath.[4]

Within this highly specialized domestic layout, the most important
arena for the expression of character was the parlor, which *Godey's Lady's
Book* called "the *face* of the house—the most noticeable part—and that
from which visitors take their impressions of the whole." Here family
and visitors formally met and laid claim to character through a careful
adherence to the elaborate social conventions of Victorian etiquette.
This "genteel performance" required a careful separation of the parlor
stage from the private regions of the house; the kitchen and its environs,
including the back staircase, were hidden from sight so that the back
regions of the house might be preserved for relaxation from the rigorous
demands of formal Victorian conduct. Even the front stairway was placed
unobtrusively to indicate that visitors were not welcome upstairs. The
parlor was also protected from the public street by the front hall, which
"ceremonialized the coming and going, the entry and exit of the members of the household and their guests," serving as a testing zone where
the social claims of would-be visitors could be evaluated and those deemed
unworthy of entrance might be turned away.[5]

The same moral aesthetic that shaped the exterior style of the middle-class home also informed Victorian views of interior decoration,
especially with respect to the parlor. If the natural setting of a country
home exerts moral influence, according to an essay entitled "The Ethics of Home Decoration," then "the moral effect of interior home-dec-
oration is still greater." Christian domesticity was stated most explicitly
in the wide range of religious objects and icons used in nineteenth-

[4] Andrew Jackson Downing, "A Few Words on Rural Architecture," in *Rural Essays*,
pp. 207–8; Clark, *American Family Home*, chap. 2.
[5] *Godey's Lady's Book*, as quoted in Gwendolyn Wright, *Building the Dream: A
Social History of Housing in America* (New York: Pantheon Books, 1981), p. 113, Karen
Halttunen, *Confidence Men and Painted Women: A Study of Middle-Class Culture in
America, 1830–1870* (New Haven: Yale University Press, 1982), chap. 4; Simon J. Bron-
ner, *Grasping Things: Folk Material Culture and Mass Society in America* (Lexington:
University Press of Kentucky, 1986), pp. 23–63; Clark, *American Family Home*, chap.
2; McDannell, *Christian Home*, chap. 2; and Kenneth L. Ames, "Meaning in Artifacts:
Hall Furnishings in Victorian America," *Journal of Interdisciplinary History* 9, no. 1
(Summer 1978): 38.

century home decoration, including pious mottoes in needlework, wooden and wax crosses made to resemble marble, parlor organs, family Bible stands, Marian shrines, and prie-dieux. Furniture in the Gothic style— armchairs, tables, lounges, hallstands, and even bedroom sets and stoves— reinforced this image of the Christian home. But the moral character-istics of the nineteenth-century parlor are not always immediately evi-dent to the late twentieth-century eye. Catharine Beecher and Harriet Beecher Stowe, in *The American Woman's Home* (1869), asserted, "The decoration of houses . . . contributes much to the education of the entire household in refinement, intellectual development, and moral sensibility." They went on to extol the virtues of buff wallpaper with maroon bordering, muslin curtains, green chintz upholstery and lam-brequins (horizontal swatches of fabric draped over the tops of windows, doors, shelves, and mantels); chromolithographs such as *Barefoot Boy* and *Sunset in Yo Semite Valley*; and plaster-cast statuettes. They also encouraged the use of a variety of "natural" objects, including picture frames of pinecones, moss, and seashells; hanging baskets for plants; climbing ivy trained around the cornice; and the "Ward case," a large terrarium furnished with ferns, shells, trailing arbutus, and partridge berries, which offered "a fragment of the green woods brought in and silently growing."[6] For the Beecher sisters, such a decorative scheme was moral simply because it was beautiful; the chromolithographs and statuettes provided aesthetic uplifting, and the introduction of nature into the home offered its moral influence upon the character of those present.

The morality of the parlor seems to have resided, above all, in its standardized air of propriety. For American Victorians, character was a matter primarily of disciplined self-restraint; it was nothing if not fixed. So too, apparently, were many middle-class parlors (fig. 1). Calvert Vaux was caustically critical of "one style of best parlor to be found in Amer-ica" which he assumed that most of his "readers have also seen": it contained an uncomfortably small table with some books "in smart

[6] J. R. Miller, "The Ethics of Home Decoration," in *Weekday Religion* (Philadel-phia, 1880), p. 269, as cited in McDannell, *Christian Home*, p. 45; Clark, *American Family Home*, pp. 25–26; Catharine E. Beecher and Harriet Beecher Stowe, *The Amer-ican Woman's Home; or, Principles of Domestic Science; Being a Guide to the Formation and Maintenance of Economical, Healthful, Beautiful, and Christian Homes* (New York: J. B. Ford, 1869), pp. 84, 103.

Fig. 1 Front parlor, Abraham Lincoln house, Springfield, Ill. From *Frank Leslie's Illustrated Newspaper*, March 9, 1861. (Courtesy, Newberry Library, Chicago.)

bindings" laid on it, a "sofa, by courtesy so called," "a row of black walnut chairs, with horse-hair seats, all ranged against the white wall," a piano, a marble-top console table, a gilt mirror, and a knickknack shelf—all of which were "arranged according to stiff, immutable law." Not only were the windows and blinds kept closed, but the door itself was shut, because this room was reserved "for *company* use." In Vaux's view, such a parlor "becomes a sort of quarantine in which to put each plague of a visitor that calls; and one almost expects to see the lady of the house walk in with a bottle of camphor in her hand, to prevent infection, she seems to have such a fear that any one should step within the bounds of her real every-day home life."[7]

Although such criticism of the rigidly formal "company" parlor was not unusual at midcentury, it grew increasingly vociferous in the

[7] Calvert Vaux, *Villas and Cottages: A Series of Designs Prepared for Execution in the United States* (New York: Harper and Brothers, 1864), pp. 95–97.

decades that followed and helped transform the stiffly pious mid Victorian parlor, with its horsehair and woolen stuffs, into the riotously over-decorated late Victorian parlor. The newly transformed parlor was characterized by velvets, plushes, and lace, fringed upholstery, crocheted tidies, piano scarves and antimacassars, "fancy" chairs with gilt and ribbon, abundant oil portraits and watercolor landscapes, numerous small tables covered with heavy fringed velours, walls with flocked paper in dark tones and florid patterns, hand-painted screens and easels, wax flowers, souvenirs, and knickknacks of every variety. In the 1880s *Harper's Bazaar* exultantly compared the modern-day parlor to that of the 1840s: "What a desert was that old parlor to this! This which, if a little overcrowded, and giving scarcely rest enough to eye or mind, is yet crowded only with beauty" (fig. 2). Historian Colleen McDannell has persuasively argued, "By linking morality and religion with the purchase and maintenance of a Christian home, the Victorians legitimized

Fig. 2. Parlor, Leoni house, New York, 1894. (The Byron Collection, Museum of the City of New York: Photo, Byron.)

acquisition and display of domestic goods." Household arbiter Harriet Spofford reassured her readers, "provided there is space to move about, without knocking over the furniture, there is hardly likely to be too much in the room." But criticism of the "grave-yard parlor" or the "Sunday go-to-meeting parlor" continued. It contributed to the "artistic" ideal of the last decades of the century, which merely provided a new rationale for accumulation, adding to the clutter an indiscriminate mix of women's handiwork, rattan furniture, peacock feathers, beaded curtains, and Japanese fans. Even with the introduction of Charles Eastlake's "sincere" furniture, the spirit of the parlor remained essentially unchanged. As late as 1889, the *Domestic Cyclopaedia* felt justified in observing, "*The Parlor* is usually the most Philistine of all Philistine American institutions."[8]

A dramatic manifestation of the late Victorian reaction to the moral parlor was the popularity in the 1890s of the "cozy corner." In 1893 one of its proponents, James Thomson, explained, "We cannot forget the parlor of the not very remote past, that period which may be termed the dark age of decorative effort, when the haircloth-covered set of furniture was very much in evidence; nor can we forget with what painful precision it was distributed round the wall spaces, when everything— in what was often spoken of as the 'best' room—assumed such a funereal aspect, that one never entered without a chill, nor departed without delight." But now, he gratefully announced, artistry, taste, and originality were transforming that "funereal" apartment, and nowhere was the change more evident than in "the artistic cozy corner." The cozy corner openly violated the "stiff, immutable laws" dictating the placement of furniture along the walls of the moral parlor. A divan was placed diagonally across the corner of the room, with a rod running

[8] Meyric R. Rogers, *American Interior Design: The Traditions and Development of Domestic Design from Colonial Times to the Present* (New York: W. W. Norton, 1947), p. 145; Russell Lynes, *The Domesticated Americans* (New York: Harper and Row, 1963), p. 140; Harvey Green, *The Light of the Home: An Intimate View of the Lives of Women in Victorian America* (New York: Pantheon Books, 1983), chap. 4; *Harper's Bazaar,* as quoted in Wright, *Building the Dream*, p. 111; McDannell, *Christian Home*, p. 49; Harriet Spofford, *Art Decoration as Applied to Furniture* (New York: Harper and Brothers, 1877), p. 222; Clarence Cook, *The House Beautiful: Essays on Beds and Tables, Stools and Candlesticks* (New York: Scribner, Armstrong, 1878), p. 277; "Letter to the Editor," *Ladies' Home Journal* 1, no. 12 (November 1884): 4; Todd S. Goodholme, ed., *Goodholme's Domestic Cyclopaedia of Practical Information* (New York: Charles Scribner's Sons, 1889), p. 223.

Fig. 3. Turkish corner, drawing room, Hughes house, New York, 1899. (The Byron Collection, Museum of the City of New York: Photo, Byron.)

overhead from which "Bagdad" curtains were draped, looped back in a calculatedly asymmetrical fashion. The divan was piled with cushions and usually decorated with some mix of Japanese, East Indian, Turkish, and Egyptian motifs, suggesting what was popularly regarded as "the sluggish, luxurious temperament of the Orient." The desired effect of the cozy corner was "one which invites repose and freedom from conventionality" by offering a place to sprawl and lounge at ease (fig. 3).[9] The Turkish, or cozy, corner was thus intended to provide, within the parlor itself, a semisecluded retreat from the rigid requirements of polite parlor conduct—a retreat, in other words, from the demands of character.

By the 1890s, however, a much larger change was taking place in the arrangement of middle-class social space, one that would extend the spirit of the cozy corner to the entire front region of the house: the replacement of the parlor with the living room. Architecturally one

[9] James Thomson, "Cozy Corners and Ingle Nooks," *Ladies' Home Journal* 10, no. 12 (November 1893): 27; Mrs. Barnes Bruce, "Embroideries for a Dining-Room," *Ladies' Home Journal* 11, no. 2 (January 1894): 9; William Martin Johnson, "The House Practical," *Ladies' Home Journal* 16, no. 6 (May 1899): 27.

important Victorian source of the living room was the "living hall" of the "Queen Anne" house, which first appeared in the 1870s and was scaled down to middle-class size in the 1880s. This hall, based loosely on the Elizabethan great hall, was the center and core of the house, an open and informal living area—often equipped with a large fireplace flanked by an inglenook—that served the combined functions of entry and stair hall, reception room, family gathering place, and circulation center of the house. By 1893, when the *Ladies' Home Journal* household editor was asked how to decorate the hall, she assumed that the reader intended to make her hall "a sort of living-room."[10]

More generally, despite its intensive specialization of space—its division of the first-floor front region into reception room, parlor or drawing room, sitting room, library, and dining room (names that were precisely stated but whose exact functions were unclear)—the Victorian house offered many opportunities for opening up interior space: by opening sliding doors, whose virtue was that they disappeared into the walls; by throwing back the heavy portieres hung in doorless doorways; or simply by removing the folding screens placed in or near doorways. Increasingly toward the end of the century, rooms were opened up into one another through wide, doorless archways, and house pattern books began to praise the interior "vistas" and the "feeling of spaciousness" in their plans. Some older houses were structurally modified: in 1898, for example, *House Beautiful* explained how one homeowner removed the wall dividing his small library from his small parlor to make "one good-sized living room."[11] As this story demonstrates, the term *living room* was increasingly used to designate the largest and most open room in the front regions of the house.

The gradual transformation of the highly specialized and intensely

[10] Maria Parloa, "Everything about the House," *Ladies' Home Journal* 10, no. 1 (December 1893): 33. For discussions of the living hall, see Vincent J. Scully, Jr., *The Shingle Style: Architectural Theory and Design from Richardson to the Origins of Wright* (New Haven: Yale University Press, 1955), pp. 4–5; John Maass, *The Victorian Home in America* (New York: Hawthorne Books, 1972), pp. 176–77; and Lynes, *Domesticated Americans*, pp. 101–2.

[11] Florine Thayer McCray, "Mary Jane Holmes," *Ladies' Home Journal* 5, no. 2 (January 1888): 3; Elmer Grey, "Some Considerations of the Home," *House Beautiful* 7, no. 3 (February 1900): 157; "Prize Competition: Honorable Mention," *House Beautiful* 5, no. 2 (January 1899): 75. On the opening of interior space in the Victorian home, see David P. Handlin, *The American Home: Architecture and Society, 1815–1915* (Boston: Little, Brown, 1979), pp. 343–48; and "Alterations of Old Houses," *House Beautiful* 4, no. 2 (July 1898): 64–65.

private Victorian house into the open and unspecialized twentieth-century house was made possible by some major changes in the nature of middle-class social life, the basic elements of which were evident in the popularity of summer homes in the 1880s and 1890s. Numerous articles in *Ladies' Home Journal* offered floor plans for summer cottages (ranging from large villas to tiny mountain cabins), suggestions on transforming a barn or stable into a summerhouse, advice on renting and fixing up an abandoned farmhouse, and discussions of summer sojourns in large tents or houseboats. According to these articles, summerhouses widely adopted the "living hall" concept, "an informal meeting place for the family, a sort of living room entered at once from the front door." Typically, this room was decorated with blue denim cushions and curtains, draped fishnet and seashells, moose heads and stuffed game birds, Indian artifacts, shooting and fishing equipment, and tennis rackets and baseball bats; it was praised for its "picnic-like character."[12]

Domestic writers averred "the most important thing in a country home is the piazza which is outside of it," which functioned as an "outdoor parlor." On the piazza, hammocks, large rockers, wicker tables and settees, rugs, decorative screens, and Japanese lanterns were in order. Alfresco entertainment was the rage, including picnics (sometimes with self-conscious rustic themes that called for costumes, such as a "Haymakers Picnic" or a "Corn Husking" party or even a "Gypsy Camp" at which the ladies were to wear their corsets laced outside their dresses), garden parties, yachting parties, and lawn-tennis teas. Social writers waxed enthusiastic about the "charming unpretentiousness about out-of-door fetes that disarms criticism and predisposes the guests to an amount of gratification which more elaborate parlor parties would never furnish." All a summer hostess needed was a nearby grove or an ample piazza to entertain her guests in "the most charming of drawing rooms."[13]

Such tongue-in-cheek identification of the summerhouse piazza

[12] See articles in *Ladies' Home Journal*: A. R. Ramsey, "Interior Decoration," 5, no. 7 (June 1888): 9; Mrs. Garrett Webster, "Furnishing a Summer Home," 11, no. 6 (May 1894): 18, and "Some Successful Country Homes," 17, no. 11 (October 1900): 3. See also Hester M. Poole, "The Best Way: Inexpensive Inland Cottages," *Good Housekeeping* 30, no. 12 (June 1900): 265.

[13] Webster, "Furnishing a Home"; in *Good Housekeeping*, see "Summer-House Furnishings," 25, no. 6 (June 1897): 261; and "Amateur Entertainments," 11, no. 11 (September 27, 1890): 249. In *Ladies' Home Journal*, see Mrs. A. G. Lewis, "Lawn Parties and Out-door Fetes," 9, no. 8 (July 1892): 2, "Entertaining in the Country," 10, no. 8 (July 1893): 10, and "Country Entertaining," 3, no. 8 (July 1886): 10.

as a "parlor" and its nearby grove of trees as a "drawing room" was clearly intended to undercut the formality of Victorian middle-class social life. What made such a breezy, informal sociability possible was that the summerhouse by its nature limited social access to invited guests. As *Ladies' Home Journal* observed, it was a place "where small groups of congenial people meet in untrammeled association."[14] There was thus no need for a front hall to exclude the undesirable or a parlor where claims to social position could be made through the formalities of the genteel performance, because those present at the summerhouse had already been screened; their claims had been assessed and accepted.

The direct impact of the social forms of the summerhouse was limited to those who could afford to buy such a house and to the friends invited to join in the summertime frolics. A far more important factor in shaping post-Victorian social life among middle-class Americans was the suburban growth stimulated by expanding commuter railroad lines and the emergence, after 1888, of the new electric streetcar. Whereas earlier suburbs of the 1840s and 1850s had represented themselves as small cities aspiring to urban greatness, by 1890 the suburban image was entirely distinct from the city. At its center was the ideal of a detached dwelling in a semirural setting, a home protected from urban noise, pollution, disease, and vice by miles of commuter tracks and separated even from its own winding, tree-lined street by an expanse of well-manicured lawn. But implicit in the new suburban ideal was the determination that there be little to fear from suburban streets. As one plan book promised, the suburb offered "houses tastefully and economically built . . . surrounded by an enterprising, high-minded, sober, industrious, refined Christian people, where health, education, culture, and a generous reward for the expenditure of talent, time, and money are assured." Since suburban residential neighborhoods tended to segregate housing by income level, they implicitly enforced middle-class standards of decorum and gentility. Although the immediate visual setting of the suburban residence seemed to promise personal independence, its larger social context provided a mechanism for mutual social supervision.[15]

The suburbs were indeed a place "where small groups of congenial people could meet in untrammeled association," secure in their understanding that the bourgeois respectability of their neighbors was largely assured. Suburban social life helped usher in what Emily Post would soon call "the era of informality." From the 1880s on, the central ceremonial ritual of the Victorian parlor—the formal call—was coming under increasing attack; by 1895, according to *Ladies' Home Journal*, it survived only in the visit of congratulation or condolence. At the same time, new social forms were emerging. Chief among these was the afternoon tea (called a kettledrum through the 1880s), whose purpose was "to dispense with formal etiquette"; other popular entertainments included the social breakfast, the ladies' luncheon ("A luncheon is ever the most cozy, friendly and informal manner of entertaining a few special favorites"), the informal dinner or "stand-up supper," and the evening party. On all such occasions, "Formality was entirely banished."[16] In their quest for novel entertainments, women's magazines offered suggestions for introducing summerhouse social forms into the suburb and even the city: holding "at homes" on the lawn or the veranda, giving alfresco dinners, even staging a "Campers' Reunion Dinner" (complete with a table centerpiece simulating a campfire) for people who had camped together the previous summer in the Adirondacks, or a "Farmers' Picnic in Winter" at which the guests were to wear denim overalls and calico dresses. As Lillian Hart Tryon observed, "Life is too full to have patience with formalities. The cry of the time is for few friends and good ones." Therefore, "we are fast becoming a parlorless nation."[17]

[16] Emily Post, *Etiquette in Society, in Business, in Politics and at Home* (New York: Funk and Wagnalls, 1922), p. 81. *Ladies' Home Journal* articles include those by Mrs. Burton Harrison, "The Small Courtesies of Social Life," 12, no. 4 (March 1895): 10; Mrs. M. E. W. Sherwood, "Afternoon Tea," 6, no. 2 (January 1889): 15; Mrs. Burton Kingsland, " 'A Forget-me-not' Luncheon," 11, no. 8 (July 1894): 22; Eliza R. Parker, "Informal Dinners," 5, no. 10 (September 1888): 11, "Informal Evening Parties," 6, no. 3 (February 1889): 11; and Mary Barrett Brown, "A Stand-up Supper," 8, no. 3 (February 1891): 31. See also Mrs. M. L. Rayne, *Written for You; or, The Art of Beautiful Living* (Detroit: Tyler, 1882), p. 218; "Company Giving and Receiving: Breakfasts," *Good Housekeeping* 12, no. 6 (June 1891): 289; "Novelties in Social Entertainments," *Good Housekeeping* 8, no. 7 (February 2, 1889): 159.

[17] Lillian Hart Tryon, as quoted in Lynes, *Domesticated Americans*, p. 154. *Ladies' Home Journal* offered suggestions by Christine Terhune Herrick, "All the Year Round in the Home," 5, no. 7 (June 1888): 2; Mrs. Roger, "Menus for Picnics, Garden Parties and Excursions," 15, no. 7 (June 1899): 30; Francis S. Hobbes, "A Novel Idea for Veranda Parties," 15, no. 9 (August 1898): 2, "Tables Set for Special Occasions," 16, no. 11 (October 1899): 9; and E. Leora Waldemen, "A Farmers' Picnic in Winter," 14, no. 4 (March 1897): 18. See also "Company Giving and Receiving: The Garden Fete," *Good Housekeeping* 13, no. 1 (July 1891): 10.

The suburban architecture of the housing boom that occurred between 1890 and 1930 both reflected and enforced this new middle-class understanding of the social function of the house. In response to both the new minimalist aesthetic and the demand for more economical housing, the ready-cut housing industry—largely responsible for the boom that approximately doubled home ownership in many communities—provided house plans that were simple in form and compact in layout. In the first major change in floor plans since the mid eighteenth century, the entrance hall dwindled and, in many houses, disappeared entirely; the vestibule was transformed into a mere closet; and the front and back parlors were merged into a single living room, which was often entered directly through the front door. By 1910 the typical two-story house had a first-floor plan consisting of living room, dining room, and kitchen. In many plans, the living room opened directly into the dining room through a wide doorway or the two rooms were fully combined. Gone was the back stairway that had concealed from the eyes of respectable guests the activities of household servants; the dramatic decline in the number of servants employed in middle-class households and the shift from live-in to live-out help made less necessary the rigid separation of the back regions of the house from the front. The person most likely to usher a visitor directly into the living room of the new suburban house was not a servant, but a member of the family.[18]

This new arrangement of domestic space was evident in the three major types of suburban houses built between 1890 and 1930—the foursquare, the homestead temple, and the bungalow—but it was best exemplified in the last and most dominant of the three. The bungalow, a small, unpretentious house with California connotations of naturalness and informality, was first promoted as an ideal summer cottage, but after 1900 it rose to prominence as a suburban housing type, expanding rapidly across the nation. It was a one- or one-and-one-half-story house with a low, sweeping roof and a veranda, generally characterized by an openness to the outdoors and an interpenetration of interior spaces, designed to generate an effect of roominess within a minimum of space. Instead of a parlor it had a living room, which was almost

[18] See Alan Gowans, *The Comfortable House: North American Suburban Architecture, 1890–1930* (Cambridge, Mass.: MIT Press, 1986), chap. 2; Clark, *American Family Home*, chap. 5, p. 191; Wright, *Building the Dream*, chap. 9; Bronner, *Grasping Things*, pp. 54–63; and David M. Katzman, *Seven Days a Week: Women and Domestic Service in Industrializing America* (Urbana: University of Illinois Press, 1981), pp. 52–55, 87–94.

always entered directly from the veranda through the front door. The living room opened through a wide archway into the dining room, beyond which the kitchen itself was often visible. This living room was not a specialized domestic space comparable to the parlor; it was regarded as the heart of the house, a casual, comfortable, homey room open to all. Henry L. Wilson's *Bungalow Book* (1910) described the living room as "the room where the family gathers, and in which the visitor feels at once the warm homelike hospitality. Everything should suggest comfort and restfulness."[19]

Between 1900 and 1930, Wilson's characterization of the living room as a place of warmth and comfort came to be widely shared. The new living room essentially combined the functions of two more specialized Victorian rooms: the parlor, where outside visitors were received; and the sitting room, where the family gathered in privacy, protected from the intrusions of outsiders by the vestibule, hall, and parlor. But in the living room, family recreation clearly took precedence over the entertainment of guests, despite its openness to invasion from without. If the parlor was the "face" of the house, the living room was repeatedly called "the heart of the house," "just the sort of cheerful, cozy, sunny, restful place you will be glad to turn to whenever the occasion arises." Most important, as one interior decorating manual after another intoned, "the living room is meant to live in." It thus required an entirely different approach to interior decoration; there was to be "no striving for effect." *House Beautiful* explained this new aesthetic in 1898: the drawing room, that "old gold-and-brocaded over-decorated horror of yesterday," was a "show-room" that violated the very concept of "home." But at last, this writer continued, it was understood that "one of the first requisites of making a home out of a house is staying in it as much as possible; living things into shape, as it were, and making them adapt themselves to look like one."[20]

---

[19] See Gowans, *Comfortable House*, pp. 74–83, chap. 4; and Henry L. Wilson, as quoted in Robert Winter, *The California Bungalow* (Los Angeles: Hennessey and Ingalls, 1980), p. 48. See also Clay Lancaster, *The American Bungalow, 1880–1930* (New York: Abbeville Press, 1985); and Clark, *American Family Home*, chap. 6.

[20] Charles E. White, Jr., *Successful Houses and How to Build Them* (New York: Macmillan, 1912), p. 101; Frank Alvah Parsons, *Interior Decoration: Its Principles and Practice* (1915; reprint, Garden City, N.Y.: Doubleday, Doran, 1931), p. 6; Jane Porter, "Looking into Other Women's Homes," *Ladies' Home Journal* 33, no. 1 (January 1916): 31; Mary Abbott, "Individuality in Homes," *House Beautiful* 3, no. 3 (February 1898): 91–92.

Here was the entering wedge of "personal decorating." Arbiters of home decoration in the 1880s and 1890s had frequently emphasized the importance of individuality and offered dozens of ways to achieve it: homemade objects, stenciled walls, photographs and albums, travel memorabilia, architectural mottoes (for example, A Man's Home Is His Castle carved over the fireplace), and the transformation of objects for new uses. Not until the late 1890s, however, was the term *personality* generally used to characterize the summum bonum of home decoration. As expressed by *House Beautiful* in 1899, people were "beginning to see that houses and furniture, no less than dress and manners, must become a part of that unspoken language by which we communicate our tastes and ideas; in short, that the *expression of personality* is the thing to be aimed at."[21] The truly lived-in house, whose heart was in the right place—in the living room—was a house that expressed not the character, but the personality of its residents.

By 1930 the concept of the "personality of homes" had become commonplace in interior decoration. Its development over time and its historical relationship to the living room may be traced through an examination of three of the most important works on interior decoration during this period: novelist Edith Wharton and Boston architect Ogden Codman's *Decoration of Houses* (1897); Elsie de Wolfe's *House in Good Taste* (1913); and Emily Post's *Personality of a House* (1930). Although *The Decoration of Houses* was expressly directed at the wealthiest classes, it sold well for many years because of the growing middle-class interest in interior decoration. Its central argument was "only a return to architectural principles can raise the decoration of houses to the level of the past." Since interior decoration should properly be considered a branch of the architectural art, any ornamentation that disguised or ignored the main lines of a room was in the poorest taste. Wharton and Codman were especially critical of such late Victorian standbys as overdressed windows, portieres, lambrequins, drapery around the fireplace, excessive bric-a-brac, and any object for a purpose other than its original

---

[21] See Clark, *American Family Home*, chap. 4; Co-operative Building Plan Association, *How to Build, Furnish, and Decorate* (New York: Robert W. Shoppel, 1883), p. 20; Abbott, "Individuality in Homes"; Alice M. Kellogg, "Individuality in Guest-Rooms," *House Beautiful* 3, no. 5 (April 1898): 170–71; "Attractive Ideas for Boys' Rooms," *Ladies' Home Journal* 16, no. 11 (October 1899): 21; and "On the Relation of Domestic Architecture to Furniture Design," *House Beautiful* 5, no. 4 (March 1899): 179.

one. As part of their quest for "architectural sincerity," Wharton and Codman also lamented the "shut-up 'best parlor' " as "a costly sham" because it was designed not for living, but "for the edification of visitors." The "dreary drawing-room" that in many town houses provided "the only possible point of reunion for the family" was too often a room of "exquisite discomfort." *The Decoration of Houses* advocated the "salon de famille," or family apartment, a "room in which people should be made comfortable" with plenty of chairs, small tables, lamps, and whatever else was necessary so that people "are not forced to take refuge in their bedrooms for lack of fitting arrangements in the drawing rooms."[22]

Despite this clear step toward the development of the living room in 1897, Wharton and Codman were severely displeased by the contemporary movement toward a more open house plan, warning, "The tendency to merge into one any two apartments designed for different uses shows a retrogression in house-planning." Privacy was "one of the first requisites of civilized life," yet privacy was lost "if the drawing-room be a part of the hall and the library a part of the drawing-room." They deplored the fate of the interior door, which had first been slid into the wall, then replaced by portieres, and finally removed entirely from interior doorways; and they felt compelled to remind their readers that "while the main purpose of the [outer] door is to admit, its secondary purpose is to exclude. The outer door, which separates the hall or vestibule from the street, should clearly proclaim itself an effectual barrier." But Wharton and Codman reserved their strongest condemnation for what they called the "abnormal development of the modern staircase-hall" into a kind of living room. They wrote that a proper hall served as "the introduction to the living-room of the house . . . like a public square in relation to the private houses around it" (fig. 4).[23]

Thus, *The Decoration of Houses* in 1897 stopped well short of accepting the new open-plan house whose heart, the living room, was open to all who entered. The enduring Victorian sensibility of Wharton and Codman resulted not only from their upper-class inclinations toward social formalism but also from their urban perspective. The houses that concerned them were located in the city, where outer doors did indeed

---

[22] Grey, "Considerations of the Home," p. 153; Edith Wharton and Ogden Codman, Jr., *The Decoration of Houses* (1897; reprint, New York: Charles Scribner's Sons, 1926), pp. 198, 62, 88, 20, 127.

[23] Wharton and Codman, *Decoration of Houses*, pp. 111–12, 22, 103, 115–16.

Fig. 4. Antechamber, Durazzo Palace, Genoa, late eighteenth century. From Edith Wharton and Ogden Codman, Jr., *The Decoration of Houses* (New York: Charles Scribner's Sons, 1926), pl. 29.

serve as barriers against the socially undesirable, even for the more solidly middle class, and where staircase halls remained testing zones for the social acceptability of applicants for admission. The proper house did not immediately open its innermost living space to just any visitor, nor did it make any personal statement about the inner life of its inhabitants. For all their concern about "sincerity," Wharton and Codman made no reference to the "personality" of interior decoration. They did observe that, in decorating a room, "the individual tastes and habits of the people who are to occupy it must be taken into account." But their primary concern was to set forth classical standards of proportion and design drawn from the past—drawn, in fact, from some of the most elaborate interiors in the history of Western civilization (rooms such as the ballroom of the Royal Palace at Genoa or a bathroom in the Pitti Palace at Florence), which provided illustrations for their text. To this day, old wealth is far more concerned with decorating homes according to classic standards of taste and propriety than with the art of personal self-expression through interior decoration.[24]

[24] Wharton and Codman, *Decoration of Houses*, p. 17; Pratt, "House as Expression."

The Decoration of Houses proved to be a major influence on the woman who largely invented the vocation of interior decorator in the first decade of the twentieth century: Elsie de Wolfe, the one-time actress and social climber whose magazine articles on interior decoration established her reputation as an influential tastemaker even before *The House in Good Taste* was published in 1913. In her book, de Wolfe drew freely and without acknowledgment from Wharton and Codman, placing her central emphasis on the principles of suitability, simplicity, and proportion and asserting that the architecture of a room should be its major decoration. She shared Wharton and Codman's attitude toward ornament, deploring the "heterogeneous mass of ornamental 'period' furniture and bric-a-brac bought to make a room 'look cozy,' " and caustically criticized the late Victorian drawing room with its "bastard collection of gilt chairs and tables, over-elaborate draperies shutting out both light and air, and huge and frightful paintings." Like Wharton and Codman, de Wolfe retained a Victorian sensibility about the specialization of interior space: "Who that has read Henry James's remarkable article on the vistas dear to the American hostess, our portiere-hung spaces, guiltless of doors and open to every draft, can fail to feel how much better our conversation might be were we not forever conscious that between our guests and the greedy ears of our servants there is nothing but a curtain!" She advised against making a living room of the hall, which "is, after all, of public access, not only to the living-rooms but to the street."[25] De Wolfe, it should be noted, lived in New York City.

Nonetheless, in 1913 de Wolfe had a more fully developed appreciation of the living room than Wharton and Codman had in 1897. "The living room!" she rhapsodized: "Shut your eyes a minute and think what that means: A room to *live* in, suited to all human needs.

[25] Elsie de Wolfe, *The House in Good Taste* (New York: Century Co., 1913), pp. 26, 84, 132. "This diffused vagueness of separation between apartments, between hall and room, between one room and another, between the one you are in and the one you are not in, between place of passage and place of privacy, is a provocation to despair. . . . Thus we see systematized the indefinite extension of all spaces and the definite merging of all functions; the enlargement of every opening, the exaggeration of every passage, the substitution of gaping arches and far perspectives and resounding voids for enclosing walls, for practicable doors, for controllable windows, for all the rest of the essence of the room-character, that room-suggestion which is so indispensable not only to occupation and concentration, but to conversation itself, to the play of the social relation at any other pitch than the pitch of a shriek or a shout" (Henry James, *The American Scene* [Bloomington: Indiana University Press, 1968], pp. 166–67).

Fig. 5. Living room, C. W. Harkness house, Morristown, N.J. From Elsie de Wolfe, *The House in Good Taste* (New York: Century Co., 1913), p. 149.

. . . Listen a minute while I tell you how I see such a room: Big and restful, making for comfort first and always; a little shabby here and there, perhaps, but all the more satisfactory for that—like an old shoe that goes on easily. Lots of light by night, and not too much drapery to shut out the sunlight by day. Big, welcoming chairs, rather sprawly, and long sofas. A big fire blazing on the open hearth" (fig. 5). In the houses of the well-to-do, such a room would not necessarily preclude a great entrance hall, a formal drawing room for receiving guests, a music room, and a more intimate boudoir. But unlike Wharton and Codman, de Wolfe mixed advice on small apartments and middle-class suburban houses with advice on the houses of the wealthy and recognized that in more modest homes the living room would serve a variety of functions: "The living-room in the modern bungalow, for instance, is often din-ing-room, library, hall, music-room, filling all the needs of the fam-ily."[26] Her recommendation for such moderate houses was that they provide some kind of smaller room—a study, library, breakfast or tea

[26] De Wolfe, *House in Good Taste*, pp. 148, 151.

room, or music room—as a retreat from the living room.

Concerning the decoration of the living room, de Wolfe was an early proponent of personal decorating: "Your living-room should grow out of the needs of your daily life. There could be no two living-rooms exactly alike in scheme if they were lived in. . . . The room will gradually find itself, though it may take years and heartache and a certain self-confession of inadequacy. It will express your life, if you use it, so be careful of the life you live in it!" Interior decoration, she observed repeatedly, expressed the personality of the woman (or, in rare cases, the man) of the house: "A house is a dead-give-away, anyhow, so you should arrange it so that the person who sees your personality in it will be reassured, not disconcerted." Like many interior decorators of the 1970s and 1980s, de Wolfe was more than a little obsessed with the self-revelatory powers of home interiors: "We are sure to judge a woman in whose house we find ourselves for the first time, by her surroundings. We judge her temperament, her habits, her inclinations, by the interior of her home." She entertained a somewhat voyeuristic fantasy of one day being admitted to a dozen similar "drawing-rooms, twelve stories deep, in a modern apartment house" to see what they would express about their inhabitants: "It isn't often our luck to see all twelve of the rooms, but sometimes we see three or four of them, and how amazingly different they are! How amusing is the suggestion of personality, or lack of it!" De Wolfe was not reticent to reveal her own "personality" in *The House in Good Taste* by offering illustrations of rooms in her own home and identifying some of them as those occupied by Elizabeth Marbury, who was probably her lover.[27] As a former actress, international traveler, and extravagant hostess, a woman celebrated for standing on her head at parties and for originating the fashion of dyeing hair blue, de Wolfe apparently had no fear that her readers would uncover any lack of personality in the rooms of her own home.

[27] De Wolfe, *House in Good Taste*, pp. 157–58, 22, 18–21, 170. For this view of the relationship between de Wolfe and Marbury, who lived together on and off for about a quarter of a century, see Jane S. Smith, *Elsie de Wolfe: A Life in the High Style* (New York: Atheneum Publishers, 1982), p. xv. I do not wish to argue that de Wolfe was making an explicit statement of her sexuality in *House in Good Taste*, although her publication of the photographs of Marbury's rooms does invite speculation in view of her assertion that a "house is a dead-give-away" of "personality," the private, idiosyncratic self. My own point is simply that de Wolfe did not shrink from opening up the private regions of her own home to the public gaze.

It is difficult to imagine Edith Wharton undertaking deliberately to reveal her "personality" by publishing photographs of her own private rooms. But de Wolfe's precedent in this matter was followed by Emily Post in a work whose title demonstrates the full arrival of "personal decorating": *The Personality of a House* (1930). Its central argument was that your house's "personality should express your personality, just as every gesture you make—or fail to make—expresses your gay animation or your restraint, your old-fashioned conventions, your perplexing mystery, or your emancipated modernism—whichever characteristics are typically yours." Post elaborated far more fully than de Wolfe the range of personal characteristics expressible in a house, including formality or casualness, sociability or solitude, the love of adventure or the love of home, and simplicity or stylishness. She also went further than de Wolfe by attributing a personality to the house itself, which she defined as "the quality that appeals not merely to our critical faculties but to our personal emotions." Most desirable in her view was "the house of inviting personality," the house of "charm" that "enchants" all who enter. To illustrate her point, in the first chapter she offered her readers a photograph of the "Front Door of Author's Massachusetts Home" and explained, "a front door of lovely design and perfect scale is like a beautiful hand held out in welcome."[28] The well-known author of *Etiquette: The Blue Book of Social Usage* (published eight years earlier, in 1922) thus warmly invited her readers to enter simultaneously her new book, her favorite house, and her own personality (fig. 6).

Not surprisingly, in light of this emphasis on the inviting quality of the house, Post largely accepted the open-house plan that had come to dominate domestic architecture by 1930. As the daughter of Bruce Price, architect and planner of Tuxedo Park in New York, Post had spent childhood summers at that exclusive country resort and was thus early accustomed to the social security of suburban living. She did, however, offer her readers a wide range of options for arranging first-floor front social space, including the formal entrance hall with dressing rooms, the reception room, the drawing room, the hall living room, and the living room. She described these options in terms of the "temperaments" of the different rooms, ranging from the utterly impersonal

[28] Emily Post, *The Personality of a House: The Blue Book of Home Design and Decoration* (New York: Funk and Wagnalls, 1930), pp. 3, 1, 10, 7.

Fig. 6. Hall, Arthur C. Holden and Associates, architects. From Emily Post, *The Personality of a House: The Blue Book of Home Design and Decoration* (New York: Funk and Wagnalls, 1930), pl. 1.

reception room (which was to contain no personal objects) to the most intensely personal option, the living room, and she advised her readers to make their choice on the basis of their own personality. But the tone of her discussion of temperamental alternatives revealed her own preference: "If you are innately formal, if you cannot endure to have anything out of place, if you like the conventional rather than the unconventional, if you have no inclination to sit otherwise than as at a dinner party or in a box at the opera," then a drawing room is for you. But if you want the company of your husband and children, she continued, and you want them to be comfortable, then you should choose the room that is "the very heart of the American home—the living room!"

Post's hymn to the living room rivaled de Wolfe's in enthusiasm as she evoked images of "a welcoming log fire," "a much-used desk and constantly sat-in chairs," plenty of books and magazines, sunshine and flowers, a dog or a cat on the rug near the hearth, and a domestic artifact that would have horrified de Wolfe: a baby playing with blocks on the floor. Post borrowed de Wolfe's old-shoe metaphor for the living room but upscaled it as befitted a woman to the manner born: "You know how well-worn, beautifully-polished hunting boots look? The perfect living-room should look the same: in no way worn through, but thoroughly easy and comfortable in fit—and with every evidence of having been long used and cared for." Such a room had more "personality" than any other, in Post's view, because it had been more lived in, and thus had been molded to the emotional temperaments of those who had lived in it, just as an old leather boot is molded to a foot. [29]

From *Decoration of Houses* through *House in Good Taste* to *Personality of a House*, changing views of the proper arrangement of domestic social space—notably the gradual acceptance of the living room as "the very heart of the American home"—were accompanied by a new approach to interior decoration that emphasized the power of the house to express the personality of its occupants. The full emergence of "personal decorating" in the first few decades of the twentieth century involved a dramatically new understanding of the meaning of domestic things, at the center of which was the concept of interior decoration as a form of language. As Frank Parsons explained in *Interior Decoration: Its Principles and Practice* (1915), "Man expresses his ideas or conveys his thoughts to others by means of language, and language consists of a set of symbols which serve to establish a standard system of communication between all persons by whom these symbols are understood." Interior decoration is one such standard system of communication: "Everything in furniture and furnishing means something. This elemental meaning is the expression of an idea, and it is quite simple to find other ideas which in combination express a whole." Parsons went on to compare interior decoration to the child's alphabet game in which the player draws a number of cardboard letters and tries to make words out of them: "Determine what you want your room to express when it is done,"

[29] See Edwin Post, *Truly Emily Post* (New York: Funk and Wagnalls, 1961), chap. 2; and Post, *Personality*, pp. 336, 340–41.

he advised, and then purchase only those "letters" that are required to make up the statement. "All this must be given in the language of colour, form, line and texture, governed by the principles which are the very structure of this language."[30]

This new semiotic approach to interior decoration involved a shift in emphasis from the Victorian concern with the moral self and its improvement to a modern concern with personal temperament and its self-expression. As *House Beautiful* had proclaimed in 1899, in the "unspoken language" of interior decoration, "the *expression of personality* is the thing to be aimed at." Early twentieth-century interior decorators believed that personal temperament was best expressed through the language of color; Amy Rolfe announced in 1917, "The whole trend of present-day decoration is toward the psychological use of color." Half a century earlier, Andrew Jackson Downing had assigned different temperamental qualities to colors—gray was formal, rose was cheerful, fawn was grave—but he had used these formulas for dictating the proper colors for different rooms: gray for the hall, rose for the drawing room, fawn for the library. By contrast, personal decorators asserted, "color lies close to the emotions" and argued, "there's a special color for every personality": red is warm, exciting, and aggressive; blue is cool, restrained, and formal; yellow is cheerful; green is serene and restful; orange is unsettling; purple is mysterious, sorrowful, and dignified. Although there was general agreement on the personal qualities of various colors, interior decorators disagreed over whether room colors should match or compensate for personal temperament. As Post put the question: "Let us say that you are a somewhat restless, overenthusiastic, excitement-loving person, and that the color you like best—as well as the one that expresses you—is orange-red. The question we now confront is whether you should be surrounded by the perpetual stimulant of red or should be grayed or quieted by the influence of blue or neutral tones instead. In other words, being yourself overcolorful by temperament, could you increase your own tendencies to the point where nervous breakdown threatens? Or could you find restfulness in other surroundings?" Post concluded that it was better to match than to complement one's own personality. But Ethel Davis Seal, author of *Furnishing the Little House* (1924), argued otherwise: "If you are despondent and inclined to be

---

[30] Parsons, *Interior Decoration*, pp. 17, 246, 247, 274.

morbid, you require plenty of happy, cheery yellow; if you are unambitious or phlegmatic, you require the tonic notes of brilliant red; if you are impulsive, nervous, inclined to be irritable or excitable, you should calm yourself with blue."[31] In either case, color was now regarded as an important kind of emotional sign within the sign system that was interior decoration and was to be chosen with reference to personality or emotional temperament.

After color, the second component of the language of interior decoration cited by Parsons was form. The new interior decorators were virtually unanimous in condemning nineteenth-century furnishings. In 1897 *House Beautiful* dismissed the entire Victorian period as "Early New Jersey," and Parsons in 1915 called it "analogous to those periods in one's life that he hesitates to discuss with anybody outside the immediate family." Even the late Victorian reactions to the excesses of the nineteenth-century parlor—Eastlake, arts and crafts, art nouveau, mission—fell under increasing criticism. But in 1918, *Handbook of Furniture Styles* announced, "At last we seem to have arrived happily at the point of realization that novelty does not necessarily mean advance, and we have begun to hark back to the best elements of the past, just as the masters of the Renaissance and the proponents of every classic revival have done."[32]

Interior decorators after 1890 turned to what they called "period" furnishings: Italian Renaissance, English Tudor and Jacobean, eighteenth-century French, and, above all, English Georgian and American colonial. To each historical period, they assigned temperamental meaning: French Renaissance represented luxury and comfort, English Tudor connoted heavy dignity, English Georgian suggested individual creativity, and American colonial radiated sincerity and hospitality. Once again, Downing half a century earlier had assigned different characteristics to period furnishings: the classical, Italian, Gothic, Romanesque, and other period styles were "each peculiarly capable of manifesting

[31] Amy L. Rolfe, *Interior Decoration for the Small Home* (New York: Macmillan, 1921), p. 6; Andrew Jackson Downing, *The Architecture of Country Houses*, ed. John C. Freeman (Watkins Glen, N.Y.: American Life Foundation, 1968), pp. 39–40; Ross Stewart and John Gerald, *Home Decoration: Its Problems and Solutions* (New York: Julian Messner, 1935), p. 53; "Do You Know How to Use Color in Your Home?" *Ladies' Home Journal* 37, no. 5 (May 1920): 206; Post, *Personality*, p. 200; Ethel Davis Seal, *Furnishing the Little House* (New York: Century Co., 1924), p. 67.

[32] Review of *The Art of the House* in *House Beautiful* 1, no. 4 (March 1897): 106–7; Parsons, *Interior Decoration*, pp. 216–17; Walter A. Dyer, *Handbook of Furniture Styles* (New York: Century Co., 1918), p. 139.

Fig. 7. "Modern" living room. From Frank Alvah Parsons, *Interior Decoration: Its Principles and Practice* (1915; reprint, Garden City, N.Y.: Doubleday, Doran, 1931), facing p. 234.

certain mental temperaments or organizations, or of harmonizing with certain tastes in the life of the individual." But he advised a unity of style within each room and suggested styles that should be adopted in particular rooms of the house: the social gaiety of the Italian style was suited to the drawing room, while the domestic gravity of the Gothic style made it appropriate for the library. By contrast, interior decorators in the early twentieth century advocated a mixture of period furnishings within each room as the best method of expressing the nuances of personality (fig. 7). *The Practical Book of Interior Decoration*, for example, criticized the "decorative archaeology" of furnishing an entire room in one period and argued that a mixture of periods would "reflect the occupant's personality, a condition that will afford vastly more interest and lively charm than any amount of simian exactitude in reproduction."[33]

[33] See Harold Donaldson Eberlein, Abbot McClure, and Edward Stratton Holloway, *The Practical Book of Interior Decoration* (Philadelphia: J. B. Lippincott Co., 1919), pt. 1; Parsons, *Interior Decoration*, chaps. 6–14; Ross Crane, *The Ross Crane Book of Home Furnishing and Decoration* (Chicago: Frederick J. Drake, 1925), p. 33; and Post, *Personality*, p. 267. Downing, *Architecture of Houses*, pp. 13, 24; Eberlein, McClure, and Holloway, *Book of Interior Decoration*, p. ix.

For this reason, interior decorating manuals began to offer detailed discussions of a wide range of period furnishings and the personal characteristics they represented, essentially providing their readers with a kind of lexicon of furniture forms from which they could select the appropriate terms in which to express their own personalities.

Although color and period furnishings were the two most important components of the new personal decorating that emerged between 1900 and 1930, interior decorators offered a number of other techniques for expressing personality in the home. One was the art of the

Fig. 8. Room with a "hunting personality," James W. O'Connor, architect. From Emily Post, *The Personality of a House: The Blue Book of Home Design and Decoration* (New York: Funk and Wagnalls, 1930), pl. 20.

"personal touch," using a few smaller articles such as pictures, photographs, objects of sentimental value, even ceramic pieces or flower arrangements, to make a personal statement. Any item that signaled personal hobbies or tastes—books, sporting prints, boat models, musical instruments—was believed to assist the domestic expression of personality. Post offered her readers an illustration of a "delightful room with a hunting personality," whose dominant decorative motif of fox hunting, detailed down to the foxtails hanging on the wall, was clearly intended to express something important about the man of the house (fig. 8).[34]

Another personal decorating technique might be called the organic method of interior decoration. It was best expressed in a *Ladies' Home Journal* article entitled "The Living Room that Grows": "I don't give much for a ready-made living room, a finished, smug, signed-and-sealed living room. . . . I like things that grow, whether they be flowers or people, souls, or homes. And as for a living room—why, the growing kind is the only kind to have!" The organic method demanded that furniture be bought separately rather than in sets; even dining room chairs should be "picked up delightfully from time to time," because a room thus furnished "is much more likely to interpret the fine personality of its owner." The organic approach assumed that every proper room was a living, breathing thing: "In every successful living-room, there must be the vital elements, some of the things that change from day to day, that have personality, life: lamps, books, flowers, open fires, mirrors, sunlight."[35]

The organic method of interior decoration was one expression of the tendency to anthropomorphize houses, rooms, and furnishings. Anna Browning Doughten wrote, "We found that rooms were like people," and Ross Crane asserted that anyone who exclaimed to the occupant, upon first seeing a room, "Why it looks just like you!" delivered "the highest possible compliment." Rolfe warned her readers that it might be some months before they could "really love" newly purchased fur-

[34] Post, *Personality*, pl. 20; Rolfe, *Interior Decoration*, p. xviii; Parsons, *Interior Decoration*, p. 249; Ekin Wallick, "The Little Personal Touch that Makes Your Home Attractive," *Ladies' Home Journal* 34, no. 10 (October 1917): 46.
[35] Ethel Davis Seal, "The Living Room that Grows," *Ladies' Home Journal* 37, no. 3 (March 1920): 205; Ethel Davis Seal, "Unmatching the Dining-Room Furniture," *Ladies' Home Journal* 37, no. 10 (October 1920): 197; Seal, *Furnishing the Little House*, p. 133.

nishings: "They may be beautiful and adapted to [your] personality and use, but there is no way to buy their friendship. The daily association, alone, can bring that." French blue, lamented Post, "is more impossible to manage than a temperamental opera singer, and more unamiable than Katherine the Shrew." Ross Stewart and John Gerald suggested arranging items on a mantel or a wall by choosing the "upward curved line" which resembles "a smiling face. The drooping line, like a frown, is to be avoided." Such anthropomorphic references are abundant in the literature of early twentieth-century interior decoration, but possibly the most revealing expression of this mentality was de Wolfe's autobiography, *After All* (1935), which made little reference either to Elizabeth Marbury or to the man de Wolfe had eventually married, but spoke emotionally of the bathroom in her Paris apartment.[36]

Even as personal decorators were learning to attribute human characteristics to rooms and furnishings, they sometimes treated the human occupants of these rooms as though they were part of the interior decoration. They did this by emphasizing the importance of interior decoration as the "background" against which "the family and one's friends must be exploited," "in varying conditions of feeling, appearance, and dress." Post stressed the importance of establishing "a background of personal becomingness," advising, for example, that a blue-eyed brunette introduce into her living room a blue cushion or chair that was "slightly deeper than the shade of her eyes." In such a case, the background of the room was clearly intended to enhance the appearance of the occupant. But Post also described a woman's boudoir decorated in shades of black, silver, orchid, magenta, and green, in which "the exotic beauty's own hair—actually, and in the portrait— would supply the missing accent of yellow-orange that completes the triad of green and orchid and magenta."[37] Here Post reversed her priority: the presence of the woman was necessary to complete the color scheme; she was the domestic artifact required to perfect the interior design.

Drawing on Philip Rieff's observation, "as cultures change so do the modal types of persons who are their bearers," Warren Susman

---

[36] Anna Browning Doughten, "Nancy's First Housekeeping," *Ladies' Home Journal* 22, no. 6 (May 1905): 31; Crane, *Book of Home Furnishing*, p. 225; Rolfe, *Interior Decoration*, p. xx; Post, *Personality*, p. 172; Stewart and Gerald, *Home Decoration*, p. 13; Smith, *Elsie de Wolfe*, p. 267.

[37] Parsons, *Interior Decoration*, p. 41; Post, *Personality*, pp. 196, 182.

argued that the transition from Victorian to modern American culture involved the replacement of the nineteenth-century concept of the self as "character" with the twentieth-century concept of "personality." The culture of character had focused on moral concerns and preached the virtues of self-control; the new culture of personality was more concerned with emotional temperament and with the techniques of self-expression. Character had embodied a uniform standard of conduct based on fixed principles; personality was more a matter of individual idiosyncrasies, personal needs, and interests. Nineteenth-century character had been associated with reputation, duty, honor, and integrity; its aim was to be respected. Twentieth-century personality connoted magnetic attraction, fascination, aura, and charm; personality endeavored to be liked. As Susman argued, this major change in the American concept of the modal self was essential to the transformation of a producer-oriented society, which rested on the virtues of self-denial, into a mass consumer society, with its new reliance on demands for self-fulfillment.[38]

Given the critical relationship between social environment and the modal self, it is not coincidental that a major transformation in domestic space occurred just as *character* was being replaced by *personality* as the goal of individual development for middle-class Americans. As folklorist Henry Glassie has observed: "The skins of houses are shallow things that people are willing to change, but people are most conservative about the spaces they must utilize, and in which they must exist. Build the walls of anything, deck them out with anything, but do not change the arrangement of the rooms or their proportions. In these volumes—bounded by surfaces from which a person's senses rebound to him—his psyche develops; disrupt them, and you disrupt him."[39] The replacement of the parlor with the living room and the larger rearrangement of domestic space surrounding that change in the period around 1900 involved a historical "psychic disruption" in the American modal self.

The nineteenth-century parlor had encouraged a clear distinction

---

[38] Susman, "Personality," p. 273; T. J. Jackson Lears, "From Salvation to Self-Realization: Advertising and the Therapeutic Roots of the Consumer Culture, 1880–1930," in *The Culture of Consumption: Critical Essays in American History, 1880–1980*, ed. Richard Wightman Fox and T. J. Jackson Lears (New York: Pantheon Books, 1983), pp. 1–38; Jackson Lears, "Beyond Veblen: Rethinking Consumer Culture in America," elsewhere in this volume. See also Bronner, *Grasping Things*; and Simon J. Bronner, "Object Lessons: The Work of Ethnological Museums and Collections," elsewhere in this volume.

between the public and the private self, demanding perfect moral restraint by those who sat erect upon its horsehair sofas and exchanged the ritualistic gestures of the formal call, yet permitting genteel guests to retreat to the sitting room or other private rooms of the house to seek freedom from self-restraint. But the living room collapsed that distinction between the public and the private self by dragging the private self out on center stage, exposing it to any and all visitors, and insisting that it be open, warm, and charming. Parlor culture, with its view of the front room as the "face" of the house, tacitly acknowledged that it was not always convenient or desirable to be "at home" to visitors. But living room culture, which insisted on throwing open the "heart" of the house to outsiders, offered no such mechanism; the "performing self" of personality was always on.[40] In short, the hidebound horsehair-and-black-walnut parlor did not merely express the ideal of character, it actually shaped character. And the cheerful, cozy, hospitable living room emerged along with the new concept of personality as a crucial mechanism for its development.

The new interior decoration that accompanied this reorganization of middle-class domestic space made its own contribution to the culture of personality by offering a new understanding of the meaning of domestic things. Ironically the full emergence of mass consumer society in the early twentieth century did not usher in a period of domestic accumulation for its own sake—called "conspicuous consumption" by Thorstein Veblen in *The Theory of the Leisure Class* (1899). The new living room was itself a product, in part, of the post-Victorian revulsion from the riotous materialism of the late nineteenth-century parlor. For the arbiters of interior decoration in the first decades of this century, less was more. But even as middle-class Americans began to foreswear the indiscriminate accumulation of domestic things, they were attributing more and more power to those things they chose to display. As the irrepressible Elsie de Wolfe announced in 1913, "I believe most firmly in the magic power of inanimate objects!"—powers of magnetism, vitality, aura, and fascination—because she saw in them a reflection of her own personality. Her love of mirrors is particularly revealing: "Whenever you can manage it, place your mirror so that it will reflect some particularly nice object," because "so much" of a house's charm is the effect

---

[40] Susman, "Personality," p. 280.

of skillfully managed reflections." Clearly, de Wolfe's mirrors not only doubled the impact of the "particularly nice objects" carefully placed in front of them; they also reflected the interior decorator herself, standing before them in admiration of her choice.[41]

Emily Post stated most directly the new connection between personality and domestic things: "The personal method of furnishing is to build each room on those objects that belong to each of us; things that would subtract from the sum of our personality were they taken away." The replacement of the parlor with the living room had collapsed the distinction between the public and the private self; the new focus of interior decoration collapsed the distinction between the self and the commodities surrounding it. *The New Interior Decoration* graphically expressed this view in 1929, noting, "this desire to adorn the place in which we live" is "an assertion of personality: like the wax comb of the bee and the thin web of the spider, our homes are in a sense a projection of ourselves."[42] The stuff of interior decoration outwardly may take the form of sofas and tables, curtains and paint, but in reality, in the twentieth-century view, it is material spun out of the personal psychic gut of those who consume such domestic things.

Victorian Americans were deeply involved with domestic things because they represented abstract ideas and sentiments, expressed timeless truths about art and truth and beauty, and purportedly contributed to the moral improvement of those who lived among them. Post-Victorians have come to revere domestic things because they "would subtract from the sum of our personality were they taken away." The self-referential quality of this view was evident in de Wolfe's exclamation on first catching sight of the Parthenon: "It's beige—my color!"[43] The conviction that the things around us are reflections of our essential, idiosyncratic selves, and that our possession of them ensures the vitality and charm of our personality, has proved a potent force behind the twentieth-century culture of consumption.

---

[41] De Wolfe, *House in Good Taste*, pp. 137, 140, 48.

[42] Post, *Personality*, p. 276; Dorothy Todd and Raymond Mortimer, *The New Interior Decoration: An Introduction to Its Principles, and International Survey of Its Methods* (New York: Charles Scribner's Sons, 1929), p. 1.

[43] Smith, *Elsie de Wolfe*, p. xv.

The Culture of Imperial Abundance

World's Fairs in the Making of American Culture

Robert W. Rydell

"World exhibitions are the sites of pilgrimages to the commodity fetish," cultural critic Walter Benjamin declared a half century ago. Over the last two decades, scholars have increasingly recognized this connection between international exhibitions and an emerging consumer society. Neil Harris has drawn attention to the close relationship between fairs and the rise of department stores and art museums, while Rosalind Williams describes fairs as fountainheads for the "dream world of mass consumption." Cultural theorist Umberto Eco has called the world's fair the "Missa Solemnis of capitalist culture." More recently, Burton Benedict and Warren Susman have addressed the ritualistic nature of fairs. Benedict, following the lead of Mary Douglas, likens fairs to potlatches—ritualistic displays of goods and power. Susman, drawing on Victor Turner's ideas about liminality, argues that fairs "were rites of passage for American society which made possible the full acceptance of a new way of life, new values, and a new social organization." Meanwhile, Alan Trachtenberg, reflecting on the 1893 World's Columbian Exposition in Chicago, has underscored the significance of that fair as "an ideal shape of an incorporated America." While agreeing with these assessments, I want to call attention to an important, perhaps overriding characteristic of America's turn-of-the-century fairs. Fairs promised material abundance and made the promise of abundance contingent on the acquisition, maintenance, and growth of empire. In the world projected by America's turn-of-the-century fairs, there was one overarching lesson: to be a "people of plenty" meant accepting "empire as a way of life."[1]

To promote this idea, exposition managers, with the active cooperation of the federal government, turned their enterprises into powerful organizing processes. First, exposition authorities organized themselves and modeled their enterprises after corporations. Second, they set up departments of publicity and promotion to keep information about the fairs in the national press. Simultaneously, exposition sponsors turned to a cadre of exhibition specialists, often trained scientists, to develop exhibit classifications for the tons of anticipated exhibit materials. Within the taxonomies of racial and material progress that scientists and businessmen created for the fairs, particular displays of "things" and people—including exhibits assembled for midway shows—were developed to give visual evidence to the equation of abundance and empire. Equally important, the process of organization spiraled down from exposition headquarters into the hands of state and local committees in communities as far away as those in Montana. In important ways, William McKinley, the president who lost his life in the cause of expositions, was right: expositions—and not just souvenirs—entered the home.

---

[1] Walter Benjamin, "Paris, Capital of the Nineteenth Century," in Walter Benjamin, *Reflections, Essays, Aphorisms, Autobiographical Writings*, ed. Peter Demetz and trans. Edmund Jephcott (New York: Harper and Row, 1978), p. 151; Neil Harris, "Museums, Merchandising, and Popular Taste: The Struggle for Influence," in *Material Culture and the Study of American Life*, ed. Ian M. G. Quimby (New York: W. W. Norton, 1978), pp. 140–74; Rosalind H. Williams, *Dream Worlds: Mass Consumption in Late Nineteenth-Century France* (Berkeley: University of California Press, 1982), pp. 58–106; Umberto Eco, *Travels in Hyper-Reality: Essays*, trans. William Weaver (1968; reprint, San Diego: Harcourt Brace Jovanovich, 1986), p. 294; Burton Benedict, *The Anthropology of World's Fairs* (Berkeley: University of California Press, 1983); Warren I. Susman, "Ritual Fairs," *Chicago History* 12, no. 3 (Fall 1983): 4–9; Alan Trachtenberg, *The Incorporation of America: Culture and Society in the Gilded Age* (New York: Hill and Wang, 1982), esp. pp. 8, 208–34; David M. Potter, *People of Plenty: Economic Abundance and the American Character* (Chicago: University of Chicago Press, 1954); William A. Williams, *Empire as a Way of Life* (New York: Oxford University Press, 1980). American fairs were not unique; see John M. Mackenzie, *Propaganda and Empire: The Manipulation of British Public Opinion, 1880–1960* (Manchester: Manchester University Press, 1984).

Finally, the material basis for the vision of the good life projected by the fairs did not vanish at the close of the expositions. In addition to much-discussed architectural forms and City Beautiful plans which framed the urban and suburban landscape of America, fairs generated tons of exhibit materials that found a permanent home in museums. One such museum, the now-forgotten Philadelphia Commercial Museum, was founded to institutionalize and perpetuate the gospel of empire and abundance promulgated at the World's Columbian Exposition and subsequent international fairs. Organized against the backdrop of depressions and industrial violence, America's fairs, like the corporations they were modeled after, moved vertically and horizontally, integrating American culture in the process.

Imperial Abundance

A common misperception of America's international fairs is that they exhibited only such commodities as dynamos, reapers, corn palaces, guns, and household furnishings and such eye-catchers as a state seal made of beans, a California mission built with oranges, or the Brooklyn Bridge constructed from soap (figs. 1, 2). These and similar items were on display and did impress visitors, but spectacles of gigantic Vulcans superintending a mining operation and examples of flush toilets, floral tea trays, and woolens existed as part of a broader universe of exhibits that included human beings. In fact, woven into the dream world of goods was a hierarchical continuum of material and racial progress that signified nothing so much as the distance traveled from "savagery" to "civilization." In a world alive with social Darwinian ideas of evolution, displays of material and natural abundance became an outward sign of inward racial "fitness" and culture.[2]

This facet of the bourgeois fantasy world, apparent at all American fairs clustered around the century's turn, came into particularly sharp focus at the 1904 Louisiana Purchase Exposition held in St. Louis. Occupying an acreage larger than any world's fair before or since, the St. Louis exposition boasted the usual array of goods on display. Visitors

[2] Examination of the fairs as vehicles for popularizing scientific racism can be found in Robert W. Rydell, *All the World's a Fair: Visions of Empire at American International Expositions, 1876–1916* (Chicago: University of Chicago Press, 1984).

Fig. 1. Corn Palace, Louisiana Purchase Exposition, St. Louis, 1904. (Library of Congress.)

took notes as they walked or were wheeled in roller chairs along miles of exhibit cases filled with commodities. These exhibits, however well attended, were not necessarily the most popular. That distinction fell to the Philippines Reservation, an exhibit of 1,200 Filipinos living at the center of the fairgrounds (fig. 3). Henry Adams may have been bewitched by the machines he saw in Machinery Hall, but oral histories conducted by the Missouri Historical Society suggest that many fairgoers were transfixed by the Filipinos, especially the scantily clad Igorots.[3]

[3] Rydell, *All the World's a Fair*, pp. 154–83; Henry Adams, *The Education of Henry Adams*, ed. Ernest Samuels (1907; reprint, Boston: Houghton Mifflin Co., 1961), p. 466.

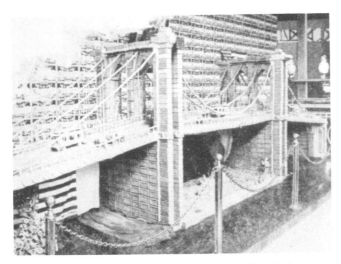

Fig. 2. Brooklyn Bridge in Soaps, World's Columbian
Exposition, Chicago, 1893. From Hubert Howe Bancroft,
The Book of the Fair, vol. 1 (Chicago: Bancroft Co., 1894),
p. 164. (Cooper-Hewitt Museum.)

The Philippines Reservation, organized by the United States government and located immediately adjacent to the American Indian Reservation, signaled the arrival of the United States as a world imperial
power. The exhibit indicated a willingness by the federal government
to compete with the colonial displays that European powers had been
building into European fairs since the 1851 London Crystal Palace
Exhibition. The magnitude of the Philippines exhibit—one of its organizers, William P. Wilson, director of the Commercial Museum, called
it "the largest and finest colonial exhibit ever made by any Government"—exalted American imperial prowess, while the juxtaposition of
the reservation to native Americans underlined continuities with America's expansionist past and with the national experience of subduing
"savage" populations. By giving the exhibit of Filipinos a central location within the broader world of goods displayed at the fair, the exhibit's
organizers created the impression that Filipinos not only would be producers and consumers in the American empire but also could be regarded
and manipulated as commodities themselves. By objectifying the Fili-

Fig. 3. Philippines Reservation, Louisiana Purchase Exposition, St. Louis, 1904. (Library of Congress.)

pinos, this exhibit also had the effect of confirming in white Americans a sense of their own racial and cultural superiority.[4]

Nonwhites on display at America's turn-of-the-century fairs were linked most closely to the natural world and were displayed as natural resources to be exploited as readily as mineral deposits. Banners above the United States government exhibit at the 1909 Alaska-Yukon-Pacific Exposition held in Seattle made that connection explicitly (fig. 4). Under the general heading Philippine Islands, two subgroups were arranged: one pointed to "The Natural Resources and the Primitive Peoples," while the other emphasized "The Development of the Natural Resources under Native Initiative." Depicted as resource rich and lacking the

[4] Richard Drinnon, *Facing West: The Metaphysics of Indian-Hating and Empire-Building* (New York: New American Library, 1980), pp. 333–51; Rydell, *All the World's a Fair*, pp. 154–83; William P. Wilson to Clarence Edwards, October 21, 1904, Records of the Bureau of Insular Affairs, file 6683–22, General Classified Files, Record Group 350, National Archives.

Fig. 4. Philippine Islands exhibit, Alaska-Yukon-Pacific Exposition, Seattle, 1909. From *Senate Document 671*, 61st Cong., 3d sess. (Washington, D.C., 1911). (Montana State University.)

material goods that anthropologists equated with civilization, "primitive" cultures on display had the effect of underwriting the predictions of a bountiful future for the "culture of abundance" and expansion of overseas markets forecast at the fair.[5]

It is important to emphasize that Filipino exhibits at the St. Louis and Seattle fairs were not unique. Beginning with the 1893 World's Columbian Exposition, every American international fair held through World War I included ethnological villages sanctioned by prominent anthropologists who occasionally organized university summer school courses around these displays. Whether one refers to the Seattle fair where schoolchildren poked Igorot women with straw or the Omaha,

[5] See, for example, *Official Catalogue: Philippine Exhibits* (St. Louis: Official Catalogue Co., 1904). The phrase "culture of abundance" is from Warren I. Susman, *Culture as History: The Transformation of American Society in the Twentieth Century* (New York: Pantheon Books, 1984), p. xx.

Buffalo, and St. Louis fairs where Geronimo sold his autograph for ten cents, the expositions, and especially the midways, gave millions of Americans firsthand experience with treating nonwhites from around the world as commodities.[6]

The midways, so important for introducing mass audiences to "junk food," "strip architecture," and an array of entertainments that would fuel the development of amusement parks, also gave world's fair audiences direct experience with an "evolving set of different relationships between advanced industrial societies and the rest of the world" that William Appleman Williams aptly targets as central to imperialism. Displayed alongside mechanical entertainments, wild animals, and thrill rides, the ethnological villages on the midways gave the impression that empire building could be fun. Set against displays of foodstuffs, clothing, and machine tools, the exhibits of "anthropology live" with "natives" working "primitive" handicrafts also created a powerful impression of foreign markets for American surplus production. To create that impression at the 1901 Pan-American Exposition in Buffalo, the managers of the Filipino village concession included several thatched-roof huts with "comfortable chairs and tables and even modern cooking stoves." Visitors could peer through the window of one hut and see a Filipino woman at work with a sewing machine.[7] Through such displays, the commodity fetish became an imperial fetish as well.

Advertising and Fairs

If the "culture of abundance" imagined by exposition promoters pivoted on dreams of empire, the success of the expositions hinged on attracting visitors and on informing the public generally about the view of the world on display at the fairs. Exposition organizers were up to the task. They established departments of publicity and promotion, usually staffed by local newspaper reporters, which flooded the nation with publicity releases, billboards, traveling shows, and speakers. The department of

---

[6] Death and disease characterized many ethnological villages; see, for example, "Hard on Eskimo," *Commercial* (Buffalo), May 8, 1901.

[7] Barbara Rubin, "Aesthetic Ideology and Urban Design," *Annals of the Association of American Geographers* 69, no. 3 (September 1979): 339–61; Williams, *Empire*, p. 7; Mable E. Barnes, "Peeps at the Exposition," 2:8–22, scrapbooks, Buffalo Historical Society.

publicity and promotion at the World's Columbian Exposition was modeled after a newspaper office and run by newspaper publisher Moses P. Handy, who hired a managing editor and a staff of trained reporters and translators to generate copy for publications around the world. As evidence of their importance, Handy's staff pointed out with pride that of the 5,314,000 words published about the fair before it opened, nearly half had come from their pens. Furthermore, Handy satisfied the demand by local editors for pictures. Reproductions of architectural plans and finished buildings were distributed to newspapers and magazines around the world. More important, Handy sponsored a competition for a bird's-eye view of the exposition grounds. Charles Graham's watercolor won the prize, and 100,000 reproductions—along with newspaper copy—were sent around the world, surprising travelers who allegedly discovered them in villages on the edge of the Sahara Desert.[8]

By the time of the St. Louis fair, the "press exploitation" bureau actually included two divisions, one devoted to domestic and the other to foreign promotion. The domestic bureau alone employed seventy-six persons, including twenty-six full-time reporters and editors, six stenographers, and numerous clerks. The director of the bureau, W. A. Kelso, summed up the scope of the bureau's activities:

[W]e furnished the press with from 10,000 to 20,000 words of reading matter daily, the average probably being 15,000 words, equivalent to over eight columns of solid non-pareil in one of our large daily papers. Mr. Stiffelmann, who had charge of the work of marking, cutting, and classifying what the domestic and foreign press had to say about our World's Fair, reports that he has filled 77 scrapbooks with clippings and partly filled 55 others, the amount of reading-matter pasted being 1,075,616 inches, or over 16 miles. Adding the loose clippings not yet pasted, we have a total of 2,009,106 inches, or nearly 32 miles of reading-matter about the World's Fair. Estimating eight lines to the inch and seven words to the line, we have 16,072,84 [*sic*] lines and 112,509,936 words. This record, as great as it is, represents only a very small portion of the newspaper publicity given the Exposition by the outside press.[9]

---

[8]Julian Ralph, "Exploiting the Great Fair," *Harper's Weekly* 36 (August 20, 1892): 806; "Advertising the World's Fair," *Monthly Review of Reviews* 7, no. 40 (May 1893): 452–53.
   [9]J. W. Buel, ed., *Louisiana and the Fair*, vol. 10 (St. Louis: World's Progress Publishing Co., 1905), pp. 3769–73.

When exposition managers tried to skimp on promotion, the results were often devastating. In the early stages of planning for Seattle's exposition, fair managers contacted the directors of the 1907 Jamestown Ter-Centennial fair and discovered that the indebtedness of the Jamestown corporation was $500,000, a sum greater than had been publicly announced. The source of the problem, they decided, had been a lack of advertising. The publicity office for the Jamestown fair had employed only a dozen press agents and had relied on five circus-style railroad cars to advertise the fair.[10]

The Jamestown experience was unusual. Buffalo's 1901 fair was advertised through a stereopticon concession at Atlantic City and by numerous 75-by-16-foot billboards located along railroad tracks in the vicinity of the city. In 1909 the number of billboards on vacant lots in Seattle became so great that residents complained to city officials. To drum up support for the 1897 Tennessee Centennial Exposition, the promotion department arranged for an exposition train to take some of the Chinese from the Chinese Village concession around Tennessee. The directors of the 1905 Portland fair hired a special agent to travel around the west promoting the Lewis and Clark Centennial. One historian of the Portland fair described the "boomer's" job, writing, "he shared worn-down hotels with traveling salesmen, showed lantern slides to the chambers of commerce, and glad-handed to editors of the weekly papers." Exposition organizers also enlisted the support of the federal government. For the World's Columbian Exposition, the United States Treasury Department issued a special commemorative half-dollar, while, for most of the expositions, the postal service issued special commemorative stamps. Portland fair promoters even convinced the local post office to postmark outgoing mail with "World's Fair 1905." Commenting on the value of the post office's stamp of approval for its 1898 Trans-Mississippi Exposition, an Omaha newspaper declared, "The issue will be not only valuable as a medium of advertising the exposition of 1898, but it gives to the project the prestige of government recognition and support."[11]

---

[10][?] Wood to Ira Nadeau, September 19, 1907, box 78, folder 12, Edmund Meany Papers, University of Washington Archives, Seattle.

[11]"The Tidings," *Pan-American Herald* 3, no. 2 (August 1900): 11; "Ten Mammoth Advertising Sign Boards," *Pan-American Herald* 1, no. 4 (October 1899): 9; "Bill Board Protests Numerous," *Seattle Times*, January 18, 1904, clipping, Alaska-Yukon-Pacific

The concern for prestige helps to explain the peculiar relationship that developed between world's fairs and advertising. Susman observed that all fairs were "great advertisements," noting that it is "characteristic of the culture of abundance that many things and institutions are in fact turned into advertisements." On the one hand, exposition managers acting as tough-minded businessmen engaged in intensive and expensive efforts to promote their expositions; on the other hand, these same managers also regarded their expositions as "meccas" and "universities" and saw themselves less as businessmen than as curates and educators who stood above the rough-and-tumble world of profit seeking. As late as 1911, Frederick J. V. Skiff, head of the Field Museum of Natural History and the "oracle" of fin de siècle world's fair authorities, advised the organizers of San Francisco's Panama-Pacific International Expositon to proceed with great caution concerning advertising. "I do not think straight advertising does the Exposition much good," Skiff told San Francisco's world's fair directors. "It is not like what the merchant would do, or what the theaters would do in the way of advertising." In Skiff's view, unprepared advertising that gave the exposition notice in important places was far better than direct advertising. For example, an article about the exposition president in the *Saturday Evening Post*, "where the advertisement of the Exposition was indirect and incidental," was worth its weight in gold. According to Skiff, the key involved persuading newspapers and magazines "to recognize that [the exposition] is a national thing." Once that was established, Skiff told fair planners that the press would "help it out as they would any other effort that all the people were concerned in." Skiff's uneasiness about prepared advertising stemmed from his conviction that the exposition, "to reach its highest position . . . should be purely educational in its character."[12]

Such uncertainty about advertising is hardly surprising. Raymond Williams and Roland Marchand have discovered that "psychological

---

Scrapbooks, Northwest Collection, University of Washington; "A Little Boy from China," *Nashville Banner*, June 30, 1897, p. 1; Carl Abbot, *The Great Extravaganza* (Portland: Oregon Historical Society, 1981), p. 25; "Exposition Postage Stamps," *Omaha Bee*, December 24, 1897, p. 4; Robert Knutson, "The White City: The World's Columbian Exposition of 1893" (Ph.D. diss., Columbia University, 1956), p. 17.

[12] Susman, "Ritual Fairs," p. 6; Harris, "Museums," p. 143; "Conference between F. J. V. Skiff, Esq., and the President and Directors of the Panama-Pacific International Exposition Company," November 24, 1911, 4:2, 40, box 3B/4A, folder 2, Panama-Pacific International Exposition Collection, Bancroft Library, University of California, Berkeley.

advertising" is a post–World War I phenomenon. Marchand recently noted that doubts about the economic value of advertising persisted through the First World War. According to Marchand, advertisers had a problem with their image. In the popular imagination, advertisers still reeked of P. T. Barnum's smoke and conjured up images of patent medicine scams.[13] For exposition planners, given their notions of expositions as bearers of civilization, advertising—however attractive as a medium for catching the public's attention—had to be treated gingerly lest it create the impression that expositions were mere business enterprises.

Throughout the fin de siècle, Skiff's ideas about advertising the fairs prevailed. Manufacturers advertised particular products and even emphasized that items had been on display at a fair (fig. 5). Prizewinning companies invoked the authority of the fairs in promoting "gold medal" products, and manufacturers actually incorporated the ethos of imperial abundance into their advertising (fig. 6). The directors of fairs held before World War I, however, did not accord advertisers full partnership in the drive to design American culture. That recognition would have to await a generation of interbella fairs, especially the fairs of the 1930s, when corporate advertising and world's fairs became inseparable. What stands out in the relationship between advertising and the fairs held before World War I is that manufacturers sought to derive legitimacy from the fairs, not the other way around. Ironically, the seeds of change were being sown at the 1915 San Francisco fair. Before the fair opened, the directors agreed to proposals by several Hollywood studios to show newsreels of the exposition in hundreds of movie theaters around the nation.[14]

While recognizing the exposition management's ambivalence about advertising, it is important not to overstate it. One contemporary of the Buffalo fair could give a knowing wink and suggest that "an exhibition of this sort is not solely for a glorification of art and the humanities for their own sake, but is a business proposition as well, and a grand adver-

---

[13] Roland Marchand, *Advertising the American Dream: Making Way for Modernity,* 1920–1940 (Berkeley: University of California Press, 1985), pp. 8–13; Raymond Williams, *Problems in Materialism and Culture: Selected Essays* (London: Verso Editions, 1980), pp. 170–95. On advertising, also consult Richard Wightman Fox and T. J. Jackson Lears, eds., *The Culture of Consumption: Critical Essays in American History, 1880–1980* (New York: Pantheon Books, 1983), esp. pp. ix–38; and Jackson Lears, "Beyond Veblen: Rethinking Consumer Culture in America," elsewhere in this volume.

[14] "Movies to Invite the World to the Exposition," *San Francisco Bulletin,* February 4, 1915, p. 8.

Fig. 5. Advertisement for watches, Robert H. Ingersoll and Bro., New York. From *Cosmopolitan* 37 (1904). (Montana State University.)

tising scheme." Businessmen in a world's fair community certainly regarded their fair as a golden opportunity to advertise the resources of their area to prospective settlers. "The Lewis and Clark Exposition could not have come at a more opportune time," declared one of Portland's urban boosters. "It will reinforce the advertising that commercial bodies are doing or propose to do, and it will be the climax of the whole plan of attracting settlers and building up the country."[15] Embossed with the imprimatur of a world's fair, the advertisement of urban development

[15] Robert Grant, "Notes on the Pan-American Exposition," *Cosmopolitan* 31, no. 5 (September 1901): 452; William Bittle Wells, "Our Point of View," *Pacific Monthly* 7, no. 4 (March 1902): 183.

Fig. 6. Advertising card, Singer Manufacturing Co., 1892.
(Exposition and Fairs Collection, Department of Special
Collections, University of California at Los Angeles.)

schemes—and the advertising business itself—could shift into high gear
and give the impression that civic improvement and advertising meant
the same thing.

In short, world's fairs accustomed fairgoers to thinking of advertising as integral to the City Beautiful. On Children's Day at the Omaha
fair, advertisers loaded down the children with business cards, product
literature, pins, and badges.[16] Despite the directors' ambivalence, fairs
had the effect of making advertising seem as "true and natural" to the
American way of life as midway exhibits of roller coasters and Ferris
wheels and ethnological ghettos of Africans, Asians, Latin Americans,
and native Americans.

Beyond the Fairgrounds

Perhaps the best evidence of the influence of America's world's fairs on
American culture is that one did not have to attend a fair to be affected
by the world's fair movement. Local newspaper stories and regional and
national magazine articles, often generated by world's fair publicity bur-

[16]"Kids Overrun the Exposition," *Omaha World-Herald*, October 23, 1898, p. 10.

eaus, together with merchandise advertising, carried the gospel of imperial abundance beyond the fairgrounds to a national audience. As
important as these promotional campaigns were, there was another,
sometimes forgotten activity that involved men, women, and children
in the process of creating and identifying with world's fairs. To secure
exhibits from various states and territories and to augment planned artistic, manufacturing, agricultural, and mineralogical displays, world's fair
authorities depended upon state legislatures to appoint state world's fair
boards comprised of locally prominent men and women. Headed by a
commissioner, these boards superintended the collection, identification, and classification of exhibit materials according to the categories
provided in the guidelines that world's fair managers sent to each state
commission. State boards, with the invaluable assistance of women's
auxiliary committees, established a network of county committees that
involved countless adults and children in the task of promoting the economic and cultural development of their state within the framework
developed by world's fair authorities.[17] For a newly organized state like
Montana, the consequences were profound.

When the World's Columbian Exposition was formally established
by an act of Congress in 1890, Montana's state legislature quickly organized the Montana Board of World's Fair Managers with Missoula
businessman Walter Bickford as executive commissioner. Bickford wasted
no time in soliciting exhibits that emphasized the richness of natural
resources—especially the mineral wealth—of the state. He took
responsibility for generating two articles each week for newspapers around
the state. On top of that, he agreed to an idea proposed by Chicago
business interests (and guaranteed by a $35,000 personal bond from
banker Lyman Gage) for a silver statue depicting Justice. With the "silver issue" dominating national politics, the silver statue "gimmick" was
a stroke of Barnumesque genius. Almost immediately upon announc-
ing the idea to the press, the statue became a rallying point for the state.
Even when it became clear that Bickford had misled people into believing that the model for the statue would be selected from Montana women
who would compete for the honor—when, in fact, the sculptor, nationally renowned Richard Henry Park, had contracted with famous actress

[17] The extent of these organizational activities is suggested by Jeanne Madeline Wei-
mann, *The Fair Women* (Chicago: Academy Chicago, 1981), pp. 125–40.

Ada Rehan to be his model—the ensuing controversy kept the fair idea in the local press for months.[18]

While Bickford publicized the fair and negotiated with Helena banker Samuel Hauser and Butte "Copper King" William A. Clark for a loan of 24,000 ounces of silver for the statue *Justice*, the Montana Board of Lady Managers concentrated their efforts on securing exhibits for the buildings devoted to women's and children's displays. Headed by Eliza Rickards, wife of Montana's governor, and made up of five equally prominent women from around the state, the board organized county committees to translate interest in the fair into actual exhibit material. "The importance of these local committees and the responsibilities assumed by the women appointed to preside over the same is apparent," declared state board member and mine owner Clara L. McAdow. "They are the medium through which must be disseminated in every city, town, village and community all essential information relative to women's work at the Columbian exposition." Once they were in place, county committees in turn organized local world's fair clubs—so-called Columbia Clubs—that met as often as every two weeks to spur local involvement in the fair.[19]

This intensive local campaigning generated a ground swell of interest in the fair—and not only among adults. Children were a particular concern of national and state world's fair officials. Once Chicago fair organizers agreed to construct a children's building, state and local committees launched drives to collect money from schoolchildren to defray costs. They were so successful in their fund-raising efforts and appeals to state pride that Montana children actually contributed double the amount requested by the Chicago Board of Lady Managers. Like their peers around the country, Montana children also served as the focus for another campaign: the introduction of the pledge of allegiance in the nation's schools as part of Columbus Day activities organized nationwide in conjunction with the dedication ceremonies for the fair in Chicago. With children generating a whirlwind of excitement, it was

[18] Dave Walter, "Montana's Silver Lady," *Montana* 76, no. 2 (March–April 1986): 68–73. Extensive information on the silver statue controversy is contained in the vertical files, Montana Historical Society, Helena (hereafter cited as MHS).

[19] "Work for Our Women," newspaper clipping, vertical files, MHS; Laura E. Howey to Walter Bickford, August 12, 1892, and L. G. Dawkins to Howey, August 22, 1892, folders D–G misc. and G–H misc., Chicago World's Columbian Exposition, Montana Board of Lady Managers Collection, MHS.

no surprise that Columbia Clubs had little difficulty securing exhibit material—much of it "tasty and elegant bric-a-brac"—for the Montana State Building and for Montana displays in buildings devoted to metallurgy, horticulture, and women.[20]

The significance of these activities can be simply stated. Long before the fair opened, the World's Columbian Exposition had become an object of immense local interest. To the extent that interest became pride, the process of generating exhibits for the fair not only facilitated popular identification with and acceptance of the directions being given to American culture at the Chicago fair by nationally prominent elites but also augmented the cultural authority of local political elites in their efforts to provide a blueprint for the economic and cultural development of Montana.

That the visions of national and state world's fair directorates coalesced is clear from ceremonies that unveiled *Justice* to the public. When the silver was cast in a south-side Chicago foundry, numerous dignitaries from the fair as well as from Montana's exposition delegation attended to underscore the value of the statue to the overall aims of the fair. Exactly what those aims were became clear at the public unveiling of the 6-foot statue, which stood on a solid-gold plinth valued at nearly $250,000. At the public ceremonies, Eliza Rickards called attention to this "silver sentiment crystalized into art. . . . Its artistic contours are mutely eloquent with the aspirations of our people. They seem to speak of the unrevealed wealth of our virgin mountains. They attest to the magnitude of an industry that has linked Montana with the financial interests of the world. They invite to an empire of resources the brain and brawn of the union." When Rickards tugged the cord that removed the red, white, and blue bunting from the statue, Montana took its place in the galaxy of world's fair states as a resource-rich internal colony that eagerly proffered the development of its natural resources in the service of enriching the imperial republic (fig. 7). Back home, Montanans read Bickford's understated evaluation: "We could not get the

[20]Weimann, *Fair Women*, p. 332. On the pledge of allegiance, see Knutson, "White City," pp. 55–56; and "Columbus Day," *Avant Courier* (Bozeman, Mont.), October 15, 1892, p. 2. Howey, secretary of the Montana Board of Lady Managers, describes the content of the exhibit and makes clear that children were asked to contribute money (Laura E. Howey, "Final Report of the Woman's Department of the Montana World's Fair Board," n.d., folder G–H misc., Montana Board of Lady Managers Collection, MHS).

Fig. 7. Montana Mining exhibit, World's Columbian Exposition, Chicago, 1893. From Hubert Howe Bancroft, *The Book of the Fair*, vol. 2 (Chicago: Bancroft Co., 1894), p. 481. (Cooper-Hewitt Museum.)

same amount of advertising for the State of Montana for a million dollars in cash."[21]

In return for their exhibit, Montanans received plenty of advertising. The silver in the statue, however, never returned to the state. After the close of the exposition, *Justice* was displayed at a series of county fairs around the nation before being reduced to bullion by an Omaha smelter in 1903.[22] What Montanans did receive was an amusement park in Butte—Columbia Gardens—that bore a strong resemblance to the Midway Plaisance at the World's Columbian Exposition (fig. 8).

The story of the transformation of Columbia Gardens from a work-

[21]"Ada Cast in Silver," *Anaconda Standard*, May 31, 1893, p. 1; "The Montana Statue," *Helena Weekly Herald*, January 19, 1893, p. 5. On Montana's role as an "internal colony," see Michael P. Malone, "The Collapse of Western Metal Mining: An Historical Epitaph," *Pacific Historical Review* 55, no. 3 (August 1986): 455–64.

[22]Walter, "Montana's Silver Lady," p. 73.

Fig. 8. Columbia Gardens, Butte, Mont. (Butte Historical Society.)

ing-class resort into an amusement park dedicated to children is the story of the sudden rise of mass entertainment to respectability. Staked out in 1876 as a mining claim, the 21-acre site became a picnic area during the 1880s before it was sold to entrepreneurs who developed it into a resort for Butte's working classes. Throughout much of the 1890s, Columbia Gardens resembled nothing so much as a preindustrial pleasure garden. That dramatically changed in 1899 when, in the midst of the fabled "War of the Copper Kings," Clark, a mining investor and former commissioner to the World's Columbian Exposition, purchased the gardens and converted them into an amusement park for workers and especially for their children. Spending more than $100,000 per year on improving his gift, Clark turned the gardens into a small-scale Midway Plaisance complete with restaurants, dance hall, zoo, and shoot-the-chutes. On one level, Clark's investment represented a bread-and-circus operation. At the very moment he made his bequest, Clark was fighting for a United States Senate seat. On another level, however,

Columbia Gardens represented less an effort to win votes than to influence leisure. Like the Midway Plaisance and Coney Island, Columbia Gardens equated fun with spending money and stood in the vanguard of national efforts to disseminate a new vision of society based on "consumption and leisure," not on the producer ethic of republican America.[23]

The World's Columbian Exposition alone left a significant legacy in Montana. But the force of the world's fair movement was deeply felt because it was cumulative. In 1884, while still a territory, Montana's agricultural and mineral resources had been represented at the New Orleans World's Industrial and Cotton Exposition. At the 1904 St. Louis fair, the Montana Building again provided exhibits designed to attract investment and settlers to the state. By the turn of the century, world's fairs had involved countless Montanans—and Americans generally—in the process of reexamining themselves in the context of the "dream worlds" of imperial abundance. Even in hotbeds of labor agitation like Butte, the result was to blunt, not to obliterate, the jagged edge of class conflict.[24]

A World's Fair Museum

Through organizational activities like those in Montana, through saturation media campaigns launched by publicity bureaus at the fairs, and through keepsakes—postcards, souvenir albums, spoons, table settings, and the like—brought home by actual exposition goers, the festivities associated with fairs (and it is important to note that these activities were repeated for all the fairs held between 1876 and 1916) acquired a momentum that swept the country. The message of the fairs persisted not only through memories of hands-on experience in organizing displays or from memories of actually visiting an exposition but also through selected exhibits from the fairs that were institutionalized in museums around the country.

Such museums as the Museum of Man in San Diego, the Field

[23] Dave Walter, "Beautiful Columbia Gardens," *Montana* 73, no. 5 (September–October 1985): 22–27. Information is also available in the vertical files, Department of Special Collections, Montana State University, Bozeman. John F. Kasson, *Amusing the Millions: Coney Island at the Turn of the Century* (New York: Hill and Wang, 1978), p. 106.

[24] *Montana at the World's Industrial and Cotton Centennial Exposition* (Helena: George E. Boos, n.d.); *Montana: Its Progress and Prosperity, Resources and Industries* . . . (St. Louis: Montana World's Fair Commission, n.d.).

Fig. 9. Commercial Museum, Philadelphia. From *National Export Museum* (n.p., n.d.). (National Museum of American History Library.)

Museum of Natural History and the Museum of Science and Industry in Chicago, the Commercial Museum in Philadelphia, and many of the Smithsonian Institution's museums, derived substantial portions of their collections from—and sometimes owed their existence to—world's fairs. These museums re-presented the ideology of imperial abundance and, in turn, became founts of exposition wisdom. Scientists like the Field Museum's Frederick J. V. Skiff, the Commercial Museum's William P. Wilson, and the Smithsonian's William P. Blake and George Brown Goode helped develop the important exhibit classification schemes for the fairs held between the end of Reconstruction and the First World War.[25] At the end of the century, a good example of this symbiotic relationship between fairs and museums could be found in the Commercial Museum (fig. 9).

[25] Attention is called to the relationship between fairs and museums in Eugene S. Ferguson, "Technical Museums and International Exhibitions," *Technology and Culture* 6, no. 1 (Winter 1975): 30–46. The relationship between fairs and the Smithsonian Institution is examined in Rydell, *All the World's a Fair.*

The Commercial Museum was the brainchild of Wilson, a University of Pennsylvania plant pathologist. The idea to organize the museum came to him while visiting the World's Columbian Exposition. When he learned that many of the natural history exhibits on display at the fair would form the nucleus of the collections for the Field Museum, he pondered the fate of the countless commercial exhibits and rushed back to Philadelphia with a proposal to organize a museum around those commercial and natural resource exhibits on display at Chicago. Fired with enthusiasm, Wilson persuaded Philadelphia politicians and businessmen to support his plan for "a great group of Museums, General, Scientific, Economic, Educational and Commercial." More specifically, this museum was intended to institutionalize one of the central lessons of the Chicago fair: the need to dominate foreign markets and to acquire overseas supplies of natural resources. By developing a museum that operated as a clearing house for information about foreign commerce and as an educational institution, Wilson saw himself as placing the gospel of imperial abundance on scientific footing.[26]

Wilson wasted no time setting his plans in motion. He returned to the fair and filled twenty-four railroad boxcars with exhibit material that he promptly shipped to Philadelphia. This was only the beginning. Over the next twenty years, Wilson obtained tons of exhibit material from American and foreign fairs and employed world's fair specialists to work at the museum. By 1899, when the permanent buildings opened on a 17-acre site between the Pennsylvania Railroad tracks and the University of Pennsylvania, the museum had become nothing less than a permanent world's fair. President McKinley declared at the museum's

[26]The history of the museum is chronicled in Ruth H. Hunter, *The Trade and Convention Center of Philadelphia: Its Birth and Renascence* (Philadelphia: City of Philadelphia for Trade and Convention Center, 1962); and Ruth H. Hunter, *The Philadelphia Civic Center* (Philadelphia: City of Philadelphia for Philadelphia Civic Center, 1971). One should also consult the annual reports from the Commercial Museum. The Commercial Museum's role in popularizing science is examined in Robert W. Rydell, "The Open (Laboratory) Door: Scientists and Mass Culture," in *High Brow Meets Low Brow*, ed. Rob Kroes (Amsterdam: Free University Press, 1987). For further discussion of the cultural role of museums during this period, see Simon J. Bronner, "Object Lessons: The Work of Ethnological Museums and Collections," elsewhere in this volume. The importance of the 1893 fair to the search for overseas markets is stressed in Justus D. Doenecke, "Myths, Machines, and Markets: The Columbian Exposition of 1893," *Journal of Popular Culture* 6, no. 4 (Spring 1973): 535–49.

dedication, "The Columbia World's Exhibition at Chicago, glorious testimonial as it was to the world's progress, was the forerunner of this less general but more permanent institution for the world's economic advance."[27]

Once the museum opened, it combined world's fair displays with operations that would be assumed a decade later by the United States Department of Commerce. Exhibits consisted of ethnological groups and "the most extensive collections of natural products in existence in any country." What made the displays unique was their arrangement. According to William Pepper, provost of the University of Pennsylvania and chairman of the board of trustees of the Commercial Museum, "[Our collections] are displayed so as to enable manufacturers or traders to study them to the best advantage, and gain the information to make the selections needed for their special interests." With its well-stocked library constantly updated with American consular reports from around the world, it is little wonder that Pepper could boast that the museum contained "the fullest, freshest, and most exact data on all trade conditions which can be obtained." The most distinctive feature of the museum, however, was its scientific laboratory which tested new products, estimated yields of agricultural crops, and provided information about potential markets for agricultural and manufactured products. One of the museum's biologists declared, "It is the earnest aim of this department to put the international commerce in raw products on a scientific basis, and to most successfully aid, with exact data, information, and investigation, international trade and industry." In theory the museum provided information to manufacturers and agriculturists around the world. But as one of the museum's publications made clear, "The object of the institution is to aid in the building up of the foreign trade of America."[28]

Until Wilson's death in 1927, the Commercial Museum continued to add to its collection from world's fairs held throughout the world. Its agents secured displays from major European fairs, including the 1896 Budapest Millennial Exhibition and the 1900 Paris Universal

[27] *Philadelphia Commercial Museums: Proceedings of the International Advisory Board* (Philadelphia: Press of the Philadelphia Commercial Museum, 1897), p. 47.

[28] *Philadelphia Museums*, pp. 52, 71; *American Trade with Siam* (Philadelphia: Press of the Philadelphia Commercial Museum, 1898), Van Pelt Library, University of Pennsylvania, Philadelphia.

Exposition. Museum staff, moreover, contributed expert advice to European governments, especially to the French, on organizing colonial exhibitions. Two of the museum's scientists, Wilson and botanist Gustavo Niederlein, bore chief responsibility for developing exhibits for the Philippines Reservation at the St. Louis fair. Rivaled only by the Field Museum and the Smithsonian Institution, the Commercial Museum, born of a world's fair, became one of the sources for expertise on international expositions.[29]

The tongue-and-groove relationship between fairs and the Commercial Museum was further evidenced by Wilson's decision to arrange an international exhibition that would draw attention to the museum. With its 5 miles of aisles lined with such displays as electric streetcars, furniture, and automobiles, the 1899 National Export Exposition could easily have been mistaken for a simple trade fair. But such was not the case. Architects joined three pavilions "so as to form one complete structure, which at first view has the appearance of a great marble palace and conveys the impression of permanency." Adorned by heroic pediments devoted to themes of abundance, international commerce, and commercial development, the Main Building mirrored similar structures at world's fairs. Two additional buildings—one devoted to transportation, the other to displays of agriculture, vehicles, and furniture—made the indebtedness to the world's fair precedent even more apparent. The full extent to which Wilson depended on world's fair blueprints became manifest when he hired Edmund Felder, one of the individuals who had been responsible for the Midway Plaisance, to develop a similar entertainment strip for the 1899 exhibition. Felder's creation, the Gay Esplanade, was a resurrected Midway Plaisance. The Gay Esplanade included the Chinese Village, the Oriental Theater, the Old Plantation—complete with "a party of Georgia Negroes, with songs, dances"—an animal circus, and the Cuban midget show. These shows were so central to the exhibition that they lined either side of the avenue leading from the main entrance to the main building.[30]

Entertainment, however, was not the sole aim of the Commercial Museum any more that it was the primary purpose of the nation's inter-

[29] Rydell, *All the World's a Fair*, pp. 168–69. The international prominence of the museum is noted in Hunter, *Trade and Convention Center*, p. 22.

[30] *National Export Exposition* (Philadelphia: National Export Exposition, Department of Promotion, 1899).

national fairs. Just as world's fair managers saw themselves as educators and their expositions as "universities," so Wilson saw himself and his institution as performing a didactic function. From the inception of the Commercial Museum, Wilson emphasized its educational mission. According to the museum's official historian, several hundreds of thousands of schoolchildren visited the museum, and countless others saw exhibits and heard presentations about displays that the museum sent to public schools around the region. Through its exhibits, daily operations, and educational mission, the Commercial Museum served as an institutional link with American fairs and perpetuated their ideological formulations. Until its slow death after World War I and transformation into the present-day Civic Center, the Commercial Museum helped translate imperial dreams into daily practice.[31]

It would be a mistake to interpret fairs as transitory spectacles that merely adorned the Gilded Age. Although America's world's fairs lasted, on average, about six months, they wove their way into American life before, during, and after their months of operation. Before an exposition opened, state committees around the nation began the arduous task of accumulating material for display. This process, directed by state elites and covered extensively in newspapers, involved numerous ordinary Americans who probably never traveled to a fair. As important as it is to remember that tens of millions of Americans actually attended fairs (by 1916 aggregate visits totaled nearly a hundred million), many uncounted Americans contributed exhibits to the network of world's fairs that stretched across the country. While it is true that numerous exhibits and staff-and-plaster buildings were demolished at the conclusion of fairs, other exhibits—both anthropological and commercial— found permanent space in museums around the country, such as in the Commercial Museum, an institution that was constructed to enshrine permanently the gospel of imperial abundance on display at the Chicago fair and at subsequent turn-of-the-century expositions.

Amid the turbulence that rocked turn-of-the-century America, world's fairs gave visible form and legitimacy to an emerging culture of abundance. Susman noted that the world's fair became "a key institution of a new culture based not like the older republican culture on principles of scarcity, limitation, and sacrifice, but on new principles of

---

[31] Hunter, *Trade and Convention Center*, pp. 32–39.

abundance, self-fulfillment, and unlimited possibilities."[32] In addition, fairs combined these new principles of abundance with new principles of empire, rooted in the racist vocabulary of social Darwinism and sanctioned by anthropologists. Tightly interwoven into an ideological double helix, the visions of materialism and imperialism at the fairs were threaded into the broader culture. By World War I, if not before, America had become a culture of imperial abundance.

[32] Susman, "Ritual Fairs," p. 6.

Object Lessons
The Work of Ethnological Museums and Collections

Simon J. Bronner

In Edward Bellamy's *Looking Backward* (1888), Dr. Leete explains to Julian West how the consumer culture of the twentieth century had triumphed over the industrial turmoil of the nineteenth: "Fifty years before, the consolidation of the industries of the country under national control would have seemed a very daring experiment to the most sanguine. But by a series of object lessons, seen and studied by all men, the great corporations had taught the people an entirely new set of ideas on the subject." Bellamy's use of the phrase *object lessons* was a powerful rhetorical strategy for turn-of-the-century writers. The concept of education in the early nineteenth century was cerebral, almost spiritual, free from the influence of object or environment. But by the late nineteenth century, increasing numbers of Americans desired a flourishing material life more than a spiritual life. Objects took on more power to educate and strengthen society as a world of exotic trinkets, labor-saving devices, and affordable fashions came to the fore.[1]

---

[1] Edward Bellamy, *Looking Backward, 2000–1887* (1888; reprint, New York: Modern Library, 1982), p. 39. For more on objects, see "Function of 'Things' in Education" and "Value of Pictures" in Robert Hebert Quick, *Essays on Educational Reformers* (1896; reprint, New York: AMS Press, 1971), pp. 476–79, 520–21; Paul Monroe, A *Text-Book in the History of Education* (1905; reprint, New York: AMS Press, 1970); "Science of Common Things" in *The Popular Art Instructor* (Windsor, Ont.: J. B. Young, 1888); Elwood P. Cubberley, "Changing Conceptions of Education (1909)," and Nicholas Mur-

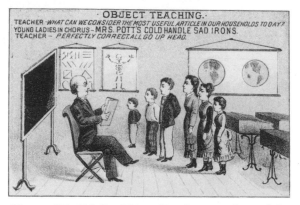

Fig. 1. W. Edell, *Object Teaching*, trade card for
Mrs. Pott's irons. Lithograph; H. 2⅝″, W. 4¼″.
(Courtesy, The New-York Historical Society,
Bella C. Landauer Collection.)

America's growth was measured not only in its geographical expanse
but also in its power to produce and consume things in increasing numbers. The pithy phrase *object lessons* drew attention to the growing
importance of things in society; moreover, it suggested that people relied
on things for their information and values (fig. 1). Reformers, advisers,
and educators repeated the phrase often to emphasize the need to make
concrete the moral imperatives of the age. One adviser declared, "Character is seen through small openings, and certainly is as clearly displayed in the arrangements and adornments of a house as in any other
way." This attitude led to constant debate over the inherent conflict of
the morally uplifting effects of tasteful material surroundings. One of
the better-known advisers, Mary Elizabeth Sherwood, made the claim
that "Indiana divorce laws may be perhaps directly traced to some frightful

ray Butler, "The Argument for Manual Training (1888)," in *Social History of American
Education, Volume II: 1860 to the Present*, ed. Rena L. Vassar (Chicago: Rand McNally,
1965), pp. 149–56; "Object Teaching" in *The Centennial Exposition* (Philadelphia: Hubbard Bros., 1876), p. 485; and E. E. Wood, "Object Lesson," *Century* 66, no. 6 (October
1903): 886–89. For secondary texts, see R. Freeman Butts, *A Cultural History of Western
Education* (New York: McGraw-Hill, 1955), pp. 473–584; Edward J. Power, *Main Cur-
rents in the History of Education* (New York: McGraw-Hill, 1962), pp. 426–97; and
Burton J. Bledstein, *The Culture of Professionalism: The Middle Class and the Development of Higher Education in America* (New York: W. W. Norton, 1976).

inharmoniousness in wall-paper. The soothing influence of an Eastlake bookcase on an irritated husband has never been sufficiently calculated." *Good Furniture* stated, "It is the duty of every educational art institution—be it museum, school, or journal—to place before the people ideals and object lessons which are useful in building in the individual an appreciation of beauty in the home."[2]

Museums devoted to displaying cultural objects arose dramatically during the late nineteenth century to provide the right kind of object lessons for a society in transition from a spiritual to a material age and from a producer to a consumer society. They became outlets for a changing vision of the future based on a changing vision of the past. In America, an energetic new breed of museum professionals, speaking for the rising middle class, helped to shape these visions. A leader of this breed was Stewart Culin, who believed that like a department store, "a museum is a place where the normal relations of things become transformed and obscured." There one teaches and influences through the power of object lessons, by using "example rather than precept." The museum and its collections, Culin established, may be made "superlatively useful," especially by proving "of value to American industry."[3] To explore these changing visions, this essay first examines the back-

[2] *Eighty Years' Progress of the United States* (Hartford, Conn.: L. Stebbins, 1868); E. Benjamin Andrews, *The History of the Last Quarter-Century in the United States, 1870–1895*, 2 vols. (New York: Charles Scribner's Sons, 1896), 2:273–99. See also David M. Potter, *People of Plenty: Economic Abundance and the American Character* (Chicago: University of Chicago Press, 1954); Daniel J. Boorstin, *The Americans: The Democratic Experience* (New York: Vintage Books/Random House, 1973); Ray Ginger, *Age of Excess: The United States from 1877 to 1914* (New York: Macmillan Publishing Co., 1965); Richard Wightman Fox and T. J. Jackson Lears, eds., *The Culture of Consumption: Critical Essays in American History, 1880–1980* (New York: Pantheon Books, 1983); Howard Mumford Jones, *The Age of Energy: Varieties of American Experience, 1865–1915* (New York: Viking Press, 1971); Alan Trachtenberg, *The Incorporation of America: Culture and Society in the Gilded Age* (New York: Hill and Wang, 1982); Robert H. Walker, *Life in the Age of Enterprise, 1865–1900* (1967; reprint, New York: Paragon/G. P, Putnam's Sons, 1979); and Edgar W. Martin, *The Standard of Living in 1860* (1942; reprint, New York: Johnson Reprint, 1970). Sara Josepha Hale, *Manners; or, Happy Homes and Good Society* (Boston: J. E. Tilton, 1868), p. 81; Mrs. M. E. W. Sherwood, "The Mission of Household Art," *Appleton's* 15, no. 358 (February 5, 1876): 179; "Bringing Art into the Home," *Good Furniture* 8, no. 4 (April 1917): 183–84.

[3] Stewart Culin, "Creation in Art," *Brooklyn Museum Quarterly* 11, no. 3 (July 1924): 94, 96; Stewart Culin, "The Road to Beauty," *Brooklyn Museum Quarterly* 14, no. 2 (April 1927): 46; Stewart Culin, "The Sources of Ornamental Design: The Relation of European Peasant Art to the Art of the Orient," *Arts and Decoration* 15, no. 8 (June 1921): 94–95, 130.

ground of the rise of ethnological exhibits and then offers an insight into the meaning of the movement by focusing on Culin's career.

By the time the Massachusetts Bureau of Statistics of Labor provided the first set of figures on American working-class spending habits in 1875, its report revealed what many already assumed: workers were spending more on manufactured "sundry expenses" from furniture to clothing. The writers of the report were especially alarmed by the consumption of liquor and entertainment in "places of amusement." To offset this trend, the report urged the pursuit of "higher" goals through the influence of material surroundings, concluding, "The comforts or luxuries of life [were] absolutely necessary for the development of the mind, of a love of beauty in the home, and of a man's social possibilities." For those able to afford amenities such as a sewing machine, a piano, books, and decorative furniture, the reward was "comfort, cheerfulness, and beauty of home and the personal and social happiness of its occupants." The report went on to criticize workers who sacrificed goods for savings; it criticized them basically for the barrenness of their existence. These workers appeared to be "in" American society, but not "of" it.[4] The reformers from Massachusetts and elsewhere called for forms of popular education to uplift tastes, to make workers part "of" American civilization by appreciating the finer things in life.

The outpouring of advisers and etiquette books between 1875 and 1925 responded to this reformist zeal and consuming vision. The authors of these books warned against haphazard consumption and decoration and set up standards of "order and beauty." There was often a sense that standards of taste, especially in a short, ignoble history like America's, were not inherited, but were set by modern-day authorities. One adviser made an analogy to city planning as "an art problem in which one man plans the layout or the groundwork of the design, and then turns it over to the public who put in the details of the composition." The authors echoed the rhetoric of most advisers by stating that "taste is molded, to a very large extent, by the things which surround one, and the family taste is trained by the objects selected by the homemaker. There is, therefore, a distinct obligation in the home to set the highest possible standards of beauty. This has become widely recognized, and there is

---

[4] See Daniel Horowitz, *The Morality of Spending: Attitudes toward the Consumer Society in America, 1875–1940* (Baltimore: Johns Hopkins University Press, 1985), pp. 13–29.

an ever growing demand for information which will help people to become more intelligent consumers." Edith Wharton and Ogden Codman, Jr., explaining the attention to the cultivation of taste through decorative objects, advised that "their intrinsic beauty is hardly more valuable than their suggestion of a mellower civilization—of days when rich men were patrons of 'the arts of elegance,' and when collecting beautiful objects was one of the obligations of a noble leisure." The decorative adviser *Good Furniture* asked, "Why not good furniture to promote greater interest and happiness in the home? If the poor man does not know what sort of furniture his family should have, why not show him?"[5]

Although the advisers gave long lectures on the principles of tasteful arrangement and purchasing—the power of the rich now made available to an elastic middle class—they wrestled with the lack of cooperation that often characterized manufacturers. *Good Furniture* warned that spreading the uplifting principles of fashion known among "better" society would require "the manufacturer to expend infinitely greater care in selecting his designs and in evolving a system of fabrication which would place durability above superficial appearance. Where is the American manufacturer who has the courage to undertake the task of supplying good furniture to the poor man?" One supporter of decorative arts geared to mass industry exclaimed, "The danger of all machine industries lies in the loss of a sense of aesthetic values." Another adviser noted, "to make beautiful the product of the machine has been the problem given to us, and unless solved, the machine will dominate the age to the detriment of the individual."[6]

The exhibits of decorative arts at expositions and world's fairs drew praise for being object lessons for consumers and manufacturers alike. Writing for *Craftsman* in 1902, Frederick Lamb expressed "hope for the future in a careful analysis of the lessons of our expositions. Here, for the first time in ages, we note a tendency to again unite the aesthetic and the practical—to redeem art by making it real and vital." Lamb

[5] Harriet Goldstein and Vetta Goldstein, *Art in Every Day Life* (1925; rev. ed., New York: Macmillan, 1932), pp. 505, 3; Edith Wharton and Ogden Codman, Jr., *The Decoration of Houses* (1897; reprint, New York: Charles Scribner's Sons, 1919), p. 187; "Why Not Good Furniture for the Poor Man?" *Good Furniture* 15, no. 8 (August 1915): 120.

[6] M. D. C. Crawford, "The Museum's Place in Art Industry," *House Beautiful* 44, no. 7 (December 1918): 368; Frederick S. Lamb, "Lessons from the Expositions," *Craftsman* 3, no. 1 (October 1902): 57.

challenged his audience to bring the object lessons of the expositions to people where they live.[7]

The lessons of the expositions were not lost on museum promoter George Brown Goode (1851–96), who began his illustrious career supervising exhibits for the Smithsonian Institution at the Centennial Exhibition of 1876 in Philadelphia. Praising the success of London's Crystal Palace Exhibition of 1851, Goode commented that the Centennial Exhibition was "almost as great a revelation to the people of the United States. The thoughts of the Country were opened to many things before undreamed of. One thing we may regret—that we have no such widespread system of museums as that which has developed in the motherland with South Kensington as its administrative center." Goode pushed the idea of establishing many local museums to promote "education of the people and the application of known facts to promoting their material welfare." His goal of democratizing museums did not go without resistance, since it shifted the emphasis of most existing museums from storehouses and meeting rooms for private collectors and elite patrons to providing muses for the masses. But Goode sold this shift to museum supporters by calling on the potential of museums for bringing rude public sentiment around to the materialistic, future-oriented views that they held dear; he sold the shift in the name of both art and science. Appealing to the evolutionary model of progress made popular by Herbert Spencer, Goode argued, "the museum of today is no longer a chance assemblage of curiosities, but rather a series of objects selected with reference to their value to investigators, or their possibilities for public enlightenment. The museum of the future may be made one of the chief agencies of the higher civilization." Calling on America to catch up with European society, Goode said, "England has had nearly forty years, however, and we but thirteen, since our exhibition. May we not hope that within a like period of time, and before the year 1914, the

---

[7] Lamb, "Lessons," pp. 49–58. At the World's Columbian Exposition in Chicago, for example, much of the decorative arts was housed alongside Manufactures in the Liberal Arts Division—"the most important educational feature of the Exposition," according to Ben. C. Truman, *History of the World's Fair* (n.p.: Ben. C. Truman, 1893), pp. 239–54; see also Trumbull White and Wm. Igleheart, *The World's Columbian Exposition, Chicago, 1893* (n.p.: J. W. Ziegler, 1893), pp. 389–404; and David F. Burg, *Chicago's White City of 1893* (Lexington: University Press of Kentucky, 1976), pp. 114–234. For the object lessons of another world's fair, see Charles Hirschfeld, "America on Exhibition: The New York Crystal Palace," *American Quarterly* 9, no. 2, pt. 1 (Summer 1957): 101–16.

United States may have attained the position which England now occupies, at least in the respects of popular interest and substantial governmental support?" Part of Goode's vision was realized as the number of museums in the United States increased dramatically between 1880 and 1914.[8]

Goode believed that museums responded to the rising visual orientation of American society:

In this busy, critical, and skeptical age each man is seeking to know all things, and life is too short for many words. The eye is used more and more, the ear less and less, and in the use of the eye, descriptive writing is set aside for pictures, and pictures in their turn are replaced by actual objects. In the schoolroom the diagram, the blackboard, and the object lesson, unknown thirty years ago, are universally employed. . . . Amid such tendencies, the museum, it would seem, should find congenial place, for it is the most powerful and useful auxiliary of all systems of teaching by means of object lessons.

Borrowing from new display techniques used by exposition and department store showcases, Goode insisted that "no pains must be spared in the presentation of the material in the exhibition halls. The specimens must be prepared in the most careful and artistic manner, and arranged attractively in well-designed cases and behind the clearest of glass." The museum would be a visually attractive place, replacing the image of a dry, dusty cabinet known more for its mummies than its muses.[9]

[8] See Edward P. Alexander, *Museum Masters: Their Museums and Their Influence* (Nashville: American Association for State and Local History, 1983), pp. 277–310; and Curtis M. Hinsley, Jr., *Savages and Scientists: The Smithsonian Institution and the Development of American Anthropology, 1846–1910* (Washington, D.C.: Smithsonian Institution Press, 1981), pp. 91–94. George Brown Goode, "Museum-History and Museums of History," in *Annual Report of the United States National Museum* (Washington, D.C.: Smithsonian Institution/Government Printing Office, 1897), pp. 65–81. The rapid growth of American museums is documented in S. F. Markham, "Impressions of American Museums," *Museums* 31, no. 7 (October 1931): 298–304; and Laurence Vail Coleman, *The Museum in America: A Critical Study*, 3 vols. (Washington, D.C.: American Association of Museums, 1939), 1:17–19, 3:663–70.

[9] George Brown Goode, "The Museums of the Future," in *Annual Report*, p. 243; Goode, "Museum-History," p. 73. For background on display techniques, see "The Spectator," *Outlook* 92 (May 29, 1909): 272–74; Edward Hale Brush, "Popularizing Anthropology: What Museums Are Doing to Make Science Attractive," *Scientific American* 84, supplement no. 2191 (December 29, 1917): 408–11; Russell Lewis, "Everything under One Roof: World's Fairs and Department Stores in Paris and Chicago," *Chicago History* 13, no. 3 (Fall 1983): 28–47; Benjamin Ives Gilman, *Museum Ideals of Purpose and Method* (2d ed.; Cambridge, Mass.: Harvard University Press, 1923), pp. 137–344; and William Leach, "Strategists of Display and the Production of Desire," elsewhere in this volume.

Relying on his prestige as a naturalist and as assistant secretary of the Smithsonian Institution, Goode spread the gospel of the public museum. American museums not only began serving the public but also started to cooperate actively with industry to design consumer goods. Museums collected objects from a supposedly lost age of handicraft which would inspire better industrial design. *The Civic Value of Museums* observed that museums also educated the consumer because "the people, as consumer, have need for firsthand knowledge of design in order to use their purchasing power to best advantage." Interest in American designs and American things contributed to reliance on museum collections for decorating ideas, as did restrictions on European goods because of World War I. Yet this was not a sudden response to a world event, for ethnological collections had set precedents for this cultural role of museums, as Goode recognized in 1897: "The study of civilization or the history of culture and of the developments of the various arts and industries have brought into being special collections which are exceedingly significant and useful. . . . Nearly every museum which admits ethnological material is doing something in this direction" (fig. 2).[10]

Ethnological collections played a "significant and useful" role by mediating between arts and industries for late nineteenth-century American society. The ethnological collections held the attention of the press and public because they spoke the primary metaphor of the day: cultural evolution. Drawing on Charles Darwin and Herbert Spencer, cultural evolution assumed that societies climbed the cultural ladder from a state of savagery to barbarism to civilization. Challenging religious education, which assumed a short path from the dawn of man to the present created by divine intervention, evolutionary thought opened a hidden, usable past operating under natural laws. Industry was viewed as the culmination of a progression of the Anglo-Saxon race from primitive roots. Vast collections of primitive objects taken from aboriginal

[10] Edward P. Alexander, *Museums in Motion: An Introduction to the History and Functions of Museums* (Nashville: American Association for State and Local History, 1979), pp. 31–32; T. R. Adam, *The Civic Value of Museums* (New York: American Association for Adult Education, 1937), pp. 34–56; A. H. Griffith, "Museums and Their Value to a City," *American City* 4, no. 5 (May 1911): 229–31; Crawford, "Museum's Place," pp. 368–70; Theodore Lewis Low, *The Educational Philosophy and Practice of Art Museums in the United States* (New York: Columbia University Bureau of Publications, 1948), pp. 17–19; Adam, *Civic Value of Museums*, p. 35; Marion Nicholl Rawson, *Candleday Art* (New York: E. P. Dutton, 1938), pp. 23–24; Goode, "Museum-History," p. 79.

Fig. 2. Collection workroom, Smithsonian Institution, ca. 1890s.
(National Anthropological Archives, Smithsonian Institution.)

and ethnic groups illustrated how civilization had progressed, measured
in middle-class material and technical terms. These collections were
presented to show how "mechanicalized" modern man genteelly
triumphed over primitive man yet retained his sensory excitement.
Craftsman reported, "Evolution is the pass-word of the hour, and studies in origin, development, and degeneration, in whatever department
found, are in chord with the spirit of the age."[11] Not yet accepted by

[11] Paul Monroe, "Possibilities of the Present Industrial System," *American Journal
of Sociology* 3, no. 6 (May 1898): 729–53; Otis Mason, "The Natural History of Folk-
lore," *Journal of American Folklore* 4, no. 13 (April–June 1891): 97–105; J. W. Powell,
"Technology; or, The Science of Industries," *American Anthropologist*, n.s., 1, no. 2
(April 1899): 319–49; Frank Hamilton Cushing, "Manual Concepts: A Study of the
Influence of Hand Usage on Culture-Growth," *American Anthropologist* 5, no. 4 (October 1892): 289–318; Alfred C. Haddon, *Evolution in Art; as Illustrated by the Life-
Histories of Designs* (1895; reprint, New York: AMS Press, 1979); Herbert Spencer, *Prin-
ciples of Sociology*, vol. 3 (New York: Appleton, 1896); Edward Burnett Tylor, *Primitive*

the universities, anthropologists entered natural history museums and later ethnological museums to do their evolutionary studies. The Museum of Natural History opened in 1869, the United States National Museum in 1879, the University Museum of the University of Pennsylvania in 1887, and the Brooklyn Museum and the Field Museum in 1893.

Among the most popular ethnological exhibits in the country after the turn of the century was the Museum of Natural History's Arctic Life exhibition drawn from the exploration of Robert Peary. Set in the forefront were the primitive Eskimo industries (fig. 3). Further fueling interest in the evolution of modern industry, Otis Mason of the Smithsonian Institution published *Origins of Invention*, Charles Abbott of the University Museum published *Primitive Industry*, and Thomas Wilson of the Smithsonian used Abbott's title for an influential essay. They were popular advisers relying on science for their authority. Answering the charge that modern industrial men and women had broken sharply with the past, other ethnologists wrote in city dailies to explain the origins of everything from play to war. Well-placed exhibits at world's fairs and control of midway attractions served to further the popularity of anthropology. Fletcher Bassett was not exaggerating when he announced at the 1893 World's Columbian Exposition in Chicago that anthropology had become the "subject of the day."[12]

The University of Pennsylvania's ethnological collection received the ultimate compliment of the day when Lee Vance called it an "object

---

Culture, 2 vols. (1871; reprint, Gloucester, Mass.: Peter Smith, 1980); Lewis Henry Morgan, *Ancient Society: Researches in the Lines of Human Progress through Barbarism to Civilization* (1877; reprint, Gloucester, Mass.: Peter Smith, 1974); J. W. Powell, "From Barbarism to Civilization," *American Anthropologist* 1, no. 2 (April 1888): 97–123. For secondary texts, see Fred W. Voget, *A History of Ethnology* (New York: Holt, Rinehart and Winston, 1975), pp. 41–310; Marvin Harris, *The Rise of Anthropological Theory: A History of Theories of Culture* (New York: Harper and Row, 1968), pp. 80–216; Simon J. Bronner, *American Folklore Studies: An Intellectual History* (Lawrence: University Press of Kansas), pp. 1–53; George W. Stocking, Jr., *Race, Culture and Evolution: Essays in the History of Anthropology* (1968; rev. ed., Chicago: University of Chicago Press, 1882), pp. 69–132; and Robert M. Young, *Darwin's Metaphor: Nature's Place in Victorian Culture* (New York: Cambridge University Press, 1985).

[12] "The Life History of a Design," *Craftsman* 1, no. 4 (January 1902): 33–40; Otis Mason, *Origins of Invention: A Study of Industry among Primitive Peoples* (1896; reprint, Freeport, N.Y.: Books for Libraries Press, 1972); Charles Abbott, *Primitive Industry* (Salem, Mass.: George A. Bates, 1881); Thomas Wilson, "Primitive Industry," in *Smithsonian Institution Annual for 1892* (Washington, D.C.: Smithsonian Institution/Government Printing Office, 1893), pp. 521–34. See also George Wharton James, "Primitive Inven-

Fig. 3. Robert Peary exhibit of Arctic life, National Museum of Natural History, Smithsonian Institution, 1908. (Library of Congress: Photo, George Grantham Bain.)

lesson": "Very interesting are those implements used for divination and fortune telling and those manipulated in games. Thus, the evolution of the playing card is shown; so too the games of chess and backgammon are displayed in their various forms or types. Nor have the games and toys and dolls of children been overlooked. They are all there—even Noah's ark, with its beasts and birds, two and two."[13] Responsibility for the collection fell to Stewart Culin (1858–1929), a leader of the museum

tions," *Craftsman* 5, no. 2 (November 1903): 125–37; and Thorstein Veblen, *The Instinct of Workmanship and the State of the Industrial Arts* (1914; reprint, New York: Augustus M. Kelley, 1964). Robert W. Rydell, *All the World's a Fair: Visions of Empire at American International Expositions, 1876–1916* (Chicago: University of Chicago Press, 1984); Robert W. Rydell, "The Culture of Imperial Abundance: World's Fairs in the Making of American Culture," elsewhere in this volume; Fletcher S. Bassett, "The Folk-Lore Congress," in *The International Folk-Lore Congress of the World's Columbian Exposition*, ed. Helen Wheeler Bassett and Frederick Starr (1898; reprint, New York: Arno Press, 1980), p. 20; and Frederick Starr, "Anthropology at the World's Fair," *Popular Science Monthly* 43 (September 1893): 610–21.

[13] Lee J. Vance, "Folk-Lore Study in America," *Popular Science Monthly* 43 (September 1893): 589.

Fig. 4. Stewart Culin, ca. 1900. (National Anthropological Archives, Smithsonian Institution.)

movement in ethnology as well as material culture studies (fig. 4).

Culin deserves special attention from cultural and intellectual historians because, on the one hand, he represented the evolutionary fervor for industrial progress common to the late nineteenth century; on
the other hand, he was responsible for establishing display techniques
now taken for granted in museums. Culin was born in Philadelphia to
a middle-class family of colonial American stock. Upon graduating from
Nazareth Hall at the age of seventeen, where his favorite instructor was
historian S. J. Blum, who regaled his students with American Indian
tales, Culin entered his father's merchant business. Much of the business was in the China trade, and Culin took an interest in Chinese
customs and artifacts. In his business as well as his avocation, he was
especially drawn to decorative items that were resplendent with culturally rich color, ritual, and design. Culin shared in the sentiment expressed
by Henry Childs Merwin in *Atlantic Monthly* that "savages and chil-

dren" had maintained a natural excitement that had been sacrificed in the progress of higher civilization. According to Merwin, the appreciation of ethnological material had a therapeutic value, for "everybody knows that these colors [of savages and children] tend to raise the spirits, and therefore to improve the health. . . . This natural, healthy sense of color may of course be cultivated and trained, so that those who possess it can learn to appreciate the beauty of more delicate shades; and in such persons there will be a happy union of natural taste with cultivation." Thus Culin's early studies exposed the colorful, emotional experience of traditional children's games, oriental ceremonies, and primitive art. With the merchant's care for detail and accurate record-keeping, Culin collected goods that showed custom and color in commerce, religion, and play.[14] He amassed a private collection of coins, costumes, toys, ritual objects, and musical instruments. He joined and later became

[14]Henry Childs Merwin, "On Being Civilized Too Much," *Atlantic Monthly* 79, no. 476 (June 1897): 838–46. For biographical background on Culin, see Temple Scott of Brentano's, New York, to Stewart Culin, September 16, 1915, Ira Jacknis, "Biographical Sketch," October 1985, and Culin's personal scrapbook, in Stewart Culin Papers, Brooklyn Museum; "Stewart Culin," in *University of Pennsylvania: Its History, Influence, Equipment and Characteristics*, ed. Joshua L. Chamberlain (Boston: R. Herndon, 1902), pp. 466–67; and Culin to Henry Mercer, July 14, 1925, Bucks County Historical Society, Doylestown, Pa. For examples of Culin's studies of games and ceremonies, see "American Indian Games with Especial Reference to Their Revival and Employment by Boy Scouts" and "Puzzles" (typescripts), Culin Papers; articles in *Journal of American Folklore*, including "Street Games of Boys in Brooklyn, N.Y.," 4, no. 14 (July–September 1891): 221–37, "Exhibition of Objects Connected with Folk-Lore," 5, no. 17 (April–June 1892): 165–58, "Exhibit of Games in the Columbian Exposition," 6, no. 22 (July–September 1893): 205–27, "Concerning Negro Sorcery in the United States," 3, no. 11 (October–December 1890): 281–87, and "Retrospect of the Folk-Lore of the Columbian Exposition," 7, no. 24 (January–March 1894): 51–59; articles in *American Anthropologist*, "Hawaiian Games," n.s., 2, no. 2 (April 1899): 201–47, and "Phillipine Games," n.s., 2, no. 5 (October–December 1900): 643–56; "The Value of Games in Ethnology," *Proceedings of the American Association for the Advancement of Science* 43 (August 1894): 355–58; *Korean Games with Notes on the Corresponding Games of China and Japan* (Philadelphia: University of Pennsylvania, 1895); and Alyce Cheska, "Stewart Culin: An Early Ethnologist of Games," *Association for the Anthropological Study of Play Newsletter* 2, no. 3 (Fall 1975): 4–13. For Culin's studies on primitive art and design, see "The Magic of Color," *Brooklyn Museum Quarterly* 12, no. 2 (April 1925): 99–103; "Primitive American Art," *University Bulletin* 4, no. 7 (April 1900): 191–96; "Creation in Art," pp. 91–100; and "Ornamental Design," pp. 94–95, 130. On Culin's collecting, see his *Bulletin of the Free Museum of Science and Art* articles, "A Summer Trip among the Western Indians," 3, no. 3 (May 1901): 143–75, and "The Indians of Cuba," 3, no. 4 (May 1902): 185–225; Craig D. Bates and Brian Bibby, "Collecting among the Chico Maidu: The Stewart Culin Collection at the Brooklyn Museum," *American Indian Art* 8, no. 4 (Autumn 1983): 46–54; and Simon J. Bronner, "Stewart Culin: Museum Magician," *Pennsylvania Heritage* 11, no. 3 (Summer 1985): 4–11.

secretary of the Numismatic and Antiquarian Society of Philadelphia, where he found many of Philadelphia's elites engaged in some kind of collecting passion. At monthly meetings, members brought new acquisitions before the group to show and discuss.[15]

As a member of the Numismatic and Antiquarian Society, Culin was influenced by its president, Daniel Brinton, who attracted international acclaim for his prolific writings in archaeology, linguistics, mythology, and religion. Brinton, a physician by training, enjoyed the distinction of becoming the first university professor of anthropology in the United States. As a medical doctor, Brinton assisted Culin in his study of Chinese drug stores and, as an anthropologist, supported Culin's publication in 1887 of a paper entitled "The Religious Ceremonies of the Chinese," read before the Numismatic and Antiquarian Society. Culin's work drew the praise of the *Philadelphia Inquirer*, which commented, "he is still a young man of studious habits, with the prospect of a brilliant future before him." The newspaper also hinted at the increasing demands of his cultural studies, however, when it stated somewhat in amazement, "Mr. Culin's researches in this line have been prosecuted during his business hours."[16]

Again Brinton stepped in to influence Culin's next move. During

[15] *Report of the Proceedings of the Numismatic and Antiquarian Society of Philadelphia, 1887–89* (Philadelphia: Privately printed, 1890); see also Stewart Culin, "Indian Fortune Telling with Dice," "Syrian Games with Knuckle Bones," and "Tip Cats," in *Report of the Proceedings of the Numismatic and Antiquarian Society of Philadelphia, 1890–91* (Philadelphia: Privately printed, 1892), pp. 65–72, 121–24, 125–26. Several of ʹe society members, including A. J. Drexel, Henry Phillips, and Richard Vaux, are ·iscussed in E. Digby Baltzell, *Philadelphia Gentlemen: The Making of a National Upper Class* (1958; reprint, Philadelphia: University of Pennsylvania Press, 1978), pp. 107–29.

[16] Stewart Culin, "Chinese Drug Stores in America," *American Journal of Pharmacy* 59, no. 12 (December 1887): 593–98; Stewart Culin, "The Practice of Medicine by the Chinese in America," *Medical and Surgical Reporter* 56, no. 12 (March 19, 1887): 355–57. These essays are reprinted and annotated in Simon J. Bronner, ed., *Folklife Studies from the Gilded Age* (Ann Arbor, Mich.: UMI Research Press, 1987), pp. 87–103. See also Stewart Culin, *The Religious Ceremonies of the Chinese in the Eastern Cities of the United States* (Philadelphia: Privately printed, 1887). For Culin's other studies of the Chinese, see *Journal of American Folklore* articles, "Chinese Secret Societies in the United States," 3, no. 8 (January–March 1890): 39–43, and "Customs of the Chinese in America," 3, no. 10 (July–September 1890): 191–200; *China in America: A Study in the Social Life of the Chinese in the Eastern Cities of the United States* (Philadelphia: Privately printed, 1887); *Popular Literature of the Chinese Laborers in the United States* (Philadelphia: Privately printed, 1894); *Overland Monthly* articles, "Divination and Fortune-Telling among the Chinese in America," 25, no. 146 (February 1895): 165–72, "Palmistry in China and Japan," 23, no. 137 (May 1894): 476–80, and "'Tsz' Fa or 'Word Blossoming': A Lottery among the Chinese in America," 24, no. 141 (September 1894): 249–53;

the late 1880s, Culin's mentor envisioned a museum at the university to undertake the collection, display, and study of cultural objects. At Brinton's urging, Culin left his business in 1889 to become the first secretary of the oriental section of the new museum. A business associate of Culin's wrote him with the foretelling message, "I am very sorry to part with you as a business friend, but I know you will succeed in your new undertaking, and the field will be much larger than in a mercantile life." Almost immediately upon taking the new position, Culin became an outspoken critic of museums that were not in step with the consumer age, complaining, "Popular taste in collecting does not often receive the approval of scientific men, and 'curiosities' which many people treasure, valued often on account of their associations, are little prized by the critical student, who even condemns many of our public museums as mere depositories for bric-a-brac." Culin continued his criticism in an address to high school teachers of art in New York: "Unlike the chemical laboratory, where a single sniff of the familiar odors stirs new flights of my imagination, museums depress and annoy me. Sometimes in unguarded moments I have expressed my feelings, but I have continued on with no other thought than of making things tell me their story, and then in trying to coax and arrange them to tell this story to the world. Museums, like libraries, have grown up as catch-alls, preserving what has come into their way upon the principle that some day it may be useful." Taking a swipe at Goode, Culin said, "An ideal museum has been defined as a collection of labels illustrated by specimens. Another distinguished authority spoke of it as a place where people find pegs on which to hang their intellectual concepts."[17]

What did Culin offer instead? "I should say at once that my ideal

---

"Social Organization of the Chinese in America," *American Anthropologist* 4, no. 4 (October 1891): 347–52; *Chinese Games with Dice and Dominoes* (1893; reprint, Seattle: Shorey, 1972); and *The Gambling Games of the Chinese in America* (1891; reprint, Las Vegas: Gambler's Book Club, 1972). For the life and influence of Daniel Brinton, see Regna Darnell, "Daniel Garrison Brinton: An Intellectual Biography" (M.A. thesis, University of Pennsylvania, 1967); and Daniel Brinton to Culin, 1889–99, Culin Papers. For Brinton's ethnological views, see Daniel Brinton, "The Aims of Anthropology," *Proceedings of the American Association for the Advancement of Science* 44 (May 1895): 1–17; Becky Vorpagel, "Daniel Brinton's Concept of Folklore," *New York Folklore* 9, nos. 3–4 (Winter 1983): 31–42; and "Personal Notes," *Philadelphia Inquirer*, March 2, 1889, p. 8.

[17] John C. Robertson to Culin, July 5, 1892, Culin Papers; "A Folk-Lore Museum," *Public Ledger* (Philadelphia), September 3, 1890, reprinted in Bronner, ed., *Folklife Studies*, pp. 253–55; Culin, "Road to Beauty," p. 41.

museum, above all a museum that is to represent the outcome of human activities, should be a work of art and as such the result of individual effort." He paused and then remarked, "I am reminded at this moment that we are still within the museum." He then shocked his audience by saying, "Let me reward your patience by unlocking some of the cases and putting their contents in your hands. At once you realize that these treasures, recently so remote, so dead it seemed, come again to life. How useful would be a museum where people could touch things, as they now see them." He pointed to department stores as models: "Enter one of our great department stores, and examine the fabrications of cotton and silk, of glass and metal, wood and lacquer; mere utility is quite insufficient to justify the profusion of form and color with which we are surrounded. [Department stores] made it possible for us all to participate in the creative thought of a new revolutionary era." Invoking the value of ethnological collection for this era, Culin said, "We must, indeed, turn aside to the so-called sterile and unproductive cultures, if we are to correctly understand the beginnings of man, and unravel the tangled web of modern civilization."[18]

Culin practiced what he preached with a widely publicized exhibition of the world's religious objects at the University Museum. Introducing the exhibition, the provost of the university boasted of the "great collections which have been accumulated here with such striking rapidity" and pointed to the "lessons" they provided of the "aspirations and affections which are guiding civilization painfully upwards and onwards through the stages of its evolution." Largely as a result of the show's success, Culin was appointed secretary of the American Historical Commission to the 1892 World Exposition in Madrid. He installed an exhibit of religious objects and received a gold medal.[19] Upon returning

[8] Culin, "Road to Beauty," p. 43; Culin, "Creation in Art," p. 100; note by Culin appended to letter from Booth Hubbett (store manager for Abraham and Straus) to Culin, January 27, 1928, Culin Papers; "The Origin of Ornament," *Bulletin of the Free Museum of Science and Art* 2, no. 4 (May 1900): 235–36.

[19] "Dr. Pepper's Address," in *Addresses Delivered at the Opening Ceremonies of the Exhibition of Objects Used in Worship, April 16, 1892* (Philadelphia: University of Pennsylvania, 1892), p. 1; *Report of the United States Commission to the Columbian Historical Exposition at Madrid, 1892–93* (Washington, D.C.: Government Printing Office, 1895), pp. 194–210; *Report of the Board of Managers of the Department of Archaeology and Paleontology of the University of Pennsylvania, 1892* (Philadelphia: University of Pennsylvania, 1894), p. 5; Stewart Culin, *Columbian Historical Exposition, Madrid: Archaeological Collections Exhibited by the Department of Archaeology and Paleontology of the University of Pennsylvania* (Washington, D.C.: Government Printing Office, 1895); Stewart Culin, "Madrid Saunterings," *Overland Monthly* 24, no. 139 (July 1894): 8–15.

Fig. 5. University Museum, University of Pennsylvania, Philadelphia.
(University Museum.)

to Philadelphia, Culin rose to the position of director of archaeology
and paleontology at the University Museum (fig. 5).

The University Museum was a pet project of Philadelphia department-store magnate John Wanamaker, who founded the archaeological
section and served on the museum's board of managers. Wanamaker
developed a close relationship with Culin, who shared with Wanamaker a merchant background, a love of art and history, and an attention to new display techniques. In addition, Wanamaker wanted to push
American museums into a new consumer age and past the glory of the
European museums: "In museums, most everything looks like junk even
when it isn't, because there is no care or thought in the display." For
Wanamaker, the museum needed "the use of the merchant instinct to
show it off to best advantage." Wanamaker's biographer, Herbert Gibbons, added that Wanamaker often opined: "What is not for sale is still
for sale. Whatever the possession you prize, when others see it you want
to sell it to them. You may not want to be paid with money and you
may not want to transfer the physical possession of the thing to another.
But you do want the person to whom you show it to pay for it in admiration and intelligent appreciation." Wanamaker's department store was
organized like Culin's archaeological museum with Egyptian, Greek,

Fig. 6. Paris fashions exhibit, Egyptian Hall, John Wanamaker department store, Philadelphia, October 1910. From John Wanamaker, *Golden
Book of the Wanamaker Stores* (Philadelphia: John Wanamaker, 1911),
p. 200.

Byzantine, and Oriental halls; the store paraded the world's ancient
civilizations behind an emergent American commercial culture (fig. 6).
In 1900 Wanamaker financed Culin's western collecting trip among the
American Indians and exhibited his finds in the store as well as in the
museum. According to Gibbons, Wanamaker wanted to present "everything that Dr. Stewart Culin brought back" in the name of "popular
education."[20]

     Culin's boldest stroke in the name of popular education occurred
in 1893 when he displayed "folklore objects" such as games, toys, and
charms at the World's Columbian Exposition in Chicago. The exhibit
earned Culin another gold medal and many notices in the press. Reporters

[20] Herbert Adams Gibbons, *John Wanamaker*, 2 vols. (New York: Harper and Bros.,
1926), 2:80–84; see also John Wanamaker, *Golden Book of the Wanamaker Stores* (Philadelphia: John Wanamaker, 1911), pp. 238–42; Stewart Culin, "A Summer Trip among
the Western Indians (The Wanamaker Expedition)," *Bulletin of the Free Museum of
Science and Art* 3, no. 1 (January 1901): 1–22; and Culin to John Wanamaker, June 21,
1902, University of Pennsylvania Archives.

Fig. 7. Ethnological exhibit, Stewart Culin, curator, World's Columbian Exposition, Chicago, 1893. (University Museum.)

and fairgoers marveled at the exhibit of exotic objects he had assembled in eye-catching arrangements (fig. 7). The *Chicago Record* exclaimed, "Folklore most intimately connects this age with the greatest antiquity, and of folklore no branch so directly informs us of our relation to the people of most ancient days than the games for the different stages in the history of the world." Culin agreed:

No subject within the range of scientific investigation appeals more strongly to popular interest than that so well designated as "folk-lore," and the very instinct that underlies the custom of collecting strange and curious objects is one through which much of this same lore may be accounted for. As folk-lore deals with ideas, so it would be the mission of the folk-lore museum to collect, arrange and classify the objects associated with them. Such a museum would form an essential part of a museum of ethnology, and would serve an admirable part in supplementing the existing collections of art and archaeology.[21]

Culin embarked on lengthy trips to Europe to study the collections of renowned ethnological museums such as the Pitt Rivers Museum in Oxford, England (fig. 8). (Established in the 1880s, the museum was considered one of Europe's best ethnological showcases. Culin admired

[21] "World's Fair Bureau: Folklore," *Chicago Record*, clipping dated October 21, 1893, Culin Papers; Culin, "Folk-Lore Museum," pp. 312–13.

Fig. 8. Ethnological exhibit, Henry Balfour, curator, Pitt Rivers Museum, University of Oxford, ca. 1890. (Pitt Rivers Museum.)

the museum's vision but abhorred the repetition and crowding of its displays.) Throughout his trips, Culin dispatched reports—astounding accounts of marvelous treasures and excessive displays—that were printed in the Philadelphia newspapers. Philadelphians made up an especially receptive audience for Culin's accounts because, through the nineteenth century, they had been strong supporters of museums, leading one historian to call Philadelphia the "cradle city" of the modern museum. Despite the strong headstart of European museums, Culin believed that American museums could rival and surpass them if the resourcefulness given to building American industry was applied to museum work. One model museum that embodied Culin's philosophy was the Commercial Museum, which was established in Philadelphia after the World's Columbian Exposition. Drawing on the collections of the Chicago exposition and the exhibit techniques of the University Museum, the founders—notably Wanamaker and University of Pennsylvania naturalist William Wilson—wedded exhibits to commerce: "Buyers from more than 50 countries visited The Commercial Museum during the year. Many of them were attracted by the Permanent Exhibition of Manufactured Products and by the liberal offers of assistance made to merchants in any part of the world."[22]

Such connections were also made vigorously at the many world's fairs held in America during the last decade of the nineteenth century. The popularity of ethnological exhibits at the Chicago exposition brought more requests for Culin's services. In compiling these massive exhibits, Culin worked with men who became leaders of the museum movement: Otis Mason and W. J. McGee of the Smithsonian Institution, Frederic Ward Putnam of the Peabody Museum, Franz Boas of the National Museum of Natural History, George Dorsey of the Field Museum, Henry Mercer of the University Museum, and, of course, Goode. Goode commissioned Culin to prepare an exhibit of gaming objects for the Atlanta Cotton States and International Exposition in 1895. Culin used hundreds of objects and issued a massive catalogue of the collection. With the exhibit, he taught the lesson that gaming objects evolved from religious rites; secular uses had replaced their spiritual functions.[23] His crowning triumph was his display of games for the Paris World's Exposition of 1900, bewildering the Europeans by taking the grand prize for exhibits.

The ethnological exhibits at the world's fairs drew some revealing satire from Thomas Fleming in *Around the "Pan" with Uncle Hank: His Trip through the Pan American Exposition.* Uncle Hank, a rustic taking in the modern wonders of the Buffalo exposition of 1901, stopped at the ethnological exhibit in the Government Building: "One group in particular attracted his attention. It represented an Indian teaching a

---

[22]On Philadelphia as a cradle city, see Joel J. Orosz, "Curators and Culture: An Interpretive History of the Museum Movement in America, 1773–1870" (Ph.D. diss., Case Western Reserve University, 1986); for the quotation on the Philadelphia Commercial Museum, see S. F. Markham, "Impressions of American Museums," *Museums* 31, no. 8 (November 1931), p. 341. See also Low, *Educational Philosophy*, pp. 18–19; and Rydell, "Culture of Imperial Abundance."

[23]Culin to G. Brown Goode, February 2, 1895, Smithsonian Institution Archives; Stewart Culin, "Chess and Playing-Cards: Catalogue of Games and Implements for Divination Exhibited by the United States National Museum in Connection with the Department of Archaeology and Paleontology of the University of Pennsylvania at the Cotton States and International Exposition, Atlanta, Georgia, 1895," *Report of the U.S. National Museum*, 1896 (Washington, D.C.: Smithsonian Institution/Government Printing Office, 1898), pp. 665–820.

boy to shoot with bow and arrow, and [was] intensely life-like. 'That Injun's teachin th' risin geneashun tew use ther bow an arrer,' said he, 'when he ought tew be teachin em tew wear more clothes so's tew give the Wool Trust a chance ter earn bigger dividends.' " The exhibit inspired a switch in scene to Machinery Hall, but reflecting on the earlier exhibit, Fleming invoked the object lesson metaphor: "Them's the most lifelike figgers I ever see, fer I'm a grate beelever in pictures and statoos tew educate ther people. Naow look et them figgers! Ye cud read a hull book thru and not git half the' infermation frum et thet ye cud git frum one glance et th' figgers in them show cases."[24] Fleming's jests were indeed testimony to the pervasiveness of the industrial object lessons that ethnological exhibits provided and to the popular appreciation of Culin's exhibition techniques.

Culin's frequent appearances in the limelight, and his even more frequent absences from the University of Pennsylvania for special exhibitions and collecting trips, caused resentment from some quarters of the museum. Political squabbles with Sara Stevenson, the powerful secretary of the museum, the death of Brinton in 1899, and the departures of Wanamaker from the United States from 1901 to 1903 precipitated Culin's loss of influence at the University Museum. In 1903 Culin left to take charge of the new department of ethnology at the Brooklyn Museum (originally designed as the flagship building for, and called, the Brooklyn Institute of Arts and Sciences, or simply the Brooklyn Institute) (fig. 9). He was welcomed with headlines such as "Stewart Culin Won by Brooklyn Institute, Magician Who Captures Hearts of Savages in the Interest of Ethnology, First Man in His Own Field." At Brooklyn, he had a chance to fulfill a vision that he had imagined since the 1890s: making museums centers "of the artistic industries." Toward this end, he had earlier sought funding from Wanamaker for his collecting trips, and at Brooklyn he had a similar ally in Edward Blum, president of the museum and head of Abraham and Straus, Brooklyn's leading department store. Culin organized a series of lectures at the museum on decorative objects such as "portable boxes and containers employed in conserving and transporting merchandise and household gear, bearing in mind the primitive and oriental objects I describe sup-

[24] Thomas Fleming, *Around the "Pan" with Uncle Hank: His Trip through the Pan-American Exposition* (New York: Nut Shell Publishing, 1901), pp. 165–66. Culin won a silver medal for his exhibit of American Indian artifacts at the Pan-American Exposition.

Fig. 9. The Brooklyn Museum, Brooklyn, N.Y., 1904. (Courtesy, The Brooklyn Museum.)

ply unnumbered suggestions of value to our manufactures. . . . Brooklyn is an appropriate place for this discussion, being, with its fifty-seven manufacturers, one of the principal seats of the paper box industry in America. The subject is of immediate importance, the use of boxes having increased enormously through the establishment of packing stores and their more general employment in retail trade." Especially fond of Japanese boxes, Culin offered, "commonly they are works of art in themselves and prized as such. What a world of suggestion we may gather from them!"[25]

[25]The squabble over Culin's departure from the University Museum is described in "Stewart Culin Resigns," *Philadelphia Press*, January 30, 1903, "Culin Resigns Office by Special Request," "Mr. Culin Resigns," "After Many Years at Post, Curator of University Museum Leaves the Institution," and "Curator Culin Resigns: Difference of Opinion Causes Vacancy at University Museum," clippings dated January 30, 1903, University Museum, Philadelphia; Culin to Charles Lummis, February 28, 1903, Charles Lummis Papers, Southwest Museum, Los Angeles. For Culin's opinion on museums as "centers of artistic industries," see Culin to Edward Blum, November 17, 1926, Culin Papers; and "Industrial Art Education in Germany," *Brooklyn Museum Quarterly* 11, no. 2 (April 1924): 55–64. Stewart Culin, "Boxes and Containers," pp. 1, 6, typescript, Culin Papers.

Culin apparently had his most resounding influence on game and toy manufacturers. He had a guiding hand, for instance, in the commercial packaging of the traditional game *Parcheesi* by Selchow and Righter. Almost thirty years after his triumphant exhibit of toys and games at the World's Columbian Exposition, the commercial magazine *Playthings* interviewed Culin about the exhibit and his suggestions for better-designed toys. As a result of Culin's efforts, the Brooklyn Museum had amassed the country's largest collection of toys and games, and the magazine spread the news of "How He Co-operates with American Toy Makers." He described the contribution of the Brunswick and Milton Bradley companies to his world's fairs exhibits of 1893 and 1895, and consequently, he said, "I constantly think of the possibilities of the practical adoption of games which I encountered in remote places to the requirements of our own American industry." *Playthings* noted, "Mr. Culin is delighted to see that the resources of the Brooklyn Institute Museum are now widely utilized by the makers of costumes, textiles and toys." But Culin still lamented, "the application of games to educational uses has been carried to a higher point in China and Japan than it has ever attained here."[26]

Culin made extensive efforts to carry educational uses of the museum to "a higher point" in America. He created strong ties with Pratt Institute, which eventually made the conversion from a manual labor college to a commercial art school during the 1920s. Culin wrote columns for *Men's Wear, Women's Wear,* and the *New York Times* on good fashion based on the history of textiles and primitive design, and he served as a judge for window display contests. He was also instrumental in introducing African primitive art into the United States, and he is usually credited with curating one of the first shows of such art in the country. In 1923 he organized an exhibit of African textiles simultaneously with show-window exhibits of African-inspired manufactured clothing at the fashionable Bonwit Teller store on Fifth Avenue.[27]

[26]Briesen and Knauth, counselors at law, on behalf of Selchow and Righter, Inc., to Culin, October 6, 1902, Culin Papers. See also Paula Petrik, "The House that Parcheesi Built: Selchow and Righter," *Business History Review* 60, no. 3 (Autumn 1986): 410–37; and "World's Wonder Toys at Brooklyn Museum," *Playthings* (May 1920): 105–10.

[27]Stewart Culin, *Primitive Negro Art* (Brooklyn: Brooklyn Museum, 1923); "Negro Art," *Brooklyn Museum Quarterly* 10, no. 3 (July 1923): 119–23. Culin's outpouring of articles during 1926 in *Women's Wear, Men's Wear,* and *New York Times* demonstrates his abundant writing for the fashion industry: "Gloves," April 11, and "Color in Window

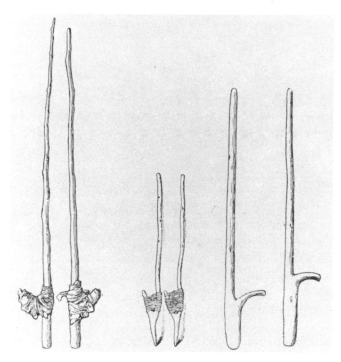

Fig. 10. Stilts from the Hopi, Shoshoni, and Zuni tribes. From Stewart Culin, *Games of the North American Indians* (1907; reprint, New York: Dover Publications, 1975), p. 732.

Much of Culin's study during the first decade of the twentieth century had revolved around American Indians (figs. 10, 11). Respond-

Display," June 9, *Men's Wear;* "Mats," May 5, "Chinese Costume," October 20, "Japanese Costume," October 27, "The Department Store in Its Relation to the Social Life of the Present Day," November 3, "Persian and Indian Costume," November 3, "European Peasant Costume," November 10, "Evolution and Importance of Gloves," November 18, "Changing Footways Bring New Shoe Types," November 24, "Women's Hats," December 1, "Buttons Descendants of Knots," December 9, and "Leather, One of Our Earliest Materials for Apparel," December 16, *Women's Wear Daily;* "Chinese Costume," November 3, and "Persia and India as Fashion Sources," November 14, *New York Times,* Culin Papers.

Fig. 11. Southwest Indian exhibit, Stewart Culin, curator, the Brooklyn Museum, 1907. From *Brooklyn Museum Report 1910*. (Courtesy, The Brooklyn Museum.)

ing to renewed industrial interest in oriental design after 1909, however, he made several trips to Japan, China, and India to collect textiles, toys, and ceremonial objects. The magazine *Asia* commented on Culin's Japanese costume exhibit: "The room that Stewart Culin has developed in the Brooklyn Institute Museum, has in my judgment no counterpart in any museum of the world. The museum offers an immense store of valuable material in such a way that the designer feels as free as though working in his own study, and it [has presented] the documents in an unusual and delightful manner. Just as the producers of costumes and textiles find inspiration, so can toy makers secure many original ideas in this Ethnological section of the great Brooklyn Institute Museum." As if to underscore the connection between curator and designer, Culin praised "the wonderful exhibitions of toys in the New York and Brooklyn department stores," and he stepped in at Bonwit Teller to assist the display of Javanese costumes at the store.[28]

[28] For Culin's contribution to American Indian studies, see his *Games of the North American Indians* (1907; reprint, New York: Dover Publications, 1975); "American Indian Games," *Bulletin of the Free Museum of Science and Art* 1, no. 3 (April 1898): 99–116;

Culin was the consummate collector, which the Brooklyn Museum acknowledged in 1967: "Culin was the ethnologist who practically filled up the Brooklyn Museum. . . . Imagine the magnitude of Culin's task in setting up thousands upon thousands of objects in meaningful installations! Imagine changing them around as wing after wing was completed!" His acquisition of objects was done in the manner of a merchant-curator; he bought objects directly from craftsmen, but more often he worked through dealers in the locales he visited to obtain the material he wanted. In "The Story of the Painted Curtain," Culin recounted his escapades in 1914 in India where he chanced upon a legendary secret treasure house. There he found "carved ivory and gilded pachisi pieces with which a king must have played." Prized possessions of the discovery were seventeenth-century painted curtains, 23 feet long and 8 feet high in brilliant colors, showing English and Portuguese merchants trading with Asians (figs. 12, 13). Both the historical and the artistic communities were excited when Culin reported his find. Clearly taking pride in his collecting escapades, Culin wrote on another occasion of acquiring Spanish columns from the Southwest:

Then we found ourselves with the column in the moonlight. We knew we must get it away without loss of time. The snoring continued, and the dogs were quiet, but at any moment they might raise an alarm. I cannot tell how it was accomplished, but I recall we let the column slide from the top of the arroya (a water course such as a stream in an arid region) so that its impetus carried it a long way to our camp, where, protected by the blue tigers and yellow rattlesnakes, we slept with it until long past our usual hour. On the following night, helped by a mercenary, a big Navajo teamster, who had neither fears nor

---

"American Indian Games," *Journal of American Folklore* 11, no. 43 (October–December 1898): 245–53; "Guide to the Southwestern Indian Hall," *Museum News* 2, no. 7 (April 1907): 105–11; "Zuni Pictures," in *American Indian Life*, ed. Elsie Clews Parsons (1922; reprint, Lincoln: University of Nebraska Press, 1967), pp. 175–78; and "Tales from the House in the Valley," *American Indian* 7, no. 4 (August 1920): 11–16. For his collections of oriental objects, see his *Brooklyn Museum Quarterly* articles "Japanese Announcements and Programmes," 5, no. 4 (September 1918): 211–17, "The Indian Stairway," 5, no. 2 (April 1918): 79–81, "The Game of Ma-Jong," 11, no. 3 (October 1924): 153–68, "Burri-Burri Gitcho: A Japanese Swinging Bat Game," 12, no. 3 (July 1925): 133–38, and "The No Drama of Japan," 5, no. 2 (April 1918): 121–23; "Art of the Chinese," *International Studio* 80, no. 332 (January 1925): 287–98; "Japanese Toys and Their Lore," *Asia* 20, no. 3 (April 1920): 295–301; and "Book Collecting in India and the Far East," *Public Libraries* 20, no. 5 (May 1915): 195–97. See also "World's Wonder Toys," pp. 105–10.

Fig. 12. Curtain panel (one of seven), India, ca. 1630–40, collected by Stewart Culin, 1914. Painted cotton; H. 108¼″, W. 37¾″. (Courtesy, The Brooklyn Museum.)

Fig. 13. Mate to panel in figure 12 (detail). (Courtesy, The Brooklyn Museum.)

scruples, we secured the remaining columns and loaded them all on his heavy wagon for an early start to the railroad.[29]

Culin took to writing fiction to reflect on the collecting experience. In "Blue Beard's Chamber," he told the story of a collecting trip to an American Indian village: "I lodged with the missionary, who gave out word I had come to buy old things. So many people came, bringing so much rubbish I rented an outbuilding as a warehouse where I worked and stored my purchases." Dissatisfied with the "utility or value" of the things they brought, the narrator determined "to try and revive some of the ancient arts and secure some of the things I really wanted." The narrative continues with a gleeful blending of the commercial and traditional:

I explained I did not want ordinary clothes, but gala attire such as their beloved Tenatsali used to wear—blue woven shirt with tight fitting knee breeches adorned with silver buttons, a belt set with large oval disks of polished silver, striped garters, leggings and immaculate moccasins. These were all. No! There should be a baldrick of deer skin with more wrought silver ornaments. I would spare no expense. I would revive an entire group of industries in a single order. In due course I learned that in consequence of the enforcement of the territorial game laws no deer had been killed by the Indians for many years and that it was necessary to send to a department store in Denver for Indian-tanned deer skins.

This collector's purpose—and Culin's—was to make "protests for variety," a variety that industry threatened to reduce. Finally he found what he was looking for in a forbidden chamber filled with ritual masks, an experience that paralleled Culin's collection of masks for the Brooklyn Museum (fig. 14). His guide asked him, "Are they not wonderful, made with all the necessary prayers and fastings. I attended to everything. Now how much will you pay for them?" Here the collector looked upon objects with depth and meaning and exclaimed, "Let us pack this stuff and get away!"[30]

Culin's "Perfect Collector" is another short piece of fiction in which he comments further on the collecting passion through the character of Mr. Greatrox:

[29] *The Brooklyn Museum Handbook* (Brooklyn: Brooklyn Museum Handbook, 1967), p. 20; Stewart Culin, "The Story of the Painted Curtain," *Good Furniture* 11, no. 9 (September 1918): 133–47; Stewart Culin, "The Story of the Carved Pilaster," *Good Furniture* 11, no. 4 (April 1918): 233–39.

[30] Stewart Culin, "Blue Beard's Chamber," typescript, Culin Papers.

Fig. 14. Stewart Culin, with American Indian ritual masks, ca. 1920s. (Courtesy, The Brooklyn Museum.)

I started in a small way and grew up much like other people until I became a collector. . . . There are collectors of cups and saucers and even tureens, but I confine myself to plates. . . . My only difficulty now is lack of room. Every day my agents report a new find. If only I had not sold the land adjacent to my house, what a collection I might have had. As it is all the servants sleep out, and I am thinking of doing over one of the cellars as a bed room, for of course even the most enthusiastic collector must have a place to sleep. I know you are going to ask if Mrs. Greatrox likes porcelain and I must tell you she dotes on it. She thinks of nothing else. Now as for myself I have such a diversity of interests! There is the church. Of course I don't have the same occasion for it as most people for I feel my life is consecrated. There so many ways we can do good. My object is to aid and instruct. Every step I take toward completing my collecting I feel that I am gaining in grace.

Later at breakfast, the separation of collecting from practical life is exposed, as Greatrox dwells on his collection of china:

I have a different set for every day in the year. Not from my collection, for that I never think of using. Nothing that is put to practical use belongs to art. I might even say nothing that could be used practically is art. Our best houses prove that. Only the other day I read some anarchist spoke of art as a byproduct of industry. Or was it a socialist? I am glad the law is to take its course with those fellows. They attack the very foundations of society. A china collector is in a peculiarly delicate position. Imagine the harm a bomb would do in this house.

Culin saw the collecting of these utilitarian items as art as a defense of the foundations of the "best" society. It was consumption revolving around consumption.[31]

Culin's fiction received far less attention than his reports of his collecting trips. Such reports of his actual adventures filled readers with envy and excited them to pursue their own finds. In addition to receiving the praise of the popular press in the first decade of the twentieth century, Culin was considered by the Smithsonian's McGee as one of the top six museum men in the country. According to McGee, what put Culin at the top of his profession was "his arrangement of material displays, that strong grasp of those general relations required for rendering a great collection attractive to the more casual visitor." Reports of valuable finds in exotic places, coupled with some danger and daring, often overshadowed the results of progressive exhibition techniques which drew imitation from museums throughout the country. In 1913 George

[31] Stewart Culin, "The Perfect Collector," typescript, Culin Papers. Culin's use of "Greatrox" is probably taken from the real-life artist Eliza Greatorex (1819–97), a blue-blooded elite who drew pictures of old New York houses and bemoaned the democratizing wave of immigration into America; see Eliza Greatorex, *Old New York from the Battery to Bloomingdale* (New York: G. P. Putnam's Sons, 1875). Greatorex was a close friend of Edward Lamson Henry's (1841–1919), another artist, New York City resident, and prominent collector of antique furniture and china; see Elizabeth Stillinger, *The Antiquers: The Lives and Careers, the Deals, the Finds, the Collections of the Men and Women Who Were Responsible for the Changing Taste in American Antiques, 1850–1930* (New York: Alfred A. Knopf, 1980), pp. 35–41, 50–51. For the rise of this kind of collecting, see Alice Morse Earle, *China Collecting in America* (New York: Charles Scribner's Sons, 1892); N. Hudson Moore, *The Old China Book* (New York: Frederick A. Stokes, 1903); Robert and Elizabeth Shackleton, *The Charm of the Antique* (New York: Hearst's International Library, 1913); Walter A. Dyer, *The Lure of the Antique* (New York: Century Co., 1910); Gardner Teall, *The Pleasures of Collecting* (New York: Century Co., 1920); and R. T. H. Halsey and Elizabeth Tower, *The Homes of Our Ancestors as Shown in the American Wing of the Metropolitan Museum of Art* (New York: Doubleday, Doran, 1925). For secondary texts, see Stillinger, *Antiquers*; Douglas and Elizabeth Rigby, *Lock, Stock and Barrel: The Story of Collecting* (Philadelphia: J. B. Lippincott Co., 1944), pp. 262–309; Wendy Kaplan, "R. T. H. Halsey: An Ideology of Collecting American Decorative Arts," *Winterthur Portfolio* 17, no. 1 (Spring 1982): 43–54; and Simon J. Bronner, *Grasping Things: Folk Material Culture and Mass Society in America* (Lexington: University Press of Kentucky, 1986), pp. 178–210.

Dorsey wrote, "When one can stand in the Japanese hall of the Brooklyn Museum and forget one is in Brooklyn—that is art, and true merit, and the genius of Stewart Culin." Dorsey noted the changes in museums Culin had made: "Museums never have enough of money or anything except trustees—and then sometimes too many. Museums also have a tendency to be musty and a disposition to bring on a headache. You can prove all this by spending an hour in a Regular Museum; then look over Culin's work in the Brooklyn Institute Museum." Dorsey's praise was not lost on the management of the Brooklyn Museum, for it bragged that Culin's department was "already being watched with envious eyes by other museums."[32]

As his career proceeded, Culin stepped even further into cooperation with manufacturers. Noting the rise of interest in traditional European designs, he traveled deep into eastern Europe in search of peasant textiles and artifacts following World War I. Culin came to believe "the patterns did not originate with the peasants themselves, but came down from some higher culture, the peasants, merely copying what they had learned but did not originate." He believed this theory could be applied to American society by encouraging elite designers to influence the taste of the masses. He encouraged art students and designers to examine the lessons from traditional goods and their makers to improve American products. Addressing the schools of fine and applied arts at Pratt Institute, Culin declared: "The traditions of craftsmanship are not to be learned from books. They are not to be taught orally either in the class room or lecture hall. They are to be acquired in a work-shop and then best if not alone from a master." In the absence of this older system, the museum stepped in as a higher cultural guild: "I would like to have you think of the museum, not as a place of antiquities and relics but as preserving the seed of things which may blossom and fruit again through your efforts." Then he called upon the "magic" which others noticed in his work: "There is something that seems akin to magic in this mastery of things, in this understanding of their language and this power to make them speak and tell their story." Culin described the magic as "the quality of life to quicken our minds and excite the creative impulse which we designate as art." He imagined that the museum would be

---

[32] W. J. McGee to Carnegie Museum, January 13, 1903, Culin Papers; George Dorsey, "Stewart Culin," *American* 45, no. 3 (June 1913): 36–37; "Ethnology at the Institute," newsletter clipping from 1904, Culin Papers.

valuable as industrialization took command, for the museum preserved models for design and a magic inspired by faraway creators filled with the compassion and immediacy of handwork.[33]

The frequent collecting trips undertaken by Culin are a rarity among collectors today (according to most reports, this work of ethnological museums has been on a long decline). Such trips were characteristic of a period in the late nineteenth and early twentieth centuries when museums, themselves on the rise, participated in the age of enterprise by unprecedented exhibiting and adventurous collecting that eventually drew imitation from history and art museums. Not all museum men felt as Culin did; for example, Franz Boas of the Museum of Natural History abandoned museum work because he felt dissatisfied with its evolutionary principles. Yet Culin was in the vanguard of a movement he shared with "scientific" men from business as well as the professions. According to at least one report by the Museums Association (Great Britain), the development of ethnological, folklore, and science museums during this period was the major American contribution to the world-wide museum movement.[34]

The rising importance of museums and museum men in this movement was a reflection of the growing importance of things and their accumulation. The sudden growth of museums in the United States was a symptom of the post–Civil War era, marked by the nation's industrial and consumptive upsurge, its need for a visible and usable past in the wake of an immigrant tidal wave, and its aspiration to greater economic and political power. It was a time of dramatic—often traumatic—changes, when traditional societies long in place seemed suddenly to give way to fierce industrialization and rampant urbanization.[35]

[33] See Stewart Culin, "Peasant Art of Central Europe," *Bulletin of the Needle and Bobbin Club* 5, no. 1 (1921): 30–35; "The Sources of Ornamental Design," pp. 94–95, 130; Culin, Field-Trip Journal, vol. 1, 1920, p. 105, Culin Papers; and Culin, "Creation in Art," pp. 91–92. For discussion of the aura of magic around consumable things, see Jackson Lears, "Beyond Veblen: Rethinking Consumer Culture in America," elsewhere in this volume.

[34] See Ira Jacknis, "Franz Boas and Exhibits: On the Limitations of the Museum Method of Anthropology," in *Objects and Others: Essays on Museums and Material Culture*, ed. George W. Stocking (Madison: University of Wisconsin Press, 1985), pp. 75–111. S. Weir Mitchell, "The Scientific Life," *Lippincott's* 15, no. 17 (March 1875): 352–56; Markham, "Impressions of American Museums," pp. 337–38.

[35] Culin's friend and fellow museum pioneer Henry Mercer avowed, for example, that in contrast to Swedish ethnological collections, museum collections "brought together here in the United States and transmuted as it were in a great cauldron [convey] a broader

Culin's displays and their objects told of ways of life becoming increasingly incomprehensible to modern Americans. His collecting trips were interpreted more as hunts in the wild as Americans thought of themselves as being more sophisticated. In his presentation of accumulated objects that seemed exotic to the Victorians, Culin offered them a sense of order in understanding the ways of life of their forebears and sought to provide a sense of continuity and comprehension of a rapidly changing world. In his push for "artistic" displays was an agenda for finding meaning and depth behind utilitarian accumulation. Culin as merchant used the museum as an adviser to industry and an educator of the public; as curator, he sought purposes and themes for objects and for his age.

Seated in a Paris bistro in 1920, Culin questioned how far the age had actually progressed according to his evolutionary belief. He watched a drunken display of jazz playing and dancing and entered the scene in his journal: "I have been among the savages, but a display like this I have never seen." Ever the "modern" scientist, he now felt old-fashioned. He struggled with an ambivalence of evolutionary ideas in a new relativistic age. Walking through his museum gallery for one of the last times, Culin wrote:

It has been my habit as an ethnologist devoted to the study of the material culture of mankind to think of the races of antiquity as younger and not older than the people of our own age; to refresh myself with such contacts as I have

---

object lesson than a similar collection would in Sweden where there has been no such influx of immigration or gathering together of other nations," in Henry Mercer, "The Tools of the Nation Maker," *A Collection of Papers Read before the Bucks County Historical Society* (Riegelsville, Pa.: B. F. Fackenthal, Jr., 1909), p. 479; chapter reprinted in Bronner, ed., *Folklife Studies*, pp. 279–91. See also Neil Harris, "The Gilded Age Revisited: Boston and the Museum Movement," in *Material Culture: Historical Agencies and the Historian*, ed. Lucius F. Ellsworth and Maureen O'Brien (Philadelphia: Book Reprint Service, 1969), pp. 158–79; and "Cultural Institutions and American Modernization," *Journal of Library History* 16, no. 1 (Winter 1981): 28–47. For examples of intellectual and cultural responses to societal changes, see T. J. Jackson Lears, *No Place of Grace: Antimodernism and the Transformation of American Culture, 1880–1920* (New York: Pantheon Books, 1981); David E. Shi, *The Simple Life: Plain Living and High Thinking in American Culture* (New York: Oxford University Press, 1985), pp. 155–214; Gunther Barth, *City People: The Rise of Modern City Culture in Nineteenth-Century America* (New York: Oxford University Press, 1980); Stephen Kern, *The Culture of Time and Space, 1880–1918* (Cambridge, Mass.: Harvard University Press, 1983), Leo Marx, *The Machine in the Garden: Technology and the Pastoral Ideal in America* (New York: Oxford University Press, 1964); and Blake McKelvey, *The Urbanization of America, 1860–1915* (New Brunswick, N.J.: Rutgers University Press, 1963).

had with their minds to feel myself younger and more vital. I have realized my dreams among savages in whose lives and thoughts I have had glimpses of the dawn of the world. I believe one should be free to choose whether the past be seen as a kind of inferno, diversified by murder and punctuated by crime, or as a joyous period of creative effort as I realize it from things of the past which I have made my friends and enticed into telling me their tales. [36]

Culin died a few months before the stock market crash in 1929. The *New York Times* devoted a full column to him, and besides recognizing that he "was internationally known for his ethnological work and for a number of authoritative studies," the paper pointed out that "one of his notable achievements was an elaborate exhibit of African art, now housed in the Brooklyn Museum." Also in New York, Allen Eaton of the Russell Sage Foundation credited Culin for inspiring the blockbuster America's Making Exposition and the book based on the exhibition, *Immigrant Gifts to American Life*. In Culin's hometown of Philadelphia, E. W. Mumford wrote the librarian of the Historical Society of Pennsylvania after hearing of his death, "Stewart Culin was really the distinguished man in his chosen field [of museums]." In Santa Fe, New Mexico, an article bearing the headline, "Dr. Culin, Who Tried to Make Museums Atractive, Dies at Age of 71 Years," described Culin as "famed for his efforts to make the rather somber museum building, somber within and without, attractive to the 'common geezer' or 'the man in the street.' [Culin] was well known all the way from New York to Peking, China. . . . He was really the pioneer in the movement to make museums attractive, . . . [and] he believed by so doing he would arouse public interest in the study of the past, and help raise funds to unearth buried cities and unlock the ancient historical treasures to the enquiring present-day peoples of the world." *Art Digest* added, "Given a free hand in Brooklyn, he had much to do with the changed attitude in American museums that has made them 'alive' instead of sepulchres of the past." *Art News* offered, "he initiated many of the practices now general in the museum field for he had a genius for installation and a profound conviction that museum collections were valuable only as they served the needs of the public." The Brooklyn Museum boasted that through the objects under Culin's control, he extended the influence of the museum into "design rooms and show windows of manu-

[36] Culin, "Road to Beauty," p. 42.

facturers and retailers all over the length and breadth of the United States." *El Palacio* noted: "under his direction the Museum attained an international reputation, not merely as a rich storehouse of ethnologic material, to which he was annually adding by trips abroad, but also as a factory of ideas . . . he encouraged in practical ways the use of the Museum material by students, designers and manufacturers, in order that the industrial and artistic life of the country might benefit from it to the full."[37]

Today Culin's innovations are taken for granted in museum accumulation and display. His name is rarely attached, although his influence, as predicted, lives on. His career illustrates the conviction of men who went far afield for museums that arose to interpret what was happening at home. Commenting on this era of growth for museums, *Scientific American* aptly described the role of museums as the "Art of Perpetuation," a translation of the "Result of Man's Acquisitiveness": "It is possible to go and with the utmost pride and self-satisfaction observe the milestones of our progress from the arrow-head to the modern rifle, from the sedan chair and hobby-horse to the motorcycle and aeroplane, from the spinning wheel to the modern loom, from the Caxton printing press to the linotype, from Stephenson's 'Rocket' to the railway express engine, from the windbag of the Roman invaders to the latest ocean greyhound in miniature. It is all there." A year after this article appeared, *Review of Reviews* pointedly asked, "What Are Museums For?" The review of prevailing thought recognized that within the last generation, museums specifically and cultural institutions generally had taken on a prominent place in American society: "Things whose merit we have hitherto taken for granted are now required to justify their existence from the standpoint of contemporary needs, or, if they cannot, to make way for others that can. We are reshaping the paraphernalia of exis-

[37] "Stewart Culin Dies; Noted Ethnologist," *New York Times*, April 9, 1929, p. 31; Allen H. Eaton, *Immigrant Gifts to American Life* (New York: Russell Sage Foundation, 1932), p. 156; E. W. Mumford to Thomas L. Montgomery, April 10, 1929, Historical Society of Pennsylvania, Philadelphia; "Dr. Culin, Who Tried to Make Museums Attractive, Dies at Age of 71 Years," clipping dated April 16, 1919, Santa Fe, University of Pennsylvania Museum Archives; "Culin Is Dead," *Art Digest* 3, no. 14 (mid April 1929): 9; "Stewart Culin," *Art News* 27, no. 28 (April 13, 1929): 12; M. D. C. Crawford, "Tribute to Robert Stewart Culin," *Brooklyn Museum Quarterly* 16, no. 2 (April 1929): 88–89; C. F. Saunders, "Death of Stewart Culin," *El Palacio* 27, no. 10 (September 1929): 108–9.

tence; whether wisely or not, the future alone can tell." Again the primary call was for the public education role of museums in the appreciation of objects, but in most museums, "the public must have no say in what it will be taught. The museums have a 'required course of study,' and this is cultural rather than practical."[38]

In the post-Victorian period, museums moved away from many of the evolutionary principles and moralistic purposes familiar to Culin and Goode. Museums, like the arts before them, were democratizing, taking "the needs and desires of the people" more into account. But the cultural education of museums, the consuming orientation toward objects in the creation of "higher civilization," had already been set in place.[39] The museums growing out of this consuming vision gave the object lessons that, while apparently democratizing society's arts, they also arbitrated its tastes.

[38] Bruce Cummings, "The Art of Perpetuation: Museums the Result of Man's Acquisitiveness," *Scientific American* 85, supplement no. 2212 (May 25, 1918): 330–31; "What Are Museums For?" *Review of Reviews* 59, no. 1 (January 1919): 97–98.

[39] "What Are Museums For," p. 98. See also "Modernizing the Museum," *Arts and Decoration* 11 (August 1919): 190–91; F. H. Sterns, "The Place of the Museum in Our Modern Life," *Scientific Monthly* 7, no. 12 (December 1918): 545–54; John Cotton Dana, "In a Changing World Should Museums Change?" *Museum* 1, no. 6 (September 1926): 82–86; and Theodore L. Low, *The Museum as a Social Instrument* (New York: Metropolitan Museum of Art/American Association of Museums, 1942). Neil Harris, "Museums, Merchandising, and Popular Taste: The Struggle for Influence," in *Material Culture and the Study of American Life*, ed. Ian M. G. Quimby (New York: W. W. Norton, 1978), pp. 140–74; Kenneth Hudson, *A Social History of Museums: What the Visitors Thought* (Atlantic Highlands, N.J.: Humanities Press, 1975), pp. 48–122; Edwin L. Wade, "The Ethnic Art Market in the American Southwest, 1880–1980," in *Objects and Others: Essays on Museums and Material Culture*, ed. George W. Stocking, Jr. (Madison: University of Wisconsin Press, 1985), pp. 167–91; and Adam, *Civic Value of Museums*, pp. 34–46.

The Collecting Self and
American Youth Movements

Jay Mechling

The white, blond-haired children dressed like American Indians and smiling in old photographs illustrate how American youth movements conceived at the end of the nineteenth century built their programs around the making and collecting of things by children (fig. 1). The uniforms and costumes of the Woodcraft Indians, Sons of Daniel Boone, Boy Scouts, Girl Scouts, Camp Fire Girls, and other groups stood for this fetish of the object, as the children often made their costumes by hand and affixed badges or other signs of rank and accomplishment on the costumes. Many of these badges, in turn, signaled that the bearer had made something or collected something to earn the badge. Both figuratively and literally, this child at the turn of the century wore his character on his sleeve.

Dressing American children in buckskins or tan drill was a sudden impulse of the late nineteenth century. Little in the treatment of American children prepares the historian for the appearance of this tactic. The simple explanation would be that these movements took the military as their model and that, accordingly, the Boy Scout uniform and the practice of earning badges and ranks were borrowed from that model. This view is reasonable when looking at Lord Baden-Powell and the origins of the Boy Scout movement in England in 1908.[1] But this expla-

[1] The most recent biography of Lord Baden-Powell is Michael Rosenthal's *Character Factory: Baden-Powell and the Origins of the Boy Scout Movement* (New York: Pantheon Books, 1986). Also useful is J. O. Springhall, "The Boy Scouts: Class and Militarism in Relation to British Youth Movements, 1908–1930," *International Review of Social History* 16 (1971): 125–58.

Fig. 1. Woodcraft Indians. From Lillian Elizabeth Roy, *Little Woodcrafter's Book* (New York: Grosset and Dunlap, 1917), frontis.

nation fails to clarify American movements. The most successful of these movements, the Boy Scouts for young men and the Girl Scouts and Camp Fire Girls for young women, originated largely in the ideas and organizations founded by men and women who were all staunchly antimilitaristic.

The reasons for the uniforms and badges must lie elsewhere, possibly in the same cultural forces that led to the emergence of American strategies of accumulation and display in the 1880s and 1890s, strategies embodied in institutions such as museums, department stores, and well-stocked parlors and halls.[2] While reading museums and department stores as American cultural texts tells us something about adult rituals of accumulation, display, and consumption, a reading of American youth movements during these same years shows how adults not only projected their own impulses upon their children but also went so far as to create institutions to socialize these impulses. To understand how American capitalism reproduces itself at a particular moment in history, we must look closely at the socialization of children. It is one thing for a group to create rituals of accumulation and consumption, surrounding itself with the material things as adjuncts to those rituals; it is another to be sure the children take their parents' rituals seriously.

Believing that they were following a reasonable strategy, American founders of youth movements from the 1890s until World War I built the movements around making, collecting, and wearing things. This essay focuses primarily on the Boy Scouts of America and two of its founders, Ernest Thompson Seton (1860–1946) and Daniel Carter Beard (1850–1941), but the insights about the Boy Scouts apply *mutatis mutandis* to girls' movements as well. Seton's movement (unlike Beard's) always included young women as well as young men, and Seton was a friend and key adviser to Luther and Charlotte Gulick and others who founded the Camp Fire Girls in 1911. The Girl Scouts, founded as the Girl Guides by Juliette Low in 1912, were fashioned even more closely than the Camp Fire Girls upon a slightly later model for the Boy Scouts, one Seton detested. The founding of the Boy Scouts of America in 1910 created a virtual monopoly as a youth program for young men, a position later secured by a charter from the United States Congress in 1915.[3]

[2] See, for example, Neil Harris, "Museums, Merchandising, and Popular Taste: The Struggle for Influence," in *Material Culture and the Study of American Life*, ed. Ian M. G. Quimby (New York: W. W. Norton, 1978), pp. 140–74; and Simon J. Bronner, "Object Lessons: The Work of Ethnological Museums and Collections," William Leach, "Strategists of Display and the Production of Desire," Jean-Christophe Agnew, "A House of Fiction: Domestic Interiors and the Commodity Aesthetic," and Karen Halttunen, "From Parlor to Living Room: Domestic Space, Interior Decoration, and the Culture of Personality," elsewhere in this volume.

[3] Ways in which a group of Boy Scouts uses its folklore and rituals to address some of the cultural contradictions of capitalism are explored in Jay Mechling, "Patois and Paradox in a Boy Scout Treasure Hunt," *Journal of American Folklore* 97, no. 383 (January–March 1984): 24–42; and Helen Buckler, Mary F. Fiedler, and Martha F. Allen,

Beard and Seton were artists and naturalists in addition to being youth-work founders. For both men, the sequence of their interests took them from art to ethology (the study of animal behavior in context), from there to ethnology (the study of human races and cultures), and eventually to youth work. Each of these fields shared what philosophers and cultural critics have come to call the "crisis of representation," the loss of confidence that our symbolic renderings of reality, from scientific accounts to art, correspond in any way with some putative objective reality. The youth program activities of making, collecting, and wearing things were conscious strategies meant to address the crisis. Not surprisingly, the new strategy of building a child's identity around material objects failed as a solution to the crisis, producing only a "collecting self" that was no more authentic or satisfying than before but that helped addict the child to the pursuit of consumer goods as a way of discovering and displaying one's emerging identity. The crisis and the response to it provide an understanding of the social psychology and cultural meanings of a distinctive, new materialism that emerged fully in American society at the beginning of the twentieth century.

Uncle Dan, Black Wolf, and the Crisis of Representation

Daniel Carter Beard's childhood in the Cincinnati home of his parents laid the groundwork for his lifelong addiction to art and nature.[4] His father, James N. Beard, was a prominent artist, and his mother's family (the Carters) enjoyed great entrepreneurial success in the Ohio valley. The Swedenborgian theology of John Chapman, better known as Johnny Appleseed, provided the moral canopy over the artistic and entrepreneurial values that Beard learned in his childhood home, as both the Beards and the Carters had converted to this faith early in the nineteenth century.

---

comps., *Wo-he-lo: The Story of the Camp Fire Girls, 1910–1960* (New York: Holt, Rinehart and Winston, 1961). The best social history of the Boy Scouts of America is David I. Macleod, *Building Character in the American Boy: The Boy Scouts, YMCA, and Their Forerunners, 1870–1920* (Madison: University of Wisconsin Press, 1983).

[4] For expanded details of Beard's life and work, see Allan Richard Whitmore, "Beard, Boys, and Buckskins: Daniel Carter Beard and the Preservation of the American Pioneer Tradition" (Ph.D. diss., Northwestern University, 1970). For his autobiography, see Daniel Carter Beard, *Hardly a Man Is Now Alive* (New York: Doubleday, Doran, 1939).

Beard first trained as a civil engineer and surveyor, but he spent as much time in the field sketching nature as he did with his engineering work. In 1878 he moved to New York City to pursue a career in art, joining the Art Students League of New York. Joining the league not only put him in the company of other young artists, including Frederick Remington and Ernest Thompson Seton, but also placed him in the center of the revolt against the art establishment dominated by the National Academy of Design.

Beard secured a position illustrating essays and stories for *St. Nicholas*, a periodical for children, but soon he added writing to his work for the magazine. His illustrated article "Snowball Warfare" appeared in the January 1880 issue, followed in March by his article "Kite Time." Over the next year, the popularity of similar articles by Beard and the urging of his brother led Beard to compile his articles into his first book, *American Boys' Handy Book: What to Do and How to Do It* (1882).[5] The book was a great success, selling a remarkable 30,000 copies by 1900 and 50,000 by Beard's death in 1941.

By 1889 Beard's fame led Samuel Clemens, writing as Mark Twain, to seek him out to illustrate *A Connecticut Yankee in King Arthur's Court*, an assignment Beard relished. The politics and morality of the novel appealed to Beard, and he was especially attracted to Twain's theme of sham and the relationship between appearance and character. Beard's illustrations for the novel became controversial because of his use of contemporary public figures (such as Jay Gould) as models for his characters as well as his explicit attacks on the church and the capitalists. In 1886 Beard had joined Henry George's single-tax movement and wrote his own single-tax novel, *Moonblight*.[6] Twain was pleased with Beard's *Connecticut Yankee* illustrations, but many critics saw the illustrations as propaganda for the single-tax movement, which created a political furor that caused Beard considerable trouble, including the blacklisting of his services as an illustrator.

Frustrated with the political and economic arena of reform, Beard returned to boys' work in 1905. William E. Annis, the new owner and

[5] D. C. Beard, *American Boys' Handy Book: What to Do and How to Do It* (New York: Charles Scribner's Sons, 1882).

[6] Whitmore, "Beard, Boys, and Buckskins," pp. 146–64, contains a discussion of the single-tax novel by D. C. Beard, *Moonblight; and Six Feet of Romance* (New York: Charles L. Webster, 1892).

publisher of *Recreation,* hired Beard as the magazine's editor. In addition to the conservationist agenda the men shared, including the conservation of American Indian cultures, Beard and Annis wanted to use the monthly magazine to launch a youth movement. The July 1905 issue introduced "The Sons of Daniel Boone," a new department of the magazine. One purpose of the new organization was to enlist young people in the magazine's conservation work. But equally important to Beard was the movement's promise to promote "manliness" through democratic organization (boys would create local chapters called "forts"), outdoor fun, the study of nature ("woodcraft"), and handicraft, the making of things as first illustrated in his *Handy Book.* There was no central bureaucracy for the movement, and Beard's monthly articles and the other materials he wrote were all that linked the local chapters. By 1908, however, 20,000 boys were members of the Sons of Daniel Boone.

Conflicts within the organization led Beard to sever his ties with *Recreation* in 1906 and join *Woman's Home Companion,* where he continued writing "The Sons of Daniel Boone." Beard's clashes with the women editors of the magazine led him to resign in 1909 and use *Pictorial Review* as the new magazine for promotion of his youth-movement ideas. A legal battle ensued with *Woman's Home Companion* over the rights to "The Sons of Daniel Boone," which was settled finally by the magazine's keeping the name but Beard's keeping the rights to his articles.[7] Beard chose Young Pioneers as the name for the new movement founded through *Pictorial Review* and filled the movement's handbook with stories of pioneer heroes like Davy Crockett and Johnny Appleseed. These movements were in place in 1910, when Beard joined Seton and others to establish the Boy Scouts of America.

Seton was born in England but moved to Canada while still a young man. His interest in natural history began at an early age. His father wanted Seton to become an artist and in 1878 sent him to the Ontario School of Art for a year of study. After a brief time homesteading in Manitoba, Seton moved to New York City in 1883 to pursue his art career, where he met Beard and others in the Art Students League. In New York, Seton also cultivated an intellectual community that included professional naturalists such as ornithologists Elliot Coues,

---

[7] The articles were collected eventually and published as D. C. Beard, *The Boy Pioneers: Sons of Daniel Boone* (New York: Charles Scribner's Sons, 1909).

Frank M. Chapman, and C. Hart Merriam (then secretary-treasurer of the American Ornithologists Union), zoologist Spencer F. Baird at the Smithsonian, and bird painter Louis Agassiz Fuertes. Coues helped Seton to secure a commission to complete the biological illustrations for the new *Century Dictionary*, and by 1890 Seton had completed a major treatise, *The Birds of Manitoba*.[8]

Scientific reaction to the Manitoba book was not kind. In the book, Seton had adopted the mixture of scientific information and narrative invention that made his stories famous but which always stood in the way of his acceptance by the scientific community. This was but one example of Seton's inability to reconcile the conflict between scientific objectivity and artistic subjectivity.[9] Pained by the response to his work, Seton fled to Europe in the summer of 1890. In London he cemented a friendship with Joseph Wolf, a German artist famous for his animal paintings, and in Paris Seton entered L'Academie Julian, where he studied under Jean-Léon Gérôme, whose students included Thomas Eakins. American painter Robert Henri was a fellow student with whom Seton spent many hours discussing art and socialism.

Seton returned to New York bolstered by the influence of Wolf and Henri. Persuasive arguments state that Seton by this time had chosen the wolf as his "symbol for nature."[10] His first entry in salon competition was *The Sleeping Wolf* (1891), a painting hung by the jury, which was reasonably well received. His second entry, *Awaited in Vain* (1892), was far more controversial. It was rejected by the jury for the Canadian exhibit at the 1893 World's Columbian Exposition in Chicago, and the Royal Canadian Academy also rejected the piece because

[8]John Henry Wadland provides a good biographical account and argues convincingly his thesis that Seton possessed an ecological consciousness, in John Henry Wadland, *Ernest Thompson Seton: Man in Nature and the Progressive Era, 1880–1915* (New York: Arno Press, 1978). Betty Keller takes Seton's life beyond the 1915 date where Wadland's book ends, but she adds little important insight into Seton, in Betty Keller, *Black Wolf: The Life of Ernest Thompson Seton* (Vancouver and Toronto: Douglas and McIntyre, 1984). Seton's autobiography is Ernest Thompson Seton, *Trail of an Artist-Naturalist* (London: Hodder and Stoughton,1951). For excerpts from Seton's journals and correspondence, see Julia M. Seton, *By a Thousand Fires* (Garden City, N.Y.: Doubleday, 1967). The English version of woodcraft is traced in Brian Morris, "Ernest Thompson Seton and the Origins of the Woodcraft Movement," *Journal of Contemporary History* 5, no. 2 (1970): 183–94.
[9]Wadland, *Seton*, p. 100.
[10]Wadland, *Seton*, pp. 117–18.

of its subject matter. The painting, which Seton preferred to call *Triumph of the Wolves*, shows a pack of wolves with the skeleton and scattered clothes of a recently devoured human who is awaited in the peaceful cabin in the background. One of the wolves is gnawing on the skull, while another gazes toward the cabin. After much political struggle within the Canadian art world, the Royal Canadian Academy finally accepted a revised version of the painting.

In 1897 Seton began what was to be the last of his scientific projects, *Life Histories of Northern Animals*, completed in 1909. From 1898 on, Seton practiced ethology not in scientific treatises, but in the realistic animal stories for which he is so famous. In 1898 he published *Wild Animals I Have Known*, a collection of his popular, early stories such as "Lobo" (1894). The attack by naturalist John Burroughs in 1903 upon Seton's animal stories led him to abandon that genre, although he completed *Life Histories of Northern Animals* at least in part as a vindication of the scientific accuracy of his animal stories.

By 1903 Seton already had work to replace the writing of animal stories. In the early 1890s Seton had formulated an idea for a youth movement based upon woodcraft and American Indian customs. In 1903 he created a small tribe of so-called Seton's Indians and adopted for himself the name Black Wolf. Rudyard Kipling urged Seton to cast his notion in the form of a novel, an idea that appealed to Seton. In May 1902 *Ladies' Home Journal* had established a new department called "American Woodcraft for Boys," which published an article by Seton monthly. The magazine printed excerpts from Seton's *Two Little Savages*, published in 1903.[11]

Seton's *Birch Bark Roll of Woodcraft* (1903) established the outline of the youth movement based upon the ideas presented in *Two Little Savages* and elaborated through many editions of *The Book of Woodcraft and Indian Lore*. For Seton woodcraft was a theory of outdoor recreation based upon human instinct. Well read in Darwinian biology and the psychological ideas of G. Stanley Hall, Seton fashioned each woodcraft activity around such instincts, the key one being the instinct to play. In *Birch Bark Roll*, Seton wrote, "Similar power and possibilities are found in the instinct of initiation, the habit of giving nicknames,

[11] Ernest Thompson Seton, *Two Little Savages; Being the Adventures of Two Boys Who Lived as Indians and What They Learned* (New York: Grosset and Dunlap, 1903).

the love of personal decoration, the propensity to carve one's name in public places, the craze to make collections of stamps, shells, specimens, etc., the compulsion of atmosphere, the power of little ceremonies, the love of romance, the magic of the camp-fire." Seton had three rules governing the fun of woodcraft:

First, your fun must not be bought with money. Make your fun; Woodcraft shows you how.

Second, your fun must be enjoyed with due decorum. No one must be hurt in body, spirit or pocketbook.

Third, the best fun is that which appeals to the imagination.[12]

Seton's Woodcraft Indians were in place in 1910 when he chaired the committee, which included Beard, that created the Boy Scouts of America. Seton wrote most of the first *Handbook for Boys* (1911), incorporating much material from *Birch Bark Roll*. Seton's relationship with the Boy Scouts soured quickly, however, as the urban bankers, lawyers, and businessmen guiding the organization moved to centralize power and create the sort of bureaucracy Seton detested. Seton's 1927 typescript, "A History of the Boy Scouts by Ernest M. T. Seton, Chief Scout, 1910–15," relates his side of the conflict with James West and the others who finally forced Seton to quit the movement in 1915. Seton wrote that West was "totally lacking any knowledge of things spiritual." The Beard and Seton egos collided increasingly in this period, each man claiming to have "invented" the basic idea for the Boy Scouts of America, but both were equally as angry at Baden-Powell for having stolen the idea for the Boy Scouts in England.

Years later Beard and Seton reconciled, as Beard was willing to concede that Seton's Indians preceded his own Boone Scouts by a few years, but Beard reminded Seton that he had invented the patrol system, the motto Be Prepared, and some other salient features of the movement. In his 1935 letter to Seton, Beard wrote: "At any rate, the ideas were not originated by any set of bankers, lawyers, or merchants. It emanated from three men, each of whom is an artist; each of whom is a writer; each of whom is an outdoor man." Indeed, Beard summarized the nature of their relationship in a 1941 letter to Seton, written

[12] Ernest Thompson Seton, *The Book of Woodcraft and Indian Lore* (Garden City, N.Y.: Doubleday, Page, 1912); Ernest Thompson Seton, *The Birch Bark Roll of Woodcraft* (21st ed., New York: Woodcraft League of America, 1927), pp. xv–xvi.

shortly before Beard died: "Our lives, willy nilly, have been linked together and we followed the same pursuits, we belong to the same clubs, and our first child was born about the same time. Some of the trail has been very rough, but, Gosh-all-hemlocks, we are made of the stuff that can travel rough roads; that's the reason we are here today." [13]

The life trajectories of Beard and Seton were remarkably similar in their sequential moves from art to ethology to ethnology to youth work. All four of these disciplines encountered a version of what has come to be called the crisis of representation by recent hermeneutical philosophers and social scientists. The crisis takes many forms, but the forms share at least two essential features. First, many Americans were facing the loss of certainty in their ability to interpret the connections between external appearances and internal states. Second, these Americans were facing the larger Western crisis that included the loss of faith in rationality, the loss of the notion of an autonomous, rational individual, the critique of knowledge as "representation," and the turn to pragmatics as the basis of knowledge. [14]

The growing inability to interpret the relationship between external appearances and internal states was rooted in the accumulating social and historical forces that were changing the cultural experiences of Americans at the end of the nineteenth century. The increasing scale of American institutions, the dramatic concentration of people in cities, the presence of large numbers of immigrants, and similar features of the modern, pluralistic life world meant that Americans sensed themselves increasingly as a community of strangers. What was becoming clear to many Americans was that they could no longer assume shared life worlds as the basis for understanding public symbols. As the social basis for a faith in the interpretability of public discourse slipped away from Americans, they felt the need to elaborate the meaning of shared contexts and to recapture at least some measure of certainty in the rela-

<hr>

[13] Daniel Beard to Ernest Seton, March 11, 1935, folder 16, Ernest Thompson Seton Papers, Seton Village, Santa Fe, N.M. The third man was E. M. Robinson, YMCA executive and cofounder of the BSA. Beard to Seton, February 12, 1941, folder 16, Seton Papers. My thanks to Dee Seton Barber and her family for their warm hospitality and access to Seton's papers.

[14] James Clifford and George E. Marcus, eds., *Writing Culture: The Poetics and Politics of Ethnography* (Berkeley: University of California Press, 1986); Kenneth Baynes, James Bohman, and Thomas McCarthy, eds., *After Philosophy: End or Transformation?* (Cambridge, Mass.: MIT Press, 1987), pp. 3–6.

tionship between external signs and internal states.[15]

The social history of natural science and philosophy in America suggests the roots of the other source of the modern crisis of representation: the loss of a faith in the autonomous, rational individual and in knowledge as representation. Scientists were having increasing difficulty sustaining a vision of an ordered world knowable through rational thought. Charles Darwin created biology's version of the crisis by overthrowing design and substituting "chance" as the central engine driving natural selection. As psychology became a Darwinian science, that discipline encountered a complex and uncertain relationship between the external behavior of the individual and its internal drives, instincts, and motives. Mathematics and the physical sciences were experiencing their own version of the crisis of representation, marked by the invention of alternative geometries and algebras, which were formal systems that could not appeal to some external reality for confirmation of their truths. Werner Karl Heisenberg's Uncertainty Principle of 1927 summarized neatly and in a name accessible to the average citizen the crisis of representation in the physical sciences.[16]

Throughout their lives, Beard and Seton encountered different versions of the era's crisis of representation. Beard and Seton entered their formal art training just as young American artists were beginning their revolt against the art establishment. This revolt against the culture of taste imposed by the "genteel tradition" matched the impressionists' impulse to free the art program from the neoclassical and later romantic representation of reality. Seton's early friendship with Henri and the experiences of both Beard and Seton in the Art Students League of New

[15] Mary Douglas relies upon Basil Bernstein's distinction between "restricted" and "elaborated" codes of communication for her grid/group model for culture; see Mary Douglas, *Natural Symbols: Explorations in Cosmology* (New York: Vintage/Random House, 1973), esp. pp. 41–45. Restricted codes draw upon a narrow range of expressions and are what E. T. Hall calls high-context codes; that is, they are dense, heavily connotative means of communicating. Douglas writes that restricted codes have " a double purpose: they convey information, yes, but they also express the social structure, embellish and reinforce it." Elaborated codes, in contrast, arise in a more complex society featuring lower levels of shared context for interpreting utterances.

[16] See, for example, Hamilton Cravens, *The Triumph of Evolution: American Scientists and the Heredity-Environment Controversy, 1900–1941* (Philadelphia: University of Pennsylvania Press, 1978); and Morris Kline, *Mathematics: The Loss of Certainty* (New York: Oxford University Press, 1980). A brief history of this revolution is found in Norbert Wiener, "The Idea of a Contingent Universe," in *The Human Use of Human Beings: Cybernetics and Society* (1954; reprint, New York: Avon Books, 1967).

York cemented their affinities for the revolt, even though neither man pursued his interest in art long enough to participate fully in the impressionist, expressionist, and other modernist experiments that moved American art away from representation.[17]

As their artistic attention to American wildlife led them to an interest in ethology, Beard and Seton encountered still another version of the crisis of representation, one stated in Darwin's *Expression of the Emotions in Man and Animals*. Rediscovered as a classic work in ethology and semiotics, Darwin's book documents his obsessive search for a scientific understanding of the relationship between external signs and internal moods in animals and humans. Besides observing infants, studying the insane, and examining classic examples of painting and sculpture, Darwin performed experiments of his own, such as showing pictures of galvanized face muscles to more than twenty people and asking them "by what emotion or feeling the old man was supposed to be agitated."[18] Darwin also circulated a questionnaire to acquaintances in other countries in order to determine if there were cross-cultural similarities in the ways humans "read" facial expressions. Darwin appeared troubled by the crisis of representation implied by his theory of natural selection.

Ethology was a science born of the crisis of representation, so it is not surprising that Seton became embroiled in the disputes that usually mark the consolidation of a community of scientific specialists. Seton's animal stories never satisfied scientists as ethological texts. Seton believed that both instinct and learning played important roles in animal behavior, and this led him to attribute moral qualities to the animal heroes of his stories. In 1897 Seton began his long-range scientific work, *Life Histories of Northern Animals*, but the stories drew fire before Seton could publish them in 1909. In addition to John Burrough's savage attack on Seton's animal stories, Theodore Roosevelt published an essay critical of what he called "nature fakers." Seton defended his stories in correspondence with naturalist friends, but even they could not pardon Seton's attributions of morality in his purportedly scientific writing.

---

[17] See, for example, John Adkins Richardson, *Modern Art and Scientific Thought* (Urbana: University of Illinois Press, 1971); and Linda Henderson, *The Fourth Dimension and Non-Euclidean Geometry in Modern Art* (Princeton: Princeton University Press, 1983).

[18] Charles Darwin, *The Expression of the Emotions in Man and Animals* (1872; reprint, Chicago: University of Chicago Press, 1965), p. 14.

Merriam praised *Life Histories* in a letter to Seton, but complained, "Then you have a whole lot to say, both in the introduction and at intervals throughout the book, about monogamy, polygamy, the Ten Commandments, Vice, Crime, Suicide, and so on. It seems a pity to blemish so good a book with such twaddle."[19]

Seton's socialist ideas stressed mutual aid as well as the tensions between the individual and the group, which he attempted to work out in his animal stories and in his more "scientific" ethological writing.[20] This issue connected naturally with Seton's interest in ethnology, specifically with the study of American Indian cultures. Seton admired Lewis Henry Morgan's ethnology of the Iroquois, which led him deep into the ethnology of all American Indian people. At first Seton's attraction to American Indian cultures provided the practical woodcraft skills and colorful ceremony that he believed met deep instincts in the child and, therefore, could be the basis for a program to develop American children's bodies, minds, spirits, and characters. *Two Little Savages* marks Seton's move from American Indian ethnology into youth work. The novel contains most of the elements of Seton's idea of woodcraft, and he filled the volume with arts, crafts, games, and ceremonies borrowed from American Indian cultures (fig. 2).

The trouble between Seton and the Boy Scouts of America in 1915 drove him to return to the woodcraft movement with increased vigor. Feeling that the Boy Scouts had abandoned the woodcraft idea, Seton began writing new woodcraft manuals for boys and girls and established a monthly magazine, *Totem Board*. Seton distinctly did not want the woodcraft movement to imitate the Boy Scout model of centralized bureaucracy and the commercialization that turned boys into little consumers. Seton's writing and lecturing was all that held together the movement from 1915 until the 1930s, when he and his second wife, Julia Buttree Seton, established the College of Indian Wisdom at their home in Santa Fe, New Mexico.

---

[19] Ernest Thompson Seton, *Life Histories of Northern Animals* (New York: Charles Scribner's Sons, 1909). A brief history of ethology is provided in Wadland, *Seton*, pp. 191–206; see also Niko Tinbergen, "Ethology," in *The Animal in Its World: Explorations of an Ethologist, 1932–1972*, vol. 2: *Laboratory Experiments and General Papers*, ed. Niko Tinbergen (Cambridge, Mass.: Harvard University Press, 1972), pp. 130–60. Ernest Thompson Seton, *The Ten Commandments in the Animal World* (Garden City, N.Y.: Doubleday, Page, 1907); C. Hart Merriam to Seton, April 3, 1910, Seton Papers.

[20] Wadland, *Seton*, p. 176.

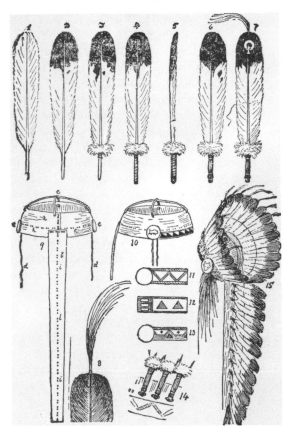

Fig. 2. "The War Bonnet." From Ernest Thompson Seton, *Two Little Savages: Being the Adventures of Two Boys Who Lived as Indians and What They Learned* (New York: Doubleday, Page, 1911).

By this time, Seton was bringing to the fore a theme that always lay in the background during his earlier use of Indian lore, when the emphasis was upon doing and making. Seton began to view woodcraft as a revitalization movement, a social movement that offered American Indian cultures as the last hope for the "sick" civilization of the whites. American Indians, especially the heroic figure Tecumseh (and, for the girls, Wetamoo, the woman Sachem of Pocassett), represented the socialist, feminist, and spiritual ideals he believed were lacking in Western civilization at the turn of the century.[21]

The experiences of Beard and Seton confirmed their belief that modern civilization suffered the destruction of a simple and easily interpretable relationship between external appearances and internal realities. It seems reasonable, therefore, to read the youth programs of these men as responses to the pressing crisis of representation. Specifically, we might ask why making, collecting, and wearing things on a special costume or uniform would seem to the early organizers of American youth movements to be a sensible basis for learning and for marking achievement in young people.

Making, Collecting, and Wearing Things in Boy Scout Culture

The handicraft and campcraft elements of American youth movements—having the youngsters *make things*—amounted to solving the crisis of representation by returning to experience as the basis of knowledge. In its earliest stages, this tactic shared much of the antimodernist sentiment found in the arts and crafts movements of the time. Beard wrote in his 1882 preface to the *Handy Book*:

> The author would also suggest to parents and guardians that money spent on fancy sporting apparatus, toys, etc., would be better spent upon tools and appliances.
>
> Let boys *make their own kites and bows and arrows;* they will find a double pleasure in them, and value them accordingly, to say nothing of the education involved in the successful construction of their homemade playthings.

In his 1916 *Woodcraft Manual for Girls,* Seton wrote a paean to "The Value of Doing":

> Our grandmothers gathered, dyed, and prepared material for their own clothes; made their rugs and carpets, their own candles, their own soap, their own medicines. Alone in the wilderness, they were sufficient unto themselves, for they were true woodcrafters—they mastered the things about them. Condi-

---

[21] For an extended discussion of Seton's view of the American Indian as feminist socialist, see Jay Mechling, "The Manliness Paradox in Ernest Thompson Seton's Ideology of Play and Games," in *Meaningful Play, Playful Meaning,* ed. Gary Alan Fine (Champaign, Ill.: Human Kinetics Publishers, 1987), pp. 45–59.

tions have changed now and most of these things have been taken from the home to the factory, so the old home training is no longer in reach.

The big value of all this knowledge was that it bestowed power. For learning to do gives more power to do, and when you let someone else do a thing for you, you eventually lose the power to do that thing.[22]

But there was more than simple nostalgia or even ideological antimodernism to the youth movement tactic of making things. Making things restored the connection between thought and action. By the time Beard wrote a new preface to the 1925 edition of *Handy Book*, he was able to express clearly this answer to the crisis of representation: "After all, there is something mighty real in thoughts—when we consider that there is nothing one can see anywhere, be it a building, painting or book, that is not an invisible thought clothed with a material body." The American assertion of the value of experience pervades American psychology and social thought during this period, but "pragmatism" is found as well in American literary expression, from Gertrude Stein's puzzling over thinking and doing in "Melanctha" (1905) to Eugene O'Neill's brute, expressionist statement in *The Hairy Ape* (1921). Americans everywhere, it seemed, were solving the crisis of representation by returning to the primacy of experience, and youth movements were no exception.[23]

After its founding in 1910, the Boy Scouts organization underwent a significant change in the sudden commercialization of the handicraft and campcraft elements of its program. Whereas Seton and Beard emphasized that youngsters should make things rather than succumb to "store bought" toys and devices, the lawyers, bankers, and businessmen who made the national organization a success steered the movement in precisely the opposite direction. The official seal of the Boy Scouts of America became a valuable imprimatur for which licensing manufac-

[22] For a discussion of the arts and crafts movement, see T. J. Jackson Lears, *No Place of Grace: Antimodernism and the Transformation of American Culture, 1880–1920* (New York: Pantheon Books, 1981), pp. 60–96; see also David E. Shi, *The Simple Life: Plain Living and High Thinking in American Culture* (New York: Oxford University Press, 1985). D. C. Beard, *The American Boys' Handy Book* (1882; reprint, New York: Charles Scribner's Sons, 1925), p. xi; Ernest Thompson Seton, *The Woodcraft Manual for Girls: The Eighteenth Birch Bark Roll* (Garden City, N.Y.: Doubleday, Page, 1920), pp. 130–31.

[23] Beard, *Handy Book*, p. v. For an overview of recent American studies scholarship on pragmatism and experience, see Jay Mechling, "William James and the Philosophical Foundations for the Study of Everyday Life," *Western Folklore* 44, no. 4 (October 1985): 301–10.

turers would pay considerable fees. The Boy Scouts insisted upon quality products and reasonable prices, but receiving the official seal in turn gave the manufacturer a monopoly in a growing market. Receiving a charter from Congress in 1915 guaranteed the organization's monopoly both as a youth movement for boys and as a marketer of official products.

The monopoly was powerful. For example, when publishing companies with lists of formula series novels for young men perceived a newly identifiable readership in the Boy Scouts, they began publishing so-called Boy Scout novels that merely took the old characters and dressed them in Scout uniforms. Boy Scout executives were alarmed that these novels, featuring boy spies, guns, and assorted other violence packaged as "action and adventure," would create false and dangerous impressions among the public. The organization fought back by condemning these novels in print and, after 1915, by legal action aimed at protecting the corporate trademark Boy Scouts. Thereafter, the Boy Scouts of America licensed a few publishers and authors to produce official Boy Scout novels that portrayed accurately and favorably the qualities of the boys in the movement.[24]

The strange turn toward commercialization touched virtually every activity that had been termed handicraft. A boy could no longer simply whittle a neckerchief slide; he now used his official Boy Scout pocket knife to whittle a prepackaged block of wood. He no longer fashioned used tin cans into camp cooking utensils; he now bought official Boy Scout cooking kits. He no longer made pin-hole cameras out of cardboard boxes; he now purchased his official Eastman Kodak Brownie camera. The corporation that was the Boy Scouts of America finally shared little with the attempts by Beard and Seton to turn American children away from the marketplace and toward their own abilities to make things.

The accumulation aspect of the youth movements founded by Beard and Seton—the part of the program based upon collecting things—differed from the handicrafts strategy as a response to the crisis of representation. At first glance, collecting things appears to be simply a continuation of the natural science tradition. Under the Enlightenment

---

[24]Over 600 Boy Scout novels were published between 1910 and the 1950s. Thornton W. Burgess and Percy Keese Fitzhugh were two of the few authors who won the official approval of the Boy Scouts of America. See Franklin K. Mathiews, "Blowing Out the Boy's Brains," *Outlook* 108 (November 18, 1914): 652–54.

paradigm of natural theology and the Great Chain of Being, the naturalist collected plant and animal specimens as part of the larger program to fill in the links of the chain, each link representing a species and each species representing an incarnation of an idea held by God. Collecting in the age of Linnaeus was only the first step in a routinized process of identifying the relevant features of a specimen for locating it in the chain, finding an appropriate binomial designation, preserving the specimen for future study, and eventually displaying it.[25]

The autobiographies of Beard and Seton recount the almost formulaic stories of nineteenth-century young boys gamboling in meadows and by streams, collecting all sorts of creatures and bones. The naturalist's heritage was demonstrated by the requirements for earning some badges in the Boy Scouts. Boy Scouts were expected to collect, name, and identify leaves, birds, insects, animal tracks, and so on in order to earn certain merit badges. Further, the boys in scouting had to *collect* a number of earned badges to achieve each rank in the movement.

Commercialization affected the collecting strategy as much as it did the making of things. While there is little systematic evidence to construct a social history of the childhood custom of trading things, it certainly seems that the nineteenth-century collecting impulse led young people to trade items from their collections. After 1910, Boy Scouts were likely customers for manufactured items to be purchased, collected, and then traded. Early collectibles included medallions, good-luck charms, tokens, patches, neckerchiefs, neckerchief slides, pins, postcards, cigarette cards, coffee mugs, and lead figures. The Boy Scouts officially licensed some of these items, while others were produced by companies taking commercial advantage of the existence of an identifiable movement and market.[26]

Just as making and collecting things were strategies adopted by Seton

[25] Some of this history is told in Charles C. Sellers, *Mr. Peale's Museum: Charles Willson Peale and the First Popular Museum of Natural Science and Art* (New York: W. W. Norton, 1980). Donna Haraway shows how taxidermy, photography, exhibition, conservation, and eugenics all came together in American Museum of Natural History to preserve a patriarchal definition of nature, in Donna Haraway, "Teddy Bear Patriarchy: Taxidemy in the Garden of Eden, New York City, 1908–1936," *Social Text*, no. 11 (1985): 20–24.

[26] Signs of the popularity of collecting Scout artifacts are J. Bryan Putman, *The Official Price Guide to Scouting Collectibles* (Orlando, Fla.: House of Collectibles, 1982), and the Scout "tradorees." Harry Thorsen, a long-time collector whose Sarasota, Fla., home is a scouting museum, publishes *Scout Memorabilia*.

and Beard in search of a solution to the crisis of representation, so was wearing things. This strategy amounts to using things as markers to say something about the bearer. The uses of uniforms, costumes, and badges in American youth movements afforded a unique solution to a very real problem in nineteenth-century America. Two aspects of clothing fascinated Americans late in the nineteenth century. First was the question of whether clothing could be relied upon as a truthful signal of something about the wearer. Second was the question of whether clothing could transform the character of the wearer.

The possibility of telling lies with one's clothing arises only in those societies where it is increasingly unlikely that people know one another. Anthropologist Marshall Sahlins writes, " 'Mere appearance' must be one of the most important forms of symbolic statement in western civilization. For it is by appearances that civilization turns the basic contradiction of its construction into a miracle of existence: a cohesive society of perfect strangers. But in the event, its cohesion depends on a *coherence* of specific kind: on the possibility of apprehending others, their social condition, and thereby their relation to oneself 'on first glance.' "[27] It is within this charged context that Beard and Seton made decisions about clothing the young members of their youth groups.

Initially, Seton and Beard chose "costumes" over uniforms for their movements. The military association of uniforms was prevalent for Americans of the 1890s, but the postbellum years also saw the increased use of uniforms among fraternal, social, and religious organizations. The professionalization of police and firefighters in large cities led to the adoption of simpler, practical uniforms, and it was during this period that other professionals (such as nurses) began to use distinctive uniforms as markers of the profession and as instantly recognizable signals of the skills that person bore.

Costumes served many of the same functions as uniforms, but without the military connotations. No doubt an important context for the meanings of costumes was the increasing theatricality of American society after the Civil War. The growth of regional playhouses and opera houses for touring companies, the success of the chautauqua, the pop-

---

[27] Marshall Sahlins, *Culture and Practical Reason* (Chicago: University of Chicago Press, 1976), p. 203. A similar point about clothing and detached attributes is made by Richard Sennett, *The Fall of Public Man* (1976; reprint, New York: Vintage/Random House, 1976), pp. 64–65.

ularity of pageants and their strange relation, the *tableau vivant*, and the growth of amateur theatricals, all combined to impress upon Americans the playfulness of costumes in contrast with the seriousness of uniforms. Costumes were colorful and romantic in a way that attracted Americans.[28]

Seton's choice of a costume for his Woodcraft Indians was the Plains Indian costume, perhaps the most dramatic choice possible, with its feathered warbonnets, bone breastplates, elaborate beadwork, and fringed leather leggings. Following the directions and ample illustrations provided by Seton in *Two Little Indians* and in the subsequent handbooks of the movement, the boy was to use Indian techniques to make each piece by hand, using authentic Indian materials if they were available. The warbonnet was especially important to the costume in that the markings on the bonnet's feathers signaled the "coups" or feats of the wearer, and these coups became the merit badges for the Scouts. Beard's Sons of Daniel Boone and Boy Pioneers wore buckskins, but Beard also required that the boys make these costumes by hand. So the strategies of making and wearing came together in the dress of these youth movements.

The Boy Scouts of America changed course on the matter of costumes. Seton lobbied heavily for the new organization to adopt a handmade costume, but Beard joined others in deciding that the organization should have a uniform in the same tradition as Baden-Powell's English Boy Scouts. Baden-Powell, a military hero, understandably adopted a military sort of uniform for his movement, which he created out of his perception that British boys needed a movement to train their bodies and their character. Seton already had a running feud with Baden-Powell over the latter's alleged piracy of portions of Seton's *Birch Bark Roll* for the British *Handbook for Boys*, and Seton found the military costume distasteful. Beard disagreed with Seton on this matter, and it was Beard who took the assignment of designing a uniform for the movement. The uniform and other aspects of the program had to be changed as part of the "Americanization" of Baden-Powell's idea.[29]

From the outset, an important rationale for having a Boy Scout uniform was that it immediately identified the boy's affiliation and signaled to others that he possessed training in first aid and other valuable

[28] See, for example, Trudy Baltz, "Pageantry and Mural Painting: Community Rituals in Allegorical Form," *Winterthur Portfolio* 15, no. 3 (Autumn 1980): 211–28.

[29] Whitmore, "Beard, Boys, and Buckskins," p. 230.

skills. The rhetoric of the movement stressed these themes of bonding and service. "The Uniform Makes All Boys Chums!" announced an advertisement for the uniform in the January 1930 issue of *Boy's Life*. The advertisement continues: "Many great men of our Country have found that the Official Boy Scout Uniform tends to bring all boys more closely together in a sense of brotherhood as it prevents any difference in appearance between the poorer boy and his more well-to-do comrade. It is a great maker for Democracy and helps all boys to be chums." [30] To reinforce the classlessness of the movement, all boys were expected to earn the money for their uniforms. But the choice was never to make one's uniform; that option died with the same turn toward commercialization that killed tin-can cooking pots and pinpoint cameras. It was the "official" Boy Scout uniform or nothing.

The second aspect to American fascination with clothing in this period involved the seemingly shared belief that "clothes made the man"; that is, that clothing might actually transform the character of the individual wearer. Charlotte Gulick voiced many of these beliefs in her foreword to a publication in 1915 introducing the ceremonial dress of the Camp Fire Girls (fig. 3). "The costume is significant for the following reasons," she wrote:

1st It is never completed. Girls can go on decorating it all their lives. . . .
2nd It is so inexpensive that all girls can have it. The poorest girl can make it as beautiful and symbolic as the richest. In Grand Councils it is impossible to tell the rich girl from the poor girl. The decorations, though, may distinguish the romantic, nature-loving girl from the artificial, shallow girl.
3rd It binds girls of all parts of the country together during the most impressionable years. It points toward the most complete team play. When Guardians let their hair down and put on this simple gown they become one of their girls. It symbolizes oneness. The girls feel it.

The Boy Scout novels of this period also express the belief in the transformative powers of the Boy Scout uniform (fig. 4). Percy Keese Fitzhugh's *Tom Slade: Boy Scout of the Moving Pictures* focuses on the transformation of street ruffian Tom Slade into the model Boy Scout, the transformation of "weak sister" Connover Bennett to the hearty manliness of scouting, and the eventual wholesale transformation of the

---

[30] Advertisement for Boy Scout uniform, "The Uniform Makes All Boys Chums," *Boys' Life* 20, no. 1 (January 1930): 67.

Girl No. II is tall and slender. The pocket, the decoration crossing the dress and brought up on the sides, and the bands on the shoulders help to break up the length. Her symbol, the frog, shows that she loves to swim. Her gown is bordered with little tents, and the two flames on her shoulders mean that, no matter what the weather, she will always have fire in her camp. She has won two National Honors, one in photography, and has placed these emblems sent her by the National Board on the side seams of her dress

Fig. 3. Ceremonial dress. From *The Book of the Camp Fire Girls* (New York: National Headquarters, 1914).

East End Gang of hoodlums into the Elk Patrol.[31] In this and other novels of the genre, the investiture ceremony—particularly the moment

[31] Gulick, as quoted in Buckler, Fiedler, and Allen, comps., *Wo-he-lo*, pp. 138–39; Percy Keese Fitzhugh, *Tom Slade: Boy Scout of the Moving Pictures* (New York: Grosset and Dunlap, 1915).

Fig. 4. "After Sending the Wireless Message, Tom Finds Himself a Hero." From Percy Keese Fitzhugh, *Tom Slade: Boy Scout of the Moving Pictures* (New York: Grosset and Dunlap, 1915), p. 195.

when the initiate dons the vestments of group identity—often marks the final transformation of the boy's character.

The systems of badges and awards created by Beard and Seton for their youth movements tell us still more about wearing things as a response to the crisis of representation. Like most workers in American youth movements of this period, Seton closely followed publications in instinct psychology and especially the child-study work of G. Stanley Hall and others. Seton considered "wearing badges" to be one of many natural instincts in the child, and he made "Personal Decoration for Personal Achievement" one of his nine "Principles of Woodcraft." The system of coups Seton created in *Two Little Savages* became the merit-badge system for the Boy Scouts. Beard also invented a system of badges or "hatch marks" for his Boone scouts. Beard established a series of awards named after famous Americans, such as the Cody Top Notch for pioneering skills, the John Muir Top Notch for walking, the Theodore Roosevelt Top Notch for heroism and daring, and the Mark Twain Top Notch for moral courage.[32]

[32] Seton, *Woodcraft and Indian Lore*, p. 6. For a discussion of Beard's hatch marks, see Whitmore, "Beard, Boys, and Buckskins," pp. 185–87.

With his uniform full of badges of office, badges of rank, merit badges of accomplishment, and special medals for heroism or other extraordinary achievement, the Boy Scout was for the knowledgeable "reader" a veritable walking story of his skills and character. The system of badges and awards, in short, worked to reunite external appearances and internal realities.[33]

The Collecting Self and the Psychology of American Materialism

The emergence of making, collecting, and wearing material objects as youth-work strategies aimed at resolving the crisis of representation provides an understanding of the social psychology of American materialism at the beginning of the twentieth century. There occurred, in the period from 1880 to 1920, a change in the ways Americans would "think with objects."

Reflection on the cultural meaning of objects in modern society owes a great deal to anthropologist Mary Douglas and economist Baron Isherwood's *World of Goods*. Douglas and Isherwood view consumption not as a matter of material welfare or display, but as a system of social communication, a system that economists cannot understand with their usual view of the "individual rational consumer." For Douglas and Isherwood, "the rational individual must interpret his universe as intelligible," so culture is, above all else, a human strategy for ordering chaos. Moreover, the individual needs the collaboration of others "to affirm and stabilize" this achieved intelligibility. In their view, goods provide a communication medium for creating the consensus necessary for a shared, intelligible world. Collective social rituals "fix" public meanings, and goods are important "ritual adjuncts" in those social dramas. Goods contribute importantly to our "metaphorical reasoning," thus "making stable the categories of culture" and, in a sense, serving as "markers" of these social categories. Douglas and Isherwood invoke a geological metaphor to describe the semiotic system of goods: "The stream of consumable goods leaves a sediment that builds up the structure of culture like coral islands. The sediment is the learned set of names and

[33] Jay Mechling, "Dress Right, Dress: The Boy Scout Uniform as a Folk Costume," *Semiotica* 64, nos. 3–4 (May 1987): 319–33.

names of sets, operations to be performed upon names, a means of thinking."[34]

The individual consumer presented by Douglas and Isherwood faces a problem of power and control; that is, a problem in attracting and holding the collaboration of others in the communication system of consumption. Class, caste, and other factors enter the system as potential barriers to the free access to the "information" one gets by participating in the communication system. The individual's problem is that "he has to be present at other people's rituals of consumption to be able to circulate his own judgments of the fitness of the things used to celebrate the diverse occasions." It is this last point that lays the foundation for the remainder of the book's analysis of the ideologies of consumption and the implications of this analysis for public policy.[35]

Douglas and Isherwood's exercise in anthropological thinking about consumption is an exciting, challenging contribution to our inquiry into the ways Americans "think" with objects. But for all the virtues of this contribution, it has two major shortcomings. First, theirs is primarily a cognitive model of consumption, lacking much insight into the affective dimension that many folklorists and anthropologists would want in a fully cultural account of the meanings of goods. The authors explain why goods are "good to think," but they do not provide much insight into why and how goods are "good to feel." Cultural geographer Yi-Fu Tuan helps fill this lacuna in his articulation of the dimension of space and place, especially what he calls "topophilia," or "love of place." Human relationships, he says, "require material objects for sustenance and deepening. Personality itself depends on a minimum of material possessions, including the possession of intimate space. Even the most humble object can serve to objectify feelings. . . . The emotion felt among human beings finds expression and anchorage in things and places."[36]

The second major deficit in Douglas and Isherwood's presentation involves their use of a model of the "rational" (albeit "culturally rational")

---

[34] Mary Douglas and Baron Isherwood, *The World of Goods: Towards an Anthropology of Consumption* (New York: W. W. Norton, 1979), pp. 81, 5, 59, 75.

[35] Douglas and Isherwood, *World of Goods*, p. 81.

[36] Yi-Fu Tuan, "Space and Place: Humanistic Perspective," in *Progress in Geography*, ed. C. Board, R. J. Chorley, and D. R. Stoddart (London: Edward Arnold, 1974), pp. 241–42.

individual. In *World of Goods*, they refer constantly to the rational individual, and in *Cultural Bias* Douglas refers to the individual actor as "a subject choosing." Douglas's semiotic anthropology requires no internalization of the shared public cosmology and "is essentially compatible with a psychology of the will." She assumes that her social actor is rational (in our everyday sense) and "free" enough to exercise choice in matters of consumption. Douglas has neglected to consider the case of the neurotic or psychotic individual who lacks the normal ability to use goods rationally and freely. If one is going to construct a communications model of the consumption of goods, as Douglas intends, then one ought to allow for pathological or disturbed communication as well as for the healthy versions. Here is where Gregory Bateson's cybernetic approach to culture nicely complements Douglas's model. Bateson paid special attention to pathologies in communication systems; however, he never concentrated his thinking on economic systems and the meanings of consumption. Bringing together the anthropological insights of Douglas and Bateson helps clarify what might go wrong in the communication system of goods and consumption. I believe that this sort of model will carry us far toward understanding the meaning of collecting and displaying things in youth movements. [37]

In my view, materialism is related to consumption in much the same way as schizophrenia is related to play. The schizophrenic individual lacks the normal person's ability to discriminate between levels of messages and to handle the inevitable, everyday paradoxes in communication. According to the double-bind theory of schizophrenia proposed by Bateson and his colleagues in the mid 1950s, the schizophrenic has been punished in the past for making those discriminations and develops pathological strategies of communication as defense mechanisms. Schizophrenic discourse, for example, confuses the literal and the metaphorical, using unlabeled metaphors as a primary defense mechanism. In contrast, play is one of the "healthy" human communication strategies for dealing with paradoxical communication. [38]

---

[37] Mary Douglas, *Cultural Bias*, Occasional Paper no. 35 (London: Royal Anthropological Institute of Great Britain and Ireland, 1978), pp. 13, 14; Gregory Bateson, "A Theory of Play and Fantasy," in *Steps to an Ecology of Mind*, ed. Gregory Bateson (New York: Ballantine Books, 1972), p. 189.

[38] Gregory Bateson, Don D. Jackson, Jay Haley, and John H. Weakland, "Toward a Theory of Schizophrenia," *Behavioral Science* 1, no. 4 (October 1956): 251–64.

By analogy, I want to distinguish materialism from Douglas and Isherwood's sense of consumption, which they define at one point as "a use of material possessions that is beyond commerce and free within the law," and at another as "a ritual process whose primary function is to make sense of the inchoate flux of events." Douglas treats consumption as normal discourse with objects. One of the characteristics of the healthy use of goods, in other words, is that the person in the person-goods system is able to distinguish and move between logical types; that is, the person is able to distinguish between the "map" that is the goods and the "territory" that is the pattern of social relations. In the healthy system of goods, as in play, the map and the territory are both equated and discriminated. Or, as Douglas and Isherwood put it, "Consumption goods are not mere messages; they constitute the very system itself. . . . The goods are both the hardware and the software, so to speak, of an information system whose principal concern is to monitor its own performance."[39]

In contrast to this normal, healthy use of objects in discourse, I reserve the word *materialism* to describe the pathological system in which a person is no longer able to distinguish between map and territory; that is, a person is no longer able to distinguish between the *literal* and the *figurative* uses of goods in communicating with others. The "materialist" confronts paradoxical communication (with and about objects) without the normal person's ability to move easily between messages of different logical types. Just as schizophrenia is a defense mechanism meant to protect the individual against the double bind, so materialism is a defense mechanism meant to defend the individual against paradoxes that arise in the use and interpretation of objects in communication.

The character of materialism as a defense mechanism is that the individual becomes supersensitive to the paradoxes that arise in contradictions between the nonverbal and the linguistic modes of communication. For example, in normal humans (using *normal* here not in some universal sense of mental health, but with reference to the normal patterns within a culture), these paradoxes may be perceived as play, falsification, humor, art, and so on. But the materialist suffers anxiety in the face of these paradoxes. Objects are no longer "props" in the

[39] Douglas and Isherwood, *World of Goods*, pp. 57, 65, 72; Bateson, "Theory of Play," p. 185.

fabrication of a performed self. Rather, objects come to be seen as extensions of the self.[40]

Like the schizophrenic, the materialist becomes addicted to the system we call materialism. More precisely, the materialist becomes addicted to materialism as a way of interpreting the self. Classes of action, like play, crime, and aggression, do not obey the ordinary rules of reinforcement. Indeed, there is good evidence that this materialism is not subject to reinforcement and extinction. More accurately, everything that happens in the class of actions called materialism reinforces the class. The materialist is never satisfied; hence, the addiction metaphor: the materialist never has enough goods.

The views of schizophrenia presented converge upon this single insight: schizophrenic styles and strategies of communication with material objects emerge when there is a breakdown in the relationships between the objects themselves and between the objects and their normal or healthy social uses. A whole social system could experience this breakdown and evidence neurotic communication strategies as a defense mechanism against the paradoxes created by this breakdown.[41]

In view of this interpretation, it can be argued that there emerged in American youth movements at the turn of the century a "collecting self" that was a neurotic solution to the crisis of representation felt by that generation. The collecting self sought to ground identity not through rational consumption, but through materialism.[42]

Viewing materialism as a pathological divergence from a normal system of human-goods interaction raises the question of origins. It is tempting to see in the biographies of Beard and Seton rich possibilities for a psychoanalytic interpretation of the origins of much of the treatment of objects in the program of the Boy Scouts. The autobiographies

---

[40] The demise of the public realm of cultural discourse and the emergence of the "intimate society" and its narcissism is chronicled in Sennett, *Fall of Public Man*, pp. 222–23. On objects as extensions of the narcissistic self, see Christopher Lasch, *The Culture of Narcissism: American Life in an Age of Diminishing Expectations* (New York: W. W. Norton, 1979), p. 84, passim.

[41] For information on the social psychiatric approach to account for how American democratic capitalism could lead to systematically neurotic personalities, see Karen Horney, *The Neurotic Personality of Our Time* (New York: W. W. Norton, 1937).

[42] I am coining the term "the collecting self" very much as an alternative to Ralph Turner's discussion of the change from a "real self" based in institution to one based in impulse, in Ralph H. Turner, "The Real Self: From Institution to Impulse," *American Journal of Sociology* 81, no. 5 (March 1976): 989–1016.

of both men provide abundant information about their formative years, including their all-important attitudes toward their fathers.[43] But we need not resort to an individual's neurotic approach to things as an expression of the self. Materialism may be a social pathology that arose in American society at the end of the nineteenth century as a perfectly workable solution or defense mechanism to a crisis in the system of goods as communication.[44]

Like other defense mechanisms, materialism could do its work only to the degree that it remained an unconscious "solution" to the crisis of representation. The problematic relationship between outward signs and inward realities was the subject of much public fiction, from the popular novels for youngsters to the realist and naturalist fiction of such authors as Twain, William Dean Howells, Edith Wharton, Henry James, and Frank Norris. These literary expressions often were able to identify the symptoms of materialism and to evoke the vague, general feeling of unease that social psychiatrists and cultural critics later came to identify as the symptoms of narcissism. But none made the therapeutic leap to engage in discourse about the breakdown in the self's ability to distin-

---

[43] Most curious is Seton's fixation upon and identification with the wolf, the same animal that appeared prominently in the dream of Sigmund Freud's young Russian patient and which in that dream stood for the patient's father. Seton found in Joseph Wolf, the German painter with whom Seton became friends during his 1890 study in London, a model for bridging art and science; see Wadland, *Seton*, pp. 103–4. On the connection between collecting, anality, and wolves, see Jay Mechling, "High Kybo Floater: Food and Faeces in the Speech Play at a Boy Scout Camp," *Journal of Psychoanalytic Anthropology* 7, no. 3 (Summer 1984): 256–68. The key interpretive text is the "Wolf Man" analysis by Sigmund Freud, "From the History of an Infantile Neurosis (1918)," in *The Standard Edition of the Complete Psychological Works of Sigmund Freud*, vol. 17, trans. and ed. James Strachey (London: Hogarth Press, 1955); see also Sigmund Freud, "Character and Anal Eroticism (1908)," in *The Standard Edition of the Complete Psychological Works of Sigmund Freud*, vol. 9, trans. and ed. James Strachey (London: Hogarth Press, 1959), pp. 167–75. Certainly wolves dominated Seton's most powerful paintings and stories, and Seton took the name Black Wolf in his "tribe" of boy Indians he founded in 1903. These brief comments do not constitute psychobiographies of Seton and Beard; such portraits would take detailed textual analysis not possible here. In lieu of complete psychobiographies, some of the themes and patterns repeated in the lives and expressive behavior of Seton and Beard are found in the psychobiographical work by Dorothy Ross, *G. Stanley Hall: The Psychologist as Prophet* (Chicago: University of Chicago Press, 1972).

[44] Frederic Jameson makes an argument similar to mine in his attempt to account for the relation between the postmodern aesthetic and the emergence of a consumer society, in Frederic Jameson, "Postmodernism and Consumer Society," in *The Anti-Aesthetic: Essays on Postmodern Culture*, ed. Hall Foster (Port Townsend, Wash.: Bay Press, 1983), pp. 111–25.

guish between itself and its material props. Not even Thorstein Veblen saw the profound change taking place in American capitalism's system of goods as a communication system.

Beard and Seton invented their youth programs during a historical moment when cultural schizophrenia was emerging as a defense mechanism against the crisis of representation. It was no longer possible to communicate normally with goods, as Douglas and Isherwood described. In late nineteenth-century American capitalism, an intense materiality and an intense literalness of experience with objects increased while, paradoxically, people found it more and more difficult to define the self with goods. Attempts to communicate with goods became obsessive as goods increasingly lost their power to demonstrate a relationship between the goods and the person's character.

A final irony in this tale of beads, bangles, and buckskins is that Beard and Seton succumbed to the cultural neurosis while they had at hand the means to resist the object schizophrenia taking over the culture. They chose to launch an antimodernist critique of their society, but, as Jackson Lears shows, such colors of antimodernism were common in the late nineteenth century and were easily assimilated by partisans of modernity.[45] The antimodern search by Beard and Seton for a return to a "sincere" relationship between objects and their maker was no more effective against the crisis of representation than was the modernist approach to accepting a "segmented self." It is not surprising, therefore, that the modern managers who took charge of the Boy Scouts of America by 1915 were able to turn the programs into commodities to be owned, bought, and sold. The important struggle during this generation was not between the modernists and antimodernists as they groped for a solution to the crisis of representation. Rather, the struggle was between official, adult versions of how to play with objects and the boys' own "folk theory" of how to play with objects.

It is only through play, ritual, art, and related forms of communication, insists Bateson, that human beings can learn a so-called healthy, normal approach to objects and how we think with them. Play is an important defense mechanism by means of which the individual can cope with the crisis of representation while, at the same time, avoiding neurotic defenses like schizophrenia.[46] In 1910 American adolescent

[45] Lears, *No Place of Grace*, p. xix.

[46] Sennett argues that the intimate society robs the individual actor of the "powers of play" in Sennett, *Fall of Public Man*, p. 264. He is on the right track, but his reliance

boys had a repertoire of folk play traditions that provided them with just such a defense mechanism to ward off the troubles of modernity, with just the sorts of skills necessary to play with objects without surrendering to those objects the power to define the boys' selves.[47] So, if left alone, the boys (and girls) of the early twentieth century could have solved the crisis of representation with their own resources.

Adults, however, were not inclined to leave adolescents alone in a period of cultural disorderliness. Adult managers of America's youth movements, including Seton and Beard, felt compelled to civilize the disorderly, unsocialized children's play they found in natural settings. Some children resisted the civilizing process, then as now, but power and time were on the side of the adults and the institutions they created to socialize children. The civilizing process for children has meant trading their healthier, play-based relationships to objects for adult neurotic, materialistic relationships. This trade is but one way in which American civilization reproduces itself.

---

on Huizinga and Piaget for an understanding of play is far inferior to that offered by Bateson, "Theory of Play," p. 193, and more recent work on play and culture, such as that in Brian Sutton-Smith and Diana Kelly-Byrne, eds., *The Masks of Play* (West Point, N.Y.: Leisure Press, 1984).

[47] A study of children's games in natural settings in this period is William Wells Newell, *Games and Songs of American Children* (1883; reprint, New York: Dover Publications, 1963).

The Evolution of Public Space in New York City

The Commercial Showcase of America

William R. Taylor

Much of the work that went into this essay was done in the research collections of the New York Public Library on Forty-second Street. To walk there from my home near Washington Square, I had to cross several parks whose present functions and dilapidated conditions would have appalled those who planned and built them. I walked past statues of military heroes unknown to my contemporaries and along thoroughfares lined by buildings of monumental character whose ornamental facades and towering campaniles interest only a few passersby. If I traveled by subway, the historical amnesia was more evident. This vast underground transportation system was the pride of New Yorkers in the opening decades of the century. The miraculous achievement of its design, engineering, and implantation in the midst of a busy, growing metropolis and the even more miraculous speed with which it transported masses of people from point to point each day is now all but forgotten in its general dereliction and neglect. Much the same could be said of Grand Central Terminal, two blocks east of the library, where I often ate lunch.

As the nineteenth century gave way to the modern age during the opening decades of the twentieth century, changing perceptions of the public on the part of business and civic leaders in New York City led to the creation of public spaces that projected a new sense of urban order and, at the same time, celebrated an emerging commercial culture. What evolved during these years was a novel kind of city, a city designed as a showcase, at once both a stimulus and a gratification to the mass of consumers, whose identity was being redefined by a new concept: "the public." A new kind of space—public space—and its architecture and iconography commands my attention in this essay. I also argue that at the center of the new urban order was a conception of what was public that was woven into the city's commercial culture.

It is scarcely surprising that before 1920, planners and architects in New York devoted much of their attention to the commercial arteries that ran through the city's center to the axes where these thoroughfares converged to form small open spaces—"squares" or "circles"—and to the creation of parks and playgrounds. After about 1890, vast new structures were designed to monumentalize these central vantage points in the commercial life of the city. The city's principal commercial institutions, department stores, newspapers, hotels, office buildings, and theaters were clustered around these axes, and architectural treatments worthy of public or ecclesiastical edifices in other societies were devised to give them a visual character and prominence.

An older order was rapidly superseded by these developments. Before about 1870, New York had grown without developing the kind of concentrated business and recreational center that began to appear thirty years later, as the commercial life of the city and its related services became compressed into the area between Thirty-fourth and Forty-second streets and continued to creep northward. Only along the central spine created by Broadway and parts of Sixth Avenue (the retail stretch known as the "Lady's Mile") was there early evidence of the complex of commercial activities that later defined the central functions of modern New York. A new, complex system of transportation filled the center of New York daily with the volume of employees and patrons necessary to assure continued commercial growth. New kinds of hotels, restaurants, and theatrical entertainment made the center increasingly enticing as a place to stay. The city was converted into a vast and efficient emporium for the handling of goods, a gigantic superstore and superwarehouse that could provide the services and offer the amenities to those who took part in the many transactions of such an entrepôt. Efficiency and visual seduction were the watchwords of the new order, which required the creation of countless service vocations—sales clerks, floorwalkers, buyers, elevator operators, drummers, copywriters, window display artists, doormen, busboys, bellhops, typewriters (as the first typists were called), and countless others.

New York soon assumed the leadership in public spatial planning. New York parks created by Frederick Law Olmsted launched a national movement for the creation of planned open spaces within major cities, but New York's pioneering role did not end with its parks. A pioneering spirit initiated a succession of services and amenities that were designed to enhance the public life of the city, encourage its commerce, and provide a comfortable, scrubbed-up aesthetic world for its citizens. Thanks to the energy and vision of architects and planners, New York's innovations were widely imitated in other American cities. In 1892 Daniel Burnham called upon New York architects and planners, including Olmsted, to design Chicago's immense World's Columbian Exposition. By the 1890s, New York had achieved a reputation for the distinction and singularity of the design of its spaces.

Only recently has this reputation been exhumed from the disgrace into which it fell at the hands of historians of modern architecture. A revival of interest in beaux arts design has awakened an appreciation for these public buildings and spaces.[1] A critique of modernism as aesthetically barren, especially in the clichéd form it assumed after World War II, has stimulated an appreciation of the architecture in New York that modernists had rejected as derivative and nonfunctional. An architectural aesthetic has now developed that, among other things, celebrates this decorative and ornamental elegance of turn-of-the-century public buildings and early skyscrapers.

Major rethinking of the historical rationale behind New York's elaboration of public space clearly seems in order. The building boom of the 1980s is altering the character of almost every focal point in the older city's design, as in the case of Times Square, which was created almost overnight by a succession of business and municipal decisions in 1904. A sense of the city's spatial past, rather than informing the

---

[1] The most denigrating estimate of New York's beaux arts buildings, one that cites the opinions of such pioneering moderns as Louis Sullivan, is in Siegfried Giedion, *Space, Time and Architecture: The Growth of a New Tradition* (5th ed.; Cambridge, Mass.: Harvard University Press, 1967). An influential recent estimate of architectural historicism has been advanced by Robert Venturi, *Complexity and Contradiction in Architecture* (2d ed.; New York: Museum of Modern Art, 1977).

debate, is rapidly being buried in the rubble created by new construction. One reason for neglecting the spatial past may lie in the mistaken assumption that the modern city of 1920 was an immense ornamental luxury at the time. Nothing could be further from the truth.[2] Those who designed New York's buildings and elaborated the city's squares and broad avenues conceived of those spaces as parts of a vast commercial city with particular needs that had to be satisfied. Among these needs were the flow of traffic—both people and vehicles—the provision of dignified recreational space for a burgeoning middle class, the enhancing and monumentalizing of commercial enterprise, and the communication of commercial values to the society at large. In a sense, the streets and squares of the city foreshadowed the airwaves that carry radio and television signals: public spaces became the vehicles used by civic and business leaders to transmit information about the city to their constituencies.

These spatial changes were made in the name of the public. Banks, insurance companies, newspapers, auditoriums, department stores, and hotels deemed it to be in the public interest to facilitate communications within the city, to speed the growth of commercial life, and to call visual attention to the parts of the city and the institutions where these activities were taking place on a rapidly expanding scale. They expanded the perception of what was public to include their own arenas, which were, strictly speaking, privately owned and administered, but which served and addressed the public in dramatic ways. Those who promoted the building of such monumental new institutions and services were referred to as "public-spirited," and they modestly held themselves to be responsive to public opinion.[3]

The concept of public opinion was scarcely a novelty in 1880, when the most intensive examination of it begins, but the growth of large cities quite suddenly placed the discussion in a strikingly different context. During most of the nineteenth century, public opinion had been employed in an almost exclusively political context. It seems most

[2] See William R. Taylor and Thomas Bender, "Culture and Architecture: Some Aesthetic Tensions in the Shaping of New York City," in *Visions of the Modern City: Essays in History, Art, and Literature*, ed. William Sharpe and Leonard Wallock (Baltimore: Johns Hopkins University Press, 1987), pp. 185–215.

[3] See, for example, Leo L. Redding, "Mr. F. W. Woolworth's Story: The Fundamentals of His Great Success—How Buying for Cash and the Proper Location of Stores Made the 5 and 10 Succeed," *World's Work* 25, no. 6 (April 1913): 662.

often to have meant the opinion expressed about public issues—res publica—rather than the thinking of any particular group.[4] A number of successive developments conspired after the 1880s (and even earlier) to modify this usage. The cumulative effect of these developments was a slow devaluation of the independence, assertiveness, and wisdom that earlier had been attributed to the "omnicompetent citizen," which gradually gave way to the "bewildered herd" as described in Walter Lippmann's *Phantom Public* in 1925, and to the machine-made opinions of the man-in-the-mass described in John Dewey's *Public and Its Problems* two years later. This conception of a mass culture emerged in discernible stages out of the interplay between changing perceptions of public space and opinion during the critical period before 1920.

The first discernible stage was the increasing tendency after the mid nineteenth century to perceive the public as a physical presence—a human aggregate—rather than simply opinion dispersed within the population. Cities as large population centers had existed previously, but never before had such numbers of people poured in and out of cities on a daily basis. Each morning ferry boats and commuter trains unloaded their human cargoes only to retrieve them the same evening. This further encouraged a second change: the perception of urban populations as fluid, circulating crowds of people. Beginning with Central Park, the facilities planned for such populations were designed to accommodate them not as static crowds, but as a mobile, circulatory flow of human beings. This appears to have been true even earlier with P. T. Barnum's American Museum of the 1840s, which was designed to keep its clientele moving through the exhibition halls. Barnum boasted in his autobiography that he had made the sign To the Egress so alluring that his crowds poured out of the museum as readily as they poured in.[5] A language of fluids became attached to all references to urban components, as in the wave of immigrants and its masses of people "streaming" in and out.

The plans for Central Park conceived by Olmsted and Calvert Vaux

[4] See, for example, W. S. Lilly, "The Shibboleth of Public Opinion," *Forum*, 10, no. 9 (November 1890): 256–63.

[5] For an interesting discussion of the evolving ideas of public space and performance, see Peter George Buckley, "To the Opera House: Culture and Society in New York City, 1820–1860" (Ph.D. diss., State University of New York at Stony Brook, 1984), esp. pp. 492ff and 632ff.

in 1858 reflect even better the changing conception of how to accommodate the town's populations, although the concept of a public as a body of people also makes its appearance here. The thinking behind this plan inverted earlier ideas concerning optimum public space. For the static arrangement of early nineteenth-century theaters, Olmsted and Vaux substituted circulation, decentralization, and distribution. A circular road was designed to carry park crowds to a wide variety of activities distributed over its 700 acres; the park could be entered at multiple points.[6]

A third stage in the changing perception of the public was manifest in the need to segregate various streams of people, a form of spatial rationalism that grew in importance toward the end of the century. First, Olmsted and Vaux segregated each form of park traffic—carriage traffic from pedestrian paths and bridle paths from both—with bridges and underpasses provided at points where these streams intersected. Perhaps even more significant was the planners' decision to sink the four east-west roads required by their commission below grade and out of sight to eliminate any contact or conflict between park crowds and the ongoing commercial traffic of the city.

Because the population at large in the city had become more ethnically mixed and more mobile by the 1880s, it was no longer possible to make the same kind of clear distinction between the coarse, vulgar stream of the city's commercial life and the public, as Olmsted and Vaux had done in their plans for Central Park. The advent of large-scale immigration from southern and eastern Europe brought into the city large groups that were perceived as wholly alien to American life and, by many, as untutored in civilized ways. Public spaces and facilities were subjected to novel mixtures of people and overwhelmed by unprecedented numbers. The spaces that were constructed reflected in their massive scale and impersonality their anticipated usage. Accordingly, new services were soon perceived as urgently needed. Finally, the vision of these massive and commercially unfledged crowds moving through the streets and ports stirred visions of unprecedented economic and political opportunities. Down the same road lay both the mass-marketing and the political movements of the twentieth century. The

---

[6] Frederick Law Olmsted and Calvert Vaux, "Greensward" (1859), reprinted in *Landscape into Cityscape: Frederick Law Olmsted's Plans for a Greater New York City*, ed. Albert Fein (Ithaca, N.Y.: Cornell University Press, 1969), p. 67.

following examples suggest some of the ways in which these developments reflected a changing perception of the public.

Grand Central Terminal opened to the public February 3, 1913. With its surrounding hotels, shops, restaurants, and offices, Grand Central was a city within a city—it was originally called Terminal City—the hub of an extensive real estate development and the capital of a railway empire that stretched from coast to coast. The terminal had been in the works since 1900, and the need for it had been felt even longer. The growing volume of passenger, freight, and commuter traffic arriving in the city had made its predecessor, Grand Central Depot—even enlarged— wholly inadequate. The increasing recognition that the Grand Central yards were occupying real estate of incalculable value and the advent of underground electrification of trains entering the city combined to encourage the terminal's designers toward the conception of an almost self-contained minicity.[7] It was purpose-built, as the English say, in the center of Manhattan, and it rapidly changed the character of the entire midsection of the city. Park Avenue stretching north to Ninety-sixth Street was one consequence; Forty-second Street as the principal east– west link between the commercial and the entertainment foci of the city was another. In its interior, Grand Central Terminal heralded a decorative space that became a harbinger of the vast hotel lobbies and atria of contemporary cities (figs. 1, 2).

The language used by the press to characterize the completed terminal suggested a changed perception of "the traveling public," as the intended clientele was described throughout the long period of design and execution. In 1904, a reporter for the *Railroad Gazette*, having seen plans for the projected terminal, commented:

In preparing the plans for the new station everything has been sacrificed to the comfort and convenience of the travelling public. The distinguishing features of the arrangement of the yards, platforms, and headhouse may be summarized as follows: Ample facilities for getting to and away from the station. Cab stand situated in most convenient place for arriving passengers. Outgoing baggage room convenient to ticket offices and incoming baggage room convenient to the exits. Separation of incoming and outgoing passengers, thus avoiding confusion. Ample waiting rooms and accessories and a grand concourse large enough to accommodate the largest holiday and excursion crowds. Separation of sub-

[7] Carl W. Condit, *The Port of New York: A History of the Rail and Terminal System from the Beginning to Pennsylvania Station* (Chicago: University of Chicago Press, 1981).

Fig. 1. Concourse, Grand Central Terminal, New York. (Museum of the City of New York.)

urban and through passengers but with arrangements for easily getting from one part of the station to the other. Comfortable waiting rooms for those desiring to meet incoming passengers. Ample baggage facilities.[8]

In the *Gazette's* language, the public was a monarch dictating what should be done. There is an obvious preoccupation with reducing the confusion of travelers by easing their transfer from one transportation system to another, providing comfortable and relaxing spaces in which to wait, and even reducing their physical exertion as they moved down an interconnecting system of sloping ramps, rather than steps, that were designed to carry pedestrian traffic down from street level by "gravity flow."

Although the design of Grand Central Terminal was interpreted as a model of utility and accommodation that catered to every need of the public, its spatial design introduced conflicting perceptions of the same public. One perception involved the fascination with quantification that

[8] Condit, *Port of New York*, p. 73.

Fig. 2. Concourse, Grand Central Terminal, north side of Forty-second Street at Park Avenue. (Museum of the City of New York.)

became evident in every description of the terminal: square and cubic footage of the terminal itself; train arrivals and departures per day; annual, weekly, and daily tons of freight and mail; and rapidly growing track mileage in the New York Central system. These descriptions were cited regularly along with the growing numbers of each kind of passenger—through, commuter, and subway—expected to use the terminal. Tables in descriptive literature also introduced the concept of the passenger mile, which reduced travelers to a mobile unit of rail-traffic measurement. In such discussions, a different sense of the public emerges—that of traveler-as-commodity. This delight in human quantification was an anticipation of the movement to study public opinion through

Fig. 3. Cross-sectional perspective, Grand Central Terminal. (Museum of the City of New York.)

sampling and polling that appeared at the end of the 1920s.[9] Such fascination with translating every feature of the project into numbers and justifying every expense through numerical projections clearly played to the company's pride in its expansion and growth.

Further illustration of the change in interpreting public space is seen in the cross-sectional drawings of the terminal and its surroundings that were produced during the ten years of planning and construction (fig. 3). In these drawings human figures serve as minuscule units of measure in depicting the scale of the structure. This kind of graphic interpretation seems closely related to the verbal discourse that grandiloquently described these spaces and crept into common usage after Grand Central Terminal's opening.[10]

Descriptions focused on the immense concourse—at the time the largest interior space ever designed for a conventional building—with its vast vaulted ceiling decorated with a zodiacal and equatorial belt to simulate the solar system. The concourse was described as "lofty," "majestic," "awesome," even "sublime."[11] This language echoes the

[9] Condit, *Port of New York*, pp. 54–100.
[10] Condit, *Port of New York*, p. 73.
[11] "Railroad Passenger Station in New York," *American Architect and Building News* 83, no. 1587 (May 26, 1900): 175.

aesthetic vocabulary commonly employed in nineteenth-century descriptions of the most dramatic aspects of nature: Niagara Falls, the western mountains, and the wildest, most rugged features of the American landscape. In its American usage, this vocabulary still retained some of the religious overtones that Edmund Burke ascribed to it in the eighteenth century, but in its application to the urban setting it quickly came to take on proprietary values for those who had constructed record-setting spaces and towers, just as it had earlier been employed to bolster a sense of American national pride. To nineteenth-century contemporaries, Grand Central's iconographic ceiling had a more specific reference. The representation of the world in the universe also spoke the language of modern global commerce with its trade routes that circled the earth and its "world" fairs. It was the same impulse that peopled the world with American missionaries and that brought "savage" peoples to be placed on display at commercial expositions.

These novel expressions all had a revolutionary effect on the perceptions of the people using these spaces. Faced with public space conceived in these terms, nineteenth-century travelers must have been awed by the commercial grandeur of the terminal and the company that had created it, Grand Central Company, as they moved through the great barrel vaulted concourse with its replica of the heavens arching overhead. As much as the facilities were designed to accommodate the public, the structure was also meant to impress—and overarch—its visitors. The company, and more specifically, the Vanderbilt family, were clearly enhanced by space that was ecclesiastical in scale.

Although its active management passed to a consortium in 1903, Grand Central Company had been the creation of three generations of Vanderbilts, who had put together their railway empire out of many local companies across the Northeast. Beginning with founder Cornelius V. ("Commodore") Vanderbilt, whose original fortune had begun with steamship lines, a succession of sons had added to the network that became Grand Central Company. Despite their great wealth and Dutch lineage, the Vanderbilts were slow to win acceptance in New York society. Spurned by society's legendary Astor family and by arbiter Ward McAlister, they did not "arrive" until well into the 1880s. The huge terminal sitting athwart Park Avenue with its many reminders of the Vanderbilt family was therefore a symbol of social as well as economic triumph in the city. Further homage was paid at the surrounding hotels— the Commodore and the Biltmore—which commemorated the proprietors' families, as did such streets as Vanderbilt Avenue. But the terminal's grandeur was also—and equally—designed to dignify the public. Nothing functional dictated such scale or height; no holiday or excursion crowds would ever require a ceiling 300 feet high that replicated the heavens.

The terminal's iconography further expressed this ambivalence toward the railway's clientele. The statue of Commodore Vanderbilt facing north along Park Avenue was clearly proprietary. Facing south over the parapet clock stood winged Mercury, symbolizing both commerce and speed. The public that worshipped technology probably saw nothing ambivalent about this kind of divine sponsorship. Theodore Dreiser's *Sister Carrie* had caught something of this overwhelming feeling about New York public spaces when one of the characters, Hurstwood, arrived in the city from Montreal and remarked, "The entire metropolitan center possessed a high and mighty air calculated to overawe the common applicant, to make the gulf between poverty and success seem both wide and deep."[12]

Grand Central Terminal served daily travelers with novel commercial services: "dressing rooms," "kissing galleries," "hair dressing parlors," "arcades," "restaurants," "post offices," and "bathtubs." It would be more accurate to say that it was designed to serve simultaneously and efficiently different groups of travelers: through-coach and Pullman passengers laying over between trains, long-run passengers terminating in New York, and daily commuters—all in all, some 250,000 people daily, not including subway riders using Grand Central as a destination or point of departure.[13]

For the most part, the various streams of travelers were separated on different levels of the terminal complex, demonstrating how a diverse public group created new spatial needs. At the same time, Grand Central Company was not alone in its efforts to reckon with these needs, nor was it alone in devising ways of both gratifying and appropriating them. Novel strategies analogous to those used by Grand Central Company for manipulating and orchestrating the public were employed by the other new institutions catering to the public.

There is probably no more revealing instance of the process of manipulation at work than the campaign launched in the 1890s to cre-

---

[12] Theodore Dreiser, *Sister Carrie* (1900; reprint, New York: Penguin Books, 1981), p. 319.
[13] Condit, *Port of New York*, p. 89.

Fig. 4. Public comfort station, Union Square, New York. (Private collection.)

ate public "comfort stations" throughout the city (fig. 4). The extent and intensity of this agitation perhaps for a time exceeded that of any other municipal reform. The volume of pamphlet literature produced over a thirty-year period supports this claim. The historic importance of this particular campaign lay in its active intervention into what had previously been considered a private, domestic realm. The revolutionary aspect was the assumption that a man's personal hygiene and cleanliness, how he provided for his intimate needs, was a matter of public import. The pamphleteers exercised this reasoning to recruit him for the burgeoning middle classes, as an early publication made clear: "To make an habitually dirty man clean is to create in his inmost soul, even if but temporarily, a desire to rise out of the squalor and filth with which he may be ordinarily encompassed." The massive campaign to create these facilities and to promote and encourage their use thus opened the way for a whole range of orchestrated intrusions into the lives of urban populations fostered under the banner of public health or welfare. This one cause finally became the focus of a whole range of related worries about urban populations, their health, their political vulnerability, their welfare, and their accommodation.[14]

[14]The New York Public Library has two bound volumes of pamphlets on the subject of public comfort stations that are probably only a fraction of what was produced and distributed. The uncatalogued collection is bound together under the title "Public Com-

It appears to have been the surge of interest during the 1890s in public health that first drew attention to the deficiency of toilets available to people moving about the city far from home.[15] Early epidemiologists pointed to the dangers of the public defecation and urination then prevalent, but a more general preoccupation with "regularity" and "the prompt elimination of poisonous residues" is clearly evident in the pamphlets. During the 1890s the agitation for comfort stations tended to form part of the larger agenda of municipal reform in New York. At the Conference on Municipal Progress held April 26, 1894, for example, the combined issue of lavoratories and mortuaries was only one of four topics discussed, the others being free baths and washhouses, neighborhood guilds, and rapid transit. The yoking together of rapid transit and issues pertaining to personal hygiene emphasizes the dual aspect of the new meaning of the public: its *embodiment* and its mobility.

A year later, a subcommittee of the powerful Committee of Seventy recommended "the establishment of adequate public baths and lavoratories for the promotion of cleanliness and increased public comfort in appropriate places throughout the city."[16] The committee epitomized the values of the emerging commercial culture. It was a citizens' collective made up of almost every private association or organization concerned with municipal reform. The committee included men prominent in business, finance, and philanthropy and enlisted the support of those active in sponsoring new monumental spaces such as Grand Central Terminal.

The subcommittee had discovered that American cities lagged far behind their English and other European counterparts in providing comfort stations, although interest in this issue rapidly spread from New York to other American cities during the next twenty years. Philadelphia had five public toilet facilities in 1895, for example, whereas there were more than 200 in Liverpool. In London, the committee reported, such stations had been placed underground at the congested junctions of major thoroughfares. More than 5 million people had used the facility in Piccadilly Circus during the first three years of its existence. Usage

---

fort Stations." Committee of Seventy, *Report of the Subcommittee on Baths and Lavoratories* (New York: By the committee, 1895), p. 111.

   [15] Committee, *Report*, p. 111.
   [16] Committee, *Report*, pp. 113–14.

of the Charing Cross Station facility had been almost equally heavy. The committee pointed out that in England and on the Continent, where these facilities had grown up in connection with the development of the underground railway systems, they were often combined with other services to travelers: bootblacking stations, barbershops, telephones, and newsstands. The committee recommended that such complexes be placed at key locations in New York where they might be combined with millinery and notion shops to help defray the cost of attendants and maintenance. Suggested locations for such complexes were Fifty-eighth Street at Eighth Avenue (Central Park West), Fifty-ninth Street at Fifth Avenue, Madison Square Park, Cooper Union Park, and Chatham Square. A later report suggested that information stations also might be located at such points to aid those seeking their way in New York.[17]

Serving travelers, however, was only one concern of the reform groups advocating comfort stations. In this sense the European example was only part of the argument. The decision not to adopt the English practice of charging a penny for the service is one indication of differing objectives. The major aim in almost every American city was to reach the "vast mass of humanity," as the Committee of Seventy report called it, that was currently at the mercy of saloonkeepers. In America saloons provided the only available toilets outside large hotels and department stores. Those lured into saloons by "nature's demand," the argument went, ended up buying a drink out of common courtesy for the service provided. A survey taken in St. Louis in 1908 found that saloonkeepers acknowledged receiving over 30 percent of their clientele in this fashion, making their toilets, in their estimation, a bigger attraction than the free lunch. The literature also emphasized another consideration that fueled the popularity of the campaign. Patrons who bought "the fatal glass of beer" were apt to end up in the meshes of machine politics because of the close association perceived between the saloons and the political boss systems. Public toilets would, therefore, emancipate this portion of the saloon clientele from Tammany's clutches.[18] In this respect,

---

[17]Donald B. Armstrong, *Public Comfort Stations: Their Economy and Sanitation* (New York: American City Pamphlets, 1914); John Joseph Cosgrove, *Standards for Public Comfort Stations* (New York: Committee of Seventy, 1913).

[18]Committee, *Report*, p. 111; *Public Comfort Station for St. Louis* (St. Louis: Street Improvement Committee of the Civic League, 1908).

those who would use comfort stations were the same group for whom bathhouses were being built during this period. It is not surprising, therefore, that the proposed locations for many of the comfort stations were in the tenement districts of the Lower East Side and analogous areas of the city: Tompkins Square, Washington Market, and Essex Market.

By 1907 New York had constructed eight comfort stations at a cost of $20,000 to $25,000 each. Annual maintenance, including attendants, was estimated at $5,000. In the eleven months between November 1907 and October 1908, almost 10 million people—8,004,309 men and 1,267,827 women—had used the facilities. Perhaps the most striking feature of this statistic is the gender ratio of roughly six to one, suggesting that far more men used these public facilities than the figures revealed by the early 1920s, when the gender ratio dropped to roughly three to one.[19] By then additional comfort stations in many different locations, some far from the city's axial thoroughfares, made comparisons a little hazardous. Moreover, women in the early 1900s were much more likely to be in the city to shop and attend the theater than for any other reason, and the large department stores and theaters prided themselves on their elaborate toilet and resting facilities for female patrons. Nonetheless, the discrepancy is too great to be accounted for by these considerations. It seems clear that the gender composition of the street population was another characteristic that was masked by the homogenizing concept of *the public*.

Only through such masking could the collectivity that became known as *the public* be expanded to include a significant proportion of the population. As rhetoric, the term became like a beacon to summon all and sundry citizens into a burgeoning middle class and to direct them through advertising to higher and higher levels of consumption. If the lure of being included as part of the public was spelled out in comfort, convenience, speed, hygiene, and civic instruction, as it was for patrons of Central Park, Grand Central Terminal, or comfort stations, such a collective designation held quite a different lure for those who did their business at street level.

A careful student of the expanding public was Frank W. Wool-

---

[19] John K. Allen, "Public Comfort Stations," *Western Architect* 12, no. 6 (December 1908): 75–76.

worth. He based his "dime store" empire on the modest resources of people moving through the streets of American towns and cities. He also based his success on his close observation of the consumer habits of ordinary people. From the time Woolworth opened his first store in upstate New York in 1879 until the completion of his skyscraper head-quarters in New York City in 1913, he had been obsessed with studying the sidewalk behavior of the public.

When interviewed in 1913, Woolworth said he had based his entire career on cash payment and people watching. He had selected store sites under the motto Take the Store to the People, choosing areas where sidewalk traffic was densest. He soon learned that stores not sited in this fashion quickly failed. A key shift in Woolworth's thinking seems to have occurred after the financial panic of the 1890s, when he opened a store in the conservative Pennsylvania "Dutch" community of Lancaster. Unable to secure one of his preferred sites, he decided to build a large, highly visible store in a location that local community leaders warned him was unpromising. His reason for taking this unwonted risk is almost as interesting as what happened.[20]

"Modern America was growing up all around Lancaster," Woolworth observed, "and it just *had* to move forward." By modern America, he left no doubt that he meant New York, where he had opened a purchasing agency on Chambers Street some ten years before. From his New York office, where he spent an increasing amount of time, Woolworth had observed the changes taking place in the city, the advent of skyscrapers and the crowds that swarmed through the streets. He therefore elected to build a large store in Lancaster that would be clearly visible some distance away. What occurred confirmed what he had shrewdly guessed: "The thing that pleased me most was that business immediately swung over to the wrong side of the street. The wrong side of the street was now the right side—it was the fashionable side and it was the prosperous side. Things grew so rapidly over there that I had to add to my new building before it was completed. I did that to accom-modate a restaurant that the public demanded."[21]

The next step in the evoluton of Woolworth's thinking about the public was his decision to build a skyscraper office building, not a store,

[20] Redding, "Woolworth's Story," p. 662.
[21] Redding, "Woolworth's Story," p. 663.

in New York. He had already surmised that an important connection existed between a merchandising operation like his own, with stores spread across the country, and a highly visible, highly publicized central headquarters in the city. His precedent was the success of Singer Sewing Machine Company with its New York headquarters. He told an interviewer in 1913: "When in Europe a few years ago, wherever I went the men with whom I came in contact asked me about the Singer Building and its famous tower. That gave me an idea. I decided to erect a building that would advertise the Woolworth 5 cent and 10 cent stores all over the world."[22]

If his intention was to provide a beacon of worldwide publicity, however, his method of choosing a site continued to be localized and old-fashioned. He acted as though he were choosing the site for a store rather than an office building. Again he took to the streets: "He looked at the crowds, watched them as they turned into side streets . . . and saw where the traffic was the most dense." Ultimately, he chose the corner of Reade and Broadway, considerably downtown from the other tall buildings and the recently completed world-record 700-foot tower of Metropolitan Life Insurance Company, which he had already decided to "overtop."[23]

The most striking feature of Woolworth's career is his progression over thirty years from stalking the public, to orchestrating it, and finally with his tower, to luring, even overwhelming it. But he never fully abandoned his earliest idea of the public as a mobile physical presence and a collective will that was discernible upon close observation, even when he chose the much more abstract course of creating an aura around his business by constructing both a Gothic cathedral of commerce and the world's tallest building. The tower of the Woolworth Building, Montgomery Schuyler observed in 1913, had been added to lighten its appearance and give it grace "at the cost of pure utility." The tower, he concluded, "commemorates [Woolworth's] sense of *civic* obligation."[24]

Schuyler's use of the word *civic* is certainly consistent with the use this term had acquired in characterizing a new form of public space: private business headquarters as architectural spectacle. Schuyler

---

[22] Redding, "Woolworth's Story," p. 664.
[23] Redding, "Woolworth's Story," p. 664.
[24] Montgomery Schuyler, "The Towers of Manhattan," *Architectural Record* 33, no. 2 (February 1913): 108 (emphasis added).

accordingly compared the Woolworth Building to both the Metropolitan Tower and the Municipal Building designed by the firm of McKim, Mead, and White across City Hall Park. Woolworth's bent toward practicality and caution about excess—he paid out $13.5 million in cash for his skyscraper—were by then legendary. What was it he intended to memorialize with such a building? Woolworth appears to have been preoccupied with communicating in spatial terms the grandeur of his own commercial triumph—hence, his choice of the Gothic style reminiscent of the Houses of Parliament, with its echo of civic and ecclesiastical power. An early photograph illustrates the degree to which the building represents a Gothic version of New York's typical campaniled towers on rectilinear bases (fig. 5). (Later construction concealed the base, and the tower now appears to rise straight up.) His first concern, beyond setting a world record, was what the public would perceive at street level. He wanted the building to be at once imposing, instructive, and self-aggrandizing. He wanted his building to serve as a model to the public through its depiction of his career and as a monument to himself.

Woolworth opened his first New York office in 1886 when he was thirty-four years old. He was in the midst of making his fortune with street-level merchandising across the Northeast. He belonged to what might be called the "sidewalk generation" that flourished from the 1890s to the 1910s—one of pedestrians, strollers, shoppers, and cyclists, keenly attuned to the panorama of goods and people provided by New York's streets. It was a generation that was both spectatorial and aggressive. This was precisely the time when the term *window shopping* entered the language, along with the word *show* for any theatrical presentation. By the 1890s the display of merchandise in department store windows was becoming a highly developed art form. The delight created by sensuous display was still fresh and unencumbered.[25] The generation of this time was the first to feel the full allure of New York at night, and the phrase "The Great White Way" was used to describe the bank of illuminated theater marquees arrayed one behind the other along Broadway from Fourteenth to Thirty-fourth streets.

---

[25] For more on display and store windows, see William Leach, "Strategists of Display and the Production of Desire," elsewhere in this volume.

Fig. 5. Woolworth Building, Broadway between Barclay St. and Park Place, New York. (Museum of the City of New York.)

By 1913 the perception of the public had clearly changed. There is probably no better symbol of this change than the moment in early February when Woodrow Wilson pressed a button in Washington, D.C., that illuminated 80,000 bulbs in the completed Woolworth Building. Some reports indicated that the flash could be seen 100 miles away. The telegraphic signal from Washington and the spectacle of an illuminated tower 60 stories high may have brought the sidewalk generation to an end. In the following days and weeks, one source estimated that some 2 million words of free publicity about Woolworth, the building, and the event filled American newspapers and magazines, as Woolworth must have confidently expected.[26] In that moment he had succeeded in shifting the focus of attention away from Metropolitan Life Insurance Company, from the sidewalk to the building's buttresses and pinnacles 792 feet above, and from goods seen at close hand in his many stores, to the more abstract image of a "brand" name. In planning his stores across the Northeast, Woolworth had emphasized the sidewalk perspective of his customers and sought to attract them by luring them into the horizontal streetlike aisles of his stores. By creating a vertical monument rather than a horizontal access route, he was dramatically adopting a new, modern strategy.

Focusing on a moment for marking such a change in perception is clearly arbitrary, since the process of change had been a long one. Even before the 1890s there had been a succession of events that issued in other vertical expressions of the evolution of the city's public spaces. These events were often compounded with related changes in communication and orchestration of public opinion, as in the welcoming celebration in 1899 for Adm. George Dewey commemorating his victory over the Spanish fleet in Manila Bay. On that occasion a barrage of newspaper publicity had produced a spectacular parade marching through the city, but it also featured a huge, electrically illuminated sign atop the Brooklyn Bridge and the vertical spectacle of searchlights probing the sky over the harbor as the naval parade moved through the night. Then in 1910 (if not earlier at the parade for Dewey) came the first ticker tape parade—that perfect dual symbol of commerce and verticality—as New York celebrated the return of Theodore Roosevelt with a march uptown from the Battery. Ticker tape dropping from the upper

---

[26] Redding, "Woolworth's Story," p. 664.

windows of the new Wall Street skyscrapers emphasized the vertical outreach of financial power.[27]

The nature of the changes signaled by these and other related events was to become more obvious by the 1920s, but already by the turn of the century there were those who sensed the connection between communications and the use of vertical space. Tall buildings, because they could be seen from afar and because their construction and design advertised the company building them, anticipated the importance of towers and other vertical structures in the transmission of telegraphic radio signals. It was no accident, for example, that New York newspapers were among the first private companies to build towers, beginning with the Tribune Building in 1876, followed by Western Union's own office tower three years later in 1879 and the campaniled Times Building in 1911.

New York today, in the midst of the largest building boom in its entire history, continues this vertical development of space unabated, but the function of tall buildings has shifted dramatically. While distinctive corporate towers such as the Citicorp Building or the AT&T Building continue to beam acronymically out of the skyline, the most characteristic tall structure is the anonymous glass commercial office building, virtually identical to its neighbor and built on speculation. The most spectacular explosion of such structures, scarcely surprising in a city now identified with financial services, has been in the Wall Street area where a high-rise glass subcity has crowded from view the pinacled silhouette that characterized lower Manhattan in the 1930s.

Across the city one can discern scores of a second genre of tall building, the so-called luxury apartment tower, equally indistinguishable one from another and aimed at New York's managerial and professional upper service tier. Even the few distinctive corporate towers function differently in the city from their counterparts fifty years earlier. The "broadcasting" function of the original towers has been successively superseded by radio, television, and electronic communications. A communications culture, of which New York is now the capital, has succeeded an older commerical culture that produced the city of the

[27] Joseph Nathan Kane, *Famous First Facts* (New York: H. W. Wilson, 1981), p. 667. Gary Jennings describes the grand celebration in 1899 for Dewey and claims that ticker tape was thrown on his parade in Gary Jennings, *Parades! Celebrations and Circuses on the March* (Philadelphia: J. B. Lippincott Co., 1966), p. 81.

1920s and 1930s. It matters little that the art-deco tower of the Chrysler Building can scarcely be glimpsed behind the new anonymous office buildings constructed on speculation by developers. The crowds that surge through the city's streets quite literally move to a different drummer.

Here and there, historical preservationists have succeeded in staking out older landmark buildings, as in the cast-iron district of Soho. Something resembling an older consumer culture still thrives in the interstices of new construction but scarcely in the way it once did. Current public space is largely confined to the atria of tall buildings like the Citicorp or Trump towers, created by builders in exchange for a relaxation of the limits on height in area building codes. Fifth Avenue continues to provide the city with luxury stores of unparalleled opulence. But these pockets of an earlier Manhattan do not evoke the pattern or ensemble of which they once formed a part.

A different urban configuration has replaced that older urban design. A series of revolutions has transformed the meaning of location and distance within the city. The Federal Reserve's vast bank clearinghouse that processes over a billion dollars daily is in one sense the hub of the city's commerce and the successor to Grand Central Terminal and the old Pennsylvania Station, but few New Yorkers know, or need to know, its location, any more than buyers need to know the geographical location of the catalogue companies from whom they order goods. An older, visible city whose arrangements could be "read" taxonomically like the display counters of the superstore that it once was, for all the bits and pieces of it that are left, has disappeared. The iconographic significance of location and elevation, so important to Woolworth, has been eroded, and circuitry has replaced district and neighborhood. New York itself, its older functions diffused by change, has become an integral part of a vast megalopolitan entity that sprawls along the East Coast from Maine to Maryland, its vital ties largely invisible.

Life, Literature, and Sociology in Turn-of-the-Century Chicago

Eugene Rochberg-Halton

In describing the technological exhibits at the World's Columbian Exposition in Chicago, Henry Adams said, "Chicago asked in 1893 for the first time the question whether the American people knew where they were driving." Adams thought the American people did not know, "but that they might still be driving or drifting unconsciously to some point in thought, as their solar system was said to be drifting toward some point in space; and that, possibly, if relations enough could be observed, this point might be fixed. Chicago was the first expression of American thought as a unity; one must start there." As Adams goes on to describe the political events in Washington surrounding the battles over the gold and silver standards, it becomes clearer that "the fixed point" toward which America was drifting was the mechanistic life of the machine and its economic extension in capitalism.[1]

Adams was wrong about Chicago as the first expression of unified American thought; if anything, what Lewis Mumford termed the "Golden Day" of transcendentalist New England in the early 1850s should count as the first flowering of "American thought as a unity." But he saw more clearly than his optimistic contemporaries that Chicago was a fast-beating pulse with which one could measure the new American dynamism: it was the city that in 1893 took as its motto, "I Will."[2]

[1] Henry Adams, *The Education of Henry Adams*, ed. Ernest Samuels (1907; reprint, Boston: Houghton Mifflin Co., 1973), p. 343.

[2] Lewis Mumford, *The Golden Day* (New York: Boni and Liveright, 1926); Perry Duis, *Chicago: Creating New Traditions* (Chicago: Chicago Historical Society, 1976).

Chicago was the quintessential American city of blind will, of the frenetic push to butcher, to stack, to railroad itself to some point in space, blindly drifting within the expansive dream of the machine. The city said "I Will" in its determination to rebuild after the great fire of 1871 and to hold the greatest exposition ever in 1893, but Chicago easily could have borrowed from Nietzsche for its motto and said, "I Will to Power," for power was its end and money its chief means.

Turn-of-the-century Chicago can be viewed as a dream of money, a dream shared by rich and poor alike, a dream that set out, for better or worse, to reshape the world. What we now consider as Chicago literature and sociology both share a fascination with the profound social upheaval and energies created by the explosion of industrial capital. Both sought to document the life of the city, which was no small task in the chaos that was Chicago. The literature of Upton Sinclair and Theodore Dreiser described the degradation that could be brought about by the new materialism. The social reform of Hull-House, opened in 1889 as one of the first social settlements in America, similarly documented the conditions of life in Chicago, while providing a humanistic alternative and the groundwork for a new sociology in the process. "Chicago sociology," although now viewed as coming into its golden age in the 1920s, should be seen as rooted in these earlier efforts and also in the broad social theories proposed by John Dewey, George Herbert Mead, and others who were not in the sociology department of the University of Chicago. Academic sociology, although now equated with Chicago sociology, emerged out of these other milieus, and although it achieved a new emphasis on urban ethnography for sociology, it may be criticized for unwarranted "scientism" in its efforts to establish itself in the academy. All these efforts can be viewed as taking their cues from life itself, particularly from the peculiar new forms of life emerging in the chaotic expansion that marked Chicago. In this way I am interpreting Chicago literature and sociology as products of the city and as indicators of its culture of materialism.

The principal themes I address in this essay are how an examination of Chicago reveals a modern materialism in the making and how the city produced a critique of the rampant consumption of the Gilded Age that is, strangely enough, the legacy of that materialism. Of primary concern here is whether Chicago literature and sociology remain forms of critique or whether they go further to create new insights or perspectives not reducible to their immediate milieu—although, perhaps, growing out of it. In other words, did Chicago literature and sociology provide a genuine and durable alternative to the consumptive materialism of Chicago?

Literature and sociology have been intimately related in Chicago since the end of the nineteenth century. Consider the irony that Upton Sinclair's fiction produced immediate social reform, whereas Thorstein Veblen's social theory of the leisure class was regarded by some as literary satire. James T. Farrell began his *Studs Lonigan* trilogy in the late 1920s while still a student at the University of Chicago, where he took courses in sociology during the central years of the department's urban ethnographical research. The list of his short stories for a composition class reads like the list of books published by members and students of the sociology department in the 1920s.[3] Even today the most celebrated Chicago author of all, Saul Bellow, has his office not in an English department, but in the noted Social Science Research Building at 1126 East Fifty-ninth Street, where he is a member of the University of Chicago's Committee on Social Thought.

The relationship between literature and sociology is further illustrated by the careers of W. I. Thomas and Robert E. Park. Thomas began his widely known sociological career at the University of Chicago as a graduate student in that key year for Henry Adams, 1893. Thomas had earlier taught English literature at Oberlin College, and he later introduced the use of "literary" materials—personal documents such as

[3] Farrell later remarked: "Most of these manuscripts related to death, disintegration, human indignity, poverty, drunkenness, ignorance, human cruelty. They attempted to describe dusty and deserted streets, street corners, miserable homes, pool rooms, brothels, dance halls, taxi dances, bohemian sections, express offices, gasoline filling stations, scenes laid in slum districts. The characters were boys, boys' gangs, drunkards, Negroes, expressmen, homosexuals, immigrants and immigrant landlords, filling-station attendants, straw bosses, hitch hikers, bums, bewildered parents. Most of the manuscripts were written with the ideal of objectivity in mind. I realized then that the writer should submit himself to objective discipline. These early manuscripts of mine were written, in the main, out of such an intention" (James T. Farrell, Introduction to *Studs Lonigan: A Trilogy* [New York: Modern Library, 1938], p. x). Compare the themes of Farrell's manuscripts to those of University of Chicago sociologists of the 1920s: Ruth Shonle, "Suicide: A Study of Personal Disorganization" (Ph.D. diss., 1926); Walter Reckless, "The Natural History of Vice Areas in Chicago" (Ph.D. diss., 1925); Paul Cressey, "The Closed Dance Hall in Chicago" (M.A. thesis, 1929); Louis Wirth, "The Ghetto: A Study in Isolation" (Ph. D. diss., 1926) (published as *The Ghetto* [Chicago, 1928]); Frederic M. Thrasher, *The Gang: A Study of 1,313 Gangs in Chicago* (Chicago, 1927); and Nels Anderson, *The Hobo: The Sociology of the Homeless Man* (Chicago, 1923).

letters and life histories—for sociological purposes in his research with
Florian Znaniecki, published between 1918 and 1920 as *The Polish
Peasant in Europe and America.* Park's complicated career included
eleven years as a newspaperman, with his last assignment coming as a
reporter and drama critic for the *Chicago Journal* from 1897 to 1898.
During this time Park also wrote an unpublished novel and several plays.
He was originally motivated to become a journalist by his study with
John Dewey, who Park said inspired him "to see and know what we call
'Life.'" Dewey also gave Park his "first great assignment": "to investi-
gate the nature and social function of the newspaper." Park went on to
study philosophy with William James, Josiah Royce, George Santay-
ana, and Hugo Muensterberg at Harvard; to take his only sociology
course with Georg Simmel in Berlin; and to work for seven years as the
personal secretary of black reformer Booker T. Washington in the South,
an unusual occupation at that time for a white man with a doctorate in
philosophy from the University of Heidelberg.[4]

The thread connecting Chicago literature and sociology is the
newspaper. Noted Chicago writers such as Dreiser, Sherwood Anderson, Ben Hecht, Carl Sandburg, Farrell, Nelson Algren, and Bellow
all worked for newspapers at some point in their careers. One can say
that "Chicago realism," although not perhaps reducible to journalism,
shows strong influences of journalism. Likewise, the series of ethnographic studies in the 1920s by graduate students of Park and Ernest
Burgess and the earlier research of Thomas and Znaniecki not only
point to the significance of communications media for sociological study
but also can be seen as using methods common to the newspaper reporter
for sociological purposes.

In Park's 1939 "Notes on the Origins of the Society for Social
Research," he describes the centrality of Thomas to the development of
academic Chicago sociology. The essence of Thomas's perspective was
for Park its "literary" quality: "Thomas' interest was always, it seems,
that of a poet (although he never, so far as I know, wrote poetry) and of
a literary man in the reportorial sense, and not that of a politician or of
a practical man. He wanted to see, to know, and to report, disinterest-
edly and without respect to anyone's policies or program, the world of

---

[4]Winifred Raushenbush, *Robert E. Park: Biography of a Sociologist* (Durham, N.C.:
Duke University Press, 1979), p. 15.

men and things as he experienced it." Although it may not seem to follow that a "literary man in the reportorial sense" is necessarily a literary man, one must remember that much of what we think of as Chicago literature is precisely literature in a reportorial sense. We should also keep in mind how essential a reportorial sense was to Park's whole conception of sociology, as he described himself:

It happened that, having been for something like ten years a newspaper reporter, I knew a good deal about the city. In fact it was, as I have frequently said, while I was a reporter and a city editor that I began my sociological studies. It was under the guidance of an extraordinary personality, Franklin Ford, himself a newspaper man, that I got my first understanding of the significance and the possibilities of the social survey as an instrument for social investigation. That must have been as early as 1893 or 1894. In the article I wrote about the city I leaned rather heavily on the information I had acquired as a reporter regarding the city. Later on, as it fell to my lot to direct the research work of an increasing number of graduate students, I found that my experience as a city editor in directing a reportorial staff had stood me in good stead. Sociology, after all, is concerned with problems in regard to which newspaper men inevitably get a good deal of first hand knowledge. Besides that, sociology deals with just those aspects of social life which ordinarily find their most obvious expression in the news and in historical and human documents generally. One might fairly say that a sociologist is merely a more accurate, responsible, and scientific reporter.[5]

One sees in this statement how strongly the impress of the newspaper made itself felt on Park and why he believed sociology needed to turn from theoretical discourse to empirical observation. One might call this type of sociology and literature "reportorial realism." Park was a key actor in the drama of twentieth-century sociology, and his self-

[5] Robert E. Park, "Notes on the Origins of the Society for Social Research," intro. Lester R. Kurtz, *Journal of the History of the Behavioral Sciences* 18, no. 4 (October 1982): 337, 338 (originally published in *Bulletin of the Society for Social Research* 1 [August 1939]: 1–5). For further information on Park and the Chicago school of sociology, see Robert E. L. Faris, *Chicago Sociology, 1920–1932* (1967; reprint, Chicago: University of Chicago Press Midway Reprint, 1979); Fred H. Matthews, *Quest for an American Sociology: Robert E. Park and the Chicago School* (Montreal: McGill-Queen's University Press, 1977); Raushenbush, *Robert E. Park*; Martin Bulmer, *The Chicago School of Sociology: Institutionalization, Diversity, and the Rise of Sociological Research* (Chicago: University of Chicago, 1984); and Lester R. Kurtz, *Evaluating Chicago Sociology: A Guide to the Literature, with an Annotated Bibliography* (Chicago: University of Chicago Press, 1984).

assigned role was to transform the sociologist from philosopher-historian to scientific reporter. He believed that sociology could become scientific through concrete reporting of empirical reality. Yet one of the potential problems in reportorial realism is that the empirical may have historical distortions embedded in it which remain relatively invisible to the reporter and which call for a different level of analysis. Chicago, for example, may not have been the generalizable model of the modern metropolis that academic Chicago sociologists believed it to be. Park's scientific materialism was itself part of the same forces of materialism which were at work in Chicago, and more generally, in modern culture. Park's reportorial realism would in turn be supplanted by a statistical sociology that viewed only itself as truly scientific: the reporter gave way to the "accountant" as the role model for scientific sociology, and the qualitative colors of city life that remained a part of the reporter's facts were excised from the quantitative conception of human science.

The Great Stockyard Machine

To understand Chicago, or "Porkopolis" as some of its citizens at the turn of the century were fond of calling it, one must appreciate to what extent it is a city of quantities. It was the fastest growing city in the world for over sixty years between the 1860s and the 1930s, frequently doubling its population in a decade. Although incorporated only about 150 years ago in 1837, Chicago had acquired 29,963 residents by 1850; 112,172 in 1860; 503,185 in 1880; and 2,701,705 in 1920. In 1892, the year before Chicago asked, as Adams noted, whether the American people knew where they were driving, Chicago drove approximately 2.5 million cattle and almost 5 million hogs to slaughter. The railroad made possible an unprecedented aggregation of capital and labor in the stockyards, one that the rationalizing tendencies of the megamachine quickly maximized, not only over the mode of production—as in the early use of assembly-line techniques—but also over every possible aspect of life, reducing everything to quanta of profit.

Chicago gave birth to the modern skyscraper, enabling a more rationalized use of limited land in the business district and an increase of light and window space. The new ideas growing out of Chicago had a profound influence on European modernist architects, which culminated in the glass and steel skeletal structures of the "second school" of

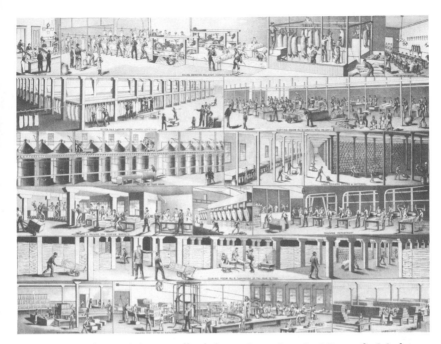

Fig. 1. Shober and Carqueville, lithographers, *Interior Views of a Modern First Class Pork Packing and Canning Establishment of the United States of America*, Chicago, 1880. (Chicago Historical Society.)

Chicago architecture led by émigré Ludwig Mies van der Rohe. Skeletal buildings are perhaps apt symbols for a city that built its reputation on the flaying and skinning of hides. Max Weber, who visited Chicago on his way to the St. Louis exposition of 1904, remarked, "With the exception of some exclusive residential districts, the whole gigantic city, more extensive than London, is like a man whose skin has been peeled off and whose entrails one sees at work." One sees the rationalized machine of the Union Stock Yards already well established in the 1880 lithograph (fig. 1). Perhaps the sight of such a display on his tour of the stockyards influenced Weber's opinion of the city as a whole. Of a somewhat more modern, but equally first-class Chicago pork packing and canning establishment, Rudyard Kipling remarked around the same time as Weber, "Then that first stuck swine dropped, still kicking, into a great vat of boiling water, and spoke no more words, but wallowed in obedience to some unseen machinery, and presently came forth at the lower end of the vat and was heaved on the blades of a blunt paddle-wheel-thing."[6]

Chicago fires of the soul burned in this "singing flame of a city," as Dreiser called it. As Upton Sinclair's *Jungle* so searingly showed, the one quality left unquantified and uncapitalized was the death squeal of the doomed pig. Citizens of Porkopolis liked to boast, "They use everything about the hog except the squeal!" Sinclair's novel is set primarily in and around the Union Stock Yards of the South Side. The Union Stock Yards were by no means named because they were organized by labor unions. Presumably named for the United States, they were founded in 1865 to consolidate meat packing in Chicago, which had risen in importance during the Civil War because Chicago was in the war zone. In many ways the Union Stock Yards can be seen as part of the victory of the machine in the Civil War, which defeated not only the human slave labor of the South but also the American vision of democratic vistas—of a free life, as Walt Whitman said, "copious, vehement, spiritual, bold"—which could transcend the merely material. It was the machine of industry that indeed appropriated the copious, vehement, spiritual, and bold to itself, leaving to life the meager, insensate, spiritless, and submissive. The Union Stock Yards, described in relentless detail in *The Jungle*, were united and cold-bloodedly efficient in attempting to destroy any opposition from the workers' unions.

In the industrialization of the American vision after the Civil War, the tensions between the romantic and the technical that characterized the exploration of the New World swung decidedly toward the technical, and a great inversion occurred: henceforth it would be the mechanism—money and the machine—that would be endowed with the romantic, leaving the hollowed-out human form to assume the qualities of the machine. When Jurgis Rudkis, the Lithuanian protagonist of *The Jungle*, toured the Durham meat-packing plant with his family shortly after their arrival in Chicago, it seemed "impossible of belief that any-

    [6]Weber, as quoted in H. H. Gerth and C. Wright Mills, eds., *From Max Weber: Essays in Sociology* (New York: Oxford University Press, 1946), p. 15; Rudyard Kipling, "How I Struck Chicago and How Chicago Struck Me," in *The American City: A Sourcebook of Urban Imagery*, ed. Anselm L. Strauss (Chicago: Aldine Publishing Co., 1968), p. 46.

thing so stupendous could have been devised by mortal man." To Jurgis it seemed almost profane to speak about the place skeptically as others did: "It was a thing as tremendous as the universe—the laws and ways of its working no more than the universe to be questioned or understood. All that a mere man could do, it seemed to Jurgis, was to take a thing like this as he found it, and do as he was told."[7]

This "thing as tremendous as the universe" was the great machine of modern capitalist industry, transcendent and omnipotent, which Sinclair later pits against a fiery socialism also transcendent and capable of defeating the bigness of the capitalist machine with the bigness of organized labor. There was a kind of transcendence in the massiveness of emergent industry itself, in its raising of human activity to the level of the gigantic, and in the smooth-flowing and metallic way it seemed ritually to transform life itself into bloodless carcass and packaged product. Perhaps only the Aztec ritual sacrifice, in which the human victim's still-beating heart was plucked out on the high steps of the pyramid and displayed to the populace, could match the ritual tours of the slaughter factories. Or perhaps the Spanish bull fight, in which living beef is agonistically skewered to the delight of the spectators, or its inverse, the annual running of the bulls in Pamplona, in which the spectators themselves are occasionally skewered by the stampeding bulls, are somewhat analogous. How many modern cities have made of their local blood baths a major tourist attraction? The stockyards were a key ingredient in the culture of display in Chicago, and they impressed on the many thousands of tourists who visited them the bloody hog-squeal symbol of a city seemingly dedicated to the mechanics and commerce of death.

The Home as a Sign of Chicago Materialism

Two representative works of Chicago literature, Sinclair's *Jungle* and Dreiser's *Titan*, illustrate the consumptive culture of the city through opposing trajectories. *The Jungle* moves from the joys of a wedding ceremony for a newly arrived immigrant couple to the depths of jail, death, destruction, and dissolution, while *The Titan* rises from divorce and jail

---

[7] Upton Sinclair, *The Jungle* (1906; reprint, New York: Penguin Books, 1965), p. 51.

to the upward reaches of unlimited power and wealth. Spiritually, however, both tell of the domination by power and bigness over purpose
and life. *The Jungle* does so through the perspective of the underclass,
and *The Titan* from that of the capitalist overlord.

Key to both works, and to an understanding of the consumptive
culture of accumulation and display, is the significance of the home.
The Jungle begins with the promise and hope of Jurgis and Ona Rudkis's
wedding, the finding of jobs for the extended family, and the purchase
of the family's new home near the stockyards. Yet the stench of the
power complex can be smelled even in these happy beginnings. The
family soon realizes that they have only signed to *rent* their home for
the next eight years with a downpayment of all their savings and that
they must pay more monthly than they had thought, or else forfeit
everything. The legal butchery of the real estate officials and lawyers
reveals itself as a form of bureaucratic slaughter parallel to that of the
stockyard factories. The house is poorly constructed, as the family dis-
covers when the cold Chicago winds begin to blow through it. The great
stockyard machine devours the lifeblood of its workers with admirable
efficiency, creating a progressive deterioration leading inevitably to the
loss of the home and of all human attributes, and eventually of human
life itself. Jurgis is at one point released from jail, where he had been
sent for a month for attacking the boss who had forced Ona into prostitution. He returns to find that while he was in jail, his house had been
sold and his family evicted. The new tenants had been told, like Jurgis
and his family, that the house was brand new. Reflecting on the house,
Jurgis realizes:

> Why, they had put their very souls into their payments on that house, they
> had paid for it with their sweat and tears—yes, more, with their very life-blood.
> Dede Antanas [the grandfather] had died of the struggle to earn that money—
> he would be alive and strong today if he had not had to work in Durham's dark
> cellars to earn his share. And Ona, too, had given her health and strength to
> pay for it—she was wrecked and ruined because of it; and so was he, who had
> been a big, strong man three years ago.
> That first lying circular, that smoothed-tongued slippery agent! That trap
> of the extra payments, the interest, and all the other charges that they had not
> the means to pay, and would never had attempted to pay! And then all the tricks
> of the packers, their masters, the tyrants who ruled them—the shut-downs and
> the scarcity of work, the irregular hours and the cruel speeding-up, the lowering

of wages, the raising of prices! The mercilessness of nature about them, of heat and cold, rain and snow; the mercilessness of the city, of the country in which they lived, of its laws and customs that they did not understand! All of these things had worked together for the company that had marked them for its prey and was waiting for its chance. And now with this last hideous injustice, its time had come, and it had turned them out bag and baggage, and taken their house and sold it again![8]

But this was not the last hideous injustice, for in the next scenes Jurgis's precious Ona dies in the process of childbirth, because of their inability to afford adequate medical treatment. Later, when his only son drowns in the mud of the street where the family lives, the last intimate tie is cut, and Jurgis abandons his remaining relatives to wander as a tramp. The process of depersonalization is complete, and Jurgis joins the homeless, with yet further depths of hell to pass through before he is redeemed by the vision of socialism.

The Titan (1914) is the second book of Dreiser's *Trilogy of Desire*, along with *The Financier* (1912) and *The Stoic* (1947, posthumous). The entire trilogy is closely modeled on the life of Charles T. Yerkes (fig. 2), the financier and street railway magnate who dominated the transit industry in late nineteenth-century Chicago. Yerkes practiced a capitalism of corruption, documented not only in Dreiser's trilogy but also in Lincoln Steffens's earlier muckraking classic *Shame of the Cities* (1904), and William T. Stead's even earlier *If Christ Came to Chicago* (1894), both of which might have influenced Dreiser. Stead described Yerkes in part 3, entitled "Satan's Invisible World Displayed": "Mr. C. T. Yerkes, erstwhile of a Pennsylvania penitentiary, now the street railway despot of Chicago, a millionaire and a resident in a handsomely furnished mansion at 3201 Michigan Avenue. Mr. Yerkes, according to the oath of the South Side Assessor, has got $1,000 worth of personal property in his residence, excluding the piano. . . . The carpets on the floor, the pictures on the walls, the plate on the table to ordinary eyes would seem to be dirt cheap at $1,000." Stead further commented on Yerkes's role in society:

> Of the predatory rich in Chicago there are plenty and to spare, but there is one man who stands out conspicuous among all the rest. . . . I refer to Mr. Charles T. Yerkes. Mr. Yerkes is a notable product of the present system. Of

[8]Sinclair, *Jungle*, pp. 213, 214.

Fig. 2. Charles T. Yerkes at home, 3201 S. Michigan Ave., Chicago, ca. 1890. (Chicago Historical Society.)

course, though Mr. Yerkes at an early stage in his career, before he was launched upon Chicago as a financier and street railway magnate, had served in a Pennsylvania penitentiary, I would not for a moment suggest that in his operations in Chicago he has brought himself within the clutches of the law. . . . It is probable, however, that Mr. Yerkes, grown insolent by the impunity with which he has ridden roughshod over the people of Chicago, has over-reached himself.

Mr. Yerkes is a significant sample of the class to which I refer. He lives in style, and apparently does not find it difficult to obtain the assistance of the gentlemen of Chicago in the managing of his companies.[9]

[9]William T. Stead, *If Christ Came to Chicago! A Plea for the Union of All Who Love in the Service of All Who Suffer* (Chicago: Laird and Lee, 1894), pp. 107–8.

Stead saw Yerkes as a "significant sample" of the predatory, as opposed to the idle, rich. This distinction was also used, somewhat differently, by Veblen in his *Theory of the Leisure Class* (1899), published shortly after Stead's book and written in, and frequently about, Chicago. The concept of a predatory elite may have been influenced by Lewis Henry Morgan's idea of evolutionary stages of savagery, barbarism, and civilization, but the metaphor of "civilized" pecuniary predation is an apt one.

The *Titan* begins with Frank Algernon Cowperwood, the Yerkes-based hero, leaving jail and relative homelessness in Philadelphia to begin his second career as a robber baron of Chicago. The novel is about power in its various manifestations in finance, sex, and acquisition and depicts a transient world in which personal force means everything. From the beginning Cowperwood buys his way into Chicago, audaciously in business and ostentatiously but not so successfully in high society. He builds a magnificent home and fills it with magnificent art. These material possessions are signs of his rise on the power and status ladder and of the magical alchemy of money, which is capable apparently of transmuting base and corrupt materials like Cowperwood and his wife, Aileen, into the gold of "the gold coast," the wealthy neighborhood then located on South Michigan and Prairie avenues.

The home in *The Titan* is, like that in *The Jungle*, a sign of achievement. But where the Rudkis home is a center of family life and death, the Cowperwood home is the center of the "higher" aspirations, or at least of the aspiration to move higher into "society." In order to do this, one must have the proper emblems and accoutrements, as described by Veblen. Perhaps the home and its belongings, including "the wife," together form the best trophy to display social standing and legitimize predatory wealth. This is particularly evident in the grand opening of Cowperwood's newly built house on South Michigan Avenue, a ritual feast of display featuring "music by a famous stringed orchestra of Chicago," "artists of considerable importance," "the important pictures" that Cowperwood had purchased in Europe, and of course the already initiated members of high society, which the Cowperwoods were seeking to join. Most prominent of the paintings were a portrait of Aileen by a Dutch artist, Jan van Beers, and "a picture of nude odalisques of the harem, idling beside the highly colored stone marquetry of an Oriental bath." The nude was "more or less 'loose' art for Chicago, shocking to the uninitiated, though harmless enough to the illuminati," who apparently had learned the correct pecuniary canons of taste.[10]

The illuminati in attendance at Cowperwood's affair would have known that the painting of fleshy, naked women was what beauty was all about and that it probably cost a bundle. And the portrait of Aileen revealed much to the onlooker: the wife taking the European trip, painted amid the Dutch countryside that symbolized a famous style of art, dressed in the latest Paris fashion, seated before a brick palace that signified her moneyed pretensions to aristocracy: "In the warm glow of the guttered gas jets she looked particularly brilliant here, pampered, idle, jaunty— the well-kept, stall-fed pet of the world." Both paintings performed their function of displaying conspicuous leisure, submission, and possession. They signified their owner's predatory manliness: he possessed "the wife" on whom he could waste conspicuously in life and in art, and he possessed "the harem" of the respectable man's desire, sublimated in the art, but also actually lived out in Cowperwood's endless romantic affairs. These paintings signified the ideal of woman and beauty in a consumer culture, "the well-kept, stall-fed pet of the world." And the paintings— all of them—were indeed a harem, which Cowperwood increasingly turned to in the name of art as his idealized narcissism increased.[11]

Although Chicago's literature is usually thought of as related to the muckraking tradition, there are also peculiar positive relations to business and capitalism. "The business of art" and the "art of business" are intertwined in Dreiser's *Trilogy of Desire*, just as they are in Sherwood Anderson's *Windy McPherson's Son* (1916), also set in and around Chicago. Perhaps one should view this attitude that business activity and art are intrinsically related and good for each other as part of the culture of gilded materialism in early twentieth-century America. This was, after all, the culture that produced such a successful businessman and great artist as Charles Ives, who combined in his person the statistical certainties of insurance with the atonal, transcendentalist longing of his 1908 musical composition, *The Unanswered Question*. But "the might of money and the entanglement of art with it—the dollar as soul's husband," as Saul Bellow's Humboldt expressed it decades later in *Humboldt's Gift*, is better viewed in the broader context of what Mumford

[10] Theodore Dreiser, *The Titan* (1914; reprint, New York: Signet Classic, 1965), p. 68.

[11] Dreiser, *Titan*, p. 68.

termed "the pragmatic acquiescence": the wholesale capitulation of higher ideals in American life to the forces of the moment, the forces of uncontrolled industrial and capitalist expansion.[12]

The word *art* appears throughout Dreiser's trilogy, frequently in inappropriate places and usually as something lofty and redeeming. But it always translates into personal force: "Truth to say, [Cowperwood] must always have youth, the illusion of beauty, vanity in womanhood, the novelty of a new, untested temperament, quite as he must have pictures, old porcelain, music, a mansion, illuminated missals, power, the applause of the great, unthinking world." The accumulation and display of art was also Cowperwood's substitute for inner spiritual experience. Through his purchase of "important" paintings and affairs with "artistic" women, he could appropriate beauty and apply it, like a salve, to the inner wasteland left by his calculating and external approach to life: "I satisfy myself" is literally Cowperwood's motto. All life's qualities and life itself become mere "satisfactions," things to be momentarily possessed and discarded. Cowperwood's desire for art and beauty and Dreiser's nebulous understanding of them are pathetic and reveal why materialism, with its underlying faith in physical sensation as the foundation of reality, must move increasingly toward power and transience.[13]

Chicago Sociologists

Although the term *sociology* originated with Auguste Comte in Europe and many of its greatest early practitioners were European, sociology is usually acknowledged to have become a fully autonomous institution at the University of Chicago. When one speaks now of Chicago sociology, one thinks particularly of the urban ethnographies and studies of "human ecology" that flourished at the university in the early decades of the twentieth century and culminated in the works of W. I. Thomas and the many publications of the 1920s by Robert Park, Ernest Burgess,

[12]Carl S. Smith, *Chicago and the American Literary Imagination*, 1880–1920 (Chicago: University of Chicago Press, 1984); Sherwood Anderson, *Windy McPherson's Son* (1916; reprint, Chicago: University of Chicago Press, 1965); Charles Ives, *The Unanswered Question*, Music for chamber orchestra, performable also as chamber music (New York: Southern Music Publishing Co., 1953); Saul Bellow, *Humboldt's Gift* (New York: Viking Press, 1975).
[13]Dreiser, *Titan*, p. 186.

and their students. Thomas is known today primarily for his development of "situational analysis" and for his multivolume series, *The Polish Peasant in Europe and America*, written with Florian Znaniecki. The authors' case-study and personal-document approaches were later criticized as insufficiently empirical by number-crunching sociologists who preferred statistical norms to situational facts. Yet *The Polish Peasant*, despite earlier controversy surrounding it, is still regarded as a pivotal work in the establishment of empirical sociology for its use of personal documents, including some 862 personal letters.

Thomas is also widely known today as one of the fathers of "symbolic interactionism" in sociology, especially for his emphasis on "the situation" as a locus for sociological analysis. His most frequently quoted statement on the situation is, "If men define situations as real, they are real in their consequences." Thomas saw that subjective factors needed to be included in analysis, and symbolic interactionists interpreted this to signify that meaning is primarily subjectively based, despite that Thomas went on to say that both subjective and objective factors are significant.[14] Thomas provides a seeming alternative to sociological positivism, yet he shares with it a prejudice for the present that devalues history. Thomas is clearly regarded today as a representative of a humanist sociology, and by the high-tech standards of robotic quantitative contemporary sociology, this view is perhaps correct. But it is important to see that Thomas himself sought to develop a scientifically grounded sociology and that his view of society was deeply imbued with the image of science wrought by the modern power complex.

According to Thomas, the nature of the individual "demanding a maximum of new experience, is in fundamental conflict with the nature of society, demanding a maximum of stability." Here the ideas of maximization and conflict are foundational, just as, perhaps not by coincidence, they are in capitalism. The individual does not possess inner capacities for stability, and society does not possess outer resources for change in this modified form of Hobbesianism. And the human sciences should emulate the natural sciences, in Thomas's view, in order to learn the "fundamental human attitudes" and thereby create the pos-

---

[14] William I. Thomas and Dorothy Swain Thomas, "Situations Defined as Real Are Real in Their Consequences" (1928), reprinted in *Social Psychology through Symbolic Interaction*, ed. Gregory P. Stone and Harvey A. Farberman (Waltham, Mass.: Ginn-Blaisdell, 1970), pp. 154–55.

sibility of social engineering. Only science, applied to a contemporary situation like Chicago, and not history (or, presumably, literature), can give us the answer:

> The very disharmony of the social world is largely due to the disproportionate rate of advance in the mechanical world. We live in an entirely new world, unique, without parallel in history. History has not helped us. It cannot help us because we do not understand it: we do not even understand an election. We must first understand the past from the present. We must view the present as behavior. We must establish by scientific procedure the laws of behavior, and then the past will have its meaning and make its contribution. If we learn the laws of human behavior as we have learned the laws of mathematics, physics, and chemistry, if we establish what are the fundamental human attitudes, how they can be converted into other and more socially desirable attitudes, how the world of values is created and modified by the operation of these attitudes, then we can establish any attitudes and values whatever. [15]

Thomas believed that the "very disharmony of the social world" could be resolved by aligning ourselves with the disproportionately advancing mechanical world that created the disharmony, a strange melody indeed. He thought that people must adjust situationally to the mechanical world of the present because history is inadequate. Only by scientifically discovering fundamental laws of behavior will "the past have its meaning and make its contribution." Then social engineering could establish "any attitudes and values whatever," as though mechanism, and not purpose, was the motive and end of human conduct. This is the voice and victory of the machine.

Park's urban sociology combined the concrete observations of social life characteristic of his earlier work as a reporter with "naturalistic" laws of ecology that underlie city life, stressing how the city is a product of human nature. The natural was nonreflective, so that certain "moral regions" of the city—vice districts, saloons, brothels, race tracks, and the like—were unplanned "natural areas." Park viewed moral regions as "part of the natural, if not normal, life of the city," and the term was intended "to apply to regions in which a divergent moral code prevails, because it is a region in which the people who inhabit it are dominated, as people are ordinarily not dominated, by a taste or by a passion or by

---

[15] William Isaac Thomas, *W. I. Thomas on Social Organization and Social Personality*, ed. Morris Janowitz (1917; reprint, Chicago: University of Chicago Press, 1966), pp. 171, 181.

some interest which has its roots directly in the original nature of the individual. It may be an art, like music, or a sport, like horse-racing. Such a region would differ from other social groups by the fact that its interests are more immediate and more fundamental."[16] Park saw the modern city as lacking the controls to keep natural inclinations in place, so that natural needs become expressed in the chaotic manifestations of vice, crime, and family life. He attempted to include a concept of life in his urban equation, yet his view of nature, like Thomas's, was derived from Thomas Hobbes, who saw nature as an underlying chaos on which is superimposed social convention to keep order. In what ways, however, could Park's Chicago, with its constantly exploding population, be said to be "natural"?

The problem with Park's view of nature, as with Hobbes's, is that it falsely assumed a one-sided, nominalistic view derivative of modern scientism, in which nature is nonrelational and nonpurposive and culture in its highest forms is denatured. The implication of this view for Park was that he could not see that there may be intentions of the system operating in the so-called moral regions. In a more explicit way than Park's scientism, Sinclair's fiction caught the fallacy of the alleged natural basis of this system when he showed how the jungle of Chicago was anything but a natural ecology.

In the Packingtown neighborhood where Rudkis lived, there was a totalitarian system of exploitation with an intentionality of its own. This systemic intentionality, the logic of unlimited rational capitalism, could be seen clearly in the planned stockyards, but it was also operating in the establishment of the check-cashing bars that lined the streets near the stockyards, the real estate people who would "eat you alive," the men who would attend a traditional wedding feast, eating and drinking according to tradition, but not giving money to the bride as was also traditional. In other words, Park and the academic sociologists of the Chicago school ignored or devalued the glaring historic, economic, and systemic purposes at work that created geographical and social areas in their own destructive image.

Chicago, the city without a history, was used as a "laboratory" for a universal scientistic-urbanism without history. It is strange that despite

[16] Robert E. Park, "The City: Suggestions for the Investigation of Human Behavior in the Urban Environment," in *The City*, ed. Robert E. Park, Ernest W. Burgess, and Roderick McKenzie (1925; reprint, Chicago: University of Chicago Press, 1967), p. 45.

Park's discussion of the tension between history and natural science, which formed the basis of the opening chapter of the widely influential introductory textbook he published with Burgess in 1921, he developed a view of the city that ignored the shaping and formative forces of history. Just as Sigmund Freud generalized from turn-of-the-century Vienna psyches to claim a universal psychology, Park and the academic Chicago sociologists such as Thomas, Burgess, and, later, Park's student, Louis Wirth, generalized from the unique and rapidly industrializing turn-of-the-century Chicago to claim a universal scientific sociology of urban life. Their fear of history and fervor for positive science were symptoms of scientism, of an ideology of science which was itself the product of modern materialism.

In seeking to legitimize sociology as a science, academic sociologists at the University of Chicago had to distinguish sharply their efforts not only from social workers and settlements but also from the research of settlement workers. Urban ethnography, demography, and ecology are now associated with academic Chicago sociology, although efforts in these areas were begun earlier in Chicago in nonacademic works such as *Hull-House Maps and Papers* (1895), works themselves influenced by earlier English social surveys. One finds sparse reference to this earlier research by the academic sociologists, and when references are made, they are frequently to distinguish the scientific nature of the academic sociology. Thus Burgess (who had actually lived at Hull-House at one point) cites *Hull-House Maps and Papers*, with some other works, as "illustrations of the careful study and keen observations of these very early efforts to determine and to take account of the many and different conditions affecting neighborhood work. This interest in the discovery of factors in the social situation may therefore be called the second stage in the trend of neighborhood work toward a scientific basis. Science, however, is concerned not with factors, but with forces."[17]

Burgess's conception of what constituted science falsely "naturalized" such forces as competition, which was supposedly an example of an ecological force rather than a by-product of industrial capitalism. Academic sociologists legitimately sought to broaden the base of sociology beyond practicing social work, but they did so with crude ideas of

[17]Ernest W. Burgess, "Can Neighborhood Work Have a Scientific Basis?" in Park et al., eds., *City*, p. 143.

scientism ultimately derived from the same power complex that created the peculiar forces of life in Chicago and that sought to repress the purposive force of community life. Even though academic Chicago sociology of the 1920s seems humane by today's standards of number-crunching machine sociology, it is the nascent technocrat of the power complex we hear in Burgess's recommendation:

> The work of neighborhood centers, like that of all other social agencies, must increasingly be placed upon the basis of the scientific study of the social forces with which they have to deal. Especially are studies desired of the actual effect and role of intimate contacts in personal development and social control. . . . Neighborhood work, by the logic of the situation, if it is to evolve a successful technique, will be compelled more and more to depend upon research into the social forces of modern life.[18]

It was precisely the scientizing and bureaucratizing of social work that devitalized the settlement concept. The model of the home was transformed into the model of the bureau as a center for social work. We see in Burgess's words the blueprint for the destruction of the organic life of Hull-House by the machine-like social forces of sociological scientism.

The academic sociologists wanted to be newspaper reporters with white laboratory coats, detached documenters. They were, in their way, every bit as reformist as Hull-House, but they saw humanism as unscientific. The people associated with Hull-House depended on the method of life, not positive science. They used the activities of life—play, art and craft, drama, work and its conditions in Chicago—as the basis of their ideas. For this reason they were in many ways more empirical than the academics precisely because they considered life in its potential fullness, rather than science, to be the foundational principle.

Jane Addams and Ellen Gates Starr opened the doors of Hull-House in 1889 with lofty ideals: they would uplift their poor neighbors in the South Halsted Street area with "object lessons" drawn from the art objects they had acquired in their European travels and through discussion of serious literature. Their initial ideas of settlement work seemed to be based on the model of bourgeois respectability, as if Dreiser's Cowperwood were to invite Sinclair's Rudkis to view his art collection! But Addams and Starr quickly readjusted their ideas, not so much

---

[18] Burgess, "Can Neighborhood Work," pp. 154–55.

by lowering their ideals as by broadening them. Hull-House, influenced by the English model of Toynbee Hall, was among the first settlement houses in an emerging movement in America, but no other settlement house so caught the fires of the imagination.

Art and social reform were interwoven in the life of drama cultivated at Hull-House. The Hull-House Players developed into the leading avant-garde theater in Chicago within about a decade after the group's founding, performing plays by George Bernard Shaw and Henrik Ibsen by 1905 and later social realist plays of John Galsworthy and Gerhart Hauptman.[19] Art was not merely a tool of counseling or a "practical activities" slot on the daily calendar; rather, it achieved a genuine life of its own which cultivated the participating community.

New forms of thought that were in the process of being created in Chicago found their forum at Hull-House; for example, Frank Lloyd Wright's famous lecture of 1903, "The Art and Craft of the Machine," wherein he challenged industrial society to take control of and put to right uses its machines, and John Dewey's close involvement with the activities of Hull-House and their influence on his developing social philosophy and philosophy of education. Both Wright's architectural outlook and Dewey's philosophy were rooted in the centrality of organic life to genuine human culture. Both believed in democratizing society and in the cultivated individual as a necessary ingredient to a living democracy.[20]

Wright specifically denied that he was giving a "sociological prescription" in his Hull-House address, yet he uttered a far better sociological description of the relations of life, individual, and society than the Hobbesian academic sociologists at the University of Chicago. Wright described how civilization could be characterized as a "dramatizing of an object," or "conventionalization," and cited the artistic use of flowers as expressions of a civilization: the acanthus and honeysuckle of ancient Greece, the chrysanthemum of Japan, or the lotus of Egypt. Far from contemporary theories of convention as inert or arbitrary code, Wright saw that conventionalizing consisted of finding in a substance "the pattern of its life-principle" and embodying it. Using the metaphor

---

[19] Stuart J. Hecht, "Social and Artistic Integration: The Emergence of Hull-House Theatre," *Theatre Journal* 34, no. 2 (May 1982): 172–82.

[20] Frank Lloyd Wright, "The Art and Craft of the Machine," in *Eighty Years at Hull-House*, ed. Allen Davis and Mary Lynn McCree (1913; reprint, Chicago: Quadrangle Books, 1969), pp. 85–88.

of the artist-craftsman who seeks to dramatize a "beloved flower" in stone and applying it to society, Wright remarked, "But the true Democrat will take the human plant as it grows and—in the spirit of using the means at hand to put life into his conventionalization—preserve the individuality of the plant to protect the flower, which is its very life, getting from both a living expression of the man-character fitted perfectly to a place in Society with no loss of vital significance. Fine art is this flower of the Man." According to Wright, art does not simply imitate life, but also creates its own life out of it. Life is not of itself formless and anarchistic, as a Hobbesian might say, but is the creative source of form and function. And democratized society is not the faceless aggregate of the "mobocracy" or "machine-made moron," but is a dramatic conventionalization that preserves and nourishes the life of the individual.

It is an understatement to say that life flourished at Hull-House: life infused everything Hull-House touched. For any serious investigation of the mind of Chicago, all roads lead eventually to Hull-House, the institution through which almost all the vital energies of Chicago seemed to pass. In the end, however, Hull-House did not remake Chicago. Yet the image of Hull-House, like the Greek acanthus or the Japanese chrysanthemum, remains as a "guide to the imagination." Walter Lippmann wrote in 1913, "If Hull-House is unable to civilize Chicago, it at least shows Chicago and America what a civilization might be like. Friendly, where our cities are friendless, beautiful, where they are ugly; sociable and open, where our daily life is furtive; work a craft, art a participation—it is in miniature the goal of statesmanship."[21]

The Triumph of Antilife

The journalistic realism found in turn-of-the-century Chicago fiction and academic sociology provides a picture of society in which the events of the moment loom large, but history and the sense of inner vision are given short shrift. In the end then, Chicago literature and academic sociology of the early twentieth century can be seen as products of the city itself and as the traces left by the culture of materialism: they doc-

---

[21] Walter Lippmann, "Well Meaning but Unmeaning," in Davis and McCree, eds., *Eighty Years at Hull-House*, p. 111.

ument the unchecked tendencies to bigness and power of modern materialism and sometimes even celebrate it, but they do not provide an
imaginative or critical alternative. They take their cues from life in the
city, from the massive social upheaval, but they are themselves stamped
with the same problems. They cannot account for the metropolis as
producer of enduring human values and civilized life or for the human
capacity to regain and create purposive organic life and form in the
modern city.

Sinclair's socialism was humane, but did not provide checks against
bureaucratization or the centralizing tendencies of the machine that
could offset the utilitarian power complex. Dreiser took the power complex itself to be that which animates the art of life. Art does not so much
imitate life as it imitates the will to power: the movers and the takers are
the makers and the shakers. Much the same view permeates Chicago's
academic sociology. Human nature is Hobbesian in the ecological views,
always seeking more and now, and the concept of life is but the philosophy of greed. The city is largely a play of transience and self-interest,
a mirror of uncontrolled capitalism, and in Louis Wirth's essay,
"Urbanism as a Way of Life," it becomes associated with the tendency
toward bigness itself.[22] American thought had indeed reached a "unity"—
the unity of the mechanistic Archimedean vanishing point: the "ghost
in the machine."

The glowing, confident White City of beaux arts buildings at the
Columbian Exposition that had provoked such dark thoughts in Henry
Adams had the same effect on another psychic seismograph of the time,
master architect Louis Sullivan:

> These crowds were astonished. They beheld what was for them an amazing
> revelation of the architectural art. . . . To them it was a veritable Apocalypse,
> a message inspired from on high. Upon it their imagination shaped new ideals.
> They went away, spreading again over the land, returning to their homes, each
> one of them carrying in the soul the shadow of the white cloud, each of them
> permeated by the most subtle and slow acting of poisons; an imperceptible miasma
> within the white shadow of a higher culture. A vast multitude, exposed, unpre-
> pared, they had not had time nor occasion to become immune to forms of
> sophistication not their own, to a higher and more dexterously insidious plau-

[22]Louis Wirth, "Urbanism as a Way of Life," in *Louis Wirth on Cities and Social
Life*, ed. Albert J. Reiss, Jr. (1938; reprint, Chicago: University of Chicago Press, 1964),
pp. 60–83.

Consuming Visions

sibility. Thus they departed joyously, carriers of contagion, unaware that what they had beheld and believed to be truth was to prove, in historic fact, an appalling calamity. For what they saw was not at all what they believed they saw, but an imposition of the spurious upon their eyesight, a naked exhibition-ism of charlatanry in the higher feudal and domineering culture, conjoined with expert salesmanship of the materials of decay.[23]

Sullivan—who, like Adams, knew that the built environment was a visible sign of a civilization—saw the death of the democratic vision in the nostalgic revivalism of the exposition's architecture. Sullivan was, in the main, correct about the downward slope of democracy, even though he could not see that those emerging nostalgic images of empire would later be replaced by a stark, ultramodern image of empire—the so-called international style—that also denied the democratic vision, but in the name of the almighty grid. Nor could he see that the two images of empire would then fuse in the "postmodern" style of the late twentieth century, signifying the depths of domination by desiccated technique and desensualized nostalgia to which the American dream had sunk. The plague foreseen by Sullivan grew to full virulence in this "post-" time when America lost any sense of history or living memory and forfeited its dreams to the fetishism of technical commodities.

As the logic of modernity, by no means necessary but surely suffi-cient, raced toward closure, even Chicago's academic sociology had to give way to more machine-like ways of thinking, to "abstracted empiri-cism," and to "grand theory," exemplified by sociologist Talcott Par-sons. The turn toward abstracted empiricism was characteristic of American sociology in general, but was signaled in particular within the sociology department of the University of Chicago by the arrival of William F. Ogburn. Ogburn not only championed quantitative tech-nique, which in itself broadened the means available to sociology and which was the reason the rest of the department hired him in 1927, but also went further to disparage that which did not fit his technical con-ception of science. He scorned social theory, social reform, "qualita-tive" methods, and seemingly everything that suggested that sociology has human interests.[24]

Oddly enough, it was Ogburn who played a significant role for the

[23] Louis H. Sullivan, *The Autobiography of an Idea* (1924; reprint, New York: Dover Publications, 1956), pp. 321–22.
[24] Bulmer, *Chicago School of Sociology*, pp. 181–84.

Fig. 3. Social Science Research Building (*center*), University of Chicago, 1126 E. Fifty-ninth St. (Eugene Rochberg-Halton.)

"Committee on Symbolism for the Social Science Research Building," which in 1929 helped decide the symbolism of the new building that would house social science at the University of Chicago (fig. 3). Although the more well known Chicago sociologists, such as Park and Burgess, had developed a sociology concerned with the physical environment and its symbolism, and although Ogburn had been at the university only less than two years, it was he who was instrumental in getting the positivistic symbolism layered on to the neo-Gothic "feudal" structure, especially expressed in a maxim derived from Lord Kelvin and incised under the large bay window of the common room: "When you cannot measure, your knowledge is meager and unsatisfactory." This inscription accurately set the tone of the rising quantifying sociology that would replace the older style of academic sociology. The new Social Science Research Building not only symbolized the turn to social science research, but in picturing titans of laissez-faire capitalism (Adam Smith), utilitarianism (Jeremy Bentham), and positivism (Auguste Comte) over its doors, and in inscribing the utilitarian view of research as a measuring cup, also symbolized the coming capitulation of social science to the ideology of scientism. Only those aspects of social life that could be counted would be considered valid for the emerging style of "American" sociology. Or put differently, only those aspects of social life capable of being run through the machine of quantification—beginning with survey forms and simple counting machines and later achieving academic centrality in the form of the computer—only those quanta of the social grid would count as valid objects of sociological research. Life itself in all its fullness would become too passionate for this dispassionate and bloodless conception of sociology. The dominant number-numbing sociology that assumed power by midcentury in America was, like the centralized stockyards that emerged in the nineteenth century, equally an avatar of the great dynamo of modernity: the life-denying machine.

The last place today that one could find the Chicago schools of sociology, philosophy, or psychology taken seriously is at the University of Chicago. The clean-fitting grid of the academy has long since replaced these modes of thought with ones stamped with the proper look of twentieth-century science. The embarrassing optimism of Chicago thought was replaced by an arrogant scientism more blindly confident of its mission, one confirmed in the religion and sects of positivism.

The open-ended pragmatism of Dewey and George Herbert Mead, centering on the human being within a live social environment—a human capable of criticism, cultivation, emergence, and continued growth in the community of interpretation—was replaced by the closed positivist dream of the end of philosophy personified by Charles Morris and Rudolph Carnap and by the new technicalism of analytic philosophy that in turn replaced positivism. The critical symbolic economics of Veblen were replaced by a second Chicago school of economics, one that believed that "there is no such thing as a free lunch," to paraphrase its chief exponent, Milton Friedman. This second school, now assumed to be *the* school, blindly ignored the possibility that there may be no such thing as a free market in its deification of uncontrolled profit stripped of social context or human purport.

It is no wonder that the economic and racist practices that nourished the corrosive sprawl of the ghetto have a stranglehold today on the city: totalitarian rationalism breeds its opposite. The blight of the megamachine and its institutionalized chaos that is Chicago's birthmark now control even those areas where organic thought once flourished as the city's own vital contribution to modernity. Perhaps the best symbolic expression of this state of affairs is the remnant of Hull-House, now a

Fig. 4. Jane Addams' Hull-House, 800 S. Halsted St., Chicago. (Eugene Rochberg-Halton.)

museum, dwarfed by the monolithic skeletal form of the black steel and glass student union of the University of Illinois at Chicago, which rises up behind Hull-House and reduces its physical presence to that of a quaint relic from the forgotten past (fig. 4). Many of the Hull-House buildings were razed to make room for the university's campus in the early 1960s, and in the mid 1980s the settlement's library was absorbed by the university library, symbolizing the final ethercalization of the organic intelligence that flowered at Hull-House. Books, this act seemed to say, must not be confused with life, and a venerable institution such as Hull-House must not be confused with living function if it is to be properly embalmed as a museum.

It is true that space was cramped in the two remaining buildings, one of which is the original structure on which the many additions to Hull-House were later added, and therefore the removal of books was perhaps "functional." But if one literally "deconstructs" a structure to arrive at a building too small to be functional as anything other than a museum, then the problem is one not simply of physical space and function but of purpose. Apparently the purposes and history embodied in the physical structure of Hull-House were at cross-purposes with the modernist premises of novelty and nonintegration with neighborhood and past embodied in the design of the "circle campus," as the university is usually called.

"The city that works" had worked to destroy the tradition-saturated Hull-House physical structure, with its many meeting, recreation, theater, dining, art, and other rooms designed expressly for communal activities. In its place, the city erected a sterile structure housing a student union with precisely the same sorts of rooms. What arrogance to destroy the greatest symbol of urban vitality in Chicago's history, in order to replace it with steel and glass buildings housing the same functions. But perhaps it is fitting that the triumph of the academy over social work, of the bureau and bureaucracy over home and neighborhood democracy, of the machine over organic thought, of the rationalization of existence over the life of the street, be honestly symbolized.

When Aristotle said that man is by nature a political animal, he had in mind a view of social relations as fundamental to the human creature and the city, or polis, as the public organ capable of expressing those fundamental human capacities for speech and self-controlled purposeful conduct. Modernity developed quite antithetical views. In its manifestation as virulent, consumptive capitalism and the power complex, modernity held competition and rational calculation to be the original beliefs of the human soul and made the city to be the gladiatorial arena: every man for himself, winner take all. In its manifestation as political communism and the power complex, modernity displaced speech and conduct with secrecy and expediency. We see the prophetic anticipation of this process in the inability of Raskolnikov of *Crime and Punishment* to break out of the secrecy of his crime, rationalized murder, and to confess his guilt in the public market. In its manifestation as Chicago, modernity rediscovered Aristotle's maxim, but diabolically inverted the meanings of *political* and *animal*. The activity of life itself was turned into a thing to be possessed. The life of the public, as *The Jungle, The Titan,* and the human ecology of Chicago's academic sociologists showed, was one of savagery, dominated by the forces of anti-life. And despite all the settlement work and muckraking, the muck has enjoyed a settled existence right down to the present.

Country Stores, County Fairs, and Mail-Order Catalogues

Consumption in Rural America

Thomas J. Schlereth

The milieu in which most American consumers lived and worked in the second half of the nineteenth century was rural. The proportion of Americans living outside cities was five out of six in 1860 and two out of three in 1900. Further, a widely accepted reckoning holds that not until 1920 did a slight majority of the United States population begin living in areas defined as urban. Prior to the 1920s, then, what roles did the large rural segment of American society play in the consumer revolution? Who formed its consuming visions? What institutions gave such visions shape and substance? Did such ideas and institutions help foster the fundamental economic and cultural change that has been labeled modernization? Did rural consumption differ appreciably from its urban counterpart? Did it simply mirror city trends, or did it also influence urban consumption? In brief, what was the historical context of consumer behavior in the countryside during what has been called "the Age of Capitalist Transformations"? What continuities did it witness, and what changes did it experience? What did it contribute to the general shift in consumer patterns in American society at large between the Civil War and World War I?[1]

[1] Bayrd Still, *Urban America: A History with Documents* (Boston: Little, Brown, 1974), pp. 352–53; David R. Goldfield and Blaine A. Brownell, *Urban America: From Downtown to No Town* (Boston: Houghton Mifflin Co., 1979), p. 382; Blake McKelvey,

If the rural domain of consumption is an often overlooked realm of cultural history, we can be easily reminded of its character by noting several predominant artifacts. I have chosen to examine the issues raised by my questions by looking at three such artifacts—the country store, the county fair, and the mail-order catalogue—as modernizing "agencies of change" in rural buying and selling in the late nineteenth and early twentieth centuries.[2] Two of these enterprises, the country store and the county fair, had been traditional cultural institutions with histories extending back into colonial times; the third, mail-order mer-

---

The Emergence of Metropolitan America, 1915–1966 (New Brunswick, N.J.: Rutgers University Press, 1968), p. 31. On the trend of consumer behavior in rural historiography, see Steven Hahn and Jonathan Prude, Introduction to *The Countryside in the Age of Capitalist Transformation: Essays in the Social History of Rural America*, ed. Steven Hahn and Jonathan Prude (Chapel Hill: University of North Carolina Press, 1985), pp. 3–21; and Robert P. Swierenga, "Theoretical Perspectives on the New Rural History: From Environmentalism to Modernization," *Agricultural History* 56, no. 3 (July 1982): 495–502. In addition to the preceding essays in this volume, the consumer "revolution" or "transformation" is also surveyed in general studies such as Daniel Horowitz, *The Morality of Spending: Attitudes toward the Consumer Society in America, 1875–1940* (Baltimore: Johns Hopkins University Press, 1985); Richard Wightman Fox and T. J. Jackson Lears, eds., *The Culture of Consumption: Critical Essays in American History, 1880–1980* (New York: Pantheon Books, 1983); Peter E. Samson, "The Emergence of a Consumer Interest in America, 1870–1930" (Ph.D. diss., University of Chicago, 1980); and John E. Hollitz, "The Challenge of Abundance: Reactions to the Development of a Consumer Economy, 1880–1920" (Ph.D. diss., University of Wisconsin–Madison, 1981).

[2] The field of rural consumption, particularly during the Gilded Age, remains a large (and largely unplowed) terrain deserving of historical analysis. Historians of American consumption usually neglect the study of retail buying and selling in the countryside. Historians of rural life, likewise, rarely pursue research on the material accumulation and display of what Lewis Mumford called "the good life" in his *Technics and Civilization* (New York: Harcourt, Brace, 1934), p. 105. Exceptions to the mutual neglect of rural consumption would include Deborah J. Hoskins, "Brought, Bought, and Borrowed: Material Culture on the Oklahoma Farming Frontier, 1889–1907," in *At Home on the Range: Essays on the History of Western Social and Domestic Life*, ed. John Wunder (Westport, Conn.: Greenwood Press, 1985), pp. 121–36; Robert P. Swierenga, "Agriculture and Rural Life: The New Rural History," in *Ordinary People and Everyday Life: Perspectives on the New Social History*, ed. James B. Gardner and George Rollie Adams (Nashville: American Association for State and Local History, 1983), pp. 91–113; Robert P. Swierenga, "Symposium on the History of Rural Life in America," ed. Barbara R. Cotton, *Agricultural History* (Special Issue) 58, no. 3 (July 1984): 207–488. In examining the three artifacts, I take methodological inspiration from two masterpieces of European scholarship on nineteenth-century rural history: Eugen Weber, *Peasants into Frenchmen: The Modernization of Rural France, 1870–1914* (Stanford: Stanford University Press, 1976); and Jerome Blum, *The End of the Old Order in Rural Europe* (Princeton: Princeton University Press, 1978). The "agencies of change" that these authors describe include a market economy, roads and railroads, national political campaigns, educational institutions, seasonal and international labor migration, compulsory military service, and war.

chandising, first made its national impact beginning in the 1870s. Each served as cause and consequence of the dramatic commercialization of the countryside that expanded in the crucial decades between 1880 and 1920, and each transformed and, in turn, was transformed by rural consumership.

Before turning to a closer analysis of these three manifestations and motivators of countryside consumership, a few generalizations about rural consumption in the Gilded Age and the Progressive Era are appropriate. Admittedly, these claims must allow for regional variations and historical exceptions. Rural life in America was never monolithic; the pace and purpose of rural consumption varied among farmers growing tobacco in North Carolina's piedmont, families engaged in small-scale mixed agriculture in Vermont, hog and corn producers in Iowa, bonanza wheat entrepreneurs in the Red River valley, or citrus growers in California.[3]

Nevertheless, in even these diverse instances, and assuredly in rural America as a whole, one thing seems clear: when compared with earlier periods of American history, the level and scope of rural consumption was rising by the turn of the twentieth century. Country people increasingly purchased more of the goods and services that they had once either produced for themselves or simply had done without. Despite the economic depressions of 1873 and 1893, fluctuating land and commodity prices, and an increase in farm tenancies and foreclosures, consumer buying slowly increased for the two generations of Americans who lived in rural environments from 1860 to 1920.[4]

[3] A sense of this geographical and economic diversity is evident in John Brinckerhoff Jackson, *American Space: The Centennial Years, 1865–1876* (New York: W. W. Norton, 1972), as well as several monographic treatments of rural life: Stephan J. DeCanio, *Agriculture in the Postbellum South: The Economics of Production and Supply* (Cambridge, Mass.: MIT Press, 1974); Roger L. Ransom and Richard Sutch, *One Kind of Freedom: The Economic Consequences of Emancipation* (Cambridge: Cambridge University Press, 1977); Hal S. Barron, *Those Who Stayed Behind: Rural Society in Nineteenth-Century New England* (New York: Cambridge University Press, 1984); Allan G. Bogue, *From Prairie to Corn Belt: Farming on the Illinois and Iowa Prairies in the Nineteenth Century* (Chicago: University of Chicago Press, 1963); Stanley N. Murray, *The Valley Comes of Age* (Fargo, N. Dak.: Institute for Regional Studies, 1967); Gilbert C. Fite, *The Farmer's Frontier, 1965–1900* (New York: Holt, Rinehart and Winston, 1966); Cletus E. Daniel, *Bitter Harvest: A History of California Farmworkers, 1870–1941* (Ithaca, N.Y.: Cornell University Press, 1981).

[4] Evidence of an acceleration in rural consumer patterns from 1880 to 1920 has been monitored by scholars studying a variety of locales. See, for example, Jacqueline S. Reinier, "Concepts of Domesticity on the Southern Plains Agricultural Frontier, 1870–

The generation of the 1880s and 1890s witnessed this increased consumption in the transformation of several everyday life activities: the abandonment of candles for modern kerosene lighting, the substitution of new water supply technologies for the spring pole and the windlass, the replacement of open-hearth cooking with cast-iron ranges, and the increasing introduction of packaged and canned groceries into a diet formerly composed largely of home-prepared foodstuffs. The generation that followed, one that participated in the country's general prosperity following 1900 and agricultural America's boom after 1910, exhibited its consumer interest in more durable goods: telephones, suites of parlor and bedroom furniture, washing machines requiring prepackaged laundry products, residential remodeling, and automobiles.[5]

1920," in Wunder, ed., *At Home on the Range*, pp. 57–70; Wayne D. Rasmussen, "The Impact of Technological Change on American Agriculture, 1862–1962," *Journal of Economic History* 22, no. 4 (December 1962): 578–91; Susan Atherton Hanson, "Home, Sweet Home: Industrialization's Impact on Rural Households, 1865–1925" (Ph.D. diss., University of Maryland, 1986); Harold F. Williamson, "Mass Production for Mass Consumption," in *Technology in Western Civilization: The Emergence of Modern Industrial Society to 1900*, ed. Melvin Kranzberg and Carroll W. Pursell, Jr. (New York: Oxford University Press, 1967), pp. 678–91; Norton Juster, *So Sweet to Labor: Rural Women in America, 1865–1895* (New York: Viking Press, 1979); Angel Kwolek-Folland, "The Elegant Dugout: Domesticity and Moveable Culture in the United States, 1870–1900," *American Studies* 25, no. 2 (Fall 1984): 21–37.

[5] On typical consumer choices by the first generation 1870–1900, see Hanson, "Home, Sweet Home," pp. 131–56, 170–216; Katherine C. Grier, "The Popular Illuminator": *Domestic Lighting in the Kerosene Era, 1860–1900* (Rochester, N.Y.: Strong Museum, 1985); Kenneth L. Ames, "Material Culture as Nonverbal Communication: A Historical Case Study," *Journal of American Culture* 3, no. 4 (Winter 1980): 619–41; Peter Cousins, "Tall Timber, Wheat, and Wrinkly Sheep: Three Generations of Ohio Farmers," and Nancy Villa Bryk, "Creating a House 'Where Taste Dwells in Unity with Utilities and Home,'" in *Henry Ford Museum and Greenfield Village Herald* 14, no. 2 (1985): 3–27, 34–41; Earl Lifeshey, *The Housewares Story: A History of American Housewares Industry* (Chicago: National Housewares Manufacturers Assn., 1973); Richard Osborn Cummings, *The American and His Food: A History of Food Habits in the United States* (Chicago: University of Chicago Press, 1940). The further expansion of rural consumerism in the early twentieth century has been examined by Donald F. Hadwiger and Clay Cochran, "Rural Telephones in the United States," *Agricultural History* 58, no. 3 (July 1984): 221–38; Sally Ann McMurry, "American Farm Families and Their Houses: Vernacular Design and Social Change in the Rural North" (Ph.D. diss., Cornell University, 1984); Clifford Edward Clark, Jr., *The American Family Home, 1800–1960* (Chapel Hill: University of North Carolina Press, 1986); Susan Strasser, *Never Done: A History of American Housework* (New York: Pantheon Books, 1982); David P. Handlin, *The American Home: Architecture and Society, 1815–1915* (Boston: Little, Brown, 1979); Robert S. Lynd and Helen M. Lynd, *Middletown: A Study in Contemporary American Culture* (New York: Harcourt, Brace, 1929); Joseph Interrane, "You Can't Go to Town in a

What general economic and cultural trends account for this piece-meal but persistent increase in the general level of rural consumption? Several factors influenced the growth of consumer buying in the countryside. First, consumer patterns were not new to rural folk. As historian Timothy Breen has demonstrated, a rural consumer ethic had strong and widespread roots in the colonial American experience. The romantic notion of isolated frontier families hand producing all their household tools, commodities, and furnishings from local materials has been proved false by several students of early American culture. Rural consumption had a long established tradition in western Massachusetts, the Connecticut River valley, the Pennsylvania cultural hearth, and the Chesapeake region.[6]

In Victorian America, however, the number of rural consumers doubled. Agricultural employment increased 50 percent between 1860 and 1890, a period when rural Americans put 431 million acres of virgin land under the plow, an average of 14.4 million acres of new tillage being added each year. By 1900 this expanded population cohort was producing up to 150 percent more of the staples—cotton, wheat, corn—than they had in 1870, which influenced patterns of consumption elsewhere throughout American economic life in the form of cheaper and more abundant ready-made clothing and preprocessed convenience foods.[7]

Bathtub: Automobile Movement and the Reorganization of American Space, 1900–1930," *Radical History Review* 21 (March 1980): 151–68.

[6]Timothy H. Breen, "The Meaning of Things: The Consumer Culture of Eighteenth Century America and the Coming of the Revolution" (Address presented at the 27th Winterthur Conference, Winterthur Museum, Winterthur, Del., November 1986). Studies of early rural consumption include Carole Shammas, "How Self-Sufficient Was Early America?" *Journal of Interdisciplinary History* 13, no. 3 (Autumn 1982): 247–72; Richard D. Brown, "The Emergence of Urban Society in Rural Massachusetts," *Journal of American History* 61, no. 2 (June 1974): 29–51; James A. Henretta, "Families and Farms: *Mentalité* in Pre-Industrial America," *William and Mary Quarterly*, 3d ser., 35, no. 1 (January 1978): 3–32; Christopher Clark, "The Household Economy, Market Exchange and the Rise of Capitalism in the Connecticut Valley, 1800–1860," *Journal of Social History* 13, no. 2 (Winter 1979): 169–89; Michael Merrill, "Cash Is Good to Eat: Self-Sufficiency and Exchange in the Rural Economy of the United States," *Radical History Review* 3 (Spring 1977): 42–71; Joseph T. Ellis, "Culture and Capitalism in Pre-Revolutionary America," *American Quarterly* 31, no. 2 (Summer 1979): 169–86; and Lorena S. Walsh, "Urban Amenities and Rural Sufficiency: Living Standards and Consumer Behavior in the Colonial Chesapeake, 1643–1777," *Journal of Economic History* 43, no. 1 (March 1983): 107–17.

[7]William L. Barney, *The Passage of the Republic: An Interdisciplinary History of Nineteenth-Century America* (Lexington, Mass.: D. C. Heath, 1987), p. 297; Joseph R.

Innovations in transportation and communication also affected buying and selling patterns. The railroads, particularly their regional networks, transformed both the physical and the cultural landscapes. Simultaneously seen as messiah and menace by rural dwellers, railroads effectively opened the entire nation to a market economy in almost every line of consumer goods. For example, the furniture trade catalogues received by retailers in the 1870s and 1880s make it clear that region was no longer a significant limiting factor in distributing household goods wholesale to the hinterland. Country store retailers in small villages and crossroad communities located in New Hampshire, Maryland, and Wisconsin, all received furniture shipped by rail from manufacturers around the country.[8]

The expansion of the agricultural and popular rural press helped promote such merchandising since, in addition to its technical and marketing information, it promulgated commercial advertisements advocating new machinery, gadgets, and services. Founded in 1886, Leonidas L. Polk's *Progressive Farmer* campaigned relentlessly against insects and ignorance, for improved soils and homes, and for a network of county and state fairs displaying family conveniences. The journal had the largest circulation of any publication in North Carolina. Polk— farmer, state legislator, storekeeper, patent medicine inventor, and town developer—used his paper to argue the case for sending children of farming families to agricultural colleges, where, for example, rural girls would learn that homemaking and nutrition were matters of rational management and that the savings from home canning could purchase the comforts of an indoor commode.[9]

Conlin, *The American Past: A Survey of American History* (New York: Harcourt Brace Jovanovich, 1984), p. 544; Fred A. Shannon, *The Farmer's Last Frontier, Agriculture, 1860–1897* (New York: Farrar and Rinehart, 1945); Claudia B. Kidwell and Margaret C. Christman, *Suiting Everyone: The Democratization of Clothing in America* (Washington, D.C.: Smithsonian Institution Press, 1974); Robert C. Alberts, *The Good Provider: H. J. Heinz and His 57 Varieties* (New York: Houghton Mifflin Co., 1973).

[8] E. Richard McKinstry, "The Trade Catalogue Collection in the Library of the Winterthur Museum," in Deborah Anne Federhen et al., *Accumulation and Display: Mass Marketing Household Goods in America, 1880–1920* (Winterthur, Del.: Henry Francis du Pont Winterthur Museum, 1986), pp. 3–8.

[9] Mary Elizabeth Johnson, ed., *Times Down Home: 75 Years with Progressive Farmer* (Birmingham, Ala.: Oxmoor House, 1978). See also Allen W. Jones, "Voices for Improving Rural Life: Alabama's Agricultural Press, 1890–1965," *Agricultural History* 53, no. 3 (July 1984): 209–20; and Albert Lowther Demaree, *The American Agricultural Press* (New York: Columbia University Press, 1941).

An increase in discretionary income likewise contributed to rural consumer spending. By the early twentieth century, many Americans living in the country, like their urban counterparts, had more money to spend on new goods and special conveniences other than those deemed necessities. General statistics for the period 1880 to 1920 show an increase in many farm family incomes, particularly after 1900. Susan A. Hanson's study of the upper South noted that a 47 percent rise in farm income took place throughout the region between 1910 and 1920. Often this extra income went into labor-saving technology for agricultural operations, but it also went to pay for new kitchen appliances, floor and wall coverings for the farmhouse, a child's bicycle, or a Kodak camera for the family.[10]

An active federal government conditioned rural consumption in several ways. Government initiatives—the creation of a national system of land-grant colleges by the Morrill Act of 1862, the establishment of a federal Office of Agricultural Experiment Stations in 1888 (eventually including consumer divisions), the elevation of the United States Department of Agriculture to cabinet status in 1889, the creation of a federal Bureau of Public Roads in 1893, and President Theodore Roosevelt's creation of a national Country Life Commission in 1908—changed the economic, social, and cultural horizons of rural Americans and their children. Each of these initiatives encouraged technological change as a positive good and promoted modernization as a means to an improved standard of living.[11] Other federal actions—specifically

[10] Hanson notes that the development of market garden crops (fruits and vegetables) for urban consumers was one way rural folk expanded their family income which, in turn, enabled them to expand their purchases of consumer goods such as Kodak or other available cameras for home photography, in Hanson, "Home, Sweet Home," pp. 38–41. For another statistical analysis of income rates in the period, see Stanley Lebergott, "Wage Trends, 1800–1900," in *Trends in the American Economy in the Nineteenth Century* (1960; reprint, New York: Arno Press, 1975).

[11] Dale E. Hathaway, *Government and Agriculture: Public Policy in a Democratic Society* (New York: Macmillan Co., 1963); Gladys L. Baker et al., *Century of Service: The First Hundred Years of the United States Department of Agriculture* (Washington, D.C.: Government Printing Office, 1963); Harold T. Pinkett, "Government Research concerning Problems of American Rural Society," *Agricultural History* 58, no. 3 (July 1984): 365–72; Milton Conover, *The Office of Experiment Stations, Its History, Activities and Organization* (Baltimore: Johns Hopkins University Press, 1924); Gladys L. Baker, *The County Agent* (Chicago: University of Chicago Press, 1939); Clayton S. Ellsworth, "Theodore Roosevelt's Country Life Commission," *Agricultural History* 34, no. 4 (October 1960): 155–72.

the Pure Food and Drug Act of 1906, the Smith-Lever Act of 1914 formalizing cooperative agricultural extension work at the county level, and the legislation establishing the national Rural Free Delivery (1896) and Parcel Post (1912) systems—had an immediate and direct impact on rural consumership, particularly as promoted by country stores, county fairs, and mail-order catalogues.

The combined forces of a tradition of consumer behavior, an expanded rural population, an extensive transportation and communication network, increases in discretionary income, and direct government involvement in rural affairs merged with a final factor, perhaps more difficult to document but no less important, in countryside consumership. This factor involved a growing desire for greater access to the comforts and conveniences of a standard of living that scholars have identified as emblematic of a new middle-class consciousness and consensus emerging in the late nineteenth and early twentieth centuries. While there have been a number of formulations of this shift in cultural identity, Walter Nugent has summarized it in language appropriate for the rural American. In Nugent's terms, there was a gradual shift in the era from 1870 to 1920, a time he sees as "The Great Conjuncture" of American history that produced a transformation in aspirations from "land-hunger" to "home-ownership-hunger, money-hunger, or durable-goods-hunger."[12]

To be sure, this quest for "middling" status among rural folk had some of its origins in antebellum America where, as David Jaffee and others have shown, rural artisans became market-oriented purveyors of "cultural commodities" such as portraits and daguerreotypes as well as carpets, clocks, and furniture for farmers who aspired to urbane gentility in a rural idiom. The "taste for scarce commodities" that Jaffee attributes to the village and countryside "new bourgeoisie" continued and

[12] Discussions of the new middle-class consensus can be found in Walter Nugent, *Structures of American Social History* (Bloomington: Indiana University Press, 1981), pp. 114–16, as well as in Stuart M. Blumin, "The Hypothesis of Middle-Class Formation in 19th Century America: A Critique and Some Proposals," *American Historical Review* 90, no. 2 (April 1985): 299–338; Warren I. Susman, *Culture as History: The Transformation of American Society in the Twentieth Century* (New York: Pantheon Books, 1984), p. xxi; Burton J. Bledstein, *The Culture of Professionalism: The Middle Class and the Development of Higher Education in America* (New York: W. W. Norton, 1976); Karen Halttunen, *Confidence Men and Painted Women: A Study of Middle-Class Culture in America, 1830–1870* (New Haven: Yale University Press, 1982); and Horowitz, *Morality of Spending*, pp. 68–69, 199.

accelerated for an expanding middle class with the widening of industrialization, the maturing of a market economy, and the increased mass production of quality goods following the Civil War. Kenneth Ames has argued that the cultural preoccupations of this broadened "middle market" of Victorian America—a like-minded cadre of both rural and urban consumers—included, at least in part, that people are what they own; that by possessing certain objects, they might demonstrate their gentility and respectability, their cosmopolitanism and modernity.[13]

The rural middle class shared with their urban cousins the fascination with the proliferation of available goods, be they modern kitchen utensils, heating systems, lawn furniture, musical instruments, or tourist souvenirs. Recent material culture research also shows this growing rural middle class as anxious to validate its achievement or its aspirations through additional artifacts, some perhaps more indigenous to countryside accumulation; hence, the rural vogue of photographic albums of the family manse's formal rooms and grounds during the 1870s, lithographs of the farmstead and its holdings in the county atlases of the 1880s (fig. 1), and newly furnished "progressive" sitting rooms or special children's "playrooms" in farm homes of the 1890s.[14]

Three agencies of change—the country store, the county fair, and the mail-order catalogue—helped stimulate and satisfy such new consumer choices for rural Americans by the turn of the century. Each prompted a significant change in the number, variety, complexity, form,

---

[13] Jaffee's argument is found in David Jaffee, "A Correct Likeness: Culture and Commerce in Nineteenth-Century Rural America," in *Folk Art and Art Worlds,* ed. Simon J. Bronner and John Michael Vlach (Ann Arbor, Mich.: UMI Research Press, 1986), pp. 53–84; and David Jaffee, " 'One of the Primitive Sort': Portrait-Makers in the Rural North, 1760–1900," in Hahn and Prude, eds., *Countryside,* pp. 103–38. Supporting data for antebellum commercial activity in the rural environment is also in Mary P. Ryan, *Cradle of the Middle Class: The Family in Oneida County, New York, 1790–1865* (Cambridge: Cambridge University Press, 1981); and Halttunen, *Confidence Men,* pp. 14–48. See also Kenneth L. Ames, "Trade Catalogues and the Study of Culture," in Federhen et al., *Accumulation and Display,* pp. 8–14.

[14] George Talbot and Joan Severa, *At Home: Domestic Life in the Post-Centennial Era, 1876–1920* (Madison: State Historical Society of Wisconsin, 1978); Ted Daniels, "Advertisements for American Selves: Nineteenth-Century Pennsylvania County Atlases," *Landscape* 29, no. 3 (Spring 1987): 17–23; Michael P. Conzen, "Purveying the Agrarian Dream: Commercial Development and Social Transformation of the County Landownership Map in America, 1814–1939" (Paper presented to the Tenth International Conference on the History of Cartography, Dublin, Ireland, August 1983); McMurry, "American Farm Families," pp. 217–58, 285–316.

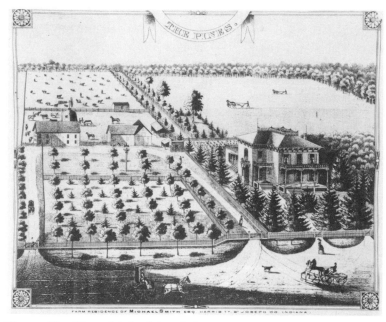

Fig. 1. The Pines, Michael Smith farmstead, St. Joseph Co., Ind. From *Illustrated Historical Atlas of St. Joseph County* (Chicago: Higgins, Belden, 1875).

and use of artifacts that rural Americans increasingly came to rely on to do their work and to regulate their social relations with one another. They were "modernizing institutions" within the context of rural consumption in that they contributed to the dynamic of modernization, a historical process and interpretive framework, which I take to encompass a broad range of human activities, including industrial production, commercial agriculture, technological innovation, capital accumulation, market economies, urban consciousness, bureaucratic organization, specialization of skills, and intensive education.[15] The remainder of this essay documents the shape and substance of the contribution made by these agencies of rural consumerism. I have treated them here in the order of their contribution to the transformation of American rural society.

[15] Applications of modernization theory can be found in Richard D. Brown, *Modernization: The Transformation of American Life, 1600–1865* (New York: Hill and Wang,

The Country Store

While historians debate the exact origins of the American country store, all agree that it predates the opening in 1811 of the first county fair in Pittsfield, Massachusetts, organized by Elkanah Watson, as well as the appearance in 1872 of the first modern mail-order catalogue issued by Montgomery Ward in Chicago. Since its decline in the 1930s, stemming from mail-order, chain-store, and supermarket merchandising, as well as a changing credit structure, the country store has either evolved into a general convenience store or become a museum piece of rural nostalgia. No frontier historical site, nineteenth-century village, or outdoor agricultural museum is complete without one. In such interpretations more attention is given to the store's social mores than its consumer practices. Paeans are sung to its legendary front porch, its inspirational cracker barrel, and its hospitable potbellied stove rather than its innovative merchandising displays, special bargain packaging, or widespread use of national-brand advertising.[16]

Even those who have surveyed the myriad of products available in a "typical" general store usually provide little sense of a real store's actual stock or how it changed over time. Only recently have researchers begun to rectify this problem in their examinations of nineteenth-century store ledgers and archaeological evidence. Fortunately, some museum historians have also recognized the need for a closer evaluation of the

1976); Fernand Braudel, *Capitalism and Material Life, 1400–1800*, trans. Miriam Cochan (New York: Harper and Row, 1973); Harvey Green, "The Ironies of Style: Complexities and Contradictions in American Decorative Arts, 1850–1900," in *Victorian Furniture: Essays from a Victorian Society Autumn Symposium*, ed. Kenneth L. Ames (Philadelphia: Victorian Society in America, 1983), pp. 17–34; and Richard D. Brown, "Modernization: A Victorian Climax," *American Quarterly* 27, no. 4 (Fall 1977): 534–48.

[16] Literature useful in dating the emergence of the American country store includes Gerald Carson, *The Old Country Store* (New York: Oxford University Press, 1965); Lewis E. Atherton, *The Frontier Merchant in Mid-America* (Columbia: University of Missouri Press, 1971); and Thomas D. Clark, *Pills, Petticoats, and Plows: The Southern Country Store* (Norman: University of Oklahoma Press, 1944). Research on contemporary country stores includes: Clifford Allan Lockyer, "The Survival of Country Stores in Eastern Maine" (Ph.D. diss., University of Northern Colorado, 1986); Jane Beck, *The General Store in Vermont: An Oral History* (Montpelier: Vermont Historical Society, 1980); Richard Bauman, "The La Have Island General Store: Sociability and Verbal Art in a Nova Scotia Community," *Journal of American Folklore* 85, no. 338 (October–December 1972): 330–43. An example of the nostalgic interpretation of the country store is Laurence A. Johnson, *Over the Counter and on the Shelf: Country Storekeeping in America, 1620–1920* (Rutland, Vt.: Charles E. Tuttle, 1961).

Fig. 2. Gibson's Store, Main St., Bennington, Vt., 1895. (Images from the Past/Weichert-Isselhardt Collection: Photo, Madison E. Watson.)

actual consumer practices and patterns of country stores and have begun to revise their exhibition interpretations accordingly.[17]

Most twentieth-century re-creations tend to depict the nineteenth-century country store as a chaotic jumble of goods, smells, and images. In practice, the store was a fairly ordered, coordinated shopping environment, a planned space where customers had ample opportunity to see, feel, and taste the goods (fig. 2). In addition to the customary spatial arrangements—devoting counters and shelves along the store's right side to dry goods, the left side to groceries, tobacco, sundries, and patent medicines, and the rear to kerosene, whiskey, and sugar and meat barrels—by the 1890s store merchants were using many display techniques to showcase merchandise such as packaged foods, cuckoo clocks,

---

[17] For recent empirical studies, see research by Sandra Morton Weizman, "The Radway General Store: An Inventory of Historical Bargains," *Muse* 17, no. 4 (Autumn 1985): 26–29; William Hampton Adams and Steven D. Smith, "Historical Perspectives on Black Tenant Farmers' Material Culture: The Henry C. Long General Ledger at Waverly Plantation, Mississippi," in *The Archaeology of Slavery and Plantation Life*, ed. Theresa A. Singleton (New York: Academic Press, 1985), pp. 309–34; and Hanson, "Home, Sweet Home." Two laudable examples of revisionist interpretation of country-store trade practices and consumer demands are Charles Alan Watkins, "The John Ward General Store Exhibit," in "Background of the Appalachian Cultural Center" (Typescript, Appalachian Cultural Center/Appalachian State University, Boone, N.C., 1986), pp. 5–9; and John Patterson, "Commercializing the American West" (Application for Indian Heritage Research Grant, Conner Prairie Museum, Noblesville, Ind., 1986), pp. 1–4.

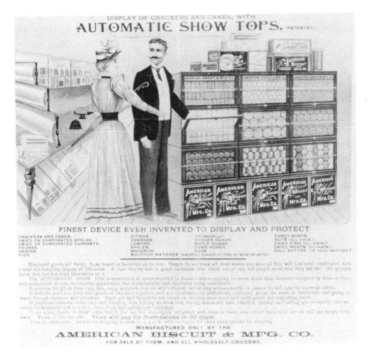

Fig. 3. Advertisement for Automatic Show Tops, American Biscuit and Manufacturing Co., 1890. (The Archives, National Brands, Inc.)

ceramics, spectacles, art reproductions, cutlery, soaps, stereoscopes, and jewelry (fig. 3). Display cases had glass fronts, shaped like mansard roofs or curving back from the customer, with the glass set in shining German silver frames. Dye companies, candy firms, and chewing-gum manufacturers provided stores with colorful dispensers of their products, as did thread companies. For example, a great cylinder of thread whirled around, showing all the gauges and colors of "Merrick's Six Cord Soft Finish Spool Cotton." Seed companies, such as those of the Shakers, contributed chromolithographed counter exhibits to enhance a store's seasonal displays. [18]

[18] Clark, *Pills, Petticoats, and Plows*, pp. 159–71; Carson, *Country Store*, p. 201; Warren C. Scoville, *Revolution in Glassmaking: Entrepreneurship and Technological Change in the American Industry, 1880–1920* (Cambridge, Mass.: Harvard University

The commercialization of Christmas took place in rural country emporiums as well as in urban department stores. In southern stores, for instance, special displays in various geometric shapes were made of coconuts, apples, and nutmegs. Children's toys and Christmas ornaments were suspended from the ceiling, while special promotions of suitable gift ideas (Martha Washington's Perfume Waters selling for $1.05 or a Harrington and Richardson pistol for $2.98) were erected near the main counter's credit book. Prominently arranged around the store were firecrackers, explosive torpedoes, black powder, and Roman candles—material culture even the poorest rural southerner deemed essential to a festive Christmas celebration.[19]

By the 1890s many country store merchants had installed a "five-and-ten-cent counter." Imitating the merchandising concept pioneered by F. W. Woolworth in 1879, country storekeepers began displaying a tempting assortment of items—crocheting needles, wash basins and dippers, thimbles, facial soap, baby bibs, watch keys, and harmonicas—that could be bought for the smallest units of change. Butler Brothers in Boston, general jobbers to the country trade, specialized in providing the country merchant with cartons of mixed goods to be displayed on special counters where each item sold for the same low price of, for example, five, ten, or twenty cents.[20] With the introduction of the five-cent coin (nickel) to United States currency during the 1880s, merchants found the price-lined counter an especially useful marketing strategy.

Besides implementing urban selling techniques in their stores, country merchants often sold by example. In rural communities, merchants were the first to install a telephone, buy a new style office desk or wall clock, use a box camera, or add window screens to their stores. Their informal endorsement of these and other new products (samples

Press, 1948), pp. 78–83, 103–4, 253–59. On the use of glass in late nineteenth-century consumer displays, see William Leach, "Transformations in a Culture of Consumption: Women and Department Stores, 1890–1925," *Journal of American History* 71, no. 2 (September 1984): 32–33; and William Leach, "Strategists of Display and the Production of Desire," elsewhere in this volume.

[19] Clark, *Pills, Petticoats, and Plows*, pp. 98–113.

[20] John K. Winkler, *Five and Ten: The Fabulous Life of F. W. Woolworth* (New York: Robert McBride, 1940), pp. 20–60. The Butler brothers are described in Robert Hendrickson, *The Illustrated History of America's Great Department Stores* (New York: Stein and Day, 1979), pp. 234–35, 263; and Carson, *Country Store*, p. 188.

of which were frequently provided by jobbers) added credibility to a product's quality in an era that thrived on testimonial advertising.

Often included in consumer displays were items that were not for sale. Indeed, many country merchants were curators of informal museum collections. Deer antlers, stuffed rattlesnakes, queer-shaped eggs, carved chains and other extraordinary pieces of whittling, Indian arrowheads, Civil War relics, unusual coins, strange root growths, and seemingly every other article of wonderment were arranged to promote customer curiosity and patronage.[21]

Not satisfied with their initial monopoly of a rural region's trade and the credit liens they held over many of their customers, storekeepers widely advertised their wares, often placing large ads for special sales and seasonal promotion in local weeklies. By 1900 they were also touting their goods through the penny picture postcard, bulk mailings of handbills, free calendars, and even their own business cards. In mounting these promotional campaigns, national advertisers and traveling salesmen assisted local storekeepers. Patent medicines were the first national brands stocked by country-store owners because they became popular goods "called for" by customers who had read about them in the agricultural, religious, or regional press. Drake's Plantation Bitters or Radway's Ready Relief were also promoted by the extensive publishing network of "medical" almanacs that were sent to country merchants every November in time to stimulate holiday sales as well as mark the New Year. Storekeepers distributed the free publications to all who came to their counters. Carl Sandburg recalled that the nostrum almanacs by Hosteller or Ayer also advertised other products and came equipped with a loop of string for hanging the book on a nail in a farm kitchen corner. Besides its consumer promotions, it was a calendar, a reference work, and a compendium of doggerel verse and ethnic jokes.[22]

The national-brand advertising of consumer goods that appeared

[21] Clark, *Pills, Petticoats, and Plows*, pp. 22–23.

[22] Lewis Eldon Atherton, *Main Street on the Middle Border* (Bloomington: Indiana University Press, 1954), pp. 222–23; James Harvey Young, *The Toadstool Millionaires: A Social History of Patent Medicines in America before Federal Regulation* (Princeton: Princeton University Press, 1961), pp. 93–110, 125–43; James Harvey Young, *American Self-Dosage Medicines: An Historical Perspective* (Lawrence, Kans.: Coronado Press, 1974); Robb Sagendorph, *America and Her Almanacs: Wit, Wisdom, and Weather, 1639–1970* (Boston: Little, Brown, 1970), pp. 254–71; Carl Sandburg, *Always the Young Strangers* (New York: Harcourt, Brace, 1953), p. 228.

in almanacs and other rural publications, such as newspapers, agricultural journals, women's magazines, pocket encyclopedias, and denominational tracts, soon forced country storekeepers to join the "packaging push." Innovative store owners recognized that the artifact in which a product was boxed or bottled could be more appealing to the consumer than the article itself. The trend away from displaying generic goods in barrels, kegs, bins, and sacks to preparing individual consumer units of wrappers, packets, cartons, and containers was a gradual but continual shift in marketing by the American country store. As early as the 1870s, a local merchant could purchase in various shapes, sizes, and colors "pasteboard caddies" on which his business card could be printed and in which he could apportion tea, sugar, coffee, and other bulk staples according to the preferences of his customers. "As an advertizing medium," claimed the trade organ that promoted this, the caddies "will repay you their cost."[23] More frequently, however, the local merchant let the national manufacturer do his promotional packaging. Commodities such as Mail Pouch tobacco in individual bags instead of 40-pound loaves of plug or Quaker Oats in a 16-ounce box instead of an 80-pound sack increasingly stocked the country store shelves after 1900.

Eventually even the cracker barrel, one of the country store's revered icons, succumbed to the new consumer culture. The National Biscuit Company, founded in 1898, began marketing Uneeda Biscuits, soda crackers in a five-cent, airtight, patented, moisture-proof package. National Biscuit initiated an unprecedented, lavish, nationwide advertising campaign to sell the new item, an effort that economic historian Alfred Chandler identified as the prototype of corporate strategies for modern mass distribution of consumer commodities that became commonplace in twentieth-century marketing. Traveling salesmen from the company worked crossroads stores with a particular intensity, distributing posters and painted signs for their facades as well as for barns, livery stables, and railroad depots. These "drummers" also used various promotions and premiums to "drum up" interest in their new produce among potential rural customers, even providing Uneeda emblems, watch fobs, cuff links, and stickpins for storekeepers and their favorite clients. The campaign succeeded, and Uneeda Biscuits quickly registered monthly sales of over 10 million packages. Promoted with the trademark of a boy

[23] Carson, *Country Store*, pp. 268–69.

Fig. 4. "The Slicker Boy," National Biscuit Co., 1902. (The Archives, National Brands, Inc.)

in a yellow rain slicker and the slogan Lest You Forget, We Say It Yet, Uneeda Biscuit (fig. 4), the product inaugurated the first million-dollar advertising campaign in the United States as well as some less successful imitators such as Uwanta Beer, Itsagood Soup, and *Ureada Magazine*.[24]

In the development of rural consumership, drummers played a vital role. With trunk and carpetbag, satchel and sample case, this cadre of traveling salesmen—called variously trade interviewers, solicitors, commercial tourists, or simply commercials—acted as the conduit by which

[24] Alfred D. Chandler, *The Visible Hand: The Managerial Revolution in American Business* (Cambridge, Mass.: Harvard University Press, 1977), pp. 334–35; William Cahn, *Out of the Cracker Barrel: The Nabisco Story from Animal Crackers to Zuzus* (New York: Simon and Schuster, 1969), pp. 89–98; Stephen Fox, *The Mirror Makers: A History of American Advertising and Its Creators* (New York: Vintage, 1985), p. 39.

advertising techniques and promotional displays that developed in the city were distributed in the country. Drummers—some of whom, like Marshall Field and Montgomery Ward, went on to become merchandising giants—kept the rural merchant abreast of what they learned from trade journals, professional associations (the American Society of Commercial Travelers), and other clients they visited on their annual, semiannual, or quarterly circuits. The subject of innumerable off-color jokes about the "farmer's daughter" and yet the founder of the Gideon Bible Society, the turn-of-the-century drummer was the perfect liaison between the commercial worlds of country and city. His latest-style haberdashery, his knowledge and wit about urban sports, arts, and entertainment, and his suitcases filled with the most up-to-date city goods made his rotational visits to the country something of a community event. More important, as revealed in Charles S. Plummer's autobiography, *Leaves from a Drummer's Diary; or, Twenty-Five Years on the Road* (1889), he often served as a financial consultant, economic forecaster, market analyst, and advertising adviser to storekeepers. The typical drummer personalized some of the increasingly impersonal aspects of modern merchandising at the turn of the century. His hard sells and hunches about what goods were on their way "out" and those soon to be "in," his experience of new display techniques and urban marketing practices, and his acumen as to what "the people in the know" considered to be "modern" made him a crucial figure in the transformation of country-store buying and selling.[25]

The County Fair

In addition to his vital contribution to modernizing many country-store practices, the drummer also played a role in expanding the consumer orientation of county and state fairs. He attended many of the fairs in his selling region, and often he either purchased or was given complimentary passes or tickets to the amusements that he, in turn, distributed among his clients. By the turn of the century, his company may have also purchased exhibition space at many fairs. As host of his firm's fair

[25] Wayne E. Fuller, *RFD: The Changing Face of Rural America* (Bloomington: Indiana University Press, 1964), p. 211; Atherton, *Main Street*, pp. 34, 222–29; Carson, *Country Store*, pp. 162–67.

displays, he continued his sales pitch to clients and other fair-goers by distributing promotional leaflets, free samples, and product souvenirs. As his corporation's sales representative at the county or state level, he used the exhibition booth as a seasonal opportunity to open up his sample case of the company's newest line of products to the general public.

Agricultural fairs always afforded opportunities for commercial exchanges, beginning with sales of improved livestock. Their precise beginnings in America, however, are not certain. If a fair is defined as a weekly or monthly market held in a town center, then seventeenth-century colonists held fairs whose antecedents were in the European Middle Ages. If the definition is restricted to an exhibition of livestock and produce, then the first American fair may have taken place at George Washington Parke Custis's sheep-shearings in Virginia in 1803, which featured premiums for superior sheep, wool, and domestic manufactures; at Chancellor Robert R. Livingston's similar festivities at his Hudson River estate in 1810; or, as is usually claimed, at Elkanah Watson's Berkshire County livestock exhibition also held in 1810. Custis, Livingston, and Watson were patrician farmers with avid interests in breeding Merino sheep. Regardless of whether Watson deserves the title as the "father of the American county fair," he was a crucial figure in its diffusion. He formed the Berkshire County Agricultural Society, a body specifically designed to perpetuate annual exhibitions of rural commodities.[26] The basic format of the "Berkshire System" evolved throughout the nineteenth century into an American institution with economic, recreational, social, and educational dimensions.

True to its beginnings as a livestock show, the county fair featured an assemblage of living material culture. Fair animals are artifacts since, as James Deetz reminds us, "the scientific breeding of livestock involves the conscious modification of an animal's form according to culturally derived ideals." The same is true of fruits and vegetables, which increasingly have been hybridized to please the consumer's eye as much as his palate. These agricultural commodities, vegetable or animal, ultimately entered the marketplace when, on a fair's final "auction days,"

[26] Donald B. Marti, *Historical Directory of American Agricultural Fairs* (Westport, Conn.: Greenwood Press, 1986), pp. 2–5; Elkanah Watson, *Men and Times of the Revolution; or, Memoirs of Elkanah Watson* (2d ed.; New York: Dana, 1856), pp. 421–30, 456–58; Elkanah Watson, *History of Agricultural Societies on the Modern Berkshire System* (Albany, N.Y.: D. Steele, 1820).

the produce and products were sold to the highest bidders. Even members of the 4-H movement, founded in 1900, and the Future Farmers of America, founded in 1927, participated early on in this consumer-oriented aspect of stock raising. Although promoted primarily as educational enterprises for the fun and glory of competition, participants in these rural youth organizations received an early introduction to countryside capitalism at the bidding for their animals at the junior livestock auctions that took place at many fairs.[27]

This exhibition of living material culture had many parallels with the array of farm machinery that became a standard fixture in the agricultural halls of every major American world's fair from 1876 to 1933.[28] As might be expected, implement companies showed their latest, fastest, most powerful, versatile, and labor-saving devices. Special fair models, such as the Studebaker Brothers Carriage Works' farm wagon made of teak and mahogany, were used to attract an audience. Plowing matches and tractor pulls became rituals of competition staged as much between the corporate giants, such as John Deere and International Harvester, as between the individual drivers of their equipment.

The county fair also encouraged its patrons to buy goods and services other than fertilizers and feeders (fig. 5). In addition to farm products and implements, the first state fair held in 1841 in Syracuse, New York, featured domestic manufactures, such as kitchen utensils, cast-iron stoves, and pottery. Similar "commercial exhibits" appeared regularly at county, and particularly state, fairs. For example, the Great Granger's Annual Picnic Exhibition at Williams Grove, Pennsylvania, drew all types of consumer promotions. Begun in 1873, this major regional fair grew from a one-day event attracting 8,000 to 10,000 people to a week-long program by 1885 when over 150,000 people attended

[27] James Deetz, *In Small Things Forgotten: The Archaeology of Early American Life* (Garden City, N.Y.: Anchor Press/Doubleday, 1977), p. 24; Thomas Wessel and Marilyn Wessel, *4-H: An American Idea* (Chevy Chase, Md.: National 4-H Council, 1982), pp. 2–24; Franklin M. Reck, *The 4-H Story: A History of 4-H Club Work* (Ames: Iowa State College Press, 1951); Janice N. Friedel, "Jessie Field Shambaugh, the Mother of 4-H," *Palimpsest* 62, no. 2 (July/August 1981): 98–115; A. Webster Tenney, *The FFA at 50* (Alexandria, Va.: FFA, 1977).

[28] Justus D. Doenecke, "Myths, Machines and Markets: The Columbian Exposition of 1893," *Journal of Popular Culture* 6, no. 4 (Spring 1973): 535–49; Merle Curti, "America at the World's Fairs, 1851–1893," *American Historical Review* 55, no. 4 (July 1950): 83–56; Hugo A. Meier, "American Technology and the Nineteenth Century World," *American Quarterly* 10, no. 2, pt. 1 (Summer 1958): 116–30.

Fig. 5. Elmira Inter-State Fair, September 1–12, 1890. Chromolithograph (detail). (Genesee Country Museum.)

from twenty-nine of the thirty-eight states. Fair visitors often became temporary residents of Williams Grove as campers, renters of cottages, hotel patrons, and boarders in private homes.[29] In 1892 more than 162 persons or firms displayed 1,329 items or lots of merchandise ranging from bedroom furniture to kitchen stoves and from parlor suites to sewing machines. Frequently a consumer could do comparative shopping within the fairground, since various models and brands of the same product were often demonstrated. In 1910, for example, 37 different styles or brands of washing machines were exhibited at the Williams Grove fair.

By the turn of the century, rural consumers could view and test drive the latest automobile models on display at the Williams Grove fair. As early as 1900, a Locomobile agent exhibited his company's line

[29] Wayne C. Neely, *The Agricultural Fair* (New York: Columbia University Press, 1935), pp. 95–96; Earle D. Ross, "The Evolution of the Agricultural Fair in the Northwest," *Iowa Journal of History and Politics* 24, no. 2 (July 1926): 462; Warren J. Gates, "Modernization as a Function of an Agricultural Fair: The Great Granger's Picnic Exhibition at Williams Grove, Pennsylvania, 1873–1916," *Agricultural History* 58, no. 3 (July 1984): 264–65.

of new cars, and the fairs of 1912 through 1916 included auto shows. Newspaper comment in that decade noted the increasing number of those attending who now came by car as opposed to the hordes that formerly came by rail. Railroads, however, continued to play vital roles in rural consumption. The roads brought drummers and their companies' lines to country stores. They carried mail-order catalogues, mail orders, and mail-order merchandise between city and country. At state and regional fairs, they became the principal carriers of exhibits and exhibitors, often giving free one-way or round-trip passes to farmers attending a fair. The Long Island Railroad in 1874 carried all exhibits free of charge to and from the Queens County Fair. In that same year, the Lake Superior and Mississippi Railroad took first place with one of its displays at the Minnesota State Fair.[30]

State fairs, and some county fairs, assumed many of the characteristics of small towns by the 1920s. Invariably located on the outskirts of a major city (for example, Minneapolis and St. Paul vied for the permanent site of the Minnesota fair which was eventually located in the "Midway district" between them), the big fairs had all the artifacts of an urban world. Flimsy wooden buildings, tents, and temporary sheds and pens gave way to massive structures of brick and steel and concrete. State legislative appropriations, plus profits from the fairs, funded the building of machinery halls, administration buildings, judging arenas, children's and women's buildings, amphitheaters, opera houses, auditoriums, concession stands, nickelodeons, post offices, and retail stores. Landscape architects were called in to beautify the grounds, and sidewalks and pavements were laid. Water systems, sewer lines, and electric street lights were installed.[31]

Fairs became big businesses by the end of the 1890s. County and state fair promoters hired professional managers, supported lobbyists in Washington, and founded their own trade associations such as the International Association of Fairs and Expositions begun in 1891. One of that organization's first objectives was to coordinate a national sched-

[30] Gates, "Modernization," pp. 270–71; Neely, *Agricultural Fair*, pp. 77, 93, 98, 119, 258, 260; Ross, "Evolution," pp. 461–62.

[31] Fred Kniffen, "The American Agricultural Fair: The Pattern," *Annals of the Association of American Geographers* 39, no. 4 (December 1949): 264–82; Ray P. Speer and Harry J. Frost, *Minnesota State Fair: The History and Heritage of 100 Years* (St. Paul, Minn.: Argus Publishing Co., 1964); Neely, *Agricultural Fair*, pp. 108–9, 111–12, 117.

ule of major events that would allow popular attractions such as carnival troupes, balloonists, auto racers, chautauqua entertainers, and airplane stuntmen to visit as many fairs around the country as possible. The association then began to develop its members' skills by publishing studies of advertising, budgeting, and other business practices. It held (and still holds) instructional conferences, and in 1924 it conducted a School of Fair Management in cooperation with the University of Chicago.[32]

Professional managers sought to modernize county and state fairs by further expanding their commercial elements. In order to make fairs turn a profit, they employed various means, such as elaborate evening programs, popular vaudeville shows, baseball games, bicycling and auto races, special days (for example, "Ladies," "Youth," and "Town" days), raffles and door prizes, and free souvenirs. Professional managers also turned increasingly to national and local manufacturing, advertising, and business sponsors to mount consumer displays, many of which were only tangentially related to agricultural pursuits.

With increased attention to professionalism, bureaucracy, and the market economy—typical hallmarks of modernization—county and state fairs came to function as middle merchandising grounds between local merchants and national manufacturers. Major corporations such as Singer Sewing Machine, Royal Baking Powder, and Sapolio Soap used fair sites to showcase their national brands beginning the the late 1880s. Promoters of the new ready-to-eat or dry cereals—Henry Perky's Shredded Wheat, C. W. Post's Grape Nuts, and the Kellogg brothers' (Dr. John and W. K.) Battle Creek line—wrought their turn-of-the-century revolution in the food ways of the American breakfast by touting their new grain processes, flavors, forms, and textures at exhibit booths at county fairs as well as on country-store shelves. The Quaker Oats Company, purveyors of hot, prepared, crushed groats partially cooked in steam chambers and rolled into flakes under heavy pressure, likewise turned to fairs to maintain their share of the breakfast-food market. Their trade character—a smiling old gentleman, long hair falling to his shoulders, dressed in knee breeches, waistcoat, stock, and broad-brimmed hat and carrying a scroll labeled "Pure" in his hand—made personal appearances at fairs and expositions. The folksy, corporate personae promoted the package system of national brands using marketing strat-

---

[32] Marti, *Historical Directory*, p. 20.

Fig. 6. Modern home interior, Sears, Roebuck, Illinois State Fair, 1910.
(Sears, Roebuck, and Company.)

egies that appealed to rural consumers, such as free samples for house-
wives, cooking schools, recipe books, fancy trade cards, and coupon
premiums and prizes.[33]

    Mail-order houses also seized the neutral turf of the county fair
both to ameliorate the hostilities of storekeepers and to create new wants
and wishes among consumers. For example, in 1910 Sears, Roebuck,
and Company outfitted various cottage and bungalow models of its mail-
order housing at the Illinois State Fair (fig. 6). The company's purpose
was twofold: first, to demonstrate in a full-scale, three-dimensional form
the features of its extensive catalogue housing line; second, to illustrate
the interior design potential of its manufactured homes, especially if
furnished with the household goods also available from the general catalogue. Bungalows frequently contained leaded-glass windows, built-in

bookcases and mantels in the living room, plate rails and sideboards in the dining room, and carved staircases. Larger, more expensive homes featured decorative plasterwork, beamed ceilings, and colonnaded openings between rooms. Sears greatly expanded its offering of home furnishings between 1908 and 1925, with furniture, like its houses, ranging from solid mission-style pieces to more elaborate colonial reproductions, thus fitting a range of budgets. Cottages were shown simply furnished with several tables and chairs; larger homes were decorated with wallpaper, carpeting, and pianos.[34]

Just as Americans first introduced an amusement area to world's fairs, so they also pioneered the addition of popular entertainment to agricultural fairs. Horse racing remained a standard fixture, despite the misgivings of fair organizers. Minstrels, band pavilions, dance halls, circuses, sideshows, games-of-chance, vaudeville shows, ethnic restaurants, amusement rides, and exotic food concessions became elements of fairs by 1900.[35] Thus a fair's midway introduced country folk to the city amusement park. One could experience the switchback, a trolley tunnel, or the flip-flop railway, rides directly inspired by various urban modes of travel. Here one could purchase an ascent on a Ferris wheel, a hot-air balloon, or a barnstorming airplane. One could also buy, for the first time for many rural people, a drink of pineapple juice or root beer, a box of caramel corn, or a spun sugar nest of cotton candy. Or if more excitement was required, the farmer's son might take in a motion picture show, a burlesque review, or a panorama program recreating events such as the Chicago fire of 1871, the Galveston flood of 1900, or the San Francisco earthquake of 1906.

The bazaar of popular culture that came alive at a fair after dark was a nocturnal consumer pattern largely unknown to rural communities. First gas, then arc, and then electrical lighting set the stage. Amusement rides, dance halls, and sideshows usually remained open until midnight, as did most food concessions. Geographer Barbara Rubin argues that such midway nightlife, especially when expanded to the scale of American world fairs, was one of the spatial and cultural ante-

---

[34] Katherine Cole Stevenson and H. Ward Jandl, *Houses by Mail: A Guide to Houses from Sears, Roebuck and Company* (Washington, D.C.: Preservation Press, 1986), pp. 36–37.
[35] William Dean Howells, "Editor's Easy Chair [Fairs in America]," *Harper's Monthly* 106, no. 631 (December 1902): 163–67.

cedents of the commercial strip. Rubin claims that constant movement and colorful lighting, false-front architecture and gigantic signage, and the advertising hype and promotional hyperbole of the linear midway of pre–World War I American fairs continued in the commercial strip developments of post–World War II America.[36]

The Mail-Order Catalogue

"There's a Haynes-Cooper catalog in every farmer's kitchen," remarks a Wisconsin woman in *Fanny Herself* (1917), Edna Ferber's novel depicting the Chicago mail-order industry. "The Bible's in the parlor, but they keep the H. C. book in the room where they live." Often called "Farmer's Bibles," the mail-order catalogues of the Chicago giants—Montgomery Ward and Sears—often expressed a secular hope for salvation from want. There was, for example, the often-quoted tale of the little boy from rural Idaho who, upon being asked by his Sunday school teacher where the Ten Commandments came from, unhesitatingly replied, "From Sears, Roebuck, where else?"[37]

Mail-order catalogues were called "a department store in a book," "the nation's largest supply house," "a consumer guide," "a city shopping district at your fingertips," and "the world's largest country store." While historians usually attribute the first such catalogue to a mail circular of 1744 issued by Benjamin Franklin, the only founding father to have a chain store named after him, catalogues came into their own during the Gilded Age. Large-scale retailing through the mails, pioneered by merchants such as Charley ("Send No Money") Thompson, publisher of the *People's Literary Companion* of Bridgeport, Connecticut, and E. C. Allen of Augusta, Maine, took off under the nationwide marketing skills of Aaron Montgomery Ward. Ward claimed to have launched in 1872 the modern mail-order industry. Catalogues were distributed to people who then placed their orders by mail. The ordered goods were delivered to the customers' homes by some established ship-

---

[36] Barbara Rubin, "Aesthetic Ideology and Urban Design," *Annals of the Association of American Geographers* 69, no. 3 (September 1979): 339–61. See also Robert W. Rydell, "The Culture of Imperial Abundance: World's Fairs in the Making of American Culture," elsewhere in this volume.

[37] Viola I. Paradise, "By Mail," *Scribner's* 69, no. 4 (April 1921): 480.

ping service such as freight, express, or post.[38] Ward sought out rural consumers through a loose affiliation with the Patrons of Husbandry, or the Grange, that made his Chicago firm the farmer organization's official supply house. Richard Sears, a former Minnesota railway agent who got into the mail-order business in his spare time selling watches, launched his company in 1886. Two decades later Sears claimed his catalogue was "The Largest Supply House in the World," selling 10,000 other items in addition to a watch every minute. The key medium for displaying his merchandise was the semiannual *Consumer's Guide*, as his mail-order catalogue began to be labeled in the 1894 edition.

Numerous interpreters attest to the mail-order catalogue's impact on American rural life. The "Farmer's Wishbook" doubled as a reader, a textbook, and an encyclopedia in many rural schoolhouses. Children practiced arithmetic by adding up order sums, learned geography from its postal-zone maps, and tried figure drawing by tracing the catalogue's models. The "Big Books" served as almanacs for many adults since they usually contained inspirational readings, epigrams, poetry, and farming and household tips. (Ward recognized this function when he began issuing an annual almanac subtitled *A Book of Practical Education*.) Selected by the Grolier Society in 1946 as one of the 100 outstanding American books of all time, the mail-order catalogue has been the subject of several novels, popular songs, and parodies.[39]

[38] Thomas J. Schlereth, "Mail Order Catalogs as Resources in Material Culture Studies," in Thomas J. Schlereth, *Artifacts and the American Past* (Nashville: American Association for State and Local History, 1980), p. 49.

[39] A basic mail-order industry bibliography includes Frank B. Latham, *A Century of Serving Customers: The Story of Montgomery Ward* (Chicago: Montgomery Ward Co., 1972); Nina Baker, *Big Catalogue: The Life of Aaron Montgomery Ward* (New York: Harcourt, Brace, 1956); and *Our Silver Anniversary: Being a Brief and Concise History of the Mail-Order or Catalog Business Which Was Invented by Us a Quarter of a Century Ago* (Chicago: A. Montgomery Ward Co., 1897). On Sears, consult David L. Cohn, *The Good Old Days: A History of American Morals and Manners as Seen through the Sears, Roebuck Catalogs, 1905 to the Present* (New York: Simon and Schuster, 1940); Gordon L. Weil, *Sears, Roebuck, U.S.A.: The Great American Catalog Store and How It Grew* (New York: Stein and Day, 1977); and Boris Emmet and John E. Jeuck, *Catalogues and Counters: A History of Sears, Roebuck and Company* (Chicago: University of Chicago Press, 1950). Lovell Thompson, "Eden in Easy Payments," *Saturday Review of Literature* (April 3, 1937), pp. 15–16; Ralph Andrist, *American Century: One Hundred Years of Changing Life Styles in America* (New York: American Heritage Press, 1972); Edna Ferber, *Fanny Herself* (New York: Frederick A. Stokes Co., 1917); Harry Crews, *A Childhood: The Biography of a Place* (New York: Harper and Row, 1978); George Milburn, *Catalogue* (first published as *All Over Town* [1936; reprint, New York: Avon Books, 1977]);

As a form of buying and selling, catalogues affected every aspect of American everyday life from love and birth to loneliness and death. For example, a Kansas farmer wrote Sears in 1899, "Find enclosed one check; please send one wife Model #1242 on page 112 as soon as possible." A Minnesota consumer wrote Ward at the turn of the century about purchasing embalming fluid for her ailing husband: "When you send the stuff please send instructions with it. Must I pour it down his throat just before he dies, or must I rub it on after he is dead? Please rush."[40]

Although they eventually became long and unwieldy, mail-order catalogues easily compressed an entire country-store inventory and a county-fair exhibit into a 500-page volume. Not only did each new edition add more lines of merchandise, it also enlarged the range of selection. Unlike the country store or the county fair, where products were tangibly present for customer inspection, mail-order merchandising required constant attention to maintain credibility. Country-store merchants continually warned their customers that mail-order purchases invited disappointment, poor-quality goods, and downright fraud. To counter such charges, Sears and Ward jammed their catalogues with beguiling illustrations and detailed descriptions written in a folksy vernacular. Ward's catalogues provided instructions for ordering products in ten languages. Sears introduced early catalogues with a personal letter: "Don't be afraid that you will make a mistake," he assured potential customers. "We receive hundreds of orders every day from young and old who never sent away for goods. . . . Tell us what you want, in your own way, written in any language, no matter whether good or poor writing, and your goods will be sent promptly to you."[41]

Both Sears and Ward guaranteed customer satisfaction or an immediate cash refund. Both used their catalogue covers to depict their stores as beehives of industrious clerks filling thousands of orders daily from a seemingly unlimited abundance of products. So that skeptical customers could get a look at company operations, Sears sold cheap sets

---

"Rears and Robust Mail-Order Catalog for Spring/Summer/Fall/Winter," *Morning Call* (Wheeling, W. Va.), 1940.

[40] Hendrickson, *Grand Emporiums*, pp. 205–6.

[41] Quoted in Stuart Ewen and Elizabeth Ewen, *Channels of Desire: Mass Images and the Shaping of American Consciousness* (New York: McGraw-Hill, 1982), pp. 65–66.

of stereopticon slides showing the company's plants and warehouses. Here the mail-order catalogues followed a convention of other nineteenth-century trade catalogues where a firm's factories and offices were depicted as a machine of sorts, notable for its scale, multiplicity or complexity of parts, and orderliness. In one illustration, for example, rural people saw modernization encapsulated in a single image: an artifact assemblage that was efficient, well organized, specialized, businesslike, and prosperous, representing the most up-to-date approaches and techniques in that line of merchandising (fig. 7).[42]

In 1905 Sears improvised a plan—called his "Iowaization" scheme—to distribute catalogues and recruit customers. The company wrote to all its current customers in Iowa and asked each to pass on catalogues to friends and neighbors. The customers, in turn, sent the names of people given the catalogue to the company. The company kept track of who ordered what and gave each "distributor" premiums on the basis of the number of incoming orders from friends and relatives. Sales from Iowa soon outstripped all other states, and Sears went on to apply the concept throughout the country.[43]

Sears also manipulated networks of personal relations established, in part, by weekly visits to a country store and the annual trek to the county fair. Social and community relations became an arena within which rural neighbors became promoters and distributors of city goods. With the spread of mail-order merchandising, people who had lived, to a large extent, on a barter or an extended credit system now became immersed in a money economy. In an instance of Ferdinand Tonnies's theory of cultural change from *Gemeinschaft* to *Gesellschaft*—that is, from informal community to organized society—rural communities became engaged in impersonal, individualistic accumulation through rituals of local bonding for the primary purpose of corporate profit.

Mail-order catalogues had other effects on American rural life. They standardized the American language, inasmuch as the Chicago-based mail-order houses homogenized the nomenclature of much American material culture. For example, what is still known in the rural South as a "sling-blade" or "slam-bang" must be ordered from

---

[42] *Sears, Roebuck Catalogue* (Spring/Summer 1908): 309; Schlereth, "Mail-Order Catalogs," p. 64. On general trade catalogue conventions, see Ames, "Trade Catalogues," p. 12.

[43] Weil, *Sears, Roebuck*, pp. 5, 25–27.

Fig. 7. "A Busy Bee-Hive," advertisement for Montgomery Ward and Co., ca. 1900. Chromolithograph. (Chicago Historical Society.)

Sears by recognizing a catalogue picture in which it is labeled a "weed-cutter." The rapid diffusion of high-style artifacts into rural communities is another influence of mail-order catalogues, as demonstrated by the popularization of the arts and crafts movement. On the one hand, this aesthetic trend associated with Elbert Hubbard and Gustave Stickley in the United States symbolized a refutation of the mass-produced, ornate, machine-made goods that the mail-order houses sold by the millions; on the other hand, the mail-order catalogues helped advertise the furniture designs of Hubbard and Stickley. Sears featured three-piece "Arts and Crafts Library Suites" as well as "Mission Art Glass Lamps" that burned kerosene. As early as 1902 a version of William Morris's famous reclining chair was in a Ward catalogue.[44]

Installment buying for many rural dwellers grew out of their mail-order merchandising experience. Many products selling for $25 or more could be had for a minimal down-payment and a check or money order dispatched monthly to Chicago. By 1911 Sears offered home loans first for its manufactured mail-order homes but later for the cost of the house lot and construction labor. In so doing, it was one of the few institutions to grant mortgages without ever meeting the borrowers personally or inspecting their collateral property.[45] Unlike the highly personal, even familial, credit system of the country store, the distant mail-order catalogue company sold goods on time to anonymous individuals, identified by name and address only, as long as they merely filled out a standard form and sent in the required down payment.

Three actions of the United States Post Office in the decades between 1890 and 1920 had an enormous impact on the success of mail-order buying. The one-cent advertiser's postcard was sanctioned in 1871, rural free delivery (RFD) was instituted in 1898, and a rural parcel-post system began by 1913. Proposed in 1891 and endorsed by postmaster general and Philadelphia department-store magnate John A. Wanamaker, RFD became a national system of direct-to-the-home mail delivery (fig. 8). Championed by the Grange, other farmers' organizations, and the mail-order houses, it was fought bitterly by the express companies, local storekeepers, and the National Association of Grocers. A similar battle over parcel post was waged by similar combatants with similar results.

[44] Fred E. H. Schroeder, "Semi-Annual Installment on the American Dream: The Wishbook as Popular Icon," in *Icons of Popular Culture*, ed. Marshall Fishwick and Ray B. Browne (Bowling Green, Ohio: Bowling Green University Popular Press, 1970), pp. 73–86; Fred E. H. Schroeder, "The Wishbook as Popular Icon," in *Outlaw Aesthetics: Arts and the Public Mind* (Bowling Green, Ohio: Bowling Green University Popular Press, 1977), pp. 50–61; Russell Lynes, *The Tastemakers* (New York: Harper and Brothers, 1949), p. 190; Perry Duis, *Chicago: Creating New Traditions* (Chicago: Chicago Historical Society, 1976), p. 116.
[45] Stevenson and Jandl, *Houses by Mail*, pp. 20–23.

Fig. 8. N. C. Wyeth, *Where the Mail Goes Cream of Wheat Goes*, 1906. Oil on canvas; H. 44¼", W. 37⅞". (The Archives, National Brands, Inc.)

　　　Rural delivery made mail-ordering something to be done in the privacy of one's kitchen or parlor. "If you live on a rural route," advised the catalogues, "just give the letter and money to the mail carrier and he will get the money order at the post office and mail it in the letter for you." With the new parcel post law in effect in 1913, the catalogues told their consumers: "Packages up to 11 pounds in weight will be hand delivered like any other mail matter." By 1920 a 50-pound package could be sent by parcel post from Chicago to anywhere in the country and a 70-pound package anywhere in its first three postal zones. In 1920, of the 787 Wisconsin farm families questioned about their buying habits, 30 percent bought an annual average of $58.91 worth of mail-order goods. Another survey along a Midwest rural route showed every family received an average of seventeen mail-order parcels a year—about one every three weeks if evenly spaced.[46]

These trends changed rural consumption patterns forever. Even traditional agrarian rituals, such as the large "threshing meals" provided by farm families for the traveling threshing crews that spent time helping such families harvest their grain, bore the impact of increased mail-order merchandising. J. Sanford Rikoon's careful study of threshing folk life in the Midwest indicates that by the late 1890s special foodstuffs for threshing meals were increasingly purchased from the mail-order catalogues in order to increase the status of an already highly symbolic communal activity. In sharp contrast to the rural practice of providing homegrown and self-prepared foods for the bulk of the threshing meal, farm families began buying bottled soda pop, ice cream, cigars, bags of potato chips, canned salmon, and dried fruit by mail order to impress guests at mealtime. Rikoon comments: "Threshing ring popularity coincides with a time when goods and services of urban or industrial origin were becoming increasingly popular in rural settings. Ironic as it may seem from the present-day return to 'home-cooking,' mass-produced items often received an initially high social prestige in rural contexts."[47]

As artifacts of a new consumership, mail-order catalogues prompted heated conflict. Country storekeepers and small-town editors waged a prolonged and vitriolic anticatalogue campaign. Local merchants, such as R. E. Ledbetter in George Milburn's novel *Catalogue*, instigated townspeople and farmers to bring in their catalogues to a "Home Town Industry Jubilee and Bonfire," where store owners paid a bounty of $1

[46]*Sears, Roebuck and Co. Catalogue*, no. 113 (Spring 1904), p. 1, and no. 126 (Spring 1913), p. 2; Wayne E. Fuller, *The American Mail: Enlarger of Common Life* (Chicago: University of Chicago Press, 1972), pp. 181–85; Fuller, *RFD*, pp. 250–52; J. H. Kolb, *Service Relations of Town and Country*, Wisconsin Agricultural Experiment Station, Research Bulletin no. 58, 1923, p. 73; *Congressional Record*, 68th Cong., 2d sess., p. 340; Edmund de S. Brunner and J. H. Kolb, *Rural Social Trends* (New York: McGraw-Hill, 1933), p. 156; *Congressional Record*, 71st Cong., 3d sess., p. 5040; *Postmaster General's Report* (Washington, D.C.: Government Printing Office, 1930), p. 29.

[47]J. Sanford Rikoon, *From Flail to Combine: Threshing in the Midwest* (Bloomington: Indiana University Press, 1987), p. 149. See also Paul M. Shoger, *Threshing Rings of Kendall County*, 1875–1955 (Yorkville, Ill.: Kendall County Records, 1976), p. 20; Carl Hamilton, *In No Time at All* (Ames: Iowa State University Press, 1974), p. 87.

in trade for every new catalogue turned in to fuel the grand bonfires staged in the town's public square.[48]

Often desperate in their responses, midwestern and southern storekeepers appealed to provincialism and xenophobia among their customers. Local merchants peddled rumors to their predominantly white, Protestant clientele that Sears and Ward were black men. In response to racial innuendo, Sears published photos of its founders to prove they were not "colored." Ward offered a $100 reward for the name of the person who had initiated the rumor that he was mulatto.[49]

The country store, the county fair, and the mail-order catalogue, while different in origin, longevity, and location, had much in common. Each demanded a fairly high degree of literacy of their patrons, whether it be the notational ordering system common to country stores or the placing of a readable mail order. Each required a national postal delivery system and a continental railway network to secure and sell its wares. Each nurtured urbanity among rurality: although they began as distinct displays of goods in rural places, by the turn of the twentieth century the country store and the county fair had taken on urban characteristics. The mail-order catalogue, an urban construct at origin, brought city ways and wares directly to country environs.

As artifact assemblages, the store, the fair, and the catalogue were more than methods of display and mediums of accumulation. Each engendered a range of cultural behavior beyond its material manifestation. For example, as Thomas Clark amply documents, the country store initiated the southern male into numerous rites: "Here it was that he bought his first 'long' pants, drank his first non-home brew liquor, compared notes on his romance with a local belle, bought a postage stamp, a coffin, a wagon, a necktie, a can of sardines, or a pistol."[50] For the midwestern farmer, the county fair served, with seasonal regularity, as a festive hub of a local universe, a paradoxically competitive and communal environment that functioned as marketplace, recreational center, chautauqua, political forum, and gossip-news exchange.

[48] Milburn, *Catalog*, chap. 18. For a good contemporary summary of the various positions in the anti-mail-order campaign, see the December 1908 issue of *Outlook*, which provides an overview of the conflict; likewise, see Atherton, *Main Street*, pp. 231–33; and Cohn, *Good Old Days*, pp. 510–17.

[49] Ewen and Ewen, *Channels of Desire*, pp. 67–68; Weil, *Sears, Roebuck*, pp. 62–64; Hendrickson, *Grand Emporiums*, pp. 212–17.

[50] Clark, *Pills, Petticoats, and Plows*, p. viii.

To the western homesteader, the mail-order catalogue (often nick-named the "homesteader's bible") became a department store between book covers, a banking and credit source, an etiquette adviser, and a down-home vade mecum of modernity.

The country store, the county fair, and the mail-order catalogue functioned in collective and competitive ways as agents of modernization. In their interaction and interconnection, they sanctioned and spread a consumer ethic that equated "new" with better and "modern" with improvement. In contrast to traditional lifeways that emphasized self-reliance, homogeneity, locality, and collectivity, they offered consumer visions that championed convenience, diversity, abundance, and individuality. Their individual effect on American rural society occurred incrementally and not each to the same degree. This is understandable, however, since modernization is a process that proceeds unevenly in both time and space with the twin forces of tradition and modernity always present in varying degrees.

Country stores were hesitant to join the expanding consumer revolution, but most—particularly those that survived—did join. Some, such as the stores at Cannon Mills, even grew into corporate giants. Thorstein Veblen and other critics notwithstanding, country stores were not all primitive, exploitative, or monopolistic operations. Eventually most adopted national brands, accepted corporate advertising to promote varieties of the same product, and even acquiesced to changes in rural life prompted by county fairs and mail-order catalogues. "By the 1920s," John Jakle argues, "catalogues lay on the counters of most country stores for all to consult, with the merchant doing the ordering."[51]

County fairs, much less ambivalent about the new order of buying and selling things, frequently fostered traditional lifeways yet championed technologies that altered rural life forever. At the turn-of-the-century fairs, rural folks found re-creations of husking bees competing with demonstrations of gasoline and diesel harvesters. By 1915, a typical state fair had more honky-tonks than horseshoe tosses, more corporate farm machinery pavilions than local agricultural society booths.

---

[51] Veblen's appraisal of the regressive economics of the country store can be found in Thorstein Veblen, "The Independent Farmer," *Freeman* 7 (June 13, 1923): 321–40; and Thorstein Veblen, "The Country Town," *Freeman* 7 (July 11, 1923): 417–30. John A. Jakle, *The American Small Town: Twentieth-Century Place Images* (Hamden, Conn.: Archon Books, 1982), p. 123.

Fig. 9. Cover, Sears, Roebuck, and Company, *Consumers Guide*, no. 102 (Spring and Summer 1896).

Mail-order catalogues unequivocally endorsed the new, the novel, and the modern for the rural consumer. They unabashedly promoted the notion that rural Americans, like their urban counterparts, deserved to be a people of plenty, frequently using the icon of a never-emptying cornucopia in their advertising (fig. 9). Their claims were akin to those of American economist Simon Patten who, in arguing that modern industrialization had created nothing short of a "new basis of civilization" (1907), maintained that an economy of scarcity (the common plight of all previous cultures) was being replaced—owing to modern mass production and its handmaidens, mass promotion and mass distribution—by a new economy of abundance.[52]

Throughout the period 1880–1920, the country store, the county fair, and the mail-order catalogue acted as agencies of change where rural Americans made direct contact with the mass production and mass distribution of industrial, commercial America. In each of these contexts, rural folks encountered consumption on their own turf, at the crossroads, at the county seat, or at their mailboxes. Not all country people took to the new ways of buying and selling: some simply did not have the money to do so; others preferred more traditional ways of trading. Most, however, eventually joined the spreading consumer revolution. They did so for an assortment of reasons: to ape their urban peers, to mitigate the unremitting domestic toil of most farm wives, to achieve personal convenience and individual comfort, to merit or maintain social and economic status, to vent self-indulgence and acquisitiveness, to have more leisure and recreation time, to delight in the new and the novel, and to achieve a higher standard of living. No matter what their reasons and no matter what institution formed and followed their visions of "the good life," people who prided themselves on being producers increasingly became consumers. In this long process, people who thought of themselves as advocates of the traditional increasingly became participants in the modern.

---

[52] Simon N. Patten, *The New Basis of Civilization* (New York: Macmillan, 1907), pp. 4, 9–10.

Index

Page numbers in boldface refer to illustrations.